** VIOLENT ATMOSPHERES**

VIOLENT ATMOSPHERES

Livelihoods and Landscapes in Crisis in Southeast Asia

Edited by
**Wolfram Dressler and
Mary Mostafanezhad**

University of Hawai'i Press
Honolulu

© 2025 University of Hawaiʻi Press
All rights reserved
Printed in the United States of America

First printed, 2025

Library of Congress Cataloging-in-Publication Data

Names: Dressler, Wolfram Heinz, editor. | Mostafanezhad, Mary, editor.
Title: Violent atmospheres : livelihoods and landscapes in crisis in Southeast Asia / edited by Wolfram Dressler and Mary Mostafanezhad.
Other titles: Livelihoods and landscapes in crisis in Southeast Asia
Description: Honolulu : University of Hawaiʻi Press, 2025. | Includes bibliographical references and index.
Identifiers: LCCN 2024038715 (print) | LCCN 2024038716 (ebook) | ISBN 9780824898465 (hardback) | ISBN 9798880701230 (epub) | ISBN 9798880701247 (kindle edition) | ISBN 9798880701223 (pdf)
Subjects: LCSH: Human ecology—Political aspects—Southeast Asia. | Natural resources—Southeast Asia—Management. | Nature—Effect of human beings on—Southeast Asia.
Classification: LCC GF668 .V56 2025 (print) | LCC GF668 (ebook) | DDC 304.20959—dc23/eng/20241224
LC record available at https://lccn.loc.gov/2024038715
LC ebook record available at https://lccn.loc.gov/2024038716

Cover photograph: Stung Treng (Cambodia), March 8, 2020. Aerial view of the old Sre Kor, one of the villages that has been submerged by the water once the gates of the Lower Sesan 2 dam were closed in 2017. Thousands of families–mostly indigenous–living in Sre Kor and nearby villages were forced to relocate losing access to their ancestral lands and to the natural products that the forest and the river had provided them for generations.
© Thomas Cristofoletti/Ruom.

University of Hawaiʻi Press books are printed on acid-free paper and meet the guidelines for permanence and durability of the Council on Library Resources.

Contents

Foreword   vii
PHILIP HIRSCH

Acknowledgments   ix

Introduction: Violent Atmospheres   1
WOLFRAM DRESSLER AND MARY MOSTAFANEZHAD

Section I: Pits and Plots

1. Deathtrap Landscape: The Politics of Reclamation of East Kalimantan's Abandoned Coal Mines   25
   TESSA D. TOUMBOUROU, TIM WERNER, ANTHONY BEBBINGTON, AND MUHAMAD MUHDAR

2. The Everyday Violence of Coal-Fired Power in Shan State, Myanmar   56
   K. B. ROBERTS AND MAI

3. Quarantined Activism: COVID-19 and Extractivism in the Philippines   79
   WOLFRAM DRESSLER

Section II: Dams and Displacement

4. Violent Displacement and Volumetric Change   103
   KIMBERLEY ANH THOMAS, LISA C. KELLEY, AND ANNIE SHATTUCK

5. The Catastrophic and Slow Violence of the Xe Pian Xe Namnoy Dam in Southern Laos   125
   IAN G. BAIRD

6. Dams, Flows, and Data: Volumetric Hydropolitics in the Mekong Basin   141
   CARL GRUNDY-WARR AND CARL MIDDLETON

Section III: Aerial Entanglements

7. The Volumetric Territory of Indonesia's Peat Fires 163
   JENNY E. GOLDSTEIN

8. The Violence of Transboundary Haze:
   The Wealth/Health Paradox in Southeast Asia 181
   HELENA VARKKEY, ALISON COPELAND, AND ALYA SHAIFUL

9. Carbon Bureaucracy and Violence in Cambodia 199
   SARAH MILNE AND SANGO MAHANTY

10. Carbon Crises: Molecular Violence across and beyond Southeast Asia 220
    ANDREW MCGREGOR AND FIONA MILLER

    Atmospheric: An Afterword 243
    FRANCK BILLÉ

    Contributors 251
    Index 255

Foreword

PHILIP HIRSCH

In recent times, scholarship on socio-environmental relations has emphasized the multidimensionality of various problems, in terms of both their causes and their effects. Terms such as polycrisis, nexus, wicked problems, and so on have moved beyond positivist, linear understandings of human action and environmental response. Interdisciplinary fields such as political ecology embrace and employ complexity and interdisciplinarity as a means of understanding socio-environmental crises, including the crossing of social and natural science boundaries. However, the multiplicity of *dimensions* within these framings of key socio-environmental issues remains largely abstract, based on academic discipline, scale, and sources of causality in an increasingly interconnected world.

This collection brings a more literal dimension to bear on our understanding of socio-nature ruptures. That is, by attention to three-dimensional volume rather than two-dimensional space, the editors and chapter authors provide an expanded hermeneutic for understanding the violence incurred by the rupturing of landscapes and livelihoods in Southeast Asia. The volumetric approach takes climate change seriously, but the "violent atmospheres" that provide the title to the book eschew the neo-Malthusian crisis narratives that distance explanation of the uprooting of people's lives from more proximate as well as structural causes in which various dimensions of "development" are heavily implicated.

Each of the chapters in this book interprets what the editors refer to in their introduction as the volumetric turn in a particular way. Overall, the vertical dimension shapes the book's grouping of the studies upward from below-ground mineral extraction, on-ground piling up—and sudden release—of water behind large dams, and above-ground asphyxiating atmospheric crises and the inequitable impact of carbon cycles and bureaucratic, neoliberal-inspired climate change responses. The book thus goes beyond flatter two-dimensional understandings of crises in landscapes and associated livelihoods. But the volumetric approach goes even further. The overall analysis works with the idea that the climate crisis is a cumulative layer in socioeconomic ruptures that cannot be understood in isolation from the long-term, multifaceted accretion of encroachments on environment and livelihoods in which these ruptures are embedded. It provides a welcome move beyond the dilemma of critical scholarship on responses to the climate crisis that sometimes risks throwing out the baby with the bathwater and being marked as climate change skepticism.

In other words, a critical understanding of the climate crisis does not start and stop with the atmosphere above our heads. Collectively, the authors of this volume demonstrate the embeddedness of global warming's causes and effects in below- and on-ground perturbations, in history and in local, national, and regional contexts in Southeast Asia. The resulting overall analysis, ably brought together by the editors, has value well beyond this region.

Acknowledgments

This collection represents several years of work by dedicated authors and their committed interlocutors who contributed critical stories of lives and livelihoods in the rapidly changing frontiers of Southeast Asia. To our authors, we thank you not only for your expertise and deep knowledge of your field sites but also for sticking with us throughout the long process of bringing this book to publication. To the interlocutors who shared their stories, we thank you for your time, energy, and collaboration. Special acknowledgments go to Professor Phil Hirsch, who wrote the foreword in a last-minute frenzy, and Franck Billé, whose lucid afterword pushes the ideas introduced in the collection into new interdisciplinary terrain. We would also like to thank Nancy Peluso for her comments on the introduction. Mary Mostafanezhad acknowledges funding from the National Science Foundation, which supported her work on seasonal air pollution in Thailand and became an impetus for the theoretical developments of this book. Wolfram Dressler thanks the ARC Discovery Fund (DP220101503) for sustained financial support and the *katutubo* and activists of Palawan for sharing their stories of struggle and hope with him all of these years. Finally, we are grateful to Masako Ikeda of the University of Hawai'i Press, who supported us along the way, and to Sophie Dowling for her critical editing and formatting work that allowed us to get the collection over the finish line. Mabuhay!

Introduction

Violent Atmospheres

WOLFRAM DRESSLER AND MARY MOSTAFANEZHAD

In Southeast Asia, atmospheric violence emerges from the haze plumes of burning palm oil plantations, the invisible but powerful spread of viral flows, and the subordination of upland farmers who have long depended on fire to clear land for new crops. The volumetric character of such events is increasingly relevant to studies of social and environmental change. While critical scholars have long examined violent environments arising from conflicts over resources in intensifying capitalist political economies (Peluso and Watts 2001), emerging scholarship brings volumetrics to bear on the political ecology of livelihoods and landscapes in crisis. This volume contributes to this endeavor by accounting for the relationship between resource conflict and socio-ecological violence in Southeast Asia. By further integrating the volumetric processes of territorialization across subterranean (pits and plots), aquatic (dams and displacement), and atmospheric (aerial entanglements) socio-materialities, the chapters build on early scholarship in human geography and environmental anthropology that argued against the empty space of territory (Jerndal and Rigg 1998; Vandergeest and Peluso 1995; Winichakul 1994). Collectively, they demonstrate how a three-dimensional analysis offers new understandings of the drivers, consequences, and potential resolutions to environmentally induced violence. Beyond their two-dimensional character, human and nonhuman beings, relations, and processes are embodied and formed through "the textured [socio-materiality] and voluminous presence of spaces" comprised of the entangled surfaces, layers, and edges that make up three-dimensional worlds (Billé 2017, 2–3). We align this collection with scholars who have long argued against conceiving space as abstract and uniform (Brenner et al. 2003; Cons 2005; Lefebvre 1991; Neumann 2009; Peluso 1995; Winichakul 1994), in our foregrounding of the three-dimensional character of human-environment relations. In doing so, we scrutinize the uneven, historically situated political-economic processes that coproduce violent atmospheres in Southeast Asia. Mediated by entangled and conflicting scales, these processes contribute to modified material flows, depleted ecologies, and precarious modes of existence and governance.

Drawing on scholarship at the intersection of political ecology and the volumetric turn in the social sciences, the collection demonstrates how carbon and fire in the air, coal underground, trees that occupy both surface and subterranean spaces, and pathogens that circulate cannot be fully understood through conventional conceptions of space and territory. While political ecology accounts for the political and economic drivers of socio-environmental change, scholars of the volumetric turn offer a reorientation from two- to three-dimensional analyses of space. The people and environments of Southeast Asia increasingly experience periods of volumetrically violent atmospheres (e.g., dust tsunamis, suffocating haze, fierce fires, landscape ruptures, viral pandemics)—and often intractable efforts to govern and mitigate them—that derive from rapidly intensifying resource extraction and production.

Focusing on these internal contradictions of capital accumulation and how resource conflict has triggered recent livelihood and landscape crises in the region, the authors dive into the violent atmospheres across Southeast Asia. They challenge terrestrially bound notions of violence and conceptually push the atmosphere into new theoretical domains by exploring its scaled socio-spatial dimensions. By integrating volumetrics with political ecologies of livelihoods and landscapes in Southeast Asia, this collection accounts for the violent effects of capital overaccumulation that find powerful social and material expression not only in the region's terrestrial context of forests and plantations but also in its aerial and subterranean spaces.

The volume goes beyond earlier conceptions of territory or territoriality as a land-oriented practice of creating access and maintaining control over resources through social relations, boundaries, and enclosures (Sack 1986). Long informed by peasant and agrarian studies (Peluso 1995; De Angelis 2001; Scott 2009; Hall, Hirsch, and Li 2011; Hall 2012), the literature has described how peasant communities have become governable through technological and bureaucratic mechanisms of legibility (Scott 1998; Li 2007). By making populations legible, highland communities in Southeast Asia were more easily managed and integrated into capitalist markets and government rule (Scott 1998). However, these practices of legibility are not just about terrestrial visibilities and political control. Rather, the history of legibility in the highlands has long been a volumetric undertaking, where not only roads, but tree coverage, water flows, underground resources, tunnels, and roots, as well as topographical challenges in mountainous regions, created the need to surveil the highlands from below and above ground (Michaud 2009; McElwee 2016; Smith and Dressler 2020). Increasingly, the democratization of surveillance technologies has shifted the balance of environmental governance regimes (Nost and Goldstein 2022).

Decades ago, John Agnew (1994) alerted us to the "territorial trap" of accounting for how territoriality and state sovereignty emerge through bounded spaces. Agnew (1994) and others argued that state territoriality not only develops well beyond national borders but is also rationalized vertically through geological stratigraphies of state authority and capitalist production (Braun 2000) as well as horizontally through strategic spatial expressions of socio-political relations (see Blomley 2022). Yet as Franck Billé (2019) demonstrates, territoriality and bordering practices are also enabled through a range of nonvisual forms such as auditory, tactile, and electronic modes of transmission that cut across subterranean, surface, and aerial volumes. These volumetric forms reflect some of the limits of two-dimensional representability, a theme that is particularly poignant in increasingly disputed aerial and oceanic territories (Billé 2019). Chapter authors draw on the foundational work on territorialization and governmentality in Southeast Asia to situate their contribution to three-dimensional perspectives on the political ecologies of violence.

A Political Ecology of Volumes

Described as the "volumetric turn" in the social sciences, scholars have sought to define volumetrics to account for the three-dimensional sphere within which social and environmental phenomena take place. With a particular focus on "the production of space and how its verticality, surface, and the subterranean relate to the power and political economy" (McNeill 2020, 1), scholars of the political technology of territory (Elden 2013) have adopted the volumetric approach. Additionally, political geographers have called for a volumetric analysis of territory to account for its verticality and volume (Adey 2013a, 2013b; Billé 2017, 2020; Bridge 2013; Childs 2020; Elden 2013; Goldstein 2019; McNeill 2020; Steinberg and Peters 2015). Elden (2013, 49) observes how "thinking merely straight up and down may blind us to different angles of approach, and the function of the oblique. Only by thinking through all of these aspects can we reflect more profoundly on the politics, metrics, and power of volume."

Similarly, critical urban geographers such as Graham and Hewitt (2013) have emphasized the necessity of transcending "flat ontologies" by delving into the politics of vertical spaces that extend beyond the two-dimensional surfaces of territorial governance, which often "flatten discourses and imaginaries" in research. Graham and Hewitt (2013, 73) contend that moving beyond the implicit "horizontalism" in geography requires an analysis of the interconnected realms of volumetric existence.

A comprehensive volumetric analysis explores "the ways in which horizontal and vertical extensions, imaginaries, materialities and lived practices intersect and mutually construct each other within the subterranean, surficial and suprasurface domains" (Graham and Hewitt 2013, 75). As Rodenbiker (2019) underscores, political spaces interconnect with the complex social and physical character of atmospheric dimensions and diverse temporalities. Seldom do they neatly align with the complex realities and terrains of human-environment relations.

The chapters within *Violent Atmospheres* show how matter works through and is constituted by multiple overlapping political, economic, social, and environmental relations. The book critically engages the two-dimensional character of resource territoriality by demonstrating that territorial boundaries and territorialization are not "fixed enclosures" or "contiguous with a singular surface" (Rodenbiker 2019, x). The authors draw on mixed methods and ethnographic perspectives to describe the volumetric expressions of territorialization through the heights and depths of social, material, and gaseous atmospheres (Rodenbiker 2019; Elden 2013). Overall, the book seeks to use volumetric insights to understand the atmospheric dimensions and violence of subterranean, terrestrial, and aerial territorialization in Southeast Asia.

Among these materialities, fire is a particularly unruly character. Burning peat bogs in Indonesia are transformed by non-state corporate entities that coproduce violent atmospheres of particulate matter that traverse forests and cities as well as national borders to produce tense environmental geopolitics (Varkkey 2022). In northern Thailand, shifting cultivation continues to be vilified in ways that further disenfranchise Indigenous highlanders who are increasingly held hostage to global markets and governance, creating social atmospheres of culpability, while they become scapegoats for the aerial conditions of market integration (Mostafanezhad and Evrard 2020). Deepening this analysis, the subterranean context of coal is linked with the terrestrial landscape and, through its incineration, the aerial spaces of its particulate distribution, and the drowning of innocence (see chapter 1 in this volume, by Toumbourou et al.). By connecting the surficial with the subterranean and the aerial, the chapters reveal the recursive relationship between the material and symbolic constitution of what Guarasci and Kim (2022) describe as "ecologies of war." They note how the volumetric character of more-than-human relations and practices of war often go unrecognized through their everyday and mundane character; these "everyday experiences, material effects, and affective resonances of violence" deeply penetrate and contaminate the entirety of the environments and ecologies of places (Guarasci and Kim 2022, 1). This volume contributes to emerging scholarship that unearths how and why atmospheric violence penetrates the everyday and mundane livelihoods and landscapes in rural Southeast Asia.

Volumetric Violence

Crisis tendencies shape atmospheres through the exploitation of resources, human labor, and non-human relations. These exploitative tendencies reproduce violence in multiple forms: discursive, material, and structural. Violent atmospheres can rapidly implode. However, they are more commonly the result of slow, structural wounds driven by unequal access to land, resources, and power. These multiple forms of violence are comprehensive and drive crises of representation, overaccumulation, and dispossession in ways that fuel climate change, displacement, and resource claims and capture. Parenti (2011, 7) argues that "climate change arrives in a world primed for crisis," where blame for crises is often racialized and misplaced. The process of identifying the causes of atmospheric crises is often fueled by enduring misrepresentations and poorly targeted policy perspectives that criminalize rather than "solve" the crisis of overaccumulation. New technologies of rule and representational practices, such as remote sensing of fires and plantation concession mapping, are critical infrastructure through which culpability for fires is derived. In Indonesia, Goldstein (2019, 4) describes how these enactments "enable a smokescreen of blame for environmental crisis." As a result, the culprits of such crises, Erik Swyngedouw (2010) argues, are frequently vague and unnamed.

Governing atmospheric crisis is thus inherently ambiguous, intractable, and affective; atmospheres are laden with contestations, ideological and moral struggles, and corrosive power dynamics. But how do intensifying uses, modes of governing, and conflicts over resources trigger volumetric atmospheric crises, and when and for whom do they become a crisis? Answers to these questions lie at the center of critical political ecology: interrogating the intersection of the socio-political, economic, and biophysical changes that produce crisis and mediate judgments of crisis over time and space. Yet bridging volume with such analysis reveals the multidimensionality of how environmental governance and its judgments articulate with class, ethnicity, and locale as crisis atmospheres subsume and rupture human and nonhuman relations over time (Lowe 2010). Crisis atmospheres are a quasi-species, multispecies organizing metaphor to account for the ways that atmospheres become unruly, contagious, and authoritative (Lowe 2010). As the volumetric basis of atmospheric crisis intensifies, so too do the material and discursive elements of atmospheres. These elements produce varied forms of violence among the rural and urban poor implicated in crisis thresholds.

In contrast to vertical expressions of discursive and structural violence, the chapters in this volume show how the entanglement of material and structural violence emerges through comprehensive forms of violence. Such forms envelop, subsume, and degrade people and ecologies gradually over time.[1] Guarasci and Kim (2022, 1) refocus our attention away from the "brute force" of violence through the lens of war. They emphasize the "networks of material, social, technological and technocratic relations, including the violence caused by pastoral forms of power designed to caretake in the wake of political brutality or climatic uncertainty." In Southeast Asia, violence is enacted through a range of securitization mechanisms that surveil the rural poor, criminalize traditional practices, and justify land grabs in the name of national security and development. In the context of Indonesia's transboundary haze, Goldstein (2019, 1) notes how "territorialization plays out through surveillance-based legal and representational practices, such as laws that seek culpability for polluted transboundary airspace and satellite-based remote sensing of underground fires, in ways that obscure the economic and political objectives of such territorial strategies." These strategies of technical observation further reify the atmosphere and obscure its structural inequalities. However, gradual forms of slow violence can culminate into faster, explosive forms of violence that approximate the brute force of acute warfare. Violent atmospheres are, therefore, best understood as generating varied combinations of gradual and immediate forms of violence that work synergistically, breaching thresholds and triggering consequential and enduring harm among the poor (Peluso and Watts 2001).

Folding volume into political ecologies of violence compels us to consider what forms, intensities, and frequencies of violent atmospheres constitute a crisis and for whom. These questions are critical points of departure for political ecologists who seek to account for the three-dimensional aspects of volume in the making of and response to violent atmospheres. Yet, answers to these questions are not simple and often demand deep historical, ethnographic, and multi-scalar investigation. Recent scholarship shows how the violence of atmospheres can be personal and collective as well as sensed and felt through the body (McCormack 2014). The diffuse nature of such affective outcomes is challenging to trace and understand in multidimensional spaces (Anderson 2009). Atmospheric violence circulates across multiple locales and class formations that often pit the rural poor against urban elite. Dust along rural mining roads or the haze from plantations entering through the thatched-roofed dwellings in Sumatra and into urban skyrise condominiums in Singapore reflect this interplay. In this sense, violent atmospheres emerge from amidst the differential mobilities of sensing subjects, and the "force fields" (Stewart 2011) or "weather worlds" (Ingold 2007) that envelope a sensing subject (McCormack 2014). The diffuse, affective capacity of atmospheres can render the poor highly precarious and indeterminate. Indeed, atmospheric violence works through the mundane practices of war, the socio-ecological terrain that includes the slow violence (Nixon 2011) of particulate exposure (see chapter 8 in this volume, by Varkkey, Copeland, and Shaiful), the toxic chemicals of militarization in island spaces (Niheu et al. 2007), the structural inequality of disease exposure and treatment, such as the class and racialized suppression of the COVID-19 pandemic (Fiske et al. 2022), and the historical amnesia of the structured erasure of Indigenous ecological knowledge (Kimmerer 2013).

Our volume demonstrates how atmospheric violence is often literally in the air as a gaseous envelope of particulates of varied densities (McCormack 2018). In Southeast Asia, atmospheres of various densities can be conditioned, but are also conditioning and subject to deliberate, sometimes political, engineering (Lorimer, Hodgetts, and Barua 2019, 27) such as the monitoring and control of smallholder farmer burning practices (chapter 8 in this volume). These practices coexist with the rapid development of environmental engineering projects meant to ameliorate the violence of atmospheric exchange through, for instance, skyscraper-sized air purifier towers (*The Nation* 2023) and climate controlled safe zone clean air pavilions in urban centers (*Inhabit* 2023).

Moving beyond the crisis-induced violence of surficial spaces, *Violent Atmospheres* points to how atmospheres take on and unleash discursive and structural violence within and through volume. As Ribot (2014, 667–668) notes, vulnerability to disasters "does not fall from the sky"; rather, "while some responsibility for stressors may now travel through the sky, the renewed focus on climate hazard is clouding attention to the grounded social causes of precarity that expose and sensitize people to hazard." While critical attention to the sky is needed, so too is a commitment to recursively investigating the grounded social drivers of atmospheric violence. Such violence is socially and chemically produced and develops into unequally shared impacts of, for example, degradation, pollution, weather events, and climate change (Parenti 2011). For example, the slow violence of the particulate matter of haze in Indonesia or Thailand reflects a "creeping environmental problem" that changes "the environment in a negative, cumulative, and at least for some period of time, an invisible way" (Glantz 1999, 6). Such "slow violence" is a gradual violence that is dispersed across time and space, whereas "fast violence" is explosive and spectacular (Nixon 2011, 8). Along this trajectory and its varied conjunctures, the varied tempo of violence must be "considered as a contest not only over space, or bodies, or labor, or resources, but also over time" (Nixon 2011, 8). This collection reveals how representations of slow and fast violence are significant in how they trigger moments of rupture and judgments of crisis.

Atmospheric Matter

Social scientists have addressed atmospheres as either a feeling or meteorological context (Riedel 2019, 86). Karl Marx, for instance, identified atmospheres as "a pressure of feeling weighing down on everyone, enveloping and pressing upon bodies from all sides" (cited in Adey 2014b, 836). Today, atmospheres have become notably "difficult to pin down, yet they are often talked about and decided upon as if they were not" (Adey 2014b, 837). Lorimer, Hodgetts, and Barua (2019, 27) similarly note how the atmosphere is a "multifaceted and productively nebulous concept that is still underdeveloped." Not unlike the "environment," atmospheres are significant for how they render coherence to sometimes disparate parts in a sort of "phantasmagoria" (Lytton 1912, cited in Riedel 2019, 90). Riedel (2019, 90) notes that "as smoothing forces that evoke coherence, atmospheres are also highly political, since they paint even conflicting voices in an all-encompassing homogeneous light." Atmospheres are constituted by a multidimensional fullness and expanse that entangles and breaks down vertical and horizontal social and biophysical spheres. They are also volumetric in how they subsume scales and human and nonhuman relations (Elden 2013). While atmospheres are shared affect, they are also material entities that envelop and shape human and nonhuman existence. These characteristics prime atmospheres for their role in capital-induced crises as they are coproduced within and through social relations, livelihoods, and environmental degradation. Bringing atmospheres to bear on environmental change compels scholars to consider how atmospheres obscure the political-ecological drivers of violent materialities that effortlessly flow through their borders.

Atmospheres work as envelopes of gases and particulate matter—both immaterial and material—and as pervading political contestations, ideological orientations, and discursive violence. They also archive violence through the traces of less visible particulate matter that permeates the bodies and psyche of rural and urban residents and envelops political forms of control, coercion, or opportunity. Lorimer, Hodgetts, and Barua (2019, 31) demonstrate how atmosphere "holds a series of opposites—presence and absence, materiality and ideality, definite and indefinite, singularity and generality—in a relation of tension." Constituted of gases, physical spaces, bodies, and infrastructures, atmospheres take on affective and meteorological forms (McCormack 2014, 2018). As atmospheres are created, they also cocreate our experiences of the world in ways that provoke "collective affective qualities" (Schroer and Schmitt 2018, 1). For critical political ecologists, the atmospheres of human-environment relations remain an emergent topic of inquiry that presents unique empirical and theoretical challenges.

Violent atmospheres therefore emerge as volatile mixes of socio-political, economic, and biophysical ruptures that encompass surficial and gaseous matter across scales. As material and symbolic entities, they coproduce crises over time and space. Pervasive in character, atmospheric contours are carved out by social, political, material, and gaseous elements of extractive spaces producing new "aerographies"

(Adey 2015). Melding together subterranean, terrestrial, and aerial space, aerographies invoke permeating processes of capital accumulation, extraction, and crisis—from large-scale conflagrations to global pandemics (Adey 2015; Billé 2017, 2020; Bonilla 2017; Elden 2013). Yet, only recently have political ecologists drawn attention to the relationship between livelihoods and nonterrestrial, volumetrically shaped crises. While political ecologists have examined violent environments emerging from conflicts over resources in intensifying capitalist political economies (Peluso and Watts 2001; Mansfield 2004; Bohle and Fünfgeld 2007; Büscher and Fletcher 2018), there is still much to learn about how the discursive and material character of atmospheres co-constitute violence and crisis (Le Billon and Duffy 2018; Martinez-Alier 2003; Robbins 2012). The contributions to this book account for how atmospheres and violence co-constitute the volumetric spaces of resource conflicts. This introduction and the chapters that follow examine the volumetric character of the political ecology of atmospheric violence and the role it plays in livelihood transformations in Southeast Asia. As a whole, this book contributes to the "re-materialization" of the so-called volumetric turn in political ecology.

Toward a Political Ecology of Violent Atmospheres

By treating the atmosphere as not merely an environmental backdrop but as an active agent in socio-material relations, this volume opens new possibilities as well as challenges for political ecologists who account for the role of contemporary capitalist processes as fundamental drivers of social and environmental change (Arsel and Dasgupta 2015, 644). By disentangling political-economic and atmospheric transformations, we can better address the relational assemblages of violence, which, rather than "an isolated and localized event," are "more appropriately understood as an unfolding process, derived from the broader geographical phenomena and temporal patterns of the social world" (Springer 2011, 90). In a similar vein, violent atmospheres are expressions of unfolding socio-political, economic, and ecological relations. These volumetric relations produce the temporal and spatial contexts through which the costs and benefits of violent atmospheres are worked out with differential impacts and outcomes. By attending to the ineffective governance of bounded spheres, we can better account for how atmospheres drift within and across populations, terrain, and borders (Szerszynski 2018).

But what do violent atmospheres entail in times of profound social and environmental crisis? As the chapters illustrate, the substance and movement of atmospheric matter can lead to expansive territorial control and penetrating violence. Atmospheric violence often arises through overlapping social relations and practices of authority, power, and control, and the changing substance and character of the socio-materiality that comprises them. The fluidity and dispersal of atmospheric matter can generate new forms of territorial control over expansive (public) and smaller (private) spaces through inflicting slower and faster forms of violence upon peoples' bodies, minds, and livelihoods. In this sense, the socio-materiality of atmospheres cuts through imagined political boundaries to envelop and often powerfully influence people's health, ways of life, and ecologies. When violent atmospheres further criminalize smallholder livelihoods and local resistance, they also drive accumulation by dispossession, and/or deny wellbeing to the rural poor. In other words, they call into question the prospect for rural people to rely on land, forests, and oceans to sustain their lives and livelihoods.

While political ecologists have long shown how a crisis in capital accumulation—the threshold of intensifying "primitive accumulation" (Marx 1976)—gives rise to the overexploitation and exhaustion of (typically) land, labor, and resources—commodities beneath and on the surface—the chapters in this volume engage the interconnections within, between, and beyond surfaces, subsurfaces, and atmospheres. In Southeast Asia, as new resource frontiers are opened, the atmosphere becomes increasingly integrated into practices of "accumulation by dispossession" (Harvey 2017). As Rasmussen and Lund explain, "frontiers represent, most basically, the discovery or invention of new resources" (2018, 388). The atmosphere becomes implicated in frontier-making practices through its role as a repository for the toxic collateral damage of resource extraction. Particulate matter, carbon, and other toxicities are spewed into the sky, unevenly affecting the lives and livelihoods of residents. As Michael Watts notes, "land is only one part of the story," and shifts to incorporate atmospheric space contribute to emerging understandings of the frontier as "primarily a social space within which forms of rule and authority, and multiple sovereignties, are in question" (2017, 480).

Neglecting volumetric dimensions, analyses of crisis situations typically involve surficial ruptures and exhaustion, failing to account for how atmospheres absorb, facilitate, and drive crises with very different material and spatial qualities that literally subsume human and nonhuman beings. The various chapter contributions bridge surficial and aerial forms of crisis by analyzing the volumetric rise, character, and impact of atmospheric violence. Collectively, the chapters reveal how violent atmospheres of governance, livelihoods, and political economies engage in spaces of crisis, where varied temporalities of violence envelop and "weather" livelihoods.

A critical political ecology approach to atmospheres demonstrates how violence is volumetrically constituted through material and symbolic forms. Engagement with the volumetric turn, we argue, deepens our analysis of the political-ecological drivers of the degradation of three-dimensional environments (Adey 2013a, 2013b; Billé 2017; Elden 2013). The volumetric conditions of atmospheric change point to how atmospheres can materialize as both slow and fast violence (Adey 2014a; Billé 2017; Choy 2012; Choy and Zee 2015; Elden 2013). As Elden (2013, 1) highlights, "we all-too-often think of the spaces of geography as areas, not volumes." An entanglement of scales, volumetric space draws together the planetary to the granular (Billé 2017), and how granular or particulate matter moves through atmospheres to unleash violence. In this sense, violent atmospheres work through "volumetric spaces," or the diverse entanglement of scales: the "gaps, pockets, and multidirectional warrens of varying densities" (Elden 2013) smothering and constraining the ability of the poor to make a living in the Global South. How atmospheres drive or subdue violence is a provocative point of departure for political ecologists focused on socio-environmental ruptures and the crises they provoke (c.f. Mahanty et al. 2023).

The unruly matter of the chapters reveals the diverse spatialities of volumetric crisis. This matter materializes within a range of socio-political and ecological affects and effects that comprise violent atmospheres. They index how resources are constituted "through the triumph of one imaginary over others" (Bridge 2009, 1221). Differently positioned actors (e.g., villagers, park rangers, CEOs, tourism entrepreneurs, urban dwellers, NGO practitioners) exploit and govern contrasting socionatures and natural resources (coal, oil palm, forests, or protected areas). They ultimately perceive, interpret, and act on the uses of such spaces in diverse ways that powerfully influence the causes of, and responses to, violent atmospheres. Thus, "state and non-state actors strategically confront these material conditions as they play out underground and in the atmosphere by claiming, contesting, and disavowing such materiality" (Goldstein 2019, 6). In this context, contemporary governance regimes, forms of representation, and associated material processes render livelihoods insecure and at risk as atmospheric violence unfolds.

The Chapters

The chapters in this collection describe the violent atmospheres of mainland and insular Southeast Asia, a region experiencing intense social and environmental transformations. Southeast Asia's agrarian and resource transitions are long-standing and manifold; they are also dramatically increasing in scale and intensity (Hart, Turton, and White 1989; Nevins and Peluso 2008; Dressler et al. 2017). Building on these themes, the chapters are organized into three sections: "Pits and Plots," "Dams and Displacement," and "Aerial Entanglements." The sections aim to facilitate the overarching narrative of the collection by showing how the atmospheric violence of each sphere transcends into and intensifies the others in three-dimensional contexts. The pits of coal mining collect water in deep caverns; major rivers and tributaries are dammed in ways that cause breaches and catastrophic flows of water; and the dust plumes from coal, the haze from smoldering plantations, and viral COVID clouds entangle in the atmosphere with violent consequences on the ground.

In section 1, "Pits and Plots," the chapters reveal how coercive governance, the viral containment of activism, and extractivism converge to generate violent atmospheres that co-emerge across terrestrial, aquatic, and aerial scales with profound consequences for the rural and urban poor. Toumbourou et al. and Roberts and Mai describe how subsurface coal in East Kalimantan, Indonesia, and Tigyit, Myanmar, is extensively extracted for export and intensively burned for energy production, leaving dangerous gaping pits and dust plumes across once-forested landscapes. Their chapters speak to the direct and indirect violence of the vertical volumetrics of energy extractivism, where children accidentally drown in remnant coal pits and coal plumes darken local atmospheres. Toumbourou et al. show how affected residents mobilize to overcome the violence of the new status quo, working with the Samarinda Lawsuit Movement to file a case against the Indonesian state's negligence in managing open-pit mines, revealing how formidable countermovements to violent atmospheres can be. Dressler reveals how the political histories of violent governance repeat themselves. The reemergence of authoritarian populism in the Philippines, he demonstrates, has emboldened state actors, parastatal, and shadowy assassins to use COVID-19 health measures to justify the suppression of grassroots activism and intensify nickel mining on Palawan Island, the country's last ecological frontier. Viral clouds, harassment, murder, and the expansion of extraction reproduce violent atmospheres that degrade human rights and forest landscapes.

In section 2, "Dams and Displacement," the chapters speak to how the conversion of rivers to dams, climate change, and displacement coproduce atmospheric violence that dramatically impacts the lives and livelihoods of the poor, whose sense of autonomy and livelihoods have long relied on access to free-flowing water, lands, and forest commons in mainland Southeast Asia. Thomas, Kelley, and Shattuck "speak back" to the racialized neo-Malthusian claims concerning the assumed impacts and outcomes of climate violence and displacement in the region. Drawing on detailed case studies, they show how the accretive effects of historical violence giving rise to climate impacts, migration, and displacement can only be understood in terms of contested agrarian histories, political economies, and changing human-environment relations across localities, landscapes, and (gaseous) atmospheres.

At the edges of rivers and dams, Baird details the catastrophic and slow violence of the Xe Pian Xe Namnoy dam's rupture in southern Laos. He describes the disastrous effects of violent hydropolitics, negligence, and dam infrastructure breaching to destroy the lives and livelihoods of the rural poor living near the dam and its river systems in Laos. Yet the haunting legacy of the dam's rupture lingers as slow violence, affecting the uncompensated livelihoods and emotional well-being of those who survived the disaster.

Grundy-Warr and Middleton discuss how the intimate relationship between the Mekong River, its flood pulse, and riparian communities has been progressively ruptured by large hydropower dam construction in the Mekong Basin. Using Allen's "topologies of power" and Elden's "volumetric politics," they elaborate on how power and authority are increasingly exercised through (big) water data politics that reinforce state-capital alliances backing large hydropower dams. They challenge discourses of "sustainable hydropower," "designed flows," and hydropower as a climate change mitigation technology as symptomatic of a structural slow violence that is intended to secure the flow for hydropower and its project cycles. This occurs at the expense of those whose lives and livelihoods have long been attuned to the flows and rhythms of water cycles in the region.

In section 3, "Aerial Entanglements," the chapters reveal how intensifying resource exploitation and governance work together, above and below ground, to influence local and regional volumetric violence and the intractable efforts to govern its impacts. They describe the dust tsunamis, suffocating haze, and fierce fires emerging from "the decaying structures left scattered across . . . [the] urban and rural geographies" of capitalist ruin in Southeast Asia (Stoler 2013, ix). Echoing Anne Stoler's *Imperial Debris,* the authors explore how the rural poor negotiate the violence of the ruins in which they live from histories of capital accumulation, dispossession, and now "restorative" governance (e.g., carbon drawdown, extinguishing fire, etc.). They account for how the technological ideals and practices of restorative governance allow those in power to govern from a distance, but with little consideration of how those entangled in ruptured landscapes must negotiate new governmental practices.

As Milne and Mahanty show, even efforts to govern and mitigate climate change within forests flanking degraded lands in Cambodia can lead to bureaucratic violence through burdensome local consultations and verification processes involving Reduced Emissions from Deforestation and Forest Degradation (REDD+). Their findings show how implementing REDD+ international standards in practice can compel "project proponents"—villagers, community leaders, and local officials—to comply with ambiguous and opaque bureaucratic standards, all the while masking and reinforcing the political-economic violence that drives the illegal logging, land acquisition, and dispossession such governance is meant to curb.

Goldstein's chapter considers how forest and peatland governance in Indonesia has become definitively volumetric through new surveillance technologies such as satellites and local enforcement practices. In this "smart space," she describes how the politics of forest governance is no longer just about state territorial control over forests, timber, and the lands upon which crops grow, or about defining national ideals, discourses, and citizenship among those peoples living in forest landscapes. Rather, she argues that the politics of governing forests today involves new assemblages of state and non-state actors using sophisticated smart technologies to govern from above and below, surveilling the full socio-materialities of forests, fires, and livelihoods among the rural poor. International NGOs, domestic civil society, state actors, and industrial corporations have become entangled in a political contest of motives, ideas, and practices of how and why to govern the uses of remnant forests and, increasingly, the uncontrollable outcomes of overexploiting forestlands. The actors behind new forest surveillance technologies attempt to govern from above the intractable, hazy outcomes of clearing and firing peat forests that seem to burn forever, while struggling to contend with particulate matter affecting plantation workers and office clerks in Singapore and Jakarta. Goldstein asks: What new territorial dynamics emerge from the capacity of a multiplicity of actors to access geospatial data on political forests, and conduct forest surveillance remotely?

Varkkey, Copeland, and Shaiful's chapter offers explanations and possible answers to Goldstein's question. They describe how the seasonal haze crisis from burning forests and peatlands for plantations has become a protracted trans-scalar crisis, where the politics of origin and blame are difficult to resolve. The volumetric flow of fine particles from atmospheric haze from uncontrolled burning travels over vast political territories, crossing national boundaries and complicating interregional cooperation to "solve" transboundary haze migrations. The authors illustrate the geopolitics of the haze crisis and the diversity of actors, narratives, relationships, processes, and practices involved (Peluso and Watts 2001).

McGregor and Miller's chapter shows how the carbon flows released from resource exploitation and surplus accumulation in one region powerfully reinforce carbon flows and violence in other regions—regions with peoples who have less to do with climate change but bear the brunt of escalating carbon violence produced elsewhere with little accountability. Drawing on the notion of a "world regional" political ecology, they underscore the need for scholars to understand the origins and impacts of carbon violence beyond single case studies to show how volumetric carbon flows from one highly industrialized region (e.g., Australia) reinforce the violence of carbon upon the lives, livelihoods, and ecologies in less industrialized regions (e.g., the Philippines) in Southeast Asia. They make explicit the more-than-human dimensions affected by the rupture of "sociocarbon" cycles due to the intensifying regional impacts of climate change that cut through subterranean, terrestrial, oceanic, and atmospheric spaces.

As dust is unlocked through the keyhole of infrastructure development along the ancient Silk Road in China, so too in Indonesia particulates spew into the atmosphere from burning underground peatlands for oil palm expansion—enveloping the air that permeates the bodies of thousands of rural poor and millions in the regional cities of Singapore and Kuala Lumpur. As a spatial fix to resolve the problems associated with China's overaccumulation and exhaustion, China's Belt and Road Initiative (BRI) is having widespread socio-environmental implications across the Mekong Subregion (Summers 2016; Yeh and Wharton 2016). Yet, the plume of volumetric crises resulting from the initiative implodes horizontally and vertically, as capitalist brokers exploit and overcome crises by reorganizing, expanding, and connecting ideas, capital, and labor to create new markets and financing opportunities (Harvey 2001, 2011, 2016). Similarly, particulate matter from urban and rural environments becomes undifferentiated forms of haze that are then collectively attributed to shifting cultivation in the rural highlands of northern Thailand (Mostafanezhad and Evrard 2020). Policy demands that seek to ameliorate these material and symbolic atmospheric crises (e.g., burning bans in Indonesia, Thailand, and Vietnam) reinforce age-old structural inequalities between the country and the city (Williams 1975). While governance often depends on simplicity, the homogenizing effect of atmospheres impedes the livelihoods of vulnerable residents in ways that allow powerful actors to consolidate greater authority and control. Thus, these relations reflect a range of socio-material paradoxes: value/intensity, wealth/poverty, and intimacy/ignorance that comprise the social and drive the material basis of violent atmospheres (Bridge 2009, 1217).

The authors in this collection push political ecologies of violence into new theoretical directions by accounting for the volumetric nature of the atmospheric archives of colonial and postcolonial environments. Using diverse research methods, they account for how violent atmospheres become visible through material engagements with wars over resources, territories, and bodies. Practices of resource land grabs, land degradation, and landscape privatization take place in and through atmospheric violence. In this context, what is broadly understood as disaster "resilience" obscures these historical relations of socio-ecological inequalities that shape the social and material atmospheres of Southeast Asia.

The volume brings the political ecology of crisis to bear on atmospheric violence in Southeast Asia through chapters that account for discourse, knowledge, power, and practice. Each chapter addresses the internal contradictions of capital accumulation and how resource conflict triggers violent atmospheres and atmospheric crises. The authors document the scaled dimensions of atmosphere-induced violence and how the material and discursive production of crisis intersects with rural and urban sociopolitics, economies, and environments. They show how the political ecology of extractivism drives violent atmospheric processes and events (e.g., climate change, haze, and air pollution) that mediate governance dynamics and often challenge rural livelihoods in insular and mainland Southeast Asia. Our volume starts new conversations and opens new conceptual windows into the violent atmospheres in Southeast Asia.

Note

1. While discursive violence can involve sociocultural expressions of violence that frame things (people, nature, etc.) to legitimize and enact violence upon them (Peluso and Watts 2001; Neumann 2009), analysis tends to be either vertical or horizontal in nature and seldom multidimensional. Similarly, structural violence—the less visible, often implicit violence that is built into and harnessed from the institutions (e.g., judiciary, property rights), ideologies, and political histories in dominant society—tends to be examined in a vertical, hierarchical manner (Galtung 1969).

References

Adey, Peter. 2013a. "Air/Atmospheres of the Megacity." *Theory, Culture and Society* 30 (7–8): 291–308.
Adey, Peter. 2013b. "Securing the Volume/Volumen: Comments on Stuart Elden's Plenary Paper, 'Secure the volume.'" *Political Geography*, no. 34, 52–54.
Adey, Peter. 2014a. *Air: Nature and Culture*. Chicago: Reaktion Books.
Adey, Peter. 2014b. "Security Atmospheres or the Crystallisation of Worlds." *Environment and Planning D: Society and Space* 32 (5): 834–851.
Adey, Peter. 2015. "Air's Affinities: Geopolitics, Chemical Affect and the Force of the Elemental." *Dialogues in Human Geography* 5 (1): 54–75.
Agnew, John. 1994. "The Territorial Trap: The Geographical Assumptions of International Relations Theory." *Review of International Political Economy* 1 (1): 53–80.
Allen, John. 2016. *Topologies of Power: Beyond Territory and Networks*. London: Routledge.
Anderson, Ben. 2009. "Affective Atmospheres." *Emotion, Space and Society* 2 (2): 77–81.
Arsel, Murat, and Anirban Dasgupta. 2015. "Critique, Rediscovery and Revival in Development Studies." *Development and Change* 46 (4): 644–665.
Auyero, Javier, and Débora Alejandra Swistun. 2009. *Flammable: Environmental Suffering in an Argentine Shantytown*. Oxford: Oxford University Press.
Baird, Ian G., and Keith Barney. 2017. "The Political Ecology of Cross-Sectoral Cumulative Impacts: Modern Landscapes, Large Hydropower Dams and Industrial Tree Plantations in Laos and Cambodia." *Journal of Peasant Studies* 44 (4): 769–795.
Bigger, Patrick, and Benjamin D. Neimark. 2017. "Weaponizing Nature: The Geopolitical Ecology of the US Navy's Biofuel Program." *Political Geography* 60:13–22.
Billé, Franck. 2017. "Introduction: Speaking Volumes." Theorizing the Contemporary, *Fieldsights*, October 24, 2017. https://culanth.org/fieldsights/introduction-speaking-volumes.
Billé, Franck. 2019. "Volumetric Sovereignty." *Environment and Planning D: Society and Space*, March 3, 2019. https://www.societyandspace.org/forums/volumetric-sovereignty.

Billé, Franck. 2020. "Voluminous: An Introduction." In *Voluminous States Sovereignty, Materiality, and the Territorial Imagination,* edited by Franck Billé, 1–47. Durham, NC: Duke University Press.

Blomley, Nicholas. 2022. *Territory: New Trajectories in Law.* London: Routledge.

Bohle, Hans-Georg, and Hartmut Fünfgeld. 2007. "The Political Ecology of Violence in Eastern Sri Lanka." *Development and Change* 38 (4): 665–687.

Bonilla, Lauren. 2017. "Voluminous." Theorizing the Contemporary, *Fieldsights,* October 24, 2017. https://culanth.org/fieldsights/voluminous.

Braun, Bruce. 2000. "Producing Vertical Territory: Geology and Governmentality in Late Victorian Canada." *Ecumene* 7 (1): 7–46.

Brenner, Neil, Bob Jessop, Martin Jones, and Gordon Macleod, eds. 2003. *State/Space: A Reader.* Malden, MA: Blackwell.

Bridge, Gavin. 2009. "Material Worlds: Natural Resources, Resource Geography and the Material Economy." *Geography Compass* 3 (3): 1217–1244.

Bridge, Gavin. 2013. "Territory, Now in 3D!" *Political Geography,* no. 34, 55–57.

Büscher, Bram, and Robert Fletcher. 2018. "Under Pressure: Conceptualising Political Ecologies of Green Wars." *Conservation and Society* 16 (2): 105.

Childs, John. 2020. "Extraction in Four Dimensions: Time, Space and the Emerging Geo(-)politics of Deep-Sea Mining." *Geopolitics* 25 (1): 189–213. doi:10.1080/14650045.2018.1465041.

Choy, Timothy. 2012. "Air's Substantiations." In *Lively Capital: Biotechnologies, Ethics, and Governance in Global Markets,* edited by Kaushik Sunder Rajan, 121–154. Durham, NC: Duke University Press.

Choy, Timothy, and Jerry Zee. 2015. "Condition—Suspension." *Cultural Anthropology* 30 (2): 210–223. https://doi.org/10.14506/ca30.2.04.

Cons, Jason. 2005. "What's the Good of Mercators? Cartography and the Political Ecology of Place." *Graduate Journal of Social Science* 2 (1): 7–36.

Dalby, Simon. 2000. "Geopolitics and Ecology: Rethinking the Contexts of Environmental Security." In *Environment and Security,* edited by Miriam R. Lowi and Brian R. Shaw, 84–100. New York: Springer.

De Angelis, Massimo. 2001. "Marx and Primitive Accumulation: The Continuous Character of Capital's 'Enclosures.'" *The Commoner* 2 (1): 1–22.

Dodds, Klaus. 2021. "Geopolitics and Ice Humanities: Elemental, Metaphorical and Volumetric Reverberations." *Geopolitics* 26 (4): 1121–1149.

Dressler, Wolfram H. 2017. "Contesting Moral Capital in the Economy of Expectations of an Extractive Frontier." *Annals of the American Association of Geographers* 107 (3): 647–665.

Dressler, Wolfram H. 2021. "Defending Lands and Forests: NGO Histories, Everyday Struggles, and Extraordinary Violence in the Philippines." *Critical Asian Studies* 53 (3): 380–411.

Dressler, Wolfram H., Robert Fletcher, and Michael Fabinyi. 2018. "Value from Ruin? Governing Speculative Conservation in Ruptured Landscapes." *TRaNS: Trans-Regional and-National Studies of Southeast Asia* 6 (1): 73–99.

Dressler, Wolfram H., David Wilson, Jessica Clendenning, Rob Cramb, Rodney Keenan, Sango Mahanty, Thilde Bech Bruun, Ole Mertz, and Rodel D. Lasco. 2017. "The

Impact of Swidden Decline on Livelihoods and Ecosystem Services in Southeast Asia: A Review of the Evidence from 1990 to 2015." *Ambio* 46 (3): 291–310.
Elden, Stuart. 2013. "Secure the Volume: Vertical Geopolitics and the Depth of Power." *Political Geography* 34:35–51.
Elden, Stuart. 2021. "Terrain, Politics, History." *Dialogues in Human Geography* 11 (2): 170–189.
Fiske, Amelia, Ilaria Galasso, Johanna Eichinger, Stuart McLennan, Isabella Radhuber, Bettina Zimmermann, and Barbara Prainsack. 2022. "The Second Pandemic: Examining Structural Inequality through Reverberations of COVID-19 in Europe." *Social Science and Medicine* 292:114634.
Galtung, Johan. 1969. "Violence, Peace, and Peace Research." *Journal of Peace Research* 6 (3): 167–191.
Glantz, Michael, 1999. "Sustainable Development and Creeping Environmental Problems in the Aral Sea Region." In *Creeping Environmental Problems and Sustainable Development in the Aral Sea Basin,* edited by Michael Glantz, 1–27. Cambridge: Cambridge University Press.
Goldstein, Jenny E. 2019. "The Volumetric Political Forest: Territory, Satellite Fire Mapping, and Indonesia's Burning Peatland." *Antipode* 52 (4): 1–23. https://doi.org/10.1111/anti.12576.
Graham, Stephen, and Lucy Hewitt. 2013. "Getting Off the Ground: On the Politics of Urban Verticality." *Progress in Human Geography* 37 (1): 72–92. https://doi.org/10.1177/0309132512443147.
Guarasci, Bridget, and Eleana J. Kim. 2022. "Introduction: Ecologies of War." Theorizing the Contemporary, *Fieldsights,* January 25, 2022. https://culanth.org/fieldsights/introduction-ecologies-of-war.
Hall, Derek. 2012. "Rethinking Primitive Accumulation: Theoretical Tensions and Rural Southeast Asian Complexities." *Antipode* 44 (4): 1188–1208.
Hall, Derek, Philip Hirsch, and Tania Murray Li. 2011. "Introduction to Powers of Exclusion: Land Dilemmas in Southeast Asia." In *Powers of Exclusion: Land Dilemmas in Southeast Asia,* edited by Derek Hall, Philip Hirsch, and Tania Murray Li, 1–27. Honolulu: University of Hawai'i Press.
Hart, Gillian, Andrew Turton, and Benjamin White, eds. 1989. *Agrarian Transformations: Local Processes and the State in Southeast Asia.* Berkeley: University of California Press.
Harvey, David. 2001. "Globalization and the 'Spatial Fix.'" *Geographische Revue. Zeitschrift Literatur und Diskussion* 3 (2): 23–30.
Harvey, David. 2011. *The Enigma of Capital: And the Crises of Capitalism.* New York: Profile Books.
Harvey, David. 2016. "Crisis Theory and the Falling Rate of Profit." In *The Great Financial Meltdown: Systemic, Conjunctural or Policy Created,* edited by Turaban Subasat, 37–54. Cheltenham: Edward Elgar Publishing.
Harvey, D. 2017. "The 'New' Imperialism: Accumulation by Dispossession." In *Karl Marx,* edited by Kevin Anderson and Bertell Ollman, 213–237. London: Routledge.
Ingold, Tim. 2007. "Earth, Sky, Wind, and Weather." *Journal of the Royal Anthropological Institute* 13:S19–38.

Jerndal, Randi, and Jonathan Rigg. 1998. "Making Space in Laos: Constructing a National Identity in a 'Forgotten' Country." *Political Geography* 17 (7): 809–831.
Kimmerer, Robin Wall. 2013. *Braiding Sweetgrass: Indigenous Wisdom, Scientific Knowledge, and the Teachings of Plants*. Minneapolis, MN: Milkweed Editions.
Le Billon, Philippe, and Rosaleen V. Duffy. 2018. "Conflict Ecologies: Connecting Political Ecology and Peace and Conflict Studies." *Journal of Political Ecology* 25 (1): 239–260.
Lefebvre, Henri. 1991. *The Production of Space*. Translated by Donald Nicholson Smith. Malden, MA: Blackwell.
Li, Tania Murray. 2007. *The Will to Improve: Governmentality, Development, and the Practice of Politics*. Durham, NC: Duke University Press.
Li, Tania Murray. 2010. "To Make Live or Let Die? Rural Dispossession and the Protection of Surplus Populations." *Antipode* 41:66–93. https://doi.org/10.1111/j.1467-8330.2009.00717.x.
Lorimer, Jamie, Timothy Hodgetts, and Maan Barua. 2019. "Animals' Atmospheres." *Progress in Human Geography* 43 (1): 26–45. Lowe, C. 2010. "Viral Clouds: Becoming H5N1 in Indonesia." *Cultural Anthropology* 25 (4): 625–649.
Lytton, Edward Bulwer. 1912. *Zanoni: Zicci*. New York: Little, Brown.
Mahanty, Sango, Sarah Milne, Keith Barney, Wolfram Dressler, Philip Hirsch, and Phuc Xuan To. 2023. "Rupture: Towards a Critical, Emplaced, and Experiential View of Nature-Society Crisis." *Dialogues in Human Geography* 13 (2): 20438206221138057. https://doi.org/10.1177/20438206221138057.
Mansfield, Becky. 2004. "Neoliberalism in the Oceans: 'Rationalization,' Property Rights, and the Commons Question." *Geoforum* 35 (3): 313–326.
Martinez-Alier, Joan. 2003. *The Environmentalism of The Poor: A Study of Ecological Conflicts and Valuation*. Cheltenham: Edward Elgar Publishing.
Marx, Karl. 1976. *Capital*. Vol. 1. London: Penguin Classics.
McCormack, Derek P. 2014. "Atmospheric Things and Circumstantial Excursions." *Cultural Geographies* 21 (4): 605–625.
McCormack, Derek P. 2018. *Atmospheric Things: On the Allure of Elemental Envelopment*. Durham, NC: Duke University Press.
McElwee, Pamela D. 2016. *Forests Are Gold: Trees, People, and Environmental Rule in Vietnam*. Seattle: University of Washington Press.
McNeill, Donald. 2020. "The Volumetric City." *Progress in Human Geography* 44 (5): 815–831.
Michaud, Jean. 2009. "Handling Mountain Minorities in China, Vietnam and Laos: From History to Current Concerns." *Asian Ethnicity* 10 (1): 25–49.
Moore, Jason W. 2014. "The End of Cheap Nature, or, How I learned to Stop Worrying about the Environment and Love the Crisis of Capitalism." In *Structures of the World Political Economy and the Future of Global Conflict and Cooperation*, edited by Christian Suter and Christopher Chase-Dunn, 285–314. Zürich: Lit.
Moore, Jason W. 2015. *Capitalism in the Web of Life: Ecology and the Accumulation of Capital*. New York: Verso Books.
Mostafanezhad, Mary, and Olivier Evrard. 2020. "Environmental Geopolitics of Rumor: The Sociality of Uncertainty during Northern Thailand's Smoky Season." In

Environmental Geopolitics: A Research Agenda, edited by Shannon O'Lear, 121–135. Cheltenham: Edward Elgar Publishing.

The Nation. 2023. "EGAT Launches Air Purification Tower to Overcome PM2.5." April 20, 2023. https://www.nationthailand.com/thailand/general/40026826.

Neumann, Roderick P. 2009. "Political Ecology: Theorizing Scale." *Progress in Human Geography* 33 (3): 398–406.

Nevins, Joseph, and Nancy Lee Peluso. 2008. "Introduction: Commoditization in Southeast Asia." In *Taking Southeast Asia to Market: Commodities, Nature, and People in the Neoliberal Age,* edited by Jospeh Nevins, and Nancy Lee Peluso, 1–24. Ithaca, NY: Cornell University Press.

Niheu, K. A., L. M. Turbin, and S. Yamada. 2007. "The Impact of the Military Presence in Hawaii on the Health of Na Kanaka Maoli." *Pacific Health Dialog* 14 (1): 205–212.

Nixon, Rob. 2011. *Slow Violence and the Environmentalism of the Poor.* Cambridge, MA: Harvard University Press.

Nost, Eric, and Jenny E. Goldstein. 2022. "A Political Ecology of Data." *Environment and Planning E: Nature and Space* 5 (1): 3–17.

Olson, K. R., and D. R. Speidel. 2023. "United States Secret War in Laos: Long-Term Environmental and Human Health Impacts of the Use of Chemical Weapons." *Open Journal of Soil Science* 13 (4): 199–242.

Parenti, Christian. 2011. *Tropic of Chaos: Climate Change and the New Geography of Violence.* Lebanon: Bold Type Books.

Peluso, Nancy. 1995. "Whose Woods Are These? Counter-Mapping Forest Territories in Kalimantan, Indonesia." *Antipode* 27 (4): 383–406.

Peluso, Nancy Lee, and Michael Watts, eds. 2001. *Violent Environments.* Ithaca, NY: Cornell University Press.

Rankantha, A., I. Chitapanarux, D. Pongnikorn, S. Prasitwattanaseree, W. Bunyatisai, P. Sripan, and P. Traisatit. 2018. "Risk Patterns of Lung Cancer Mortality in Northern Thailand." *BMC Public Health* 18:1–9.

Rasmussen, M. B., and C. Lund. 2018. "Reconfiguring Frontier Spaces: The Territorialization of Resource Control. *World Development* 101:388–399.

Ribot, Jesse. 2014. "Cause and Response: Vulnerability and Climate in the Anthropocene." *Journal of Peasant Studies* 41 (5): 667–705.

Riedel, Friedlind. 2019. "Atmosphere." In *Affective Societies: Key Concepts,* edited by Jan Slaby and Christian von Scheve, 85–95. New York: Routledge.

Robbins, Paul. 2012. *Political Ecology: A Critical Introduction.* 2 ed. New York: Blackwell.

Rodenbiker, J. 2019. "Uneven Incorporation: Volumetric Transitions in Peri-urban China's Conservation Zones." *Geoforum* 104, 234–243.

Sack, R. 1986. *Human Territoriality: It's Theory and History.* Cambridge: Cambridge University Press.

Schroer, Sara Asu, and Susanne Schmitt. 2018. *Exploring Atmospheres Ethnographically.* New York: Routledge.

Scott, James C. 1998. *Seeing Like a State: How Certain Schemes to Improve the Human Condition Have Failed.* New Haven, CT: Yale University Press.

Scott, James C. 2009. *The Art of Not Being Governed: An Anarchist History of Upland Southeast Asia.* New Haven, CT: Yale University Press.
Smith, W., and W. H. Dressler. 2020. "Forged in Flames: Indigeneity, Forest Fire and Geographies of Blame in the Philippines." *Postcolonial Studies* 23 (4): 527–545.
Springer, Simon. 2011. "Violence Sits in Places? Cultural Practice, Neoliberal Rationalism, and Virulent Imaginative Geographies." *Political Geography* 30 (2): 90–98. https://doi.org/10.1016/j.polgeo.2011.01.004.
Steinberg, Philip, and Kimberley Peters. 2015. "Wet Ontologies, Fluid Spaces: Giving Depth to Volume through Oceanic Thinking." *Environment and Planning D: Society and Space* 33 (2): 247–264.
Stewart, Kathleen. 2011. "Atmospheric Attunements." *Environment and Planning D: Society and Space* 29 (3): 445–453.
Stoler, A. L. 2013. *Imperial Debris: On Ruins and Ruination.* Durham, NC: Duke University Press.
Summers, Tim. 2016. "China's 'New Silk Roads': Sub-National Regions and Networks of Global Political Economy." *Third World Quarterly* 37 (9): 1628–1643.
Swyngedouw, Erik. 2010. "Impossible Sustainability and the Post-Political Condition." In *Making Strategies in Spatial Planning: Knowledge and Values,* edited by Maria Cerreta, Grazia Concilio, and Valeria Monno, 185–205. Dordrecht: Springer.
Szerszynski, Bronislaw. 2018. "Drift as a Planetary Phenomenon." *Performance Research* 23 (7): 136–144.
Vandergeest, Peter, and Nancy Lee Peluso. 1995. "Territorialization and State Power in Thailand." *Theory and Society* 24:385–426.
Varkkey, Helen. 2022. "Emergent Geographies of Chronic Air Pollution Governance in Southeast Asia: Transboundary Publics in Singapore." *Environmental Policy and Governance* 32 (4): 348–361.
Wang, Lucy. 2023. "Futuristic Safezone Shelter Battles Air Pollution in Thailand with a Green Oasis." Inhabitat, March 18, 2023. https://inhabitat.com/futuristic-safezone-shelter-battles-air-pollution-in-thailand-with-a-green-oasis/.
Watts, M. J. 2017. "Frontiers: Authority, Precarity and Insurgency at the Edge of the State." *World Development* 101:477–488. https://doi.org/10.1016/j.worlddev.2017.03.024.
Williams, Raymond. 1975. *The Country and the City.* Oxford: Oxford University Press.
Winichakul, Thongchai. 1994. *Siam Mapped: A History of the Geo-Body of a Nation.* Honolulu: University of Hawai'i Press.
Yeh, Emily T., and Elizabeth Wharton. 2016. "Going West and Going Out: Discourses, Migrants, and Models in Chinese Development. *Eurasian Geography and Economics* 57 (3): 286–315.

SECTION I

Pits and Plots

Figure A. Coal mining pit, East Kalimantan, Indonesia. (Photo credit: Tessa D. Toumbourou, 2022)

CHAPTER 1

Deathtrap Landscape
The Politics of Reclamation of
East Kalimantan's Abandoned Coal Mines

TESSA D. TOUMBOUROU, TIM WERNER,
ANTHONY BEBBINGTON, AND MUHAMAD MUHDAR

In East Kalimantan, open-pit or surface mining for coal is the dominant form of industrial land use. Home to the majority of Indonesia's coal reserves, nearly 40 percent of the province's 12.7 Mha land area is overlain with mining permits. Surface mining involves removing all vegetation, soil, and rock overlying the coal seam—a process that produces vast, sheer-edged, and polluted mine voids and more generally does palpable, physical violence to the landscape, killing biotic life and scarring surface features. Mine voids often fill with water, forming pit lakes, many of which are located close to human settlements. As of September 2021, an estimated 1,735 coal mine voids remained unfilled in East Kalimantan, and the number of deaths in pit lakes had reached 40 (33 of which were children) and continues to grow (JATAM 2021). Driven by policies aimed at increasing domestic coal-fired energy generation, growing demand from China, and recent weakening of mining laws and environmental safeguards, coal extraction is projected to expand in Indonesia (IEA 2020).[1] Yet there remain few requirements on mining companies to conduct remediation or post-mining cleanup following extraction or closure to return land to its pre-mined conditions, and no clear legal obligations exist to refill exposed mine voids.

The hazards that former mining sites present to local communities have been the focus of local protests, lobbying efforts, and litigation and legislation reform strategies in East Kalimantan. A civil lawsuit from Gerakan Samarinda Menggugat (Samarinda Lawsuit Movement), filed through the provincial capital city of Samarinda District Court on behalf of a citizen group of plaintiffs, resulted in a court ruling that provincial and national-level government actors with mining-related responsibilities had been negligent in their management of exposed mining pits. Alongside this litigation, local social movement actors—with support from national NGOs—advocated and organized over several years, which led to the introduction of an East Kalimantan provincial regulation (Perda no. 8 of 2013) on the Management of Reclamation and Post-Mining. The regulation mandates that reclamation must be conducted to rehabilitate a mined site's ecological functions. Yet, despite this regulation and the various successes of social movements to pressure state actors, little has changed in the governance of coal mining in East Kalimantan. In this chapter, we document some of the violent legacy effects of coal mining in East Kalimantan. In doing so, we explore the discursive, administrative, and budgetary factors, as well as the political settlements, pacts, and networks (including between elites and mafia or paramilitary groups) that sustain the political economy of unregulated coal mine licensing and reclamation in the province. The asymmetries of power embodied in these political pacts generate "atmospheres" in which violence is always present: in the killing of forest and fauna, the creation of scarred landscapes of danger for human life, and the threat of physical violence against any resistance to the operation and expansion of coal mining.

In Indonesia, the extractive sector is notorious for its entrenched rent seeking and opaque licensing processes—a legacy of the Suharto era (Korte 2011). The political economy of coal sector governance and energy policy is shaped by a distribution of power and inter-elite pacts that are closely controlled by Indonesia's "highly cohesive and complex oligarchy" (Hadiz 2010, 36; Hadiz and Robison 2013). Indonesia's business class is more powerful, more liquid, and more engaged in resource industries than ever before (Warburton 2017, 2), and this is particularly the case for a mining sector dominated by national companies and investors (as opposed to transnational mining corporations). Political actors forge bargains with wealthy business actors, distributing access to government contracts and concessions for natural resource extraction in exchange for campaign funds (Berenschot 2018; Brown and Spiegel 2017). These interests hinder the implementation of laws in relation to environmental and social protections (Butt and Lindsey 2018) and mining governance reforms. A growing literature has examined the political economy factors shaping Indonesia's persistent coal use (Ordonez et al. 2021), and the obstacles to improved regulation of coal reclamation (Toumbourou et al. 2020). Funfgeld's (2016) empirical case study of a coal mine in East Kalimantan illustrates the disproportionate impacts experienced by local communities living close to sites of coal extraction.

We build and expand on this literature by drawing on satellite data and extensive spatial overlays to construct a detailed geographical profile of the extent of coal extraction and coal mining's legacies in East Kalimantan (cf. Roche et al. 2021). We reveal far-reaching environmental impacts and social risks and apparent regulatory violations indicating systemic problems with land use and mining governance in the province. By exploring mining-induced land clearing and the prevalence and impact of mining voids that extend far below the groundwater table, we draw attention to coal extraction's terrestrial and subterranean (or subsurface) implications. We combine this spatial analysis with key informant interviews and site observations conducted between December 2018 and May 2019. Twenty-one interviews were conducted by Tessa Toumbourou and Muhamad Muhdar in East Kalimantan, and two interviews in Jakarta, with respondents from a range of select institutions: national and subnational government, NGOs, social movement and community-based organizations, mining companies and industry organizations, and academia. Complementing the 2018–2019 data, the analysis also draws on thirty-two interviews conducted by Anthony Bebbington in 2016–2017 and 2018 with national (and some international) key informants working in civil society, government, international NGOs, mining companies, and the World Bank. Interview data were complemented by analysis of legal, operational, and other documents. These included relevant regulations and laws, environmental impact assessments, mine reclamation plans, and government agency reports as well as NGO investigation reports.

We show that political economic arrangements shaped over time by national elites have protected and sustained business elites with interests in mining, and enabled coal companies to avoid conducting post-extraction reclamation in East Kalimantan. In this context, we ask several interrelated questions: What do mining sector infractions reveal about extractive industry governance in East Kalimantan? What sustains a political economy of unregulated coal mine reclamation in East Kalimantan? And in what ways does this political economy of coal mining generate forms of violence on people and on the landscape that accompany everyday life in the province?

In addressing these questions, we reveal the extent of coal mining's impact in East Kalimantan. An extensive body of literature has combined land-change science with political ecology studies in "productive hybrid ways" (Turner and Robbins 2008, 308) that go beyond the limitations of each of these disciplinary approaches to provide a systematic, multi-scalar analysis of the extent of land use change, as well as an understanding of the political economy of such transformations (Baird and Fox 2015; Brannstrom and Vadjunec 2013; Lukas 2014). Informed by this scholarship, our study provides a systematic analysis of coal extraction, revealing both violations of mining laws and massive impacts to terrestrial land cover and the subterranean realm. We also explore the political economic processes that have produced the post-mining landscapes of East Kalimantan, and the power dynamics that continue to frustrate reforms and policies, to address the legacy effects of coal mining and enable mining's expansion with fewer social and environmental safeguards. These factors range from flaws in the design of regulations mandating reclamation, through constraints on capacities to adequately implement the law, and on to the extensive networks that link political actors, miners, and paramilitary organizations (*organisasi kemasyarakatan,* commonly known as *ormas*) who seek to intimidate and deter local activists and leaders.

A Political Ecology of the Volumetrics of Coal Mining in East Kalimantan

The field of political ecology (Blaikie and Brookfield 2015; Carney 1996; Robbins 2011) has paid increasing attention to the centrality of mineral and hydrocarbon extraction in contemporary environmental politics (Bebbington 2012; Andrews and McCarthy 2014). Influenced by such work, this subfield has begun to explore the vertical and volumetric relationships between the materialities of subsurface, surface, and aerial spaces (e.g., Elden 2013; Adey 2015)—going beyond earlier land change discussions (Turner and Robbins 2008) focusing mostly on the earth's surface (Bebbington and Bury 2013; Bridge 2013; Goldstein 2019; Postigo, Montoya, and Young 2013).

In this vein, this chapter brings together critical political ecology with emerging work on volumetrics to better understand the corrosive effects of capital overaccumulation that find material expression not only in terrestrial contexts but also in aerial and subterranean spaces (see Introduction). This approach makes explicit connections between ecological change beyond the immediate impact area of a development project, in multidimensional manifestations: horizontal, vertical, and over time (Postigo, Montoya, and Young 2013).[2] As Goldstein (chapter 7 in this volume) notes, for instance, large-scale conversion of forests to industrial agricultural plantations in Indonesia has created the dry conditions that enable peatland fires to spread into and through peatlands' subsurface, resulting in air pollution in territories far beyond the terrestrial areas of Indonesia's peatlands. Similarly, in chapter 2 in this volume, Roberts and Mai examine coal production in dimensions both terrestrial and subterranean, as well as the aerial dimension of the particulates released by coal's incineration in Myanmar. A volumetric perspective is thus useful for understanding the cumulative impact of post-coal mining landscapes over time. The legacies of coal mining involve significant ecological change in the form of clearing trees and brush, displacing and killing fauna, and moving surface soil and rock (known as the overburden) to create massive mine voids and hazardous chemical-filled water bodies, changing human-environment relations across these different domains. The various socio-ecological impacts unfold and accumulate over time, slowly dispossessing local people of their livelihoods, resulting in food insecurity and social inequalities. As Ojeda et al. (2022, 3) describe, extraction-induced dispossession is a "process of violent reconfiguration impacting life and living worlds, and usually involving the devastation of communities and ecologies." At the same time, extraction does violence to the subterranean worlds layered by geological and edaphic histories, rupturing their form and displacing their content from subsoil strata to piles of waste rock and overburden heaped upon other parts of the mine site.

Attending to the volumetric dimensions of post-closure coal mine landscapes invites consideration of the processes and phases of mining that work to enable the creation of hazardous mine voids and the persistent view that such landscapes are unavoidable and irreversible. We argue below that a key phase in these processes is the definition and granting of mine permits by mining authorities for what are essentially square "blocks" on maps that lack detail of village settlements, landscape features, or other land use allocations. Under Indonesian law, the state has ownership of subsoil minerals and coal, subsuming the rights of local landholders and other land use functions. Recent legal changes have reduced avenues for local communities to contest when mining is permitted on their land, or where mining occurs outside of concession areas. Following Goldstein (2019, 6), we argue that state mapping strategies that represent mining zones as "two-dimensional, [often rectilinear] enclosed mapped representations" of terrestrial land areas fail to consider the other existing ecological functions and livelihood uses of that land, and obscure the three-dimensional, long-term material implications of coal's extraction. As Rocheleau (2005, 329) notes, conventional maps can reduce complex and volumetric material realities to simple two-dimensional representations that "facilitate control of land and natural resources and that so often function as both the tools and alibis of powerful political and commercial interests." We also show that mining is not limited to these legal "blocks" on maps but occurs over residential land or river buffer zones bordering mine concessions.

Obscuring the subterranean dimensions of coal extraction with simplified two-dimensional representations enables miners and state agencies to downplay the massive, long-lasting subsurface impacts of coal extraction, and the ways in which they intersect with the politics and protection of human life on the surface. As Indonesian legislation does not explicitly mandate the refilling of mine voids, miners are able to extract with impunity, leaving massive mine voids to be generated without any obligation to meet the high cost of refilling them. While state- and private sector–aligned actors acknowledge the irreversible subterranean implications of coal mining, they still defend vaguely worded laws and mining sector practices on the grounds that refilling mine voids would be impractical.

The Politics and Political Economy of Coal Mining Expansion in East Kalimantan: Devolution and Decentralization

Coal mining first began in East Kalimantan under the Dutch colonial administration (van Bemmelen 1949; Daulay 1994), but was scaled up under the Suharto-led

New Order regime, which in 1967 introduced two major laws to cultivate the coal mining industry. The 1967 Mining Law (Law no. 11/1967) opened up the coal mining sector to foreign investment and prevented landowners from refusing to release land if mining investors offered "fair" compensation (Gandataruna and Haymon 2011, 227). The 1967 Foreign Investment Law (Law no. 1/1967) then allowed foreign investors to repatriate their earnings and protect them from expropriation. These laws left local communities with few options for veto when large-scale mining companies began to arrive in the 1970s and 1980s. Land appropriation for large-scale mines—issued with so-called Coal Contracts of Work (*Perjanjian Karya Pengusahaan Pertambangan Batubara,* or PKP2B)—involved forced but compensated land acquisition for communities residing in areas targeted for concessions (Mahy 2012).[3] Coal production increased in the decades that followed, with contracts for large-scale mining operations distributed to patronage networks in exchange for political support for the Suharto administration (McCarthy 2011). This intersection of coal, patronage, and the formation of inter-elite political pacts at both national and subnational levels has continued through to the present.

Post-1998: Reformasi-Era of Decentralization

While coal extraction grew under Suharto, it was during the *reformasi* period following his fall in 1998 that the mining boom reached full swing. *Reformasi* involved reforms promoting electoral democracy and competitive elections, together with administrative and political decentralization (O'Rourke 2002; Resosudarmo 2010). While decentralization created new spaces for political participation, it also opened new opportunities for corruption at the subnational level (Brown and Spiegel 2017). One of the later reforms, the 2009 Minerals and Coal Mining Law (Law no. 4/2009), exemplified this by changing the PKP2B contract system to a mining permit system. Under this system, mining investors now had to obtain one of three types of permit: a mining business permit (*Izin Usaha Pertambangan* [IUP]) for exploration (*IUP-Eksplorasi*) and production (*IUP-Operasi*); a special mining business permit (*Izin Usaha Pertambangan Khusus* [IUPK]); or a people's mining permit (*Izin Pertambangan Rakyat* [IPR]) (O'Callaghan 2010).[4] IUPs and IUPKs are for midsize operations, with concession areas capped at 15,000 hectares, while IPRs are for an area of 5 to 10 hectares. PKP2B contracts, which were generally for larger operations (under the former mining system, concession size was arranged by contractual negotiation), remain in place until their expiration, at which point they are transferred to the new permit system.

The 2009 Minerals and Coal Mining Law gave district head authorities control over determining access to coal deposits, meaning that mining companies had to reach agreements with these authorities to operate. This new power incentivized local bureaucrats and elites to raise revenue and collect illegal levies to fund expensive election campaigns to run for district head, a position that would (if they were elected) give them access to rents from extractive industries (Butt and Lindsey 2018; Ordonez et al. 2021; Robinson 2016). Unsurprisingly, the new powers given to district heads to control mining were not accompanied by improved regulation or protections; instead, mining practices became "unrestrained and unscrupulous" (Gandataruna and Haymon 2011, 225), with "little regard for environmental protection" (Butt and Lindsey 2018, 162). In October 2014, the Regional Governance Law (Law no. 23/2014) was introduced, which transferred mining oversight from district to provincial governments, ostensibly to improve land use governance and monitoring. Yet, by this time, permits had already been issued over most of East Kalimantan's coal rich areas (Funfgeld 2019).

As decentralization reforms were unfolding, demand from China, India, Vietnam, and elsewhere created incentives to expand coal production. This increasing demand for coal, coupled with political incentives to grant coal permits in return for political and financial support, led to a surge of mining in East Kalimantan. Following the implementation of the 2009 Minerals and Coal Mining Law, 800 mining permits were issued across the province between December 2009 and December 2010 alone (Macdonald 2017). By 2017, 1,404 mining business permits (IUPs and IUPKs) and 33 large-scale PKP2B mining contracts had been issued across East Kalimantan (see figures 1.1 and 1.2).[5] Companies that hold IUPs and IUPKs are typically medium-sized enterprises, often subsidiaries of larger holding companies, fully or partially owned by Indonesian political elites working with both domestic and international public and private financing. This rampant growth in mining concessions has been accompanied by serious environmental and human impacts, including forest loss and carbon emissions, water pollution, and risks to human health and life.

In 2014, reduced demand for low-grade coal from China resulted in a sharp drop in Indonesia's coal exports (Cornot-Gandolphe 2017). As the majority (around 70–80 percent) of Indonesia's coal production is exported (EIA 2019), fears that reduced demand would continue long term led Indonesia's coal mining sector to lobby for policies that would expand the domestic market, in particular by encouraging the government to prioritize a suite of new coal-fired power plants as part of national energy policy (Ordonez et al. 2021).[6] In the same year, President Joko Widodo announced a plan to fast-track the addition of 35 gigawatts (GW) of new generating capacity by 2019, some 20 GW of which was to be in the form of new coal plants (although this was later scaled back), with plans to add a further 15 GW of coal-based capacity by 2025 (PLN 2016; Brown and Spiegel 2017; Agrawal et al. 2018). The planned coal plants are set to use low-rank, lignite-grade coal at prices capped well below the market price (Ordonez et al. 2021), requiring that larger amounts of coal be extracted to maintain existing energy levels (Dutu 2016).

32   Chapter 1

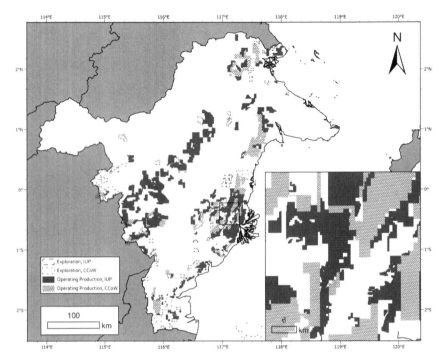

Figure 1.1. Map showing location of mine concessions in East Kalimantan at time of publication, including small- to medium-sized exploration (*IUP-Eksplorasi*) and operation (*IUP-Operasi*) mining permits, and large-scale Coal Contract of Work operational contracts. (Source: Prepared by the authors using geospatial data provided by JATAM East Kalimantan, 2018)

Post-2020: Mining Control Recentralized

After several years of flatlined production, from 2018 through 2019, coal production spiked again in Indonesia, reaching record high rates (13.76 exajoules in 2018 and 15.05 exajoules in 2019) (BP 2020). While India and China remain the major international buyers, growing domestic demand fueled Indonesian coal production (Friederich and van Leeuwen 2017). In 2020 however, the COVID-19–induced economic slowdown saw international demand for coal plummet. Another parallel impact on the coal sector was the impending expiry of seven major PKP2Bs that control as much as 70 percent of Indonesia's coal production (CNN Indonesia 2020). In response to pressure by mining elites, in 2020 the Indonesian government passed two major pieces of legislation that aimed to enable mining expansion. The first was a revision to the Minerals and Coal Mining Law, which passed through

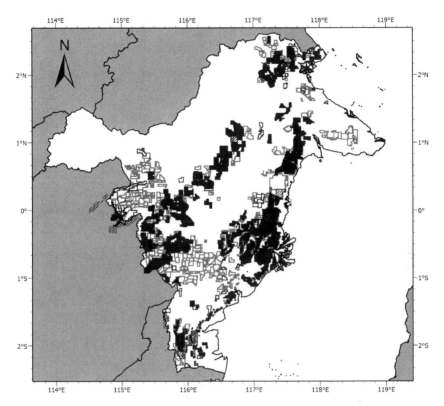

Figure 1.2. Map showing all mining permits overlaying East Kalimantan at time of publication. Black-filled areas are those with operating extraction permits, and outlined areas depict areas with exploration permits, which vary depending on the source. Grey outlines are those reported under the Nature Conservancy. Dashed areas represent Coal Contract of Work permits reported by the Indonesian Ministry of Energy and Mineral Resources, see Werner et al. (2024). (Source: Prepared by the authors using geospatial data provided by JATAM East Kalimantan, 2018)

Indonesia's parliament on May 12, 2020, with little scrutiny, as legislators took advantage of COVID-19 social distancing measures.

The 2020 Minerals and Coal Mining Law recentralizes control over mining, previously held by provincial governments, to now being the exclusive authority of the Ministry of Energy and Mineral Resources (MoEMR)—bringing industry oversight closer to national political elites. Article 196A of the revised law guarantees extensions of PKP2Bs for two consecutive ten-year periods (a total of twenty years) without an auction, giving priority to state-owned companies, as was required in the former version of the law. The new law also removes the 15,000-hectare cap for a single IUP, to benefit holders of large-scale PKP2Bs whose concessions reach up to six times this size.[7] Indeed, expansion of mining concessions is encouraged under the new mining law; Article 36A states that an IUP or IUPK holder is "obligated" to conduct exploration every year, whereas the previous law only "allowed" such activity. The revisions also further weaken the previous law's already ambiguous environmental and social obligations. While the revisions have introduced sanctions on IUP or IUPK holders for not conducting mine reclamation—five years' imprisonment and a maximum fine of IDR 100 billion (US$6.9 million)—they preserve the lack of clarity around what is meant by mine rehabilitation in the previous law, which has allowed companies to avoid refilling mining pits. Article 128A of the revised law additionally exempts large mining companies (IUPK and PKP2B holders—largely owned by politico-elites with close central government connections) from paying royalties (previously between 2 percent and 7 percent of the average selling price in a royalty period), as long as these companies "carry out [activities that] add value to coal," such as developing coal-fired power plants. Observers have argued that this vaguely worded revision does not specify the meaning of "value added," and essentially gives mining companies coal for free (Jong 2020). Royalties play a crucial role in contributing to the economic development that proponents argue mining brings to underdeveloped regions. The absence of royalties, enabled by this revision, undermines this rationale.

Another recent change affecting mining governance was the introduction of the Law on Job Creation (Law No. 11/2020 or Omnibus Law), which came into effect on November 5, 2020. The Omnibus Law introduced a suite of legislative changes (seventy-nine current laws and fifty-one implementing regulations were changed under the law), with the stated purpose of simplifying rules and administrative systems to increase foreign investment. One of the legal changes was to Law no. 32/2009 on Environmental Protection and Management, removing the current prerequisite for an environmental impact assessment (called AMDAL) to have been conducted to determine the environmental feasibility of any mine or other development. Following this change, only activities deemed "high risk" will require an AMDAL, while for moderate-risk activities there is only a recommendation for an "environmental feasibility study," and low risk activities will merely have to be registered. Criminal charges for violations of environmental regulations have been removed and replaced with administrative sanctions. The changes also remove the requirement for involvement of environmental experts or other civil society observers in the AMDAL or environmental feasibility study, an important measure to ensure transparency and rigor.

These reforms benefit mine operators but reduce protections for local communities. For example, Article 162 of the 2020 Minerals and Coal Mining Law imposes criminal sanctions and fines for anyone deemed to be hindering or interfering with mining activity. With already few processes in place for affected populations to participate in the land-licensing process for mining, local communities are currently at risk of criminalization should they express objections to mining activity on their land. This risk is further heightened by imbalances of power, lack of transparency, and violence and intimidation between state authorities and local communities. The 2020 mining law also removes sanctions set out in the previous law (Article 162) for government officials who engage in corruption related to the issuance of mining permits. Civil society observers suspect that the 2020 mining law was passed with pressure from mining elites linked to PKP2Bs that were coming up for expiry. Describing parliament's deliberation of the bill, a researcher from the national NGO Indonesia Corruption Watch stated: "The debate was rushed and held behind closed doors. Our suspicion is that mining elites who have interests in the coal business had pushed for the debate [to be held in this way]" (Rahmadi 2020). Concerns have been raised about conflicts of interest among ministers and officials involved in developing deregulation reforms (both the 2020 Job Creation Law and the 2020 Minerals and Coal Mining Law) due to their direct ties to coal mining companies (Bersihkan Indonesia 2020; Margiansyah et al. 2020). These laws were passed a year after the Corruption Eradication Commission (KPK)—which had investigated mining sector violations and corruption leading to 2,178 illegal mining permits being revoked (*Mongabay* 2017)—was also weakened by politico-elites, compromising its independence and investigative powers (Mudhoffir 2023).

By 2021, coal production was booming again in East Kalimantan, enabled by the recent deregulation reforms, and by China turning to Indonesia for its coal supply after placing unofficial sanctions on Australian products, including coal, following the Australian government's call for an inquiry into the Wuhan origins of the coronavirus pandemic (Chang 2021). Between January and March 2021, 144 million tons of coal were produced in Indonesia (Idris 2021); on January 8, 2021, the price of Indonesian coal reached US$45.56 per ton, the highest since July 2018 (Russell 2021). The global rebound in demand for coal is likely to be short-lived however, if, as predicted by the International Energy Agency (IEA 2020), coal prices flatten by 2025.

Human-Environment Transformations due to Coal Mining

Most of the coal in East Kalimantan is extracted through open-cut mining (Sasaoka et al. 2015) or surface mining (Woodbury et al. 2020). In these processes, large tracts of often-forested land are cleared to access brown surface coal. The overburden is stripped of all vegetation, then removed and deposited in a pile that, according to regulations, should be within the concession site (Fatah 2008). Open-cut mining results in major disturbances to landscapes, causing extensive deforestation (Bebbington et al. 2018), and severely damaging underground and surface hydrology and hydrological cycling (Conde and Le Billon 2017). When mining ceases, mine voids—often hundreds of meters below the natural water table—fill with groundwater, rainfall, and runoff.[8] Acid and metalliferous drainage (AMD, also known as acid mine drainage) results from the exposure of sulfide-rich crushed rock to rainfall, causing heavy metals (that would otherwise remain buried in intact rock) to discharge from water-filled mining pits into groundwater, causing it to evaporate (Geller et al. 2012; McCullough 2016). Acidic mine waters are potentially toxic to organisms living in the aquatic environment (Stephens and Ingram 2006) and to humans.

An investigation by independent journalists into the water quality in abandoned mine voids in East Kalimantan revealed dangerous amounts of heavy metals (Kompas.id 2018).[9] Coal mining has also resulted in an increase in the number and severity of floods, with the city of Samarinda being flooded 150 times between 2009 and 2014, at an estimated total cost of some US$9 million (Winn 2016). Increased flooding caused by coal mining is also a likely reason for dramatic sedimentation in three lakes in the local Mahakam River Basin, which is home to 147 indigenous species of freshwater fish. These impacts have been noted by local researchers at the East Kalimantan Development Study Centre (Pusat Studi Pembangunan Kalimantan Timur): "Thirty years ago, these lakes were 15m deep and clear; today, they are only 2m in depth and their water is murky" (cited in van Paddenburg et al. 2012, 58).

Concerns about freshwater access and quality were reflected in discussions with communities in the villages of Mulawarman and Kerta Buana, both in the Kutai Kartenegara district (an hour's and a two-hours' drive north of Samarinda, respectively), where large-scale coal mines have expanded to abut village residences. Upstream water flows have been cut off, and tailings and acidic water in waterways have reduced rice and crop yields. In interviews, villagers reflected on the negative impacts of coal mining to their livelihoods, with many observing dramatic reductions in crop yields and pollution to waterways.

Deaths in Mining Concessions Certified as "Clean and Clear"

Alongside impacts on water and soil fertility, water-filled mine pits have introduced into the landscape new risks of drowning. Between 2011 and 2021, forty deaths occurred at former coal mining sites in East Kalimantan (Burton 2016; Komnas HAM 2016; JATAM 2021; Tribunnews.com 2019). Figure 1.3 indicates the sites of these drownings, the majority of which have occurred in and around Samarinda,

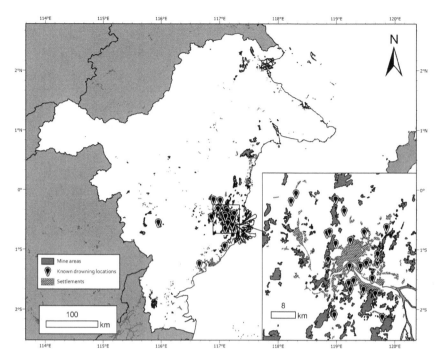

Figure 1.3. Map showing sites of drownings in mine pits in East Kalimantan. (Source: Prepared by the authors using geospatial data provided by JATAM East Kalimantan, 2018; sites of drownings determined from media reports)

where 70 percent of the municipal area is overlain with mining concessions. These deaths frequently involve children falling into and drowning in unfenced pit lakes. Our spatial analysis revealed that nearly 25 percent of village settlements in East Kalimantan are located within one meter of pit lakes, indicating that mining-induced drownings will continue without intervention. This violates a regulation that mine voids must not be within 500 meters of human settlements.[10]

Until it ended in 2018, the so-called clean-and-clear (CnC) audit was one of the few systematic mechanisms for mining sector oversight in Indonesia, involving a review of compliance with relevant environmental and other permit-related regulations.[11] A desktop exercise, the CnC audit did not require a site assessment, and as we show, it did not reflect whether company operations were adhering to environmental and human health protection laws on the ground. As illustrated in figure 1.3, drownings have frequently occurred in mine concessions granted CnC status.[12] The CnC certification system was therefore an insufficient indicator of regulatory compliance in mining. Our study also shows that violations of boundary delineations—including mining concessions located within 500 meters of human settlements—were evident on concessions with CnC certification. Furthermore, conducting reclamation was not a criterion of the CnC audit, despite the immediate and longer-term risks that abandoned mine sites pose to human health and safety. Where permits were deemed to be non-CnC, a governor or the MoEMR had the authority to revoke or amend the IUP. Interviews with mining sector representatives confirmed that revoking CnC mining permits for noncompliance transferred the cost burden of resolving "illegalities" from mining companies to the state. Thus, rather than being a punitive measure, this could perversely diminish the incentive for state agencies to enforce compliance and benefit companies whose permits were revoked as they could abandon their obligations to conduct reclamation.

Mining Drives Land Clearing in East Kalimantan

Over the past five years, mining has spread rapidly across the province of East Kalimantan, driving extensive land clearing. In the two years from 2015 to 2017, despite a flatlining in coal production, the geographical extent of mining activity grew by 9 percent in the province (from around 116,844 ha to 130,625 ha). At present rates, mining activity may reach approximately 142,348 ha by 2040. Satellite image classifications showed that land issued with an active operating permit (IUP-O) had 5.3 times more land clearing than other areas of the province where no mining is present.

We found that coal mining operations have land clearing impacts beyond their direct features—that is, beyond just the area of land disturbed for opening pits, waste treatment ponds, dumping waste rock and soil (the overburden), and basecamp and processing infrastructure. We also show that (as far as is possible to tell given data uncertainties), coal extraction and waste disposal areas regularly violate concession boundaries (see figure 1.4). Field checks and interviews with mining intermediaries and NGO activists revealed that illegal mining often takes place in what is known locally as "mining corridors"—narrow strips of residential land or river buffer zones where mining is prohibited by law. Within these areas, farmers have reported that mining's expansion nearby has had detrimental effects on ecohydrological systems, making farming increasingly difficult and reducing their crop yields (Funfgeld 2016; Muhdar, Nasir, and Nurdiana 2019). Consequently, farmers are increasingly compelled to sell or rent their land to mining intermediaries—who specifically target these mining corridors using leaked government data on coal seam locations—and often forced to settle for prices below the actual market value of their land. These intermediaries then arrange for these mine corridors to be mined, with extracted coal sold to neighboring permit-holding companies (for significantly reduced market price).

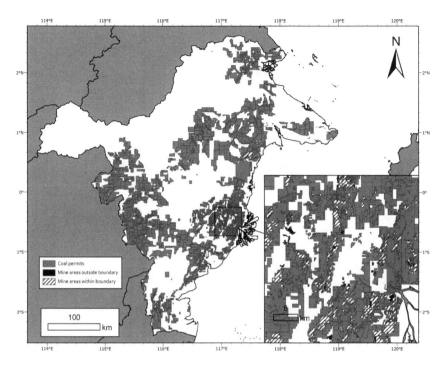

Figure 1.4. Map showing mining-induced land clearing beyond concession boundaries, East Kalimantan. (Source: Prepared by the authors using data sourced from the Nature Conservancy and the East Kalimantan mining agency, 2017)

A global assessment of deforestation driven by large-scale mining found more mining-induced forest destruction in Indonesia than in any other country of the world, with much of the forest loss occurring in East Kalimantan (Giljum et al. 2022). Forest destruction was far more extensive between 2010 and 2019 than during the previous decade. Despite its negative impacts, mining is set to continue to increase in East Kalimantan. We found that exploration mining permits (IUP-E) now cover a significant proportion of the province. In interviews, NGO actors indicated that once an IUP-E has been granted, there is a high likelihood that the same company will be granted a permit to operate. Indeed, legislation guarantees that holders of an IUP-E who have complied with permit conditions have automatic priority rights to apply for an operating permit (IUP-O) for the same area (Indonesian Mining Institute 2018). There are strong indications then that further land clearing will occur when IUP-E holders are granted an IUP-O over these concessions and extraction begins.

Mining in these areas is contingent on ensuring that mining actors have access to sufficient funds to cover the initial costs of mining, which many do not. One civil society observer explained that the extensive number of exploration permits is due to a local practice of land banking, where local brokers—who lack the technical or financial capacity to mine themselves—obtain IUPs with the purpose of selling these to investors.[13] A report by the Indonesian Mining Institute (2018, 33) corroborates this analysis, stating that more than half of the time, exploration and operational permits are awarded to applicants that do not have the technical and financial capacity to fulfill permit requirements and conduct extraction.

Land-Use Licensing Obfuscates the Subterranean Impacts of Coal Extraction

> Mining permitting is brutal, it's out of control. There is hardly any coordination between the national, provincial, and district governments. Issuance of permits between 2001 and 2010 was chaos. All the permits issued were not based on the reality of land. Almost all permits issued in East Kalimantan are in blocks, or grids, ignoring natural land features, rivers, or communities.
>
> —JATAM East Kalimantan organizer, April 6, 2018

As explained by a leading activist with JATAM (the Mining Advocacy Network) East Kalimantan, permits for coal mines are represented as two-dimensional blocks on government maps that delineate only the bounded, terrestrial area allocated for mine concessions. Our findings, indicating land clearing outside mine concession boundaries and the extensive subsurface area affected by coal voids, show that such simplified representations of mining at the licensing stage compound the extensive ongoing vertical impact of coal mining.

As in many other countries, Indonesian law privileges mining over other forms of land use, by decoupling legal control over the land's terrestrial surface and subsurface minerals.[14] Mining permits can be granted for any land area zoned for mining controlled by the state, even where other land uses exist. The legal weight given to mining interests over other land uses, reinforced by licensing and regulations that allow mining to occur with relative impunity, has resulted in extensive overlap between mining concessions and other land use allocations, with large portions of Kalimantan's land surface area overlaid with multiple concessions (Abood et al. 2015).

It was only in 2010 that mining reclamation regulations were introduced at the national level. Government Regulation no. 78/2010 on Reclamation and Post-Mining states that exploration and operation IUP holders are obligated to perform reclamation. It requires mining business permit holders to submit a reclamation and post-mining activity plan, and to set aside a reclamation guarantee in the form of a time deposit. The regulation was implemented in 2014 and does not detail requirements for treating or filling mine voids, referring only to requirements relating to revegetation of mined sites and for "managing" voids.[15] The regulation was revised in 2018 to become the Ministry for Energy and Mineral Resources (MoEMR) Regulation no. 26/2018 on the Implementation of Good Mining Rules and Supervision of Mineral and Coal Mining but was in effect the same as the earlier version. It remains the case with the 2020 changes to the mining law that no government regulation specifically requires the refilling of mine voids. The Perda no. 8 introduced in East Kalimantan in 2013 implements Government Regulation no. 78/2010, and its subsequent revisions, which require companies to meet only what was already mandated in the higher-level laws.

Political Settlements and Networks Sustaining a Political Economy of Unregulated Mining

The coal sector protects its incumbency and sustains a political economy of poorly regulated mining through a series of networks, pacts, and relationships. An NGO report links the six largest coal mining companies in Indonesia, which combined produced more than 50 percent of the country's coal in 2015, to national political elites (JATAM et al. 2019).[16] The East Kalimantan mining sector is dominated and controlled by these national elites, particularly politicians, military, and police generals with mining investments. These actors continue to frustrate laws at the national level that would damage their interests and are also able to influence budget allocation to enforcement agencies, and thus constrain their capacities to implement regulations. The highly clientelist system for electing regional heads is a factor here. Berenschot (2018) has identified the key features of Indonesia's "patronage democracy" that facilitate clientelism: the relative independence of candidates from political parties, which means that political candidates must negotiate and buy the support of a coalition of parties (Hendrawan, Aspinall, and Berenschot 2017); candidates having to build their own campaign networks and doing so by promising access to natural resources (including guaranteeing the awarding of mining permits) should they be elected (Aspinall 2014; Macdonald 2017); and the high costs of political campaigns fostering corruption and forcing political candidates to engage in clientelist deals (Hadiz 2010; Mietzner 2013).

Alongside these pact-based mechanisms, mining elites maintain extensive networks with mafia (*preman*) and paramilitary groups (*ormas*) who use intimidation or violence to protect coal-based interests (Funfgeld 2016, 2018; Atteridge, Aung, and Nugroho 2018). At times, *ormas* engage directly in mining themselves or work as contractors to mine owners, the regional police, and others. The most notorious *ormas* group—Pemuda Pancasila (Pancasila Youth), a national paramilitary group—has a strong presence in East Kalimantan in their provision of security to mining companies, and, as Bakker (2017, 134) details, a history of "clearing inhabitants from new project sites through intimidation, violence and arson." In interviews, NGO actors noted that many subsidiary mining companies in East Kalimantan are linked to senior government actors such as Luhut Binsar Pandjaitan, who was the former coordinating minister for political, legal, and security affairs, a role that oversaw the mining and energy sector.[17] Luhut was also a former military general strongly linked to local *ormas* through his previous Golkar political party links.[18,19]

Ormas have been mobilized to deal with incidents related to mine abandonment. Interviews with members of mine-affected communities revealed several examples where, following children's deaths in mining voids, families did not pursue investigations after experiencing intimidation, or being offered money by companies to avoid filing a police report.[20] JATAM East Kalimantan's office was visited several times by *preman* linked to mining companies prior to and during data collection. In another case, a young teenager, aged thirteen, had drowned in a mining pit owned by Bukit Baiduri Energi. JATAM visited the house of the victim's family and released a press release reporting the death. The following evening, around thirty men broke into JATAM's office and ransacked the property, damaging windows and a motorbike belonging to one staff member.[21] This was the second time that JATAM has had to move office due to intimidation and harassment. JATAM activists had to gather away from the office for their safety, and several activists moved house.

The deployment of *preman* and *ormas* is not limited to conflicts related to reclamation. In one transmigrant rice-farming village, residents noted that when blasts from nearby mines began to destroy houses, village efforts to blockade the mine operations were quashed by *ormas*. One village head revealed in an interview: "When there's issues [and we've taken them to the company], *ormas* are sent to scare us off. *Ormas* use intimidation." The use of *ormas* to provide mining operations protection from local communities is widespread. Local journalist investigations have revealed how, for example, in a number of locations in East Kalimantan, *ormas* are involved in protecting mining taking place illegally on sites permitted for commercial housing estates (Katadata.co.id 2019).

Discussion

There is a clear asymmetry in how laws have operated in regulating coal mining in East Kalimantan. On the one hand, a suite of laws, regulations, and policies have facilitated the expansion of the extractive industries (cf. Andrews and McCarthy 2014). These laws have reduced obstacles to investment, helped open new frontiers, and weakened instruments designed to reduce the environmental and social impacts of the sector. On the other hand, those laws, regulations, and policies, whose introduction was designed to diminish the adverse effects of mining on local communities, have not been adopted with the same vigor as those that enabled mining's rapid and unfettered expansion. The courts, regulating government agencies, and the police have all failed to hold the coal mining industry accountable for human rights harms or illegal environmental harms that have occurred on abandoned mine sites. Nefarious links between the coal sector and violent paramilitary groups remain hidden from legal scrutiny.

This asymmetry reflects the political economy of coal and the political settlement that sustains this extractive status quo. Energy policy has elevated coal within Indonesia's energy matrix, while Indonesia's legal and illegal coal exports to South and East Asia are key sources of revenue for the state and actors within the state, as well as being a critical component of bilateral relations between Indonesia, China, India, Vietnam, and other countries. At the same time, income from coal helps sustain political alliances at both national and subnational levels: these alliances in turn advocate for and defend the sector's investment interests. With the removal of international extractive companies from coal mining in Indonesia, the ties between coal, national elites and Indonesian-owned companies have become stronger. These connections have facilitated Indonesia's growing domestic consumption of coal and recent deregulation reforms further reducing social and environmental safeguards to enable the expansion of mining, leaving local communities stranded in places "stripped of the very characteristics that made it habitable" (Nixon 2011, 19) with few grievance options. In short, these political connections have enabled expanded violence to human life, to biota (especially forest cover), and to the integrity of the soil and the subsoil.

Our findings show that small- to medium-sized coal mining companies, with strong links to national elites, operate with near impunity in East Kalimantan. The violence, intimidation, and harassment applied by local paramilitary groups to gain access to coal deposits on these concessions continues (in increasingly coercive forms) to allow resource elites to maintain control over rents from coal extraction. These local actors and organizations protect the mining sector on behalf of nationally based elites who ensure that mandates for conducting reclamation are weak and poorly enforced, to keep the cost of mining relatively low. Mine voids on these concessions frequently occur in the immediate vicinity of local residences, in violation of national regulations, posing health and safety threats to local communities. In the forty drownings in "death trap" pit lakes that have occurred at the time of this writing, companies have almost entirely avoided responsibility. The limited reclamation of post-mine landscapes also presents harmful longer-term legacy effects that unfold cumulatively over time, in a form of "slow violence" (Nixon 2011). The consequences of forest clearing, contamination of surface and ground water, erosion, and increased incidences of flooding result in local farming communities losing their "ability to derive benefits from previous and potential systems of life-making" (Roberts and Mai 2021, 6). The slow violence taking place at East Kalimantan's extractive frontier is manifest in many forms, most visibly (Galtung 2004) in the death by drowning of children in sheer-edged pit lakes, but also in less visible ways, through the alteration of hydrological systems, reduced agricultural land, water pollution, and the razing of forest ecosystems that provide crucial agricultural services such as soil formation, pollination, and pest control (Karp et al. 2013; Koh 2008; Maas, Clough, and Tscharntke 2013; van Noordwijk et al. 2012). This devastation is gendered and intersectional, disproportionately affecting marginalized groups excluded from limited mining employment opportunities, leading to impoverishment (Großmann, Padmanabhan, and von Braun 2017; Lahiri-Dutt 2006; Lahiri-Dutt and Mahy 2008). Through the transformation of agricultural regions into unproductive regions, extraction further legitimizes the discourse that coal drives economic growth in underdeveloped regions (Atteridge, Aung, and Nugroho 2018; Welker 2009), supporting the expansion of coal mining and its central role in Indonesia's export economy and extractive settlement (Diprose et al. 2022; Tyson, Varkkey, and Choiruzzad 2018; Winanti and Diprose 2020). Mining reorganizes vertical relationships between materials, biota, and people; in the language of this book, it reworks volumes and volumetric violence. Biota is destroyed, underground hydrological processes are ruptured, landscapes are violated, and livelihoods and lives are changed in abrupt and irreversible ways. While some may see new opportunities, for others these transformations come accompanied by new atmospheres of fear: fear of the *ormas,* fear of your child drowning in pit lakes, fear of yet more mines being opened, and fear of retribution for speaking out. Coal mining's material damage to the subterranean inevitably brings new violence to life on the surface—directly to the water and livelihood sources of local communities and ecologies in and around sites of extraction, and indirectly to the atmosphere, where coal is burnt for energy generation (Canelas and Carvalho 2023).

An opaque licensing system, inaccurate and incomplete land use maps, and underfunded government oversight agencies have facilitated overlapping mining permits. Without clarity over where concessions begin and end, companies can act with impunity. They avoid repercussions from violating concession boundaries, deaths in their pit lakes, and the high cost of post-extraction reclamation beyond cosmetic activity. The techniques used to sustain coal's ascendancy include policy and political lobbying, pact making, idea framing, and differentiated funding of the public bureaucracy (cf. Humphreys Bebbington and Huber 2017). We have paid particular attention to the ways in which national political and economic elites exercise power in the sector. We have noted how the coal industry and its allies have been able to define the understanding of "reclamation" in mining legislation, and how public bodies that are charged with supervising mines' environmental and social performance are funded at levels that prevent them from being both effective and independent.

The cumulative effect of this situation is that coal continues to be mined, forest continues to be cleared, greenhouse gas emissions continue to rise, and the sector continues to leave in its wake pit-scarred landscapes that create dangers for the people who live in and around them. Or put another way, landscapes of overlapping violence thus continue to be reproduced: the violence of environmental destruction, the violence of pit drownings, and the violence of the *ormas*. While such violence can be, and has been, contested, there is no doubt that it constrains the possibilities of civic action and of living well for mine-affected communities in East Kalimantan.

Notes

1. On March 25, 2021, Indonesia announced a Long-Term Strategy for Reducing Carbon Emissions and Climate Resilience 2050, which sets in place a plan for Indonesia's emissions to peak in 2030, before reaching net zero by 2070. According to the strategy, coal will continue to dominate Indonesia's energy mix for the next three decades, constituting 34 percent of Indonesia's energy production in 2050.

2. The various studies in the wide-ranging volume *The Earth as Transformed by Human Action: Global and Regional Changes in the Biosphere Over the Past 300 Years* (Turner et al. 1990) also focus on all dimensions of human impact on the physical environment, including land, water, and atmosphere.

3. For example, establishing East Kalimantan's largest coal mine, Kaltim Prima Coal, required the resettlement of an entire village (Atteridge, Aung, and Nugroho 2018, 15).

4. While IUPs and IUPKs are similar permit types, an IUP is for mining conducted in areas zoned by the central government as commercial mining business areas, while an IUPK is for mining conducted in areas zoned as state reserve areas—land reserved for the "strategic national interest" (PricewaterhouseCoopers 2016, 10).

5. The 2017 figures are supplied by the East Kalimantan energy and mineral resources agency. Data varies across levels of government: according to the Ministry of Energy and Mineral Resources (MEMR), as of September 2018, East Kalimantan had 998 IUPs in operation—the most of any province in Indonesia—with 215 non-clean and clear. In July 2018, the director general of minerals and coal (*dirjen minerba*), within the Ministry of Energy and Mineral Resources documented almost eight million hectares of mine pits that have not been reclaimed to date across Indonesia.

6. Indonesia exports predominantly bituminous (middle-rank coal) and subbituminous coal (second-division low-rank coal). Its lignite coal production, however, has increased since 2010, reflecting demand for cheap sources of coal, particularly from China and India

(Cornot-Gandolphe 2017). In December 2020, Indonesia exported 12.19 million tons of coal to China, and 5.56 million tons to India.

7. The concession area of Kaltim Prima Coal, one of the bigger CCoW in the province, for example, covers 90,000 hectares (Scrivener 2013).

8. Open-cut coal mines reach the end of their economic life when the cost of resource extraction outweighs its financial value, "such as when the coal seam has dipped so far that the cost of removing rock from above is prohibitively expensive" (Walters 2016, 6).

9. Metals identified included manganese, iron, mercury, chromium, cobalt, zinc, arsenic, selenium, cadmium, barium, lead, and thallium.

10. Ministry of Environment Decree no. 4/2012 (on environmentally responsible indicators for open-pit mining operations or activities) states that the distance from the edge of a mine void must be at least 500 m from a concession boundary. This rule is also stated in the Ministry of Energy and Mineral Resources (ESDM) regulation no. 1827 K/30/MEM/2018 about the technical guidelines for the implementation of good mining.

11. In February 2018, the MoEMR issued a regulation (MoEMR regulation no. 11/2018 regarding Procedures for the Granting of Area, Licensing and Reporting on Mineral and Coal Mining Activities), which states that IUPs that have been issued with a clean-and-clear audit status shall remain valid, but IUPs issued after the enactment of this regulation no longer require clean-and-clear status.

12. The clean-and-clear certification system is set out in a MoEMR issued regulation (Ministerial Regulation no. 32/2013 regarding the Procedures for Issuing Special Permits for Mineral and Coal) issued on November 19, 2013, which set out the requirement for IUP permit holders to obtain a clean-and-clear certificate (Velentina 2020). This was amended on December 30, 2015, with an MoEMR regulation (Ministerial Regulation no. 43/2015 regarding Procedures to Evaluate the Issuance of Mining Business Permits). The MoEMR regulatory amendments also set out an audit process for determining whether companies meet minimal legal requirements relevant to permit holders. The regulation sets various criteria for assessing compliance with relevant laws, including that miners have no outstanding royalty obligations or tax debts, have fulfilled environmental commitments, have no property delineation issues and have obtained any necessary forestry permits (Atteridge, Aung, and Nugroho 2018, 18).

13. Investors have been known to be foreign actors who lack the legal eligibility to apply for an IUP.

14. The 1967 Mining Law and subsequent regulations and amendments, through to the 2020 Mining Law, grants the state the right to subsurface minerals. Mining companies do not have to have a land permit over an area to acquire a mining permit.

15. MoEMR regulation no. 7/2014 concerning Reclamation and Post-Mining in Mineral and Coal Mining Business Activity.

16. These companies are Bumi Resources (who owns Kaltim Prima Coal and Arutmin Indonesia), Adaro Energy, Kideco Jaya Agung, Indo Tambangraya Megah, Berau Coal, and Tambang Batu Bara Bukit Asam.

17. Luhut recently admitted to owning a 6,000-hectare coal mine in East Kalimantan (*Jakarta Post* 2019). As many as fifteen mine voids in East Kalimantan are reportedly linked to holding company Toba Sejahtra, which is majority owned by Luhut (Apriando 2017).

18. Golkar (Golongan Karya) was the political party of the authoritarian Suharto regime. Other influential political elites involved in coal mining and linked to the Golkar political party include Aburizal Bakrie, a former cabinet minister and chair of the Golkar political party, who is

majority owner of Bumi Resources holding company, which owns Kaltim Prima Coal, Indonesia's biggest coal mine with a 90,000-hectare concession in East Kalimantan.

19. In East Kalimantan, the provincial branch head of Pemuda Pancasila, Said Amin, has close links to Golkar, and the former Samarinda mayor, Achmad Amins (formerly of the Golkar party) (Maimunah 2018), who was found to have approved sixty-three mining permits over Samarinda's municipal area without any environmental impact assessment (Hardjanto and Rahmad 2014).

20. One police report documents a case following a child's death by drowning in 2016, where a family canceled the police investigation in agreement with the mining company, Multi Harapan Utama, who owned the concession where the child had drowned in a mine void.

21. See *Jakarta Post* (2018); also detailed in a report by the United Nations (UN) Working Group on Human Rights and Transnational Corporations and Other Business Enterprises (United Nations 2019, 3).

References

Abood, Sinan A., Janice Ser Huay Lee, Zuzana Burivalova, John Garcia-Ulloa, and Lian Pin. 2015. "Relative Contributions of the Logging, Fiber, Oil Palm, and Mining Industries to Forest Loss in Indonesia." *Conservation Letters* 8 (1): 58–67. https://doi.org/10.1111/conl.12103.

Adey, Peter. 2015. "Air's Affinities: Geopolitics, Chemical Affect and the Force of the Elemental." *Dialogues in Human Geography* 5 (1): 54–75. https://doi.org/10.1177/2043820614565871.

Agrawal, Sumali, Anthony J. Bebbington, Aviva Imhof, Mai Jebing, Nonette Royo, Laura Aileen Sauls, Rini Sulaiman, Tessa Toumbourou, and Arief Wicaksono. 2018. *Impacts of Extractive Industry and Infrastructure on Forests: Indonesia*. San Francisco: Climate and Land Use Alliance. http://www.climateandlandusealliance.org/wp-content/uploads/2018/12/Indonesia-Impacts-of-EII-on-Forests-1.pdf.

Andrews, Eleanor, and James McCarthy. 2014. "Scale, Shale, and the State: Political Ecologies and Legal Geographies of Shale Gas Development in Pennsylvania." *Journal of Environmental Studies and Sciences* 4:7–16.

Apriando, Tommy. 2017. "Who Owns Indonesia's Deadly Abandoned Coal Mines?" *Mongabay*, May 25, 2017. https://news.mongabay.com/2017/05/who-owns-indonesias-deadly-abandoned-coal-mines/.

ASM Haze Task Force. 2018. *ASM Local and Trasnbundary Haze Report*. Edited by H. Varkkey. Kuala Lumpur Akademi Sains Malaysia.

Aspinall, Edward. 2014. "Indonesia's 2014 Elections: Parliament and Patronage." *Journal of Democracy* 25 (4): 96–110. https://doi.org/10.1353/jod.2014.0070.

Atteridge, Aaron, May Thazin Aung, and Agus Nugroho. 2018. *Contemporary Coal Dynamics in Indonesia*. Stockholm: Stockholm Environment Institute. https://www.sei.org/wp-content/uploads/2018/06/contemporary-coal-dynamics-in-indonesia.pdf.

Baird, Ian G., and Jefferson Fox. 2015. "How Land Concessions Affect Places Elsewhere: Telecoupling, Political Ecology, and Large-Scale Plantations in Southern Laos and Northeastern Cambodia." *Land* 4 (2): 436–453. https://doi.org/10.3390/land4020436.

Bakker, Laurens. 2017. "Militias, Security and Citizenship in Indonesia." In *Citizenship and Democratization in Southeast Asia,* edited by Ward Berenschot, H. G. C. (Henk) Schulte Nordholt, and Laurens Bakker, 125–154. Leiden: Brill.

Bebbington, Anthony, ed. 2012. *Social Conflict, Economic Development and Extractive Industry Evidence from South America.* New York: Routledge.

Bebbington, Anthony, and Jeffrey Bury, eds. 2013. *Subterranean Struggles: New Dynamics of Mining, Oil, and Gas in Latin America.* Austin: University of Texas Press.

Bebbington, Anthony, Denise Humphreys Bebbington, Laura Aileen Sauls, John Rogan, Sumali Agrawal, César Gamboa, Aviva Imhof, Kimberly Johnson, Herman Rosa, Antoinette Royo, Tessa Toumbourou, and Ricardo Verdum. 2018. "Resource Extraction and Infrastructure Threaten Forest Cover and Community Rights." *Proceedings of the National Academy of Sciences* 115 (52): 13164–13173. https://doi.org/10.1073/pnas.1812505115.

Berenschot, Ward. 2018. "The Political Economy of Clientelism: A Comparative Study of Indonesia's Patronage Democracy." *Comparative Political Studies* 51 (12): 1563–1593. https://doi.org/10.1177/0010414018758756.

Bersihkan Indonesia. 2020. *Omnibus Law: Oligarch's Legal Holy Book; Mining Businessmen and Dirty Energy behind Omnibus Law: Their Roles, Conflicts of Interests, and Track Record.* Available at: https://drive.google.com/file/u/0/d/1zpBmvXcemwQj5kyKE0GWyBg1g3qg-Atz/view?usp=embed_facebook. Accessed May 30, 2023.

Blaikie, Piers, and Harold Brookfield, eds. 2015. *Land Degradation and Society.* London: Routledge. https://doi.org/10.4324/9781315685366.

BP. 2020. "Statistical Review of World Energy." 2020. 69th ed. www.bp.com/content/dam/bp/business-sites/en/global/corporate/pdfs/energy-economics/statistical-review/bp-stats-review-2020-full-report.pdf. Brannstrom, Christian, and Jacqueline M. Vadjunec. 2013. "Notes for Avoiding a Missed Opportunity in Sustainability Science: Integrating Land Change Science and Political Ecology." In *Land Change Science, Political Ecology, and Sustainability: Synergies and Divergences,* edited by Christian Brannstrom and Jacqueline M. Vadjunec, 1–23. London: Routledge.

Bridge, Gavin. 2013. "Territory, Now in 3D!" *Political Geography,* no. 34, 55–57.

Brown, Benjamin, and Samuel J. Spiegel. 2017. "Resisting Coal: Hydrocarbon Politics and Assemblages of Protest in the UK and Indonesia." *Geoforum* 85:101–111. https://doi.org/10.1016/j.geoforum.2017.07.015.

Burton, B. 2016. *Indonesian Human Rights Commission Finds Coal Mining Pit Deaths Were Human Rights Abuses.* https://endcoal.org/2016/12/indonesian-human-rights-commission-finds-coal-mining-pit-deaths-were-human-rights-abuses/.

Butt, Simon, and Tim Lindsey. 2018. *Indonesian Law.* Oxford: Oxford University Press.

Canelas, Joana, and António Carvalho. 2023. "The Dark Side of the Energy Transition: Extractivist Violence, Energy (In)Justice and Lithium Mining in Portugal." *Energy Research and Social Science* 100:103096. https://doi.org/10.1016/j.erss.2023.103096.

Carney, Judith. 1996. "Rice Milling, Gender and Slave Labour in Colonial South Carolina." *Past and Present* 153 (1): 108–134. https://doi.org/10.1093/past/153.1.108.

Chang, Charis. 2021. "China's Unofficial Ban on Australian Products Fails to Inflict Significant Damage." *News.com.au,* April 8, 2021. https://www.news.com.au/finance

/economy/australian-economy/chinas-unofficial-ban-on-australian-products-fails-to-inflict-significant-damage/news-story/1858bb05a6030bfcad0bcf2a3aacef62.

CNN Indonesia. 2020. "Faisal Basri: RUU Minerba 'Karpet Merah' Pengusaha Batu Bara" [Faisal Basri: Minerba bill "red carpet" for coal entrepreneurs]. April 15, 2020. https://www.cnnindonesia.com/ekonomi/20200415172426-85-493883/faisal-basri-ruu-minerba-karpet-merah-pengusaha-batu-bara.

Conde, Marta, and Philippe Le Billon. 2017. "Why Do Some Communities Resist Mining Projects While Others Do Not?" *Extractive Industries and Society* 4 (3): 681–697. https://doi.org/10.1016/j.exis.2017.04.009.

Cornot-Gandolphe, Sylvie. 2017. *Indonesia's Electricity Demand and the Coal Sector: Export or Meet Domestic Demand?* Oxford: Oxford Institute for Energy Studies. https://doi.org/10.26889/9781784670795.

Daulay, Bukin. 1994. "Tertiary Coal Belt in Eastern Kalimantan, Indonesia: The Influence of Coal Quality on Coal Utilisation." PhD diss., University of Wollongong. https://ro.uow.edu.au/theses/1413.

Diprose, Rachael, Nanang Kurniawan, Kate Macdonald, and Poppy Winanti. 2022. "Regulating Sustainable Minerals in Electronics Supply Chains: Local Power Struggles and the 'Hidden Costs' of Global Tin Supply Chain Governance." *Review of International Political Economy* 29 (3): 792–817. https://doi.org/10.1080/09692290.2020.1814844.

Dutu, Richard. 2016. "Challenges and Policies in Indonesia's Energy Sector." *Energy Policy* 98:513–519. https://doi.org/10.1016/j.enpol.2016.09.009.

EIA (US Energy Information Administration). 2019. "Indonesia." https://www.eia.gov/international/overview/country/IDN.

Elden, Stuart. 2013. "Secure the Volume: Vertical Geopolitics and the Depth of Power." *Political Geography* 34:35–51.

Fatah, Luthfi. 2008. "The Impacts of Coal Mining on the Economy and Environment of South Kalimantan Province, Indonesia." *ASEAN Economic Bulletin* 25 (1): 85–98.

Friederich, Mike C., and Theo van Leeuwen. 2017. "A Review of the History of Coal Exploration, Discovery and Production in Indonesia: The Interplay of Legal Framework, Coal Geology and Exploration Strategy." *International Journal of Coal Geology* 178:56–73. https://doi.org/10.1016/j.coal.2017.04.007.

Funfgeld, Anna. 2016. "The State of Coal Mining in East Kalimantan: Towards a Political Ecology of Local Stateness." *Austrian Journal of South-East Asian Studies* 9 (1): 147–162. https://doi.org/10.14764/10.ASEAS-2016.1-9.

Funfgeld, Anna. 2018. "Just Energy? Structures of Energy (In)Justice and the Indonesian Coal Sector." In *Routledge Handbook of Climate Justice*, edited by Tahseen Jafry, Michael Mikulewicz, and Karin Helwig, 222–236. Abingdon: Routledge.

Funfgeld, Anna. 2019. "Hegemony and Varieties of Contestation: Social Movements and the Struggle over Coal-Based Energy Production in Indonesia." In *Rule and Resistance Beyond the Nation State: Contestation, Escalation, Exit,* edited by Felix Anderl, Christopher Daase, Nicole Deitelhoff, Victor Kempf, Jannik Pfister, and Philip Wallmeier, 89–114. London: Rowman and Littlefield.

Galtung, Johan. 2004. "Violence, War, and Their Impact. On Visible and Invisible Effects of Violence." *polylog* 5. https://ictlogy.net/bibliography/reports/projects.php?idp=4407.

Gandataruna, Kosim, and Kirsty Haymon. 2011. "A Dream Denied? Mining Legislation and the Constitution in Indonesia." *Bulletin of Indonesian Economic Studies* 47 (2): 221–231. https://doi.org/10.1080/00074918.2011.585951.

Geller, Walter, Martin Schultze, Robert Kleinmann, and Christian Wolkersdorfer. 2012. *Acidic Pit Lakes: The Legacy of Coal and Metal Surface Mines*. New York: Springer Science and Business Media.

Giljum, Stefan, Victor Maus, Nikolas Kuschnig, Sebastian Luckeneder, Michael Tost, Laura J. Sonter, and Anthony Bebbington. 2022. "A Pantropical Assessment of Deforestation Caused by Industrial Mining." *Proceedings of the National Academy of Sciences* 119 (38): e2118273119. https://doi.org/10.1073/pnas.2118273119.

Goldstein, Jenny E. 2019. "The Volumetric Political Forest: Territory, Satellite Fire Mapping, and Indonesia's Burning Peatland." *Antipode* 52 (4): 1060–1082. https://doi.org/10.1111/anti.12576.

Großmann, Kristina, Martina Padmanabhan, and Katharina von Braun. 2017. "Contested Development in Indonesia: Rethinking Ethnicity and Gender in Mining." *Advances in Southeast Asian Studies* 10 (1): 11–28. https://doi.org/10.14764/10.ASEAS-2017.1-2.

Hadiz, Vedi R. 2010. *Localising Power in Post-Authoritarian Indonesia: A Southeast Asia Perspective*. Redwood, CA: Stanford University Press.

Hadiz, Vedi R., and Richard Robison. 2013. "The Political Economy of Oligarchy and the Reorganization of Power in Indonesia." *Indonesia* 96:35–57. https://doi.org/10.5728/indonesia.96.0033.

Hardjanto, Yustinus S., and Rahmadi Rahmad. 2014. "Fokus Liputan: Bencana Tambang di Samarinda" [Coverage focus: Mining disaster in Samarinda]. *Mongabay*, August 31, 2014. https://www.mongabay.co.id/2014/08/31/fokus-liputan-bencana-tambang-di-samarinda/.

Hendrawan, Adrianus, Edward Aspinall, and Ward Berenschot. 2017. "Parties as Pay-Off Seekers: Pre-Electoral Coalitions in a Patronage Democracy." *Electoral Studies* 69. https://doi.org/10.1016/j.electstud.2020.102238.

Humphreys Bebbington, Denise, and Celina Grisi Huber. 2017. "Political Settlements, Natural Resource Extraction, and Inclusion in Bolivia." Effective States and Inclusive Development (ESID) Working Paper no. 77. University of Manchester. https://justice-project.org/wp-content/uploads/2017/08/esid_wp_77_humphreys_bebbington_grisi_huber.pdf.

Idris, Muhammad. 2021. "10 Perusahaan Paling Banyak Mengeruk Batubara di Indonesia Halaman all" [10 companies that extract the most coal in Indonesia]. KOMPAS.com, July 2, 2021. https://money.kompas.com/read/2021/07/02/134329326/10-perusahaan-paling-banyak-mengeruk-batubara-di-indonesia.

IEA (International Energy Agency). 2020. "Coal 2020: Analysis and Forecast to 2025." Paris: International Energy Agency. https://www.iea.org/reports/coal-2020.

Indonesian Mining Institute. 2018. "Indonesia—Mining Sector Diagnostic." https://openknowledge.worldbank.org/bitstream/handle/10986/33087/Report-on-Indonesia-Mining-Sector-Diagnostic.pdf?sequence=1andisAllowed=y.

Jakarta Post. 2018. "Island Focus: Govt Should Protect JATAM Activists: NGO." November 29, 2018. https://www.thejakartapost.com/news/2018/11/29/govt-should-protect-jatam-activists-ngo.html.

Jakarta Post. 2019. "Luhut Admits Owning 6,000-ha Coal Mine in East Kalimantan." February 27, 2019. https://www.thejakartapost.com/news/2019/02/27/luhut-admits-owning-6000-ha-coal-mine-in-east-kalimantan.html.

JATAM. 2021. "Ditengah pembahasan konferensi Iklim COP 26, Jatuh lagi Korban Lubang Tambang ke 40" [In the midst of discussions at the COP 26 climate conference, the fortieth mine hole victim falls]. JATAM, November 3, 2021. https://www.jatam.org/ditengah-pembahasan-konferensi-iklim-cop-26-jatuh-lagi-korban-lubang-tambang-ke-40/.

JATAM, Greenpeace Southeast Asia, Indonesia Corruption Watch, and Auriga. 2019. "COALRUPTION: Shedding Light on Political Corruption in Indonesia's Coal Mining Sector." https://auriga.or.id/wp-content/uploads/2018/11/COALRUPTION-EN-1.pdf.

Jong, Hans Nicholas. 2020. "Indonesian Officials Linked to Mining and 'Dirty Energy' Firms Benefiting from Deregulation Law." *Mongabay,* October 26, 2020. https://news.mongabay.com/2020/10/indonesia-coal-mining-energy-omnibus-deregulation-law-oligarch/.

Karp, Daniel S., Chase D. Mendenhall, Randi Figueroa Sandí, Nicolas Chaumont, Paul R. Ehrlich, Elizabeth A. Hadly, and Gretchen C. Daily. 2013. "Forest Bolsters Bird Abundance, Pest Control and Coffee Yield." *Ecology Letters* 16 (11): 1339–1347. https://doi.org/10.1111/ele.12173.

Katadata.co.id. 2019. "Investigasi Batu Bara: Ragam Modus Batu Bara Ilegal di Kalimantan Timur" [Investigating coal: Various methods of illegal coal in East Kalimantan]. February 11. https://katadata.co.id/berita/2019/02/11/ragam-modus-batu-bara-ilegal-di-kalimantan-timur.

Koh, Lian Poh. 2008. "Can Oil Palm Plantations Be Made More Hospitable for Forest Butterflies and Birds?" *Journal of Applied Ecology* 45 (4): 1002–1009. https://doi.org/10.1111/j.1365-2664.2008.01491.x.

Komnas HAM (National Commission on Human Rights). 2016. "Komnas HAM 2016." https://www.komnasham.go.id/files/20170110-laporan-pelanggaran-ham-di-bekas-%24ZWDM.pdf.

Kompas.id. 2018. "Dangers of Abandoned Mines." Kompas.id, December 18, 2018. https://kompas.id/baca/english/2018/12/18/dangers-of-abandoned-mines/.

Korte, Nina. 2011. "It's Not Only Rents: Explaining the Persistence and Change of Neopatrimonialism in Indonesia." German Institute of Global and Area Studies (GIGA) Working Paper no. 167. https://ciaotest.cc.columbia.edu/wps/giga/0022161/f_0022161_18228.pdf.

Lahiri-Dutt, Kuntala. 2006. "Globalization and Women's Work in the Mine Pits in East Kalimantan, Indonesia." In *Women Miners in Developing Countries: Pit Women and Others,* edited by Kuntala Lahiri-Dutt and Martha Macintyre, 349–370. Abingdon: Ashgate.

Lahiri-Dutt, Kuntala, and Petra Mahy. 2008. "Impacts of Mining on Women and Youth in Indonesia: Two Mining Locations." Canberra: ANU Enterprise. http://202.131.4.17/uploads/files/miningimpactsreport.pdf.

Lukas, Martin C. 2014. "Eroding Battlefields: Land Degradation in Java Reconsidered." *Geoforum* 56:87–100. https://doi.org/10.1016/j.geoforum.2014.06.010.

Maas, Bea, Yann Clough, and Teja Tscharntke. 2013. "Bats and Birds Increase Crop Yield in Tropical Agroforestry Landscapes." *Ecology Letters* 16 (12): 1480–1487. https://doi.org/10.1111/ele.12194.

Macdonald, Karunia F. 2017. "The Risk Assessment of Corruption in the Awarding of Mining Permits in Indonesia." Transparency International Indonesia. https://transparency.org.au/wp-content/uploads/2019/10/Indonesia-report_English.pdf.

Mahy, Petra K. 2012. "Gender Equality and Corporate Social Responsibility in Mining: An Investigation of the Potential for Change at Kaltim Prima Coal, Indonesia." PhD diss., Australian National University. https://openresearch-repository.anu.edu.au/bitstream/1885/9234/1/02Whole_Mahy.pdf.

Maimunah, Siti. 2018. "Rezim Ekstraksi, Oligarki dan Lubang Tambang" [Extraction regimes, oligarchies and mine pits]. *Mongabay,* November 7, 2018. https://www.mongabay.co.id/2018/11/07/rezim-ekstraksi-oligarki-dan-lubang-tambang/.

Margiansyah, Defbry, Fachri Aidulsyah, Fuat Kurniawan, Dwiyanti Kusumaningrum, Yulinda Aini, Kanetasya Sabilla. 2020. "Peta Berbisnis di parliament: Potret oligarki di Indonesia" [Map of doing business in parliament: Portrait of oligarchy in Indonesia]. Marepus Corner Working Paper no. 01. https://doi.org/10.13140/RG.2.2.31169.17765.

McCarthy, John F. 2011. "The Limits of Legality: State, Governance and Resource Control in Indonesia." *Social Science Research Network.* 10.2139/ssrn.2281591.

McCullough, C. D. 2016. "Key Mine Closure Lessons Still to Be Learned." In *Mine Closure 2016: Proceedings of the 11th International Conference on Mine Closure,* edited by A. B. Fourie and M. Tibbett, 25–33. Perth: Australian Centre for Geomechanics. https://papers.acg.uwa.edu.au/p/1608_23_mccullough/.

Mietzner, Marcus. 2013. *Money, Power, and Ideology: Political Parties in Post-Authoritarian Indonesia.* Singapore: NUS Press.

Mongabay. 2017. "Coal Miners Owe the Indonesian Government Hundreds of Millions of Dollars." May 8, 2017. https://news.mongabay.com/2017/05/coal-miners-owe-the-indonesian-government-hundreds-of-millions-of-dollars/.

Mudhoffir, Abdil Mughis. 2023. "The Limits of Civil Society Activism in Indonesia: The Case of the Weakening of the KPK." *Critical Asian Studies* 55 (1): 62–82. https://doi.org/10.1080/14672715.2022.2123019.

Muhdar, Muhamad, Mohamad Nasir, and Juli Nurdiana. 2019. "Risk Distribution in Coal Mining: Fighting for Environmental Justice in East Kalimantan, Indonesia." *Preprints,* 2019080058. https://doi.org/10.20944/preprints201908.0058.v1.

Nixon, Rob. 2011. *Slow Violence and the Environmentalism of the Poor.* Cambridge, MA: Harvard University Press.

O'Callaghan, Terry. 2010. "Patience Is a Virtue: Problems of Regulatory Governance in the Indonesian Mining Sector." *Resources Policy* 35 (3): 218–225. https://doi.org/10.1016/j.resourpol.2010.05.001.

Ojeda, Dianna, Padini Nirmal, Dianne Rocheleau, and Jody Emel. 2022. "Feminist Ecologies." *Annual Review of Environment and Resources* 47 (1): 149–171. https://doi.org/10.1146/annurev-environ-112320-092246.

Ordonez, Jose Antonio, Michael Jakob, Jan Christoph Steckel, and Anna Fünfgeld. 2021. "Coal, Power and Coal-Powered Politics in Indonesia." *Environmental Science and Policy* 123:44–57. https://doi.org/10.1016/j.envsci.2021.05.007.

O'Rourke, K. 2002. *Reformasi: The Struggle for Power in Post-Soeharto Indonesia.* Sydney: Allen & Unwin.

PLN (Perusahaan Listrik Negara). 2016. "PLN Plan for the Provision of Electricity for 2016–2025." Perusahaan Listrik Negara, National Electricity Company. http://www.djk.esdm.go.id/pdf/RUPTL/RUPTL%20PLN%202016-2025.pdf.

Postigo, Julio, Mariana Montoya, and Kenneth R. Young. 2013. "Natural Resources in the Subsoil and Social Conflicts on the Surface: Perspectives on Peru's Subsurface Political Ecology." In *Subterranean Struggles: New Dynamics of Mining, Oil, and Gas in Latin America,* edited by Anthony Bebbington and Jeffrey Bury, 223–240. Austin: University of Texas Press.

PricewaterhouseCoopers. 2016. "Mining in Indonesia: Investment and Taxation Guide—May 2016." 8th ed. PricewaterhouseCoopers. https://www.pwc.com/id/en/energy-utilities-mining/assets/May%202016/PwC%20Indonesia-mining-in-Indonesia-survey-2016.pdf

Rahmadi, May. 2020. "Understanding How the Revised Mining Law Favors Mining Giants." *Ekuatorial,* June 17, 2020. https://www.ekuatorial.com/en/2020/06/understanding-how-the-revised-mining-law-favors-mining-giants/.

Resosudarmo, Budy. 2010. "Reformasi, Environmental Security and Development in Indonesia." In *Development in an Insecure and Gendered World: The Relevance of the Millennium Goals,* edited by Jacqueline Lekie, 195–212. Farnham: Ashgate.

Robbins, Paul. 2011. *Political Ecology: A Critical Introduction.* Hoboken, NJ: John Wiley and Sons.

Roberts, K. B., and Mai. 2021. "Everyday Violence: Tigyit Coal Mine and Coal-Fired Power Plant in Shan State, Myanmar." *Geoforum* 124 (August): 392–399. doi:10.1016/j.geoforum.2021.03.002.

Robinson, Kathryn. 2016. "Mining, Land and Community Rights in Indonesia." In *Land and Development in Indonesia: Searching for the People's Sovereignty,* edited by John F. McCarthy and Kathryn Robinson, 141–166. Singapore: ISEAS Publishing.

Roche, Charles, Lian Sinclair, Rochelle Spencer, Hanabeth Luke, Martin Brueckner, Sally Knowles, and Megan Paul. 2021. "A Mining Legacies Lens: From Externalities to Wellbeing in Extractive Industries." *Extractive Industries and Society* 8 (3): 100961. https://doi.org/10.1016/j.exis.2021.100961.

Rocheleau, Dianne. 2005. "Maps as Power Tools: Locating Communities in Space or Situating People and Ecologies in Place?" In *Communities and Conservation: Histories and Politics of Community-Based Natural Resource Management,* edited by Peter J. Brosius, Anna. L. Tsing, and Charles Zerner, 327–362. Walnut Creek, CA: Altamira.

Russell, Clyde. 2021. "China's Ban on Australian Coal Forces Trade Flows to Realign: Russell." Reuters, January 12, 2021. https://www.reuters.com/article/column-russell-coal-asia-idUSL1N2JN0B4.

Sasaoka, Takashi, Hiroshi Takamoto, Hideki Shimada, Jiro Oya, Akihiro Hamanaka, and Kikuo Matsui. 2015. "Surface Subsidence Due to Underground Mining Operation under Weak Geological Condition in Indonesia." *Journal of Rock Mechanics and Geotechnical Engineering* 7 (3): 337–344. https://doi.org/10.1016/j.jrmge.2015.01.007.

Scrivener, Alexander. 2013. *Banking While Borneo Burns: How the UK Financial Sector Is Bankrolling Indonesia's Fossil Fuel Boom.* World Development Movement. https://www.banktrack.org/download/banking_while_borneo_burns/banking_while_borneo_burns.pdf.

Stephens, F. J., and Ingram, M. 2006. "Two Cases of Fish Mortality in Low Ph, Aluminium Rich Water." *Journal of Fish Diseases* 29 (12): 765–770. https://doi.org/10.1111/j.1365-2761.2006.00772.x.

Toumbourou, Tessa, Muhamad Muhdar, Tim Werner, and Anthony Bebbington. 2020. "Political Ecologies of the Post-Mining Landscape: Activism, Resistance, and Legal Struggles Over Kalimantan's Coal Mines." *Energy Research and Social Science* 65:101476. https://doi.org/10.1016/j.erss.2020.101476.

Tribunnews.com. 2019. "Komnas HAM Endus Ada Pelanggaran HAM di Kalimantan Timur, Sebab Lubang Tambang Batu Bara" [Komnas HAM detects human rights violations in East Kalimantan, due to coal mine pits]. July 19, 2019. https://www.tribunnews.com/regional/2019/07/31/komnas-ham-endus-ada-pelanggaran-ham-di-kalimantan-timur-sebab-lubang-tambang-batu-bara.

Turner, B. L., W. C. Clark, R. W. Kates, J. F. Richards, J. T. Mathews, and W. B. Meyer. 1990. *The Earth as Transformed by Human Action: Global and Regional Changes in the Biosphere over the Past 300 Years.* Cambridge: Cambridge University Press with Clark University.

Turner, B. L., and Paul Robbins. 2008. "Land-Change Science and Political Ecology: Similarities, Differences, and Implications for Sustainability Science." *Annual Review of Environment and Resources* 33 (1): 295–316. https://doi.org/10.1146/annurev.environ.33.022207.104943.

Tyson, Adam, Helena Varkkey, and Shofwan Al Banna Choiruzzad. 2018. "Deconstructing the Palm Oil Industry Narrative in Indonesia: Evidence from Riau Province." *Contemporary Southeast Asia* 40 (3): 422–448. https://doi.org/10.1355/cs40-3d.

United Nations. 2019. Report of the United Nations Working Group on Human Rights and Transnational Corporations and Other Business Enterprises. Geneva: United Nations. https://spcommreports.ohchr.org/TMResultsBase/DownLoadPublicCommunicationFile?gId=24296.

van Bemmelen, R. W. 1949. *The Geology of Indonesia.* The Hague: Government Printing Office.

van Noordwijk, Meine, Hesti Lestari Tatal, Jianchu Xu, Sonya Dewi, and Peter Minang. 2012. "Segregate or Integrate for Multifunctionality and Sustained Change through Rubber-Based Agroforestry in Indonesia and China." In *Agroforestry—The Future of Global Land Use,* edited by P. K. R. Nair and D. Garrity, 69–104. Dordrecht: Springer Netherlands.

van Paddenburg, Annawati, Andrea M. Bassi, Eveline Buter, Christopher E. Cosslett, and Andy Dean. 2012. "Heart of Borneo: Investing in Nature for a Green Economy." Jakarta: WWF Heart of Borneo Initiative. https://d2ouvy59p0dg6k.cloudfront.net/downloads/heart_of_borneo_green_economy_main_report_2012.pdf.

Velentina, Rouli Anita. 2020. "Legal Certainty for Foreign Investors in Coal Mining in Indonesia." *Jurnal Hukum dan Pembangunan* 49 (4): 923. https://scholarhub.ui.ac.id/jhp/vol49/iss4/10/.

Walters, Adam. 2016. "The Hole Truth: The Mess Coal Companies Plan to Leave in NSW." Energy and Resource Insights (erinsights.com), commissioned by the Hunter Communities Network. http://downloads.erinsights.com/reports/the_hole_truth_LR.pdf.

Warburton, Eve. 2017. "Resource Nationalism in Post-Boom Indonesia: The New Normal?" *Lowy Institute for International Policy,* April 27, 2017. https://www.lowyinstitute.org/publications/resource-nationalism-post-boom-indonesia-new-normal.

Welker, Marina A. 2009. "'Corporate Security Begins in the Community': Mining, the Corporate Social Responsibility Industry, and Environmental Advocacy in Indonesia." *Cultural Anthropology* 24 (1): 142–179. https://doi.org/10.1111/j.1548-1360.2009.00029.x.

Winanti, Poppy S., and Rachael Diprose. 2020. "Reordering the Extractive Political Settlement: Resource Nationalism, Domestic Ownership and Transnational Bargains in Indonesia." *Extractive Industries and Society* 7 (4): 1534–1546. https://doi.org/10.1016/j.exis.2020.08.015.

Winn, Paul. 2016. "Deadly Coal Pits of Samarinda." *Waterkeeper Alliance,* August 16, 2016. https://waterkeeper.org/death-pits-of-samarinda/.

Woodbury, David, Ishak Yassir, Arbainsyah Insya, Danica Doroski, Simon Queenborough, and Mark S. Ashton. 2020. "Filling a Void: Analysis of Early Tropical Soil and Vegetative Recovery under Leguminous, Post-Coal Mine Reforestation Plantations in East Kalimantan, Indonesia." *Land Degradation and Development* 31 (4): 473–487. https://doi.org/10.1002/ldr.3464.

CHAPTER 2

The Everyday Violence of Coal-Fired Power in Shan State, Myanmar

K. B. ROBERTS AND MAI

On a cool December morning in 2017, students in the mountainous city of Taunggyi, the capital of Shan State in northern Myanmar, bundled themselves up in sweaters and scarves. Nervous energy pervaded the room as they waited to give group presentations. After four weeks of coursework, field trips, and lectures, these young adults prepared to share their own experiences with the extractive industries in Myanmar. As the morning fog began to dissipate, we heard stories of violence. Taunggyi serves as a hub for many organizations and individuals working in the less accessible and frequently restricted parts of south and east Shan State. To the south of Taunggyi, the Tigyit coal mine produces nearly 2,000 tons of lignite coal daily (see figure 2.1). The students connected the operations of the Tigyit coal mine and coal-fired power plant in southern Shan State to comprehensive everyday harm against women, education, health, livelihoods, religion, and ecosystems. These youth explained how violence occurs not just through physical acts of conflict and warfare, but also through slow acts of negligence and cumulative acts of environmental degradation. They talked about environmental degradation as a human rights violation, and they asked us, Roberts and Mai, to share their insights and experiences of this everyday violence. In this chapter, the violence we discuss results from the material effects, or what we refer to as byproducts, of building and operating a coal mine and coal-fired power plant and the structural impacts of the policies and practices that enable its operation.

At Tigyit, local and foreign individuals, civil society and nongovernmental organizations (NGOs), state and non-state militaries collide with nationalist, development, capitalist, and activist interests. The Myanmar Electric Power Enterprise began building the Tigyit coal-fired power plant in 2001. In 2005, the Chinese state-owned China National Heavy Machinery Corporation, along with local Myanmar companies Eden Group and Shan Yoma Nagar, started operating the power plant (Aung Shin 2016; Kritsanavarin and Vrieze 2015). The Tigyit coal mine, which supplies the power plant, is the largest coal mine in Myanmar (EJAtlas Southeast Asia Team n.d.; Students and Youth Congress of Burma 2018). In 2014,

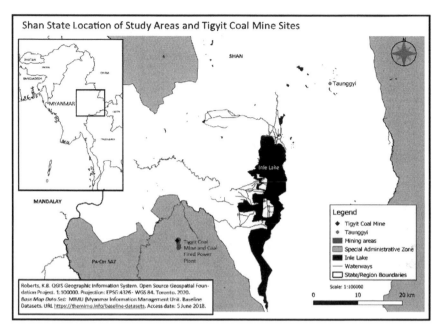

Figure 2.1. Map showing study areas and Tigyit coal mine sites.

amid a public backlash over harm to people's health and the environment from pollution, President U Thein Sein's administration closed the Tigyit power plant (Shan Herald Agency for News 2017); however, the Chinese company Wuxi Hua Guang Electric Power Energy was granted a twenty-two-year license to restart operations and reopened the plant in 2016 (Chan Mya Htwe 2018; Kyi Kyi Sway 2016; *Shan Herald Agency for News* 2017).

Everyday violence from the Tigyit coal mine and power plant results in the loss of ability to derive benefits from previous and potential systems of life-making. This everyday violence produces impacts across scales. It restricts access to clean and safe drinking water, as well as water for agriculture and livestock. It also contributes to global climate change and local and regional air and water pollution. This everyday violence began from the inception of the mine, with explosions that destroyed important cultural and religious sites. The violence continued through the dispossession of land and livelihoods, decreased access to education and health, and the pollution of air and waterways. In this way, everyday violence impacts the whole of a person's life, affecting their present and future.

To understand everyday violence, we first draw on theorizations of violence within geography and political ecology, before explaining our research methods.

We then illustrate how historical patterns of civil conflict and contested sovereignty have shaped resource extraction in Myanmar and resulted in structural forms of violence at Tigyit. Next, we discuss how the operations of the mine and power plant perpetuate everyday violence that negatively effects the atmosphere, waterways, human health, livelihoods, cultural practices, and education. The bulk of the research for the chapter occurred prior to the military coup that took place on February 1, 2021, in Myanmar; however, following our discussion of the Tigyit coal mine and power plant and their byproducts, we include a brief section on the effect of the 2021 coup on Tigyit.

The Everyday Violence of Resource Extraction

In their 2011 report "Poison Clouds," the Pa-Oh Youth Organization[1] (PYO) warns: "If the Tigyit coal mine continues to go ahead, nearly 12,000 people living within five miles of the mine and workers will face health problems and breathing difficulties similar to the Mae Moh communities of northern Thailand. Villagers losing their traditional livelihoods and farmlands day by day will become impoverished and displaced. Polluted water from the coal mine flowing into Balu Creek will contaminate Burma's cherished Inle Lake" (PYO 2011, 47). The term "violence" frequently conjures up images of bodily harm and armed conflict. Indeed, decades of civil war between various configurations of ethnic armed organizations (EAOs) and the Myanmar military have resulted in deaths, extrajudicial killings, forced labor, rape, and injuries (SWAN 2002; SHRF 1998; Jolliffe 2015).[2] Yet, violence extends beyond the parameters of immediate bodily harm. In this discussion, we contribute to political ecologies of violence (see Bohle and Fünfgeld 2007; Le Billon and Duffy 2018; Peluso 2008; Peluso and Vandergeest 2011; Peluso and Watts 2001; Watts 2013) by highlighting how civil society organizations (CSOs) and activists conceptualize resource extraction harm. As the students described it to us and as we see it, resource frontier violence is rooted in dispossession and accumulation and the material byproducts of resource extraction activities. However, this violence also flows through interconnected webs of life making to create a schism in "what could have been and what is" (Galtung 1969, 68). Le Billon (2001, 561) writes about how violence can be expressed in "the subjugation of the rights of people to determine the use of their environment and the brutal patterns of resource extraction and predation." In this sense, coal mining and power plant activities at Tigyit enact violence not only through armed conflict, but by restricting people's access to and use of those same spaces (Roberts 2019).

Scholars have long discussed resource frontiers and sites of resource extraction as spaces where previous systems of property, governance, and socioeconomic relations are destroyed and remade in favor of new ways (Rasmussen and Lund 2018, 389). This zone of destruction predicates on the process of primitive accumulation, an ongoing process in which, according to Marx, "conquest, enslavement, robbery, murder, briefly force, play the great part" (1992, 359). Resource extraction sites are inherently violent. Literature on resource frontiers and extraction often emphasizes the strategic use of force, coercion, law, discourse, neglect, political economic relations, institutions, and systemic histories to establish access and rights (Cons and Eilenberg 2019; Le Billon 2001; Rasmussen and Lund 2018; Ribot and Peluso 2003). However, less attention is given to how violence manifests in the everyday (Berman-Arevalo and Ojeda 2020, 1589; Springer and Le Billon 2016). Following anthropologist Kikon's (2019) ethnographic work on living with coal and oil in Northeast India, we call attention to how people live with and experience resource extraction (Jenss 2020).

Geographers use the phrase "everyday violence" to articulate the spatially connected, day-to-day, and embodied aspects of violence (Bhagat 2018; Bhide 2020; de Leeuw 2016; Jenss 2020; Piedalue 2019). This everyday violence is experienced in the spaces and bodies of people living with resource extraction (Berman-Arevalo and Ojeda 2020; Elden 2013; Zaragocin 2019). We define the everyday violence associated with resource extraction as a loss in benefits derived from previous and potential systems of life making, with everyday material consequences. We emphasize the diverse mechanisms through which that violence occurs and the diverse impacts on day-to-day life. This violence operates in slow and fast ways, with long-term cumulative effects (Blake and Barney 2018; Davies 2019; Li 2010; Nixon 2011; Zaragocin 2019). This violence also impacts peoples' ability to determine their own use of the resources around them (Le Billon 2001; Roberts 2019) and inhibits their ability to access and benefit from forms of life making and world making (Bhide 2020; Galtung 1969, 1990; Piedalue 2019; Ribot and Peluso 2003). This violence unevenly impacts not only local communities, but specifically women and children (de Leeuw 2016; Lamb et al. 2017; Zaragocin 2019). This critical intervention into the violence of resource extraction draws attention to the unevenly experienced impact of that violence and makes visible everyday forms of violence caused by extractive industries like the Tigyit coal mine and power plant within southern Shan State.

Methods

Primary research for this chapter took place between December 2017 and March 2018 in Taunggyi, Myanmar. We met the youth mentioned at the start of this chapter in December of 2017, while teaching a two-day research methods training course. These youth, aged between twenty and twenty-five, were two-thirds of the way through a two-month sustainable development leadership program. At the time of the training, Roberts and Mai had worked together as research partners for two years. Mai is from the region and conducts research with local and regional organizations on environmental and human rights issues. Roberts is from North America and has worked with similar organizations along the borderlands of Myanmar and Thailand since 2007.

Although we had previously worked together researching resource extraction, the students were the first to teach us about what was occurring in Tigyit. Inspired by their knowledge and concerns, we then sought to learn more about Tigyit and the CSOs engaging with the impacts of the coal mine and power plant. Research for this chapter draws on participant observation and presentations by the students, as well as interviews with eleven local CSOs. Interviews took place in Shan, Burmese, and English. Mai translated and interpreted for interviews in Burmese and Shan. Informed consent was given for all interviews and participatory observation, including student presentations. However, to protect the identities of our informants, including co-author Mai and the CSOs, we have used pseudonyms and a numbering system. Even prior to the 2021 coup, the situation in Myanmar was precarious for many activists and human rights organizations (Suhardiman, Rutherford, and Bright 2017).

In addition to participant observation and interviews, data collection included an extensive literature review of relevant topics involving land, investment, mining, environmental and water policies, and laws, pending and present, as well as state and non-state reports and publications. Interviews and reports were coded using QSR NVivo 11 software. Codes were developed based on discussions between Mai and Roberts, CSO interviews, student presentations, and gray documents to draw out themes connected to the operations of the coal mine and power plant and their effect on water and air quality, health, education, and livelihoods. From those recorded and transcribed conversations came the focus of this chapter on everyday violence. Following the 2021 military coup, we have made additions to this chapter to incorporate some of the ramifications of the coup for Tigyit.

Conflict, Fragmented Sovereignty, and Resource Extraction in Myanmar

The everyday violence discussed in this chapter is embedded in the colonial and racialized histories of Myanmar.[3] Everyday violence at Tigyit does not occur without the structures in place, or lack thereof, that enable that violence. These structures stem from policies, governance practices, and laws that perpetuate the dispossession of marginalized people from land and that enable harm to ecosystems. Conflict, fueled in part by competition over natural resources and political power struggles, has inhibited coherent and cohesive rule throughout Myanmar, particularly across rural and mountainous regions in the ethnic states of the country (Bryant 1997; Callahan 2009; Sai Aung Tun 2009).[4] Since independence from Britain on January 4, 1948, territorial disputes in Myanmar have fed civil wars. After fourteen years of tenuous democracy, General Ne Win's 1962 military coup inaugurated decades of successive socialist and authoritarian dictatorships in Myanmar (Jolliffe 2015, 15). In the late 1980s, after facing economic challenges and increased pressure from disgruntled EAOs (often seeking autonomy or federalism), Ne Win's junta all but collapsed. A new military government, the State Law and Order Restoration Council (SLORC), later transformed into the State Peace and Development Council (SPDC), took control in 1988, turning away from socialist policies.

In 2010, Myanmar held its first election since 1990. Despite the SPDC 2008 constitutional mandate that the military could hold up to 25 percent of the seats in parliament, this was a significant step toward demilitarization and democratization of the country and led to the inauguration of President U Thein Sein (a former military general) in 2011 (Pedersen 2011).[5] The subsequent 2015 elections then brought a further shift in power. The National League for Democracy (NLD) party, which had boycotted the 2010 elections, ran and won by a large margin. In March of 2016, Daw Aung San Suu Kyi was appointed state counselor, and Htin Kyaw was sworn in as president. Aung San Suu Kyi became the de facto head of state, despite the 2008 constitution barring her from becoming president.

During the military regime years, 1962–2010, resource extraction fueled and funded conflict between armed actors, sustaining insurgencies and ethno-nationalism (Han 2019). In the late 1980s, bilateral agreements between Myanmar and China increased trade (legal and illegal) of natural resources across borders (EIA 2015). Additionally, through ceasefire agreements between EAOs and the government of Myanmar, many former combatants became business partners, accelerating resource extraction (Woods 2011). These renegotiated state-armed military-private partnerships resulted in the leasing of state sovereignty over natural resources, usually to the disadvantage of local populations and smaller ethnic minority groups (MacLean 2010; Meehan 2015; Sturgeon 2004; Woods 2011).

This history has produced "fragmented sovereignties," which include the Myanmar government (Union Government), the Myanmar military, and dozens of ethnic armed organizations (EAOs), some of whom have ceasefire agreements and some of whom are still engaged in active conflict.[6] As a result, multiple governance actors influence resource extraction throughout the country, including in Shan State (Callahan 2007, 2009; Jolliffe 2015; Jones 2014; Mark 2016; Meehan 2015; Woods 2019).

Tigyit exemplifies these fractured governance models and tensions between local and national interests. The Tigyit coal mine and coal-fired power plant are within the boundaries of a Pa-Oh self-administered zone (SAZ), and Pa-Oh ethnic organizations remain critical to the history and governance of the zone. The Pa-Oh National Organization (PNO) has its roots in the first Pa-Oh nationalist armed movement that began in 1949 and is among one of the oldest armed groups within Myanmar (Jolliffe 2015, 61). On April 11, 1991, the PNO was given State Special Region 6 territory in their ceasefire agreement (Jolliffe 2015, 19). As a SAZ, the Pa-Oh legislative body is comprised entirely of PNO officials. However, the national General Administration Department (GAD) undermines these subnational governments and SAZs by limiting their authority (Jolliffe 2015, 3). The Pa-Oh SAZ does not have governance authority or autonomy over security, education, and natural resource management, and the national Union government performs land management–related functions (Baver et al. 2013; Jolliffe 2015, 37). According to interviews, there is some leeway regarding agricultural products; however, the Pa-Oh governing body has no influence or authority over Union government development projects like the Tigyit coal mine and power plant (Interview 10, January 5, 2018). Instead, governance and management stem from a series of negotiations between the previous military government, U Thein Sein's Union government, and the companies involved in construction and operations for the mine and power plant.

Everyday Violence: The Tigyit Coal Mine and Its Byproducts

Since the mine's inception, its operations have had impacts on religious sites, livelihoods, and ecosystem services. Part of the everyday violence that results from the mine and power plant arises from the biophysical properties of coal itself. The Tigyit coal reserves that supply the power plant are younger, closer to the surface, and more frequently extracted through open-cast mining (also known as open-pit mining). To access this coal economically, the state forced the relocation of some households and confiscated farmland (PYO 2011). In September 2001, the Myanmar military regime's vice-senior general, Maung Aye, instructed local military to confiscate over one hundred acres of local farmland (PYO 2011, 23). Since that time, over five hundred acres of farmland in Tigyit, Taung Pola, Pyin Thar, Lai Khar, and Bar Min Kone villages were confiscated for open-cast mining. In some instances, the Ministry of Mining directly confiscated the land; in other instances, people received nominal compensation for the farmland (PYO 2011, 32). Reports also suggest that at the time, with support from some local village-level authorities, the Shan Yoma Nagar and Shwe Than Lwin companies pressured farmers into selling their land. While the land could produce up to 300,000 kyat (US$300) per acre annually, farmers only received 8,000 kyat (US$8) to 30,000 kyat (US$30) per acre in compensation from the mining companies (Kritsanavarin and Vrieze 2015; PYO 2011, 32–33). Two villages were also relocated for the mine. Relocation of affected villagers occurred during the rainy season, despite requests to postpone. The mining companies did not provide a resettlement program and offered only minimal compensation, which, according to residents, did not even cover transportation costs (PYO 2011, 28). Affected villagers stated that they received at most 150,000 kyats (US$150) per household, with smaller households receiving less. People from nearby villages had to help those affected to relocate onto land from two adjacent villagers (PYO 2011, 29). Moreover, while the mining companies promised clinics, a library, and schools, as of 2018, those promises were not fulfilled (Interview 4, January 13, 2018; PYO 2011). As a result of this forced displacement during a hazardous time of year, with little assistance, residents experienced a form of violence, further perpetuated through daily loss of income and livelihood access.

This violence builds on the legacy of economic reforms and resulting changes to land tenure and access in Myanmar following the SLORC military regime change. Despite nominal protections for farmland, the 1988 land policy introduced by SLORC shifted from a socialist emphasis on peasant farmers to one of economic growth through market reform, relaxing control of domestic and foreign investment. In 2012, U Thein Sein's Union government introduced a series of laws that further defined the process of land acquisition by individuals and investors. The 2012 Farmland Law offers land tenure security through a land use certificate and registration system, which is not universally in place in the Shan State (Kattelus, Rahaman, and Varis 2014, 90; Oberndorf 2012, 8). While the Settlement and Land Records Department (SLR) conducted some land surveys, dispossessed villagers around Tigyit did not have land documents. The limited expansion of the land certificate system created a situation where villagers could lose access to their land and resources with little to no legal recourse. Even when smallholder farmers do have land leases, the Farmland Law often allows bigger businesses to acquire their land (Oberndorf 2012, 8–9). Articles 28–29 of the law allow the state to expropriate farmland for projects considered to benefit "the national interest," although there is ambiguity on whether mining activities meet this criteria (Myanmar Centre for Responsible Business 2018).

In addition to the impacts of dispossession and forced relocation, the process of extracting coal also has consequences for important religious and cultural practices and beliefs. In 2002, heavy machinery bulldozed brush and trees and removed top layers of soil to access the coal underneath. Workers also used dynamite to create an open pit in the ground. The blasts generated residual shocks that cracked buildings in Tigyit village and damaged several pagodas (Chan Mya Htwe 2018; PYO 2011). This not only created safety concerns and economic impacts in terms of rebuilding and repair costs, but also had important cultural ramifications. In interviews with PYO representatives, villagers talked about how they believed that the coal project was upsetting local spirits near the pagoda: "When the pagoda collapsed, a fight between villagers and company workers almost broke out. Most villagers were so angry, some were crying. We always celebrate our traditional festival at the pagoda and many people join; it's a time for a reunion among relatives. Now we have nowhere to hold the festival. One monk said we should rebuild the pagoda but now the land is not strong enough to support it" (Interview 10, January 5, 2018; PYO 2011). This destruction of the pagoda led to an everyday loss of access to religious practices. Residents continue to fear land collapses at religious sites and at agricultural fields (PYO 2011, 35).

The operations of the coal mine and coal-fired power plant also affect water quantity and quality. The processing requirements of coal mining, particularly in water-scarce areas, frequently result in a disruption to the watershed (Thurber 2019, 57). Water shortages in southern Shan State during the dry season (February–April) are common. However, according to one CSO, Tigyit villagers complain that the water they rely on has dried up (Interview 3, January 13, 2018). In terms of wastewater, in 2015, when Wuxi Hua Guang was granted a twenty-two-year license by U Thein Sein's government, the company pledged to upgrade the plant and follow waste management procedures (Chan Mya Htwe 2018). However, water from the plant still discharges into a nearby river, and the process of digging for coal in the open pit mine continues to further disrupt local water sources (Interview 6, January 14, 2018). Wastewater from the mine and power plant also flows into Inle Lake, a UNESCO Biosphere Reserve since 2015 and an important tourist site, via Tigyit creek and Balu creek (PYO 2011, 42). The Waterkeeper Alliance analyzed a report dated April 6, 2018, provided by Advancing Life and Regenerating Motherland and a second report dated April 5, 2018, from the Analysis Department of the Government of the Republic of Myanmar on water and soil samples collected in and around the village of Tigyit. Samples from thirteen different sites around Tigyit were shown to have high levels of heavy metals including selenium, cadmium, lead, and arsenic. Two samples containing arsenic concentrations were five times the WHO guidelines for safe drinking water (Earth Rights International et al. 2018b). These impacts on water quality and quantity from the Tigyit coal mine and power plant are in clear violation of the 2018 Myanmar Mining Rules. Under the rules, mining projects are not allowed to deprive any persons of access to local water sources (Mining Rule 153) and mines are not allowed to pollute surface or groundwater.

The 2015 Law Amending the Myanmar Mines Law of 1994 is the country's main legislation governing the mining sector. Under this amendment, mining projects must adhere to the 2012 Environmental Conservation Law and 2015 Environmental Impact Assessment (EIA) procedure. While Article 13e states that permit holders must "ensure not to harm the socioeconomic wellbeing of local people and to minimize environmental damage and reserve a fund for annual environmental conservation" (Valentis Resources 2016), there is still inconsistency surrounding the requirements for conducting an EIA (Myanmar Centre for Responsible Business 2018). Yet, as CSO reports and interviews indicate, it is evident that harm to the socioeconomic wellbeing of local people has occurred. This lack of enforcement of policy and protection of water quality and access for local communities perpetuates the everyday violence people face from the operations of the coal mine and power plant.

The mining of and burning of coal also generate byproducts that pollute airways. The stage that a reserve has reached in the process of transformation from swamp to peat bogs to coal (through heat, burial, and pressure) determines its type, which not only influences how that coal is mined, but also the amount of greenhouse gas emissions, and the type of air and water pollutants it generates (Thurber 2019). The lignite and subbituminous coals found at Tigyit are brown or "soft" coals, which have lower carbon content and higher amounts of hydrogen and oxygen. These "dirtier" coals have a low heat value, are less efficient to transport, and reduce the thermal efficiency of the steam boilers that use these coals (Thurber 2019, 18).

Coal-fired power plants can release a range of air pollutants, including fly ash and other volatile organic compounds, sulfur dioxide (SO_2), oxides of nitrogen (NO_X), and other particulate matter, which scientists have connected to a range of health conditions from respiratory problems, stroke, and heart conditions to cancers (Earth Rights International 2018a). As the most carbon-rich fossil fuel, coal also emits a high level of CO_2, between 93 and 104 kg CO_2 per mmBTU, with subbituminous coal at 97.17 and lignite at 97.72 kg CO_2 per mmBTU. In comparison, motor gasoline releases 71.26, and natural gas releases 53.06 kg CO_2 per mmBTU (USEIA 2011). Coal produces nearly 30 percent of global emissions, making coal power plants a significant contributor to global environmental change (IPCC 2014; Thurber 2019). In addition to CO_2, mining and burning coal emits other atmospheric pollutants, including methane (CH_4) and nitrous oxide (N_2O). Not all greenhouse gases are alike. While CO_2 is a significant byproduct of coal, it is not the most potent in relation to global warming potential. Direct global warming potential (DGWP) refers to a greenhouse gas's warming potential in relation to CO_2, which has a DGWP of 1. Importantly, N_2O and CH_4, two pollutants of coal mining and burning, have significantly higher DGWP than CO_2; N_2O has a DGWP of 298 and CH_4 of 25 (IPCC 2014).

Climate change contributes to current and ongoing violence for people near Tigyit; however, the power plant also produces other air pollutants that cause immediate and accumulating harm to everyday life. A 2018 assessment of the twenty-four-hour concentrations of NO_2, SO_2, particulate matter (PM) 2.5, and PM 10 found that PM 2.5 levels in the sample area were three to four times higher than Myanmar's guidelines for a twenty-four-hour period, and PM 10 levels were more than two times as high. SO_2 levels were twelve–fifteen times higher than the guidelines, and NO_2 levels also surpassed the twenty-four-hour period Myanmar guidelines. All of these pollutants, measured around Tigyit, exceeded levels commonly found in China and the United States, and surpassed Myanmar's national guidelines (Earth Rights International 2018a). Some of these pollutants, such as fine particulate matter (PM2.5), ozone (O_3), SO_2 and NO_X can be reduced by using flue gas desulfurization and selective catalytic reduction of nitrogen oxides. However, in a contribution to everyday violence through neglect, the Tigyit coal-fired power plant does not use these techniques (Earth Rights International 2018a, 6).

Coal-fired power plants also emit coal ash, also known as fly ash. This ash is a byproduct of the combustion process, which is released through a smokestack into the atmosphere (PYO 2011, 13). Elevated levels of ash are associated with less energy production and more residue and harmful pollutants (Thurber 2019, 18). Depending on the source of the coal, fly ash usually contains heavy metals and toxins such as arsenic, lead, mercury, and cadmium, among many others (Earth Rights International 2018b), which can result in immediate and cumulative health impacts. Reports suggest that over the past ten years, communities around Tigyit have suffered from increased rates of health problems, including high blood pressure, headaches, premature and underweight births, rashes, and other skin problems (Students and Youth Congress of Burma 2018). According to the PYO report "Poison Clouds," roughly 50 percent of the nearby population suffers from skin rashes (PYO 2011, 37). Moreover, as is common with the extractive industries, these effects have a disproportionate impact on minority populations and women (Chan Mya Htwe 2018; Hnin Wut Yee 2016). According to an interviewee, before the power plant was operational, in the villages within five miles of Tigyit, roughly three women would have a miscarriage each year. Yet, in 2017, about 130 women had miscarriages (Interview 6, January 14, 2018). This interviewee also reported that children as young as three or four years old suffered from high blood pressure, and that many women and children had skin conditions from the pollutants from the coal-fired power plant (Interview 6, January 14, 2018). In an anonymous interview in a 2018 Students and Youth Congress of Burma report, one respondent shared, "I am very worried about the impacts of coal on the health of pregnant women, children, youth, and old people. Life expectancy will be reduced." In their group presentations to us, students also stressed this disproportionate impact on women and children from the coal mine and power plant.

The effects of pollutants, however, are not limited to health. Residents also talked about a decrease in income from farming activities. Before the Tigyit mine and power plant, the students reported that 60 percent of household incomes within Pinlaung township were derived from growing corn; however, this has since dropped to just 20 percent of household incomes. Fluctuating international and national commodity markets and a drop in the price of corn from 2,000 kyat per kilo to 750 kyat per kilo contributed to this loss of income; however, residents also blame the decrease in income on the fly ash and pollution from the power plant. Farmers have told CSO organizers that "crops from their farmlands are not of a high quality anymore, and because of this they cannot generate income from the crops and cannot get the market price for the crops" (Interview 3, January 13, 2018). Everyday violence emerges as the fly ash lands on the leaves of the vegetables, desiccating the plants and eroding livelihoods (Interview 6, January 14, 2018). According to PYO, "When farmers tried to complain to the company about their cabbages being destroyed, the company sent a Captain from the Burma Army to talk to the villagers. He told them: 'Pesticides get stuck on the vegetable skins and you wash and eat them anyway. In the same way you can wash away the coal dust covering your cabbages and it is no problem'" (PYO 2011, 38). This disregard for the concerns of the villagers further perpetuates an everyday loss of access to livelihoods, health, and cultural traditions. This decrease in income also makes it more difficult for families to pay for their children to attend school. Those children who can still attend school face other barriers to access created by the mine. For instance, during the rainy season, fly ash on the roads makes it dangerous for students to walk to school:

> Some of the children, when they go to school, need to cross the coal mine and it's really difficult for them. In the rainy season the fly ash, when mixed with water, gets really slippery. So, some of the children go to school in the early morning, but when they arrive there, they've already fallen, and they get dirty, and they don't want to go to the school anymore. Sometimes, they also cannot be on time at school, because the trucks carrying the coal to the power plant are big trucks and they make it unsafe for the children to cross the road. (Interview 6, January 14, 2018)

For these communities, pollution from the coal-fired power plant and the operations of the mine challenge their immediate livelihoods, but also harm the future life and livelihoods of their children through increased health risks and decreased access to education.

Laws do exist in Myanmar that offer protection for communities, including the 2015 Protection of the Rights of Ethnic Nationalities legislation. Article 5 of this law requires that ethnic nationalities receive "complete and precise" information about extractive industry projects and other business activities in their area before project implementation so that negotiations between groups and the government/companies can take place. Yet enforcement of these laws, as well as other environmental laws, remains patchy (Myanmar Centre for Responsible Business 2018), as one activist described: "If you look at the government situation right now, we consider that they are not aware, and do not understand the law anymore. Because if you look at Tigyit . . . mostly the projects should do the EIA first and they can run the project, but right now they are running the project first and then doing the EIA at the same time. It is so different from the procedure they have right now" (Interview 1, 13 January 2018). Residents have accused local officials of breaking their promises to shut down the power plant. According to U Soe Soe Zaw, secretary of the Shan State government, tests run in October of 2016 were conducted for review purposes only, to assess the effects of the plant on the environment (Kyi Kyi Sway 2016; Ye Mon 2016). Nevertheless, Shan, Danu, Pa-Oh, and Dara-ang people from around the Tigyit area protested the potential reopening of the plant (*Shan Herald Agency for News* 2017). In an interview with the *Myanmar Times,* villager U Sein Thaung expressed frustration over the lack of transparency around the tests and reopening of the coal-fired plant: "The company should have told us they were going to run tests, but they don't care about us. And the Shan State government told us they wouldn't allow the plant to reopen if we objected. It looks like they broke their promise" (Ye Mon 2016). Despite its location within a Pa-Oh SAZ, the Union government maintains control over Tigyit coal mine and power plant. Laws and policies that promote a "Burmanization" practice then enact a form of violence against the communities around Tigyit through subjugating their voices and limiting their access to good health, livelihood, and education.[7]

Although officials have asserted that the tests and running of the plant are for review purposes only and not an official restarting of the plant (Kyi Kyi Sway 2016; Ye Mon 2016), residents believe that the plant was fully operational in 2018 and are angered by this apparent lack of procedural compliance. One CSO employee who works near Tigyit explained: "Right now [Wuxi Hua Guang] has permission from the government to run the power plant and to do the EIA for one year for tests. So, the local people are really angry. Why do they test the local people like this? To run the EIA, do we need to die for it? We are people, not animals" (Interview 6, 14 January 2018). Laws and policies such as the 2006 Conservation of Water

Resources and Rivers Law, or the 2014 Environmental Conservation Rules and 2015 Environmental Quality Guidelines, should protect communities from the more harmful effects of a nearby project (Kattelus, Rahaman, and Varis 2014, 90; Ministry of Environmental Conservation and Forestry Myanmar 2014; Myo Nyunt 2008; Urban et al. 2013). Yet, many of these laws favor national economic development over local needs, further perpetuating systemic pathways of violence.

Tigyit and the (Post-coup) Future

On February 1, 2021, on the morning that newly elected members of parliament were meant to be sworn in, Myanmar's military staged a military coup. The military breached its own 2008 constitution (*Al Jazeera* 2021; ICJ 2021) and justified the coup through claims of election fraud during the November 2020 elections (Thant Myint-U 2021)—claims that have been delegitimized by independent election monitoring bodies (Sarma and Kapur 2021). Within weeks of the coup, massive peaceful demonstrations erupted in all corners of the country. These protests have shown the solidarity of the Myanmar people. Thousands of public servants are participating in a civil disobedience movement (CDM) that has inspired people from different ethnic backgrounds (Aye Min Thant and Yan Aung 2021): a key development in a country governed by the roughly two-thirds majority ethnic Burman nationalities (Min Zin 2021). Young people, doctors, and nurses have mostly led the ongoing protests. The CDM aims to disrupt the military regime's ability to control the country, and to give the power back to the elected government (Aye Min Thant and Yan Aung 2021). The military has been extremely violent toward protestors and dissidents. As of August of 2022, more than 2,230 people had been killed and over 15,200 people detained since the coup.[8] Atrocities were committed around the country, including extrajudicial killings and the destruction of personal property. According to the UNHCR (2022), as of August 8, 2022, due to armed conflict and insecurity since the coup, over 903,000 people have been internally displaced. Many of the activists, CSO workers, politicians, community leaders, and lawyers who have not been detained by the military are in hiding or have fled to neighboring countries.

The 2021 coup, CDM protests, and the resulting military violence have justifiably garnered much international and diplomatic attention, directly impacting resource frontiers within Myanmar. In times of conflict, resources have experienced both an increase and decrease in extraction in relation to their accessibility, geographic location, and distribution (Koubi et al. 2014; Le Billon 2001). In Myanmar, resource abundance has alternately funded the Myanmar military and EAOs. Prior to 2011, during active conflict between EAOs and the Myanmar military, commercial logging of high–market-value timber products decreased, only to increase after ceasefire agreements were signed (Khin Sandar Aye and Khin Khin Htay 2019).

Since the 2021 coup, the Hong Kong-based VPower group have declined to renew contracts for Myanmar power stations (*Myanmar Now* 2021a), and an Australian company has divested from a lead, silver, and zinc mine in north Shan State (*Myanmar Now* 2021b). International sanctions have pressured some companies to divest and loosen economic ties with the junta (*Myanmar Now* 2021c); however, for some companies, the coup offers new opportunities. Journalists have reported growing concerns over an increase in environmental degradation as a result of the coup (Cowan 2021a; Nachemson 2021), including an increase in logging and illegal timber trade practices (Alberts 2021; Cowan 2021b, 2021c). Evidence of an increase in illegal rare earth extraction has also been reported (*The Irrawaddy* 2021). At Tigyit, the Shan Herald Agency for News (SHAN) reported on March 6, 2021, on the unlicensed expansion of the coal mine occurring amidst the diversion of nationwide protests. Among community members and CSOs, there is also a growing concern over an increase in arrests of environmental activists (Bociaga 2021).

The current and ongoing threat of increased and unregulated resource extraction exacerbates the everyday violence discussed above for communities living in and around Tigyit, making their future lives and livelihoods all the more precarious. Impacts from the coal mine and power plant are not always direct, and everyday violence manifests in a myriad of ways. As Springer (2011, 91) states, violence is an unfolding process, not just a moment in time. It can occur through traumatic events like the dispossession of people from their lands or negligence in enforcing policies and laws or through the accumulative effects of ill health. As the students argued, this is a violence that does not distinguish between health, environment, education, and livelihood. It occurs in the everyday. This everyday violence is grounded in the physical properties and demands of coal production itself, and it flows through the airways, waterways, and terrestrial spaces (Elden 2013). It bleeds into people's everyday and future lives. The enforcement of protections through the rule of law or the application of technologies to limit pollutants could have minimized the violence caused by this plant. Unfortunately, there is nothing exceptional about this coal project and the harm it has caused; yet, within a country with fragmented sovereignties and with unenforced laws and policies, the unnecessary everydayness of the violence it perpetuates stands out. As Galtung (1969) and Tyner and Rice (2016) suggest in their definitions of violence, the operations of and the byproducts of the Tigyit coal mine and power plant are violent because they are not inevitable.

Notes

1. The Pa-Oh Youth Organization was founded by Pa-Oh women, monks, and young people in Shan State in the late 1990s.

2. We use "Myanmar military" to refer to both the Myanmar military as an armed institution and as a government regime that currently refers to itself as the State Administrative Council (SAC), but in the past has included General Ne Win's Revolutionary Council, the Burma Socialist Program Party (BSPP), State Law and Order Restoration Council (SLORC), and State Peace and Development Council (SPDC). The military as a government regime is also commonly referred to as the "Junta," which we also occasionally use. Unless used in quotes or in the bibliography, we have not used the oft-invoked term "Tatmadaw" to refer to the military. Tatmadaw is the institution's self-titled honorific term, meaning the Royal/Great "Tat" (the army). After the February 2021 coup, many Myanmar citizens, in a citizen-led effort to refuse to refer to the military with its honorific title, prefer to use other terms, such as "Sit-tat" (the "War army"), instead of the "Tatmadaw." In this chapter, we have thus used "Myanmar military" in recognition of and respect for the citizens' plural terms for the military and the government.

3. British colonization left a legacy of new forms of ethnic racism and ethno-nationalism. Prior to colonization, understandings of race and ethnicity differed. In Burmese, the term *lumyo* conveyed a meaning of a "type of person" in relation to their social status or class distinction, not to language or ethnicity as it does today. When the British census commissioners surveyed the population of the Province of Burma, they focused on different language groups, tying language to race or tribe and ultimately changing the meaning of *lumyo* (Ferguson 2021, 44–49; Thant Myint-U 2001; Winichakul 1994, 12–16). European notions of biologically determined race and ethnicity were built into the racialized narratives of upland people groups, like Shan and Pa-Oh, as "wild and uncivilized" (Lieberman 2003, 131–132). In Shan State, the ethno-nationalist project for political power and autonomy against the Myanmar government marries the connection between sovereignty, territory, capitalist endeavors, and racialization.

4. Today, Myanmar is divided into seven divisions and seven states. The seven states are named for the major ethnic nationalities: Chin (Chin people), Shan (Shan people), Kachin (Kachin people), Kayin (Karen peoples), Kayah (Karenni people), Mon (Mon people), and Rakhine (Arakan people). Within the eight nationality groups of Myanmar (including ethnic Burman), there are 135 officially recognized subgroups (Ferguson 2021, 22).

5. This mandate cannot be changed without a greater than 75 percent majority in parliament.

6. Within Myanmar, however, a ceasefire agreement doesn't guarantee an actual ceasefire, as the increase in armed conflict in Kachin, Kayin, and Shan areas with signed ceasefires demonstrate (see Kiik 2020). Many of the ceasefire attempts remained non-inclusive of a majority of the ethnic players, and were thus unsuccessful (Tønnesson, Min Zaw, and Lynn Aung 2021).

7. Ne Win's military government institutionalized Burmanization policies, seeking to construct "a highly centralized, culturally homogenous Burman state" (Cockett 2015, 76–77).

8. See Assistance Association for Political Prisoners (Burma), https://aappb.org/.

References

Al Jazeera. 2021. "Dr Sasa: Army leaders 'Underestimate' the People of Myanmar." *Talk to Al Jazeera,* March 27, 2021. https://www.aljazeera.com/program/talk-to-al-jazeera/2021/3/27/dr-sasa-army-leaders-underestimate-the-people-of-myanmar.

Alberts, E. 2021. "Myanmar's Troubled Forestry Sector Seeks Global Endorsement After Coup." *Mongabay,* February 8, 2021. https://news.mongabay.com/2021/02/myanmars-troubled-forestry-sector-seeks-global-endorsement-after-coup/.

Aung Shin. 2016. "Chinese Firm to Restart Myanmar's Only Coal Plant." *Myanmar Times,* December 3, 2016. https://www.mmtimes.com/business/20010-chinese-firm-to-restart-myanmar-s-only-coal-plant.html.

Aye Min Thant and Yan Aung. 2021. "How the CDM Can Win." *Frontier Myanmar,* March 4, 2021. https://www.frontiermyanmar.net/en/how-the-cdm-can-win/.

Baver, Jesse, Benoit Jonveaux, Ran Ju, Keisuke Kitamura, Pushkar Sharma, Lila Wade, and Shinji Yasui. 2013. "Securing Livelihoods and Land Tenure in Rural Myanmar: With a Case Study on Southern Shan State." New York: UN-Habitat and Columbia University School of International and Public Affairs. https://sipa.columbia.edu/sites/default/files/UN-HABITATFinalReport_17May2013.pdf.

Berman-Arevalo, Eloísa, and Diana Ojeda. 2020. "Ordinary Geographies: Care, Violence, and Agrarian Extractivism in 'Post-Conflict' Colombia." *Antipode* 52 (6): 1583–1602. https://doi.org/10.1111/anti.12667.

Bhagat, Ali. 2018. "Forced (Queer) Migration and Everyday Violence: The Geographies of Life, Death, and Access in Cape Town." *Geoforum* 89:155–163. https://doi.org/10.1016/j.geoforum.2017.07.028.

Bhide, Amita. 2020. "Everyday Violence and Bottom-Up Peace Building Initiatives by the Urban Poor in Mumbai." *International Development Planning Review* 42 (1): 57–71.

Blake, David J. H., and Keith Barney. 2018. "Structural Injustice, Slow Violence? The Political Ecology of a 'Best Practice' Hydropower Dam in Lao PDR." *Journal of Contemporary Asia* 48 (5): 808–834. https://doi.org/10.1080/00472336.2018.1482560.

Bociaga, Robert. 2021. "Ethnic Communities in Myanmar Opposing a Coal Plant See Their Fight Get Harder." *Mongabay,* July 29, 2021. https://news.mongabay.com/2021/07/ethnic-communities-in-myanmar-opposing-a-coal-plant-see-their-fight-get-harder/.

Bohle, Hans-Georg, and Hartmut Fünfgeld. 2007. "The Political Ecology of Violence in Eastern Sri Lanka." *Development and Change* 38 (4): 665–687. https://doi.org/10.1111/j.1467-7660.2007.00428.x.

Bryant, Raymond L. 1997. *The Political Ecology of Forestry in Burma: 1824–1994.* Honolulu: University of Hawai'i Press.

Callahan, Mary. 2007. *Political Authority in Burma's Ethnic Minority States: Devolution Occupation and Coexistence.* Washington, DC: East Wester Center.

Callahan, Mary. 2009. "Myanmar's Perpetual Junta: Solving the Riddle of the Tatmadaw's Long Reign." *New Left Review* 60:27–63.

Chan Mya Htwe. 2018. "Residents Still Unhappy over Tigyit Coal Project." *Myanmar Times,* September 11, 2018. https://www.mmtimes.com/news/residents-still-unhappy-over-tigyit-coal-project.html-0.

Cockett, Richard. 2015. *Blood, Dreams and Gold: The Changing Face of Burma*. New Haven, CT: Yale University Press.
Cons, Jason, and Michael Eilenberg. 2019. "Introduction: On the New Politics of Margins in Asia: Mapping Frontier Assemblages." In *Frontier Assemblages: The Emergent Politics of Resource Frontiers in Asia*, edited by Jason Cons and Michael Eilenberg, 1–18. Hoboken, NJ: Wiley.
Cowan, Carolyn. 2021a. "Myanmar Junta's Growing Reliance on Extractives for Cash Raises Concerns." *Mongabay*, June 18, 2021. https://news.mongabay.com/2021/06/myanmar-juntas-growing-reliance-on-extractives-for-cash-raises-concerns/.
Cowan, Carolyn. 2021b. "Deforestation Surge Continues amid Deepening Uncertainty in Myanmar." *Mongabay*, August 23, 2021. https://news.mongabay.com/2021/08/deforestation-surge-continues-amid-deepening-uncertainty-in-myanmar/.
Cowan, Carolyn. 2021c. "Will Myanmar's Press Crackdown Cover Up Environmental Crimes?" Global Investigative Journalism Network, September 15, 2021. https://gijn.org/2021/09/15/myanmar-environmental-crimes/.
Davies, Thom. 2019. "Slow Violence and Toxic Geographies: 'Out of Sight' to Whom?" *Environment and Planning C Politics and Space* 40 (9): 239965441984106.
de Leeuw, Sarah. 2016. "Tender Grounds: Intimate Visceral Violence and British Columbia's Colonial Geographies." *Political Geography* 52:14–23. https://doi.org/10.1016/j.polgeo.2015.11.010.
Earth Rights International, L. Myllyvirta, P. Winn, and Paung Ku. 2018a. "Air Pollution Assessment Report."
Earth Rights International, L. Myllyvirta, P. Winn, and Paung Ku. 2018b. "Water Quality Assessment Report."
EJAtlas Southeast Asia Team. n.d. "Tigyit Coal Mine and Power Plant, Shan State, Myanmar." Accessed December 4, 2018. https://ejatlas.org/print/tigyit-coal-power-plant-shan-state-myanmar.
Elden, Stuart. 2013. "Secure the Volume: Vertical Geopolitics and the Depth of Power." *Political Geography* 34:35–51.
Environmental Investigation Agency (EIA). 2015. *Organized Chaos: The Illicit Overland Timber Trade between Myanmar and China*. London: EIA. https://eia-international.org/report/organised-chaos-the-illicit-overland-timber-trade-between-myanmar-and-china/.
Ferguson, Jane M. 2021. *Repossessing Shanland: Myanmar, Thailand and a Nation-State Deferred*. Madison: University of Wisconsin Press.
Galtung, Johan. 1969. "Violence, Peace, and Peace Research." *Journal of Peace Research* 6 (3): 167–191.
Galtung, Johan. 1990. "Cultural Violence." *Journal of Peace Research* 27 (3): 291–305.
Han, Enze. 2019. *Asymmetrical Neighbors: Borderland State Building between China and Southeast Asia*. Oxford: Oxford University Press.
Hnin Wut Yee. 2016. "Implications on Women's Lives and Livelihoods: A Case Study of Villages to be Affected by the Mongton Dam Project in Shan State." In *Conference Proceedings: International Conference on the Mekong, Salween and Red Rivers: Sharing Knowledge and Perspectives across Borders, 12 November 2016*, 303–333. Bangkok:

Centre for Social Development Studies, Faculty of Political Science, Chulalongkorn University.
ICJ (International Commission of Jurists). 2021. "Myanmar: Military Coup D'état Violates Principles of Rule of Law, International Law and Myanmar's Constitution." *International Commission of Jurists,* February 8, 2021. https://www.icj.org/myanmar-military-coup-detat-violates-principles-of-rule-of-law-international-law-and-myanmars-constitution/.
IPCC. 2014. *Climate Change 2014: Synthesis Report. Climate Change 2014: Synthesis Report. Contribution of Working Groups I, II and III to the Fifth Assessment Report of the Intergovernmental Panel on Climate Change.* Geneva: IPCC. https://doi.org/10.1017/CBO9781107415324.
The Irrawaddy. 2021. "Illegal Rare Earth Mines on China Border Multiple Since Myanmar's Coup." April 26, 2021. https://www.irrawaddy.com/news/burma/illegal-rare-earth-mines-china-border-multiply-since-myanmars-coup.html.
Jenss, Alke. 2020. "Global Flows and Everyday Violence in Urban Space: The Port-City of Buenaventura, Colombia." *Political Geography* 77:102113. https://doi.org/10.1016/j.polgeo.2019.102113.
Jolliffe, Kim. 2015. *Ethnic Armed Conflict and Territorial Administration in Myanmar.* San Francisco: Asia Foundation.
Jones, Lee. 2014. "Explaining Myanmar's Regime Transition: The Periphery Is Central." *Democratization* 21 (5): 1–23. https://doi.org/10.1080/13510347.2013.863878.
Kattelus, Mirja, Muhammad Mizanur Rahaman, and Olli Varis. 2014. "Myanmar under Reform: Emerging Pressures on Water, Energy and Food Security." *Natural Resources Forum* 38 (2): 85–98. https://doi.org/10.1111/1477-8947.12032.
Khin Sandar Aye and Khin Khin Htay. 2019. "The Impact of Land Cover Changes on Socio-economic Conditions in Bawlakhe District, Kayak State." In *Knowing the Salween River: Resource Politics of a Contested Transboundary River,* edited by Carl Middleton and Vanessa Lamb, 239–258. SpringerLink Open Access. https://doi.org/10.1007/978-3-319-77440-4.
Kiik, Laur. 2020. "Inter-National Conspiracy? Speculating on the Myitsone Dam Controversy in China, Burma, Kachin, and a Displaced Village." *Geopolitics* 28 (1): 72–98. https://doi.org/10.1080/14650045.2020.1808886.
Kikon, Dolly. 2019. *Living with Oil and Coal: Resource Politics and Militarization in Northeast India.* Seattle: University of Washington Press.
Koubi, Vally, Gabriele Spilker, Tobias Böhmelt, and Thomas Bernauer. 2014. "Do Natural Resources Matter for Interstate and Intrastate Armed Conflict?" *Journal of Peace Research* 51 (2): 227–243. https://doi.org/10.1177/0022343313493455.
Kritsanavarin, S., and P. Vrieze. 2015. "Shan State Coal Mine Brings Misery for Villagers, Environmental Degradation." *Unearth Myanmar,* August, 2015. https://www.unearthmyanmar.com/stories/shan-state/coal-mining-shan/.
Kyi Kyi Sway. 2016. "Official Speaks Out against Coal Power." *Myanmar Times,* November 10, 2016. https://www.mmtimes.com/national-news/23574-official-speaks-out-against-coal-power.html.

Lamb, Vanessa, Laura Schoenberger, Carl Middleton, and Borin Un. 2017. "Gendered Eviction, Protest and Recovery: A Feminist Political Ecology Engagement with Land Grabbing in Rural Cambodia." *Journal of Peasant Studies* 44 (6): 1217–1236. https://doi.org/10.1080/03066150.2017.1311868.

Le Billon, Philippe. 2001. "The Political Ecology of War: Natural Resources and Armed Conflicts." *Political Geography* 20:561–584.

Le Billon, Philippe, and Rosaleen V. Duffy. 2018. "Conflict Ecologies: Connecting Political Ecology and Peace and Conflict Studies. *Journal of Political Ecology* 25 (1): 239–260.

Li, Tania Murray. 2010. "To Make Live or Let Die? Rural Dispossession and the Protection of Surplus Populations." *Antipode* 41:66–93. https://doi.org/10.1111/j.1467-8330.2009.00717.x.

Lieberman, Victor. 2003. *Strange Parallels: Southeast Asia in Global Context, c 800–1830.* Vol. 2. Cambridge: Cambridge University Press.

Maclean, Ken. 2010. "The Rise of Private Indirect Government in Burma." In *Finding Dollars, Sense, and Legitimacy in Burma*, edited by Susan L. Levenstein, 40–52. Washington, DC: Woodrow Wilson International Center for Scholars. Retrieved from http://www.wilsoncenter.org/topics/pubs/ASIA_092010_Burma_rpt_for web.pdf.

Mark, S. 2016. "'Fragmented Sovereignty' over Property Institutions: Developmental Impacts on the Chin Hills Communities." *Independent Journal of Burmese Scholarship* 1 (1): 131–160. https://repub.eur.nl/pub/93533.

Marx, Karl. 1992. "Primitive Accumulation." In *Capital*, vol. 1, *A Critique of Political Economy*, part 7. London: Penguin.

Meehan, Patrick. 2015. "Fortifying or Fragmenting the State? The Political Economy of the Opium/Heroin Trade in Shan State, Myanmar, 1988–2013." *Critical Asian Studies* 47 (2): 253–282. https://doi.org/10.1080/14672715.2015.1041280.

Min Zin. 2021. "The Real Kingmakers of Myanmar." *New York Times,* June 4, 2021. https://www.nytimes.com/2021/06/04/opinion/myanmar-ethnic-armed-groups.html?searchResultPosition=1.

Ministry of Environmental Conservation and Forestry Myanmar. 2014. *Environmental Conservation Rules, Ministry of Environmental Conservation and Forestry Notification No. 50/2014.* Myanmar.

Myanmar Centre for Responsible Business. 2018. "Main Laws Applicable to the Mining Sector in Myanmar." *Myanmar Centre for Responsible Business.* https://www.myanmar-responsiblebusiness.org/pdf/SWIA/Mining/Main-Myanmar-E_and_S-Laws-Mining-Sector.pdf.

Myanmar Now. 2021a. "Hong Kong's VPower Ends Involvement in Two Myanmar Power Projects." August 31, 2021. https://www.myanmar-now.org/en/news/hong-kongs-vpower-ends-involvement-in-two-myanmar-power-projects.

Myanmar Now. 2021b. "Australian Company Divests from Bawdwin Mine in Northern Shan State." August 20, 2021. https://www.myanmar-now.org/en/news/australian-company-divests-from-bawdwin-mine-in-northern-shan-state.

Myanmar Now. 2021c. "US Adds New Sanctions against Myanmar Junta." July 2, 2021. https://www.myanmar-now.org/en/news/us-adds-new-sanctions-against-myanmar-junta.

Myo Nyunt. 2008. "Development of Environmental Management Mechanism in Myanmar." *Asia Europe Journal* 6 (2): 293–306. https://doi.org/10.1007/s10308-008-0182-2.

Nachemson, Andrew. 2021. "Myanmar's Environmental Record Was Weak but Improving. Then Came the Coup." *Mongabay,* March 18, 2021. https://news.mongabay.com/2021/03/myanmars-environmental-record-was-weak-but-improving-then-came-the-coup/.

Nixon, Rob. 2011. *Slow Violence and the Environmentalism of the Poor.* Cambridge, MA: Harvard University Press.

Oberndorf, Robert B. 2012. "Legal Review of Recently Enacted Farmland Law and Vacant, Fallow and Virgin Lands Management Law: Improving the Legal and Policy Frameworks Relating to Land Management in Myanmar." Forest Trends Food Security Working Group paper. Washington, DC: Forest Trends. https://www.forest-trends.org/wp-content/uploads/imported/fswg_lcg_legal-review-of-farmland-law-and-vacant-fallow-and-virgin-land-management-law-nov-2012-eng-2-pdf.pdf.

Pedersen, Morten B. 2011. "The Politics of Burma's 'Democratic' Transition." *Critical Asian Studies* 43 (1): 49–68. doi:10.1080/14672715.2011.537851.

Peluso, Nancy Lee. 2008. "A Political Ecology of Violence and Territory in West Kalimantan." *Asia Pacific Viewpoint* 49 (1): 48–67. https://doi.org/10.1111/j.1467-8373.2008.00360.x.

Peluso, Nancy Lee, and Peter Vandergeest. 2011. "Political Ecologies of War and Forests: Counterinsurgencies and the Making of National Natures." *Annals of the Association of American Geographers* 101 (3): 587–608. https://doi.org/10.1080/00045608.2011.560064.

Peluso, Nancy Lee, and Michael Watts, eds. 2001. *Violent Environments.* Ithaca, NY: Cornell University Press.

Piedalue, Amy D. 2019. "Slow Nonviolence: Muslim Women Resisting the Everyday Violence of Dispossession and Marginalization." *Environment and Planning C: Politics and Space* 40 (2): 373–390. https://doi.org/10.1177/2399654419882721.

PYO (Pa-Oh Youth Organization). 2011. "Poison Clouds: Lessons from Burma's Largest Coal Project at Tigyit." Pa-Oh Youth Organization (PYO) and the Kyoju Action Network (KAN). https://burmacampaign.org.uk/images/uploads/PoisonClouds.pdf.

Rasmussen, Mattias Borg, and Christian Lund. 2018. "Reconfiguring Frontier Spaces: The Territorialization of Resource Control." *World Development* 101:388–399. https://doi.org/10.1016/j.worlddev.2017.01.018.

Ribot, Jesse C., and Nancy Lee Peluso. 2003. "A Theory of Access." *Rural Sociology* 68 (2): 153–181. https://doi.org/10.1111/j.1549-0831.2003.tb00133.x.

Roberts, K. B. 2019. "Powers of Access: Impacts on Resource Users and Researchers in Myanmar's Shan State." In *Knowing the Salween River: Resource Politics of a Contested Transboundary River,* vol. 27, edited by Carl Middleton and Vanessa Lamb, 205–221. SpringerLink Open Access. https://doi.org/10.1007/978-3-319-77440-4.

Sai Aung Tun. 2009. *History of the Shan State: From Its Origins to 1962.* Chiang Mai: Silkworm Books.

Sarma, Jasnea, and Roshni Kapur. 2021. *The Myanmar Coup, Resistance and India's Response: Fractured between Words and Deeds.* ISAS Special Report. Singapore: National

University of Singapore Institute of South Asian Studies (ISAS). https://www.isas.nus.edu.sg/papers/the-myanmar-coup-resistance-and-indias-response-fractured-between-words-and-deeds/.

Shan Herald Agency for News. 2017. "Public Skips Meeting on Tigyit Coal-Fired Power Plant." *Burma News International,* May 3, 2017. https://www.bnionline.net/en/news/shan-state/item/2989-public-skips-meeting-on-tigyit-coal-fired-power-plant.html.

Shan Herald Agency for News. 2021. "Coal Mining Companies Ramp Up Illegal Extractions Amid Protests." March 6, 2021. https://english.shannews.org/archives/22523.

SHRF (Shan Human Rights Foundation). 1998. *Dispossessed: A Report on Forced Relocation and Extrajudicial Killings in Shan State, Burma.* Chiang Mai: SHRF.

Springer, Simon. 2011. "Violence Sits in Places? Cultural Practice, Neoliberal Rationalism, and Virulent Imaginative Geographies." *Political Geography* 30 (2): 90–98. https://doi.org/10.1016/j.polgeo.2011.01.004.

Springer, Simon, and Philippe Le Billon. 2016. "Violence and Space: An Introduction to the Geographies of Violence." *Political Geography* 52:1–3. https://doi.org/10.1016/j.polgeo.2016.03.003.

Students and Youth Congress of Burma. 2018. "Statement Opposing the Planned Restarting of the Tigyit Coal Red Power Plant." *SYCB News.* http://www.sycbyouth.org/statement-opposing-the-planned-restarting-of-the-tigyit-coal-fired-power-plant/.

Sturgeon, Janet C. 2004. "Border Practices, Boundaries, and the Control of Resource Access: A Case from China, Thailand and Burma." *Development and Change* 35 (3): 463–484. https://doi.org/10.1111/j.1467–7660.2004.00361.x.

Suhardiman, Diana, Jeff Rutherford, and Saw John Bright. 2017. "Putting Violent Armed Conflict in the Center of the Salween Hydropower Debates." *Critical Asian Studies* 49 (3): 349–364. https://doi.org/10.1080/14672715.2017.1328284.

SWAN (Shan Women's Action Network). 2002. *License to Rape: The Burmese Military Regime's Use of Sexual Violence in the Ongoing War in Shan State.* Chiang Mai: SWAN.

Thant Myint-U. 2021. "What Next for Burma?" *London Review of Books blog,* March 18, 2021. https://www.lrb.co.uk/blog/2021/march/what-next-for-burma.

Thurber, Mark C. 2019. *Coal.* Cambridge: Polity Press.

Tønnesson, Stein, Min Zaw Oo, and Ne Lynn Aung. 2021. "Non-Inclusive Ceasefires Do Not Bring Peace: Findings from Myanmar." *Small Wars and Insurgencies* 33 (3): 313–349. doi:10.1080/09592318.2021.1991141.

Tyner, James A., and Stian Rice. 2016. "To Live and Let Die: Food, Famine, and Administrative Violence in Democratic Kampuchea, 1975–1979." *Political Geography* 52:47–56. https://doi.org/10.1016/j.polgeo.2015.11.004.

UNHCR. 2022. "Myanmar Emergency Overview Map: Number of People Displaced since Feb 2021 and Remain Displaced." *Reliefweb,* August 8, 2022. https://reliefweb.int/map/myanmar/myanmar-emergency-overview-map-number-people-displaced-feb-2021-and-remain-displaced-08-aug-2022.

Urban, Frauke, Johan Nordensvärd, Deepika Khatri, and Yu Wang. 2013. "An Analysis of China's Investment in the Hydropower Sector in the Greater Mekong Sub-Region." *Environment, Development and Sustainability* 15 (2): 301–324. https://doi.org/10.1007/s10668–012–9415-z.

USEIA (US Energy Information Administration). 2011. "Carbon Dioxide Emissions Coefficients Detail Factors." USEIA. http://eia.gov/environment/emissions/archive/coefficients.php.

Valentis Resources. 2016. "Myanmar Mine Laws: Unofficial Translation and Comparison Yangon, Myanmar." Valentis Resources, January 27, 2017. https://s3.amazonaws.com/rgi-documents/51750b60d4e26f1f6572958fbc2eb602e63fcb16.pdf.

Watts, Michael. 2013. *Silent Violence: Food, Famine, and Peasantry in Northern Nigeria: With a New Introduction.* Athens: University of Georgia Press.

Winichakul, Thongchai. 1994. *Siam Mapped: A History of the Geo-Body of a Nation.* Honolulu: University of Hawai'i Press.

Woods, Kevin. 2011. "Ceasefire Capitalism: Military-Private Partnerships, Resource Concessions and Military-State Building in the Burma-China Borderlands." *Journal of Peasant Studies* 38 (4): 747–770. https://doi.org/10.1080/03066150.2011.607699.

Woods, Kevin. 2019. "Rubber out of the Ashes: Locating Chinese Agribusiness Investments in 'Armed Sovereignties' in the Myanmar-China Borderlands." *Territory, Politics, Governance* 7 (1): 79–95. https://doi.org/10.1080/21622671.2018.1460276.

Ye Mon. 2016. "Residents Fear Restart of Coal Power Plant." *Myanmar Times,* October 25, 2016. https://www.mmtimes.com/national-news/23280-residents-fear-restart-of-coal-power-plant.html.

Zaragocin, Sofia. 2019. "Gendered Geographies of Elimination: Decolonial Feminist Geographies in Latin American Settler Contexts." *Antipode* 51 (1): 373–392.

CHAPTER 3

Quarantined Activism
COVID-19 and Extractivism in the Philippines

WOLFRAM DRESSLER

For much of 2020 and 2021, parts of Southeast Asia saw deepening authoritarian populism and the COVID-19 pandemic intersect in ways that reinforced the suppression of human rights, dismantled environmental protections, and intensified resource extraction. Resurgent authoritarian regimes created conditions of impunity in which state and non-state actors could intensify political campaigns against diverse activists (hereafter "defenders") upholding human rights and environmental protections (Beban, Schoenberger, and Lamb 2020; Middeldorp and Le Billon 2019; Neimark et al. 2019).[1] Since 2020, the outbreak of SARS-CoV-2 (Severe Acute Respiratory Syndrome Coronavirus 2) and the COVID-19 pandemic enabled "strongman" leaders, state actors, and shadowy hitmen to foment violent atmospheres of control and suppression across the region. These actors worked opportunistically, exploiting the edges of fraying legal orders and co-opting public health measures to further restrain activism, contain Indigenous livelihoods, and intensify illegal resource uses. In this chapter, I critically examine national media and policies to explore how the election of former Philippine president Rodrigo Duterte generated punitive agendas of political control and violence, which intersected with public health measures during the COVID-19 pandemic to suppress human rights and environmental defenders in the country.

In 2020, the United Nations Human Rights Council released a damning report documenting that between 2015 and 2019, at least 248 human rights and environmental defenders had been murdered in their pursuit of social and environmental justice in the Philippines (OHCHR 2020). The harassment, intimidation, and murder of so-called leftist defenders escalated significantly after President Duterte assumed office. Elected in 2016, Duterte built upon exploitative resource policies and growth agendas to exercise repressive political control with revanchist rhetoric and practices against those in civil society critical of his rule. Partly emboldened by the president's violent rhetoric, state actors, political elites, and hitmen intensified the long-standing practice of crushing activist dissent and social movements in order to enable private and state-financed resource grabbing and extractive development (mining, palm oil production, etc.), which often intersected with and exacerbated communist and Moro-Islamic insurgencies in "commodity frontiers" such as Mindanao and Palawan (Holden, Nadeau, and Jacobson 2011; Moore 2000). With Duterte's ostensive pivot to the "East," Chinese-backed loans continued to finance his mega-infrastructure initiatives. They also expanded palm oil plantations, roads, and hydropower projects further into these frontier areas (Bello 2019; Heydarian 2017) and increased the bloodshed of defender deaths. The violence of the past has continued under the newly elected president, Bongbong Marcos, the son of the former dictator Ferdinand Marcos.

The Beginnings

In September 2016, barely six weeks after his election, Duterte declared a nationwide state of emergency due to multiple insurgent bombings in Mindanao. This state of emergency culminated in a declaration of martial law for the island in May 2017, criminalizing diverse defenders as terrorists and subjecting them to curfews, monitoring, arrests, and murder (Aspinwall 2020a). Duterte's Philippines soon became one of the most dangerous countries in the world for human rights and environmental defenders. According to the domestic NGO Kalikasan People's Network for the Environment (KPNE 2019), forty-six defenders were killed in 2019 alone, with the majority being activist farmers and/or plantation workers, followed by municipal officials, Indigenous peoples, and forest rangers—an "accounting" that most likely underreported the numbers of killings and failed to lay bare the violent atmospheres behind the executions and harassment leading up to them.

While human rights and environmental activists have experienced harassment and murder under previous administrations, President Duterte's brutish populism further emboldened the military, police, and hitmen to unleash violence across the countryside. Many of these actors intensified the decades-old practice of "red-tagging" defenders as leftist "anti-capitalists" and sympathizers of the New People's Army (NPA)—the armed wing of the Communist Party of the Philippines (CPP) (Rutten 2008; Holden, Nadeau, and Jacobson 2011). Red-tagging and similar schemes became ever more entrenched as broader surveillance and intimidation campaigns across the country under Duterte.

About six months after martial law was "lifted" in Mindanao, the state's freshly drafted Anti-Terrorism Act (RA no. 11479) further conflated terrorism and activism in law and practice, reinforcing the ongoing suppression of citizens' rights and freedoms (Aspinwall 2020b).[2] Under the law, the military and police retained sweeping powers to determine what constitutes terrorism, obliging "suspects" to prove they have no connections with the CPP-NPA or other insurgency groups (most of whom have since been branded as terrorists) (Aspinwall 2020b). With little independent judicial oversight, enforcement agencies, politicians, and others have indiscriminately red-tagged almost anyone with activist inclinations—whether priest, farmer, or fisher—as a potential terrorist threat (Chavez 2020; Batac 2020).

After March 2020, however, the strategies and struggles of environmental and human rights defenders entered the increasingly violent sphere of the COVID-19 pandemic. Between March 7 and 12, 2020, after a sudden increase in local virus transmission in Manila (a megacity of twenty-four million residents), health authorities suspended air, sea, and land travel into and out of the National Capital Region (Palo, Rosetes, and Cariño 2020, 169–170). In haste, President Duterte declared the first "enhanced community quarantine" (ECQ) for Metro Manila on March 17 to contain the initial outbreak, with hard lockdowns imposed across the rest of the country from early April (Aspinwall 2020c). Scheduled to end on April 12, the ECQ was extended twice and continued until June 1, 2020, after which restrictions were loosened under the general community quarantine scheme (Palo, Rosetes, and Cariño 2020). However, various types of community quarantine continued across the country for the duration of the pandemic. Under these emergency orders, the already dangerous work of defender activism was further threatened by additional monitoring and restrictions.

As certain state actors' use of pandemic restrictions suppressed activism and breached social and environmental protections, political elites, private sector actors, and local *illegalista* became emboldened to grab land, poach timber and non-timber forest products, and illegally harvest marine resources with fewer barriers in place. By quarantining, containing, and threatening those who defend human rights and the environment, illegal operators took advantage of lulls in monitoring and enforcing environmental safeguards to accelerate resource plunder and threaten the resource base and livelihoods of local and Indigenous peoples. In other cases, the state and private sector exploited COVID-related suppressions of activism to further expand mining and palm oil plantations into upland areas as part of the president's so-called pandemic economic recovery.

In examining the quarantining of activism, I show how the violent conjunctures of political oppression and COVID-19 strictures unfolded together to intensify as comprehensive and deeply penetrating violent atmospheres in a literal and figurative sense. I describe how the harassment and containment of defender activism was amplified under COVID-19, and how such suppression (and the ostensive push for economic recovery) intensified the exploitation of timber and nickel in the mountains of Palawan Island. I shed light on the plight of defenders during the pandemic and what this portends for the future of activism in the Philippines.

Methods

Data for this chapter were drawn from online media sources from March to December 2020, with the sourcing of content related to specific incidents of defender activism (concerning environmental degradation, land grabs, agrarian reform, and human rights abuses, etc.) involving state and non-state suppression and COVID-19 public health restrictions.[3]

Using Google Advanced Search, a research assistant and I ran a detailed search of mainstream, national, state-owned, and alternative news media for these incidents from March to December 2020. This scaled search invariably picked up cases of activist suppression involving COVID-19 measures, which were then categorized and examined in greater detail (see table 3.1).

Table 3.1. Keyword search terms and strings

Step 1—Identify keywords for Google Search	
Main keyword	**Related phrases used in news media**
Environmental defender	Environmentalist, activist, NGO, community worker, Indigenous
Violence against	Arrested, harassed, dead, killed, threatened, detained, shot
COVID-19	Pandemic, quarantine restrictions, lockdown, activists
Step 2—Formulate keyword strings for Advanced Search	
#1 Activist	Arrested OR dead OR killed OR threatened OR detained OR shot
#2 Environmentalist	Arrested OR dead OR killed OR threatened OR detained OR shot
#3 NGO	Arrested OR dead OR killed OR threatened OR detained OR shot
#4 Indigenous group	Arrested OR dead OR killed OR threatened OR detained OR shot
#5 Community leader	Arrested OR dead OR killed OR threatened OR detained OR shot
#6 Forest ranger	Arrested OR dead OR killed OR threatened OR detained OR shot
#7 Farmer	Arrested OR dead OR killed OR threatened OR detained OR shot
#8 COVID-19	Pandemic/activist OR quarantine/activist OR lockdown/activist/detained

We then began an advanced search involving a content analysis of textual material related to the arrests, harassment, and/or killing of defenders, both independent of and in the context of the pandemic. The content analysis was further broken down into incident type and number, number of persons involved, and specific cases involving COVID-19 restrictions. To capture outlier cases, we used MS Excel to document and examine provincial media sources. We looked for and collated key patterns in the search across each media source to inform the broader narrative and details of specific cases in the chapter. Independent of the structured media review, I also drew on case material from the local broadsheet, the *Palawan Times*, involving defenders being subjected to COVID-19 lockdowns and the associated rise in resource exploitation on Palawan. I contextualize these media cases with my own insights from my long-term research on the island (see Dressler 2021).

Authoritarianism and the Violence of Viral Conjunctures

The global surge in authoritarian populism this past decade has extended political control and violence over peoples and territories and further intensified the expansion of ideology, capital accumulation, and resource exploitation (Scoones et al. 2018; McCarthy 2019; Middeldorp and Le Billon 2019). Based on his own reflections on authoritarian populism in the UK from the 1970s–1980s, Stuart Hall's (1979) critique and conceptualization of authoritarian populism resonates with the political and economic conjunctures in the Philippines that led to the rise of Duterte and of dictator Ferdinand Marcos before him, in 1965. In Hall's formulation, authoritarian populism amounts to "an exceptional form of capitalist state—which, unlike classical fascism, has retained most (though not all) of the formal representative institutions in place, and which at the same time has been able to construct around itself an active popular consent" (Hall 1979, 15). In the Philippines under Duterte, this active popular consent was (and continues to be) upheld by Filipinos of contrasting ethnic, gender, and class positions who gave the former president consistently high levels of popular support (Curato 2016). Recent scholarly work on authoritarian populism emphasizes core traits exemplified by Duterte: *political performance* and *enactment* engendered by certain styles and rhetorical practices imbued with unbridled revanchism and chauvinism (Moffitt and Tormey 2014; Theriault 2020).

Duterte's brand of authoritarian populism often relied heavily on "performative repertoires" in his claims to represent "the people" or "the nation" (Moffitt and Tormey 2014, 387–388) as he and others like him rely on varied tools of repression (militarized violence, diminishing civil liberties, etc.) and harness the often-vague rhetorical tone of populism for instrumental means and ends (Bugaric 2019). Some scholars have even suggested that recent forms of authoritarian populism reflect a newer confrontational style that aims to meld and accentuate the aspirations and sentiments of broader public grievances, however real or superficial, as part of coordinated rhetoric, alliance, and political movements (Canovan 2004). Duterte was one such "new populist" who claimed to "represent the right source of legitimate power—the people, whose interests and wishes have been ignored by self-interested political and politically correct intellectuals" (Canovan 2004, 242). As McCoy (2017a) notes, such populism takes on a distinctly moral tone as populist leaders claim to act for a "genuine public" against a "corrupt elite" that denies the "will of the people."

Duterte's deliberate use of vulgar, sexist, confrontational, and violent language to demonstrate his charisma and power to get the "job done" at any cost (e.g., controlling crime and activism) and to distance himself from the "political establishment" of Manila, despite also hailing from a wealthy political family, is well documented (McCoy 2017a). Among countless media scrums and policy addresses, Duterte's violent rhetoric, exemplified through statements such as, "Just because you're a journalist you are not exempted from assassination, if you're a son of a bitch," which he made in response to the death of a journalist, has given state and non-state actors a sense of legitimacy and impunity to unleash terror against progressive members of civil society (Lewis 2016). Since 2020, the tempo and scale of authoritarian violence against defenders was dramatically amplified by the pandemic's viral conjunctures.

Viral Conjunctures

The violence that defenders endured arose from the conjunctural crisis of authoritarianism intersecting with COVID-19 restrictions and constraints: a process involving a "number of forces and contradictions, which are at work in different key practices and sites in a social formation, com[ing] together or 'con-join[ing]' in the same moment and political space" (Hall 2011, 705). As the case shows, conjunctural dynamics reflect "period[s] when different social, political, economic and ideological contradictions that are at work in society and have given it a specific and distinctive shape come together, producing a crisis of some kind" (Hall and Massey 2012, 55). The intensity of a conjunctural crisis depends on how constraints, contradictions, and violence emerge, collide, and compress over time (Hall 2011, 705).

In the last decade, different conjunctural crises have yielded both slower and faster forms of violence against defenders in the Philippines. Slower forms of violence may be gradual and incremental, infrequent, or hidden; it is a violence of "delayed destruction that is dispersed across time and space, an attritional violence that is typically not viewed as violence at all" (Nixon 2011, 2). Slow violence is particularly damaging in how it manifests and intensifies to envelop NGOs, defenders, families, and communities. While slow violence sometimes dissipates, the harassment and intimidation of defenders frequently increases in tempo to coemerge as faster explosive violence (Nixon 2011), often culminating in murder. In the viral sphere of COVID-19, both slow and fast violence coemerged volumetrically through atmospheric particles, mining pits and dust, and uneven political economies working through and corroding the bodies and lives of defenders.

Under Duterte's rule, the management of COVID-19 reinforced the underlying inequality of predatory capitalist relations and violent atmospheres through securitization, suppression, and vulnerability among the poor and those defending them and their environments (Lowe 2010). In rural and urban areas, defenders and other activists who once ensured their own safety by changing travel routes, seeking refuge in "safe houses," and doing their work under comrades' protection, were now spatially fixed—locked down—as easy targets by state and non-state actors monitoring and containing them. The violence of the virus and those exploiting it to suppress defenders enveloped, contained, and disrupted the everyday lives of activists, while politicians mused about expanding mining. These viral conjunctures penetrated defenders' lives and suppressed resistance.

Political Economies of Violence in the Philippines Post-independence Era

Despite the fall of dictator president Ferdinand Marcos (1965–1986)—Duterte's "strong-man" idol—the suppression of agrarian reform movements, insurgencies, and activism remains entrenched across the country. Under martial law from 1972 until 1981, Marcos consolidated state and elite control over land, minerals, and forest resources in the public domain and under private title, reinforcing landlords' usury practices over tenants, dispossession of Indigenous peoples, and the killing of those resisting his regime (Putzel 1992; Vitug 1993). At that time, the Marcos regime contended with a "reformed" CPP, which, in 1968–1969, drew on Maoist principles and armed resistance through the NPA. With public land increasingly controlled by political elites and militia for commercial agriculture (Kimura 2006), tenant farmers were evicted and marginalized, while agrarian reform activists and insurgents were killed for defending their rights to land and livelihoods. In response, the CPP-NPA insurgency, peasant struggles, and student movements have resisted (violently and nonviolently), asserting basic human rights and rights to land and livelihood (Kimura 2006; Dressler and Guieb 2015). Other NGOs and peoples' organizations went underground to forge covert coalitions to resist state subordination and violence (Putzel 1992; Clarke 1998; Borras and Franco 2005). The disappearance and deaths of hundreds of activists, the visible levels of corruption, and then the execution of Marcos's political opponent, Benigno "Ninoy" Aquino, in 1983, caused public frustrations to boil over and culminated in the popular uprising, the People Power Revolution, which forced Marcos into exile in 1986 (Dressler and Guieb 2015).

The wife of Ninoy, Cory Aquino, led the post-Marcos administration from 1986 to 1992, ushering in new political freedoms and constitutional amendments supporting diverse civil society and state partnerships that forged progressive policies on forest conservation, agrarian reform, and Indigenous rights (Dressler 2009). Sustained pressure from NGO and peasant movements ultimately created political openings under the Aquino government's reform agenda, including in 1988 the Comprehensive Agrarian Reform Program (CARP) (Putzel 1992; Borras and Franco 2005). The CARP initiative was considered an essential policy intervention to quell simmering political tensions and conflicts between landed elites, their military apparatus, and landless classes by redistributing (private and state) *hacienda* plantation lands to tenant and landless farmers through acquisition and voluntary land transfers (Borras and Franco 2005, 336; Borras 2008). Despite some initial success, the program was slowed by landed political elites willing to give up only small portions of their land, usually in line with market-oriented land reforms and redistribution (Borras 2008). Many more prominent haciendas thus remained the "local authoritarian enclaves" that have long entrenched unequal land holdings and fueled peasant grievances, organized social struggles, and retaliatory activist murders (Borras 2008; Wright 2019).

Policies to abate extractivism on Indigenous lands have similarly struggled. Despite new laws being drafted to protect Indigenous peoples' rights to land, resources, and social protections under the much-celebrated Indigenous Peoples Rights Act 1997, the issuance of "native titles" through de jure Certificates of Ancestral Domain Title (CADTs) ultimately did less than was hoped for in protecting "tribal lands" from the expansion of agribusiness and mining in the country (Theriault 2019). Regardless, CADTs and associated people's organizations continued to serve as the political and institutional basis for NGOs and Indigenous land rights defenders, whose work increasingly collided with the violence of extractive accumulation (Dressler 2009; Theriault 2019).

Neoliberal extractivism and violence against defenders and insurgents across the country were particularly pronounced under the presidency of Gloria Macapagal Arroyo from 2001 to 2010 (Bello et al. 2004; Singh and Camba 2016). Arroyo pushed multiple biofuel production initiatives and consolidated peasant and Indigenous lands in Mindanao and Palawan for palm oil plantations, fueling local land struggles, social movements, and insurgencies (Montefrio and Dressler 2016; Miller 2017).[4] In the early 2000s, as extractivism and the associated repression of insurgencies expanded, so too did the murder of activists and rebels who resisted ongoing patterns of accumulation by dispossession (Harvey 2017; Dressler 2017, 2021).[5]

The late Benigno "Noynoy" Aquino III (2010–2016) sustained Arroyo's neoliberal policies when he succeeded her. While the political economy of state repression was somewhat less overt, NGOs and defenders still contended with elite politics reproducing itself through violent subnational political dynasties, local "political entrepreneurs," and associated militia and hitmen enabling extractivism (Fegan 2002; McCoy 2002). After Noynoy's six-year term ended, Duterte's 2016 campaign platform of peace and order, resource redistribution, and bypassing the "Manila elite" tapped into growing public discontent about the country's weakening welfare state, fraying infrastructure, and rising criminality from decades of neoliberalism (Putzel 2020; Theriault 2020). However, rather than transcending neoliberalism, Duterte pushed for a "deregulated" form of authoritarian developmentalism (Jayasuriya 2020; Ramos 2021) and associated extralegal practices that would "get the job done" for Filipinos (Arsel, Adaman, and Saad-Filho 2021)—that is, the criminalization and eradication of critical media, drug users, leftist NGOs, and activists (Putzel 2020). Over time, Duterte's performative violence further emboldened a suite of state and non-state actors to harass and kill with impunity defenders resisting the expansion of Chinese-financed infrastructure (e.g., the Kaliwa dam), palm oil plantations, and mining into frontier areas (McCoy 2017a, 2017b). The COVID-19 pandemic soon reinforced the suppression of activism in the country.

Quarantined Activism: Red-Tagging, COVID-19, and Resource Plunder

In the lead-up to the Duterte government signing the Anti-Terrorism Act (RA no. 11479) into law on July 3, 2020, human rights and environmental defenders contended with the convergence of intensifying red-tagging and the violent atmosphere of COVID-19 (Batac 2020; Chavez 2020). In March 2020, after the first ECQ was implemented in Metro Manila to contain the COVID-19 outbreak, strict lockdowns were then imposed across the islands of Luzon, Mindanao, and the rest of the country in early April, as enforcement agencies and politicians continued to red-tag almost any activist as a potential terrorist (Aspinwall 2020c, 2020d). In areas known for human rights, land, and environmental activism, ECQ restrictions were soon paired with military and police surveillance, harassment, and arrests (Jennings 2020). After going into lockdown, many activists received unexpected visits from enforcement units, with often violent consequences. Frequent arrests occurred at police checkpoints, in quarantine "boundary zones," and during household visits late at night while "suspects" were sleeping under lockdown.[6]

State enforcers used the new Anti-Terror Act in conjunction with ECQ restrictions to enhance their monitoring and containment measures. Pandemic restrictions were arbitrarily imposed upon defenders, enabling their further suppression by claiming they breached quarantine rules (Aspinwall 2020c). Based on the national and subnational news media analysis (covering center-left and right-wing national media and alternative far left-wing media), from March to December 2020, when quarantine measures were strictest, forty-four incidents occurred. These incidents ranged from individual and group arrests to harassment and deaths of defenders involving a total of 134 people. From the forty-four incidents, thirteen cases were directly associated with authority figures taking advantage of quarantine measures (see table 3.2).

Table 3.2. COVID-19–related violence against defenders in 2020

Type of incident	No. of incidents reported	No. of persons involved	Cases involving COVID-19 restrictions
Arrest	12	91	5
Death	16	27	2
Detention	1	3	1
Kidnapping	1	1	1
Other harassment	3	Not specified	2
Smear campaign	2	9	1
Intimidation	4	2	1
Assault	1	1	
Environmental degradation and harassment	4		
Total	**44**	**134**	**13**

The pattern of arrests typically involved police detaining and arresting smaller and medium-sized groups of activists who were on their way to (or were actively) protesting the deaths and harassment of fellow defenders. Five of these cases were justified on the basis that activists had allegedly breached COVID-19 lockdown rules. The high number of deaths (twenty-seven individuals from sixteen incidents) was partly due to smaller groups (three–five) of armed and unarmed activists being slain by police and/or the military, and individual activists being assassinated.

Based on the media analysis, thirteen reported incidents were directly associated with state authorities (e.g., national police) using pandemic restrictions and public health measures to arrest, relocate, and/or harass/intimidate activists involved in social and environmental justice campaigns. Among all types of incidents, arrests (allegedly with insufficient evidence) were particularly prominent, and the main method of containing activists during regional lockdowns from March to June 2020. Indeed, it was at this time, during a national address, that Duterte warned both leftist groups and violators of the ECQ not to challenge the government: "Don't do anything foolish and go on a riot because I will order you detained, and I will let you go after this COVID-19 . . . Don't test the Filipino. Do not try to test it. You know, we are ready for you. Violence or shooting or killing, I will not hesitate to order my soldiers to shoot you. I will not hesitate to order the police to arrest and detain you" (Esguerra 2020).

Given that the media search most likely identified prominent cases deemed worthy of media attention, the figures in table 3.2 likely underestimate the actual number of incidents that occurred during and after lockdown measures were in place. Below I illustrate some of the more prominent cases. Most of the examples involve the police using quarantine restrictions to detain and arrest activists for allegedly disseminating anti-government, communist propaganda material (embedded in pandemic relief goods).

On May 1, 2020, in Iloilo, the Visayas, the Philippine National Police reportedly arrested forty activists attempting to protest the recent murder of Bayan Muna coordinator Jory Porquia, citing their violation of COVID-19 quarantine rules (*Rappler* 2020a). Porquia was shot by armed men in Iloilo City while working as a coordinator for the political organization Bayan Muna, an affiliated member of the leftist political party Makabayan. Before his murder, Porquia claimed that he was repeatedly harassed by local police for leading relief operations and education campaigns on COVID-19 in poor communities in Iloilo City (*Rappler* 2020b). Those planning to protest his murder were allegedly arrested after agreeing to disperse. The police carried off in a lorry about forty young activists for "processing."

On June 18, 2020, the Armed Forces of the Philippines detained two young Indigenous Lumad students during pandemic restrictions after they had left school and tried to avail of the government's *balik-probinsiya* (B2P) program in Sarangani, Mindanao. The program aimed to reverse rural peoples' migration to Metro Manila and other urban areas (San Juan 2020). The father of the two students (they were siblings) was arrested by the same unit after inquiring about his children's whereabouts. Shortly thereafter, the Lumad organization Save Our Schools issued an alert that the three were last seen boarding a police vehicle in the vicinity. Authorities allegedly used the pandemic as a pretext to detain "wayward" Lumad youth, often (erroneously) linked to the NPA and other leftist groups opposing mining and plantation expansion. The incident highlighted how the pandemic's securitization intersected with broader representations of all Lumad being leftists who resist "development."

In an even more brazen case, between April 19 and April 21, 2020, several volunteers from the left-wing rights group Anakpawis—a party list of the electoral wing of the radical trade union movement Kilusang Mayo Uno and the peasant group Kilusang Mangbubulid ng Pilipinas—were arrested and charged by state authorities for alleged violation of a pandemic-related law (the Republic Act 11332 or the Mandatory Reporting of Notifiable Diseases and Health Events of Public Health Concern Act) and for "Inciting to Sedition" (Conde 2020). Bulacan police stopped at a checkpoint a group of six volunteers, who were then brought to a municipal police station where their food pass (for food relief distribution), along with copies of activist newspapers, was allegedly confiscated. The group was reportedly detained for supposedly giving out anti-government propaganda material (Luna 2020). The Department of Interior and Local Government undersecretary accused them of using an unauthorized government-issued pandemic food pass in an attempt to spread "seditious, subversive propaganda" and to conduct a mass gathering under the broader guise of a pandemic food relief operation. An Anakpawis member who attempted to negotiate the release of the volunteers was also charged. A lawyer for the peasant rights group SENTRO disputed the arrest, calling it unlawful, citing that the group did not violate the law, as they were providing food relief with an official pass. The food drive was part of a larger food relief effort organized by a diverse coalition of rights groups, peasant farmer groups, and other advocates to link fresh farm produce with the poor affected by the pandemic lockdown.

In Bacoor, Cavite—a commuter megacity near Metro Manila—community leaders opposing coastal land reclamation for a new Chinese-financed international airport and residential development were met with early-morning police patrols. Local fisherfolk and leftist NGOs, such as Pamalakaya, which supports fisher rights and livelihoods, claimed that the land reclamation would infill coastal areas, demolish local residences, and destroy remnant mangrove areas, critical spawning habitats for declining marine species that poor families often depend upon for food and income. Local activists also claimed that the state Department of Environment and Natural Resources (DENR) took advantage of the COVID-19 lockdown to fast-track the issuance of the Environmental Clearance Certificate needed to allow the development to proceed, while organized protests at the development sites were banned and suppressed, supposedly because of community quarantine policies (Aspinwall 2020e). Former Pamalakaya members and consultants, such as Randall Echanis, who had resisted the developments, were repeatedly red-tagged as communist terrorists. Echanis was ultimately stabbed to death in Manila in August 2020 (Aspinwall 2020d).

The harassment and intimidation of defenders in the cases above reflect the culmination of historical struggles between peasant movements, activists, landed elites, and politicians who use the military, police, and paramilitary to do dirty work on their behalf. Similar struggles have ensued over violent land grabs, dispossession, and murders on Palawan Island, where the politically powerful retain and accumulate land and capital at the expense of the poor.

COVID-19, Censure, and Resource Plunder on Palawan Island

The following cases from Palawan reveal how state actors, corporate brokers, local henchmen, and criminals have used COVID-19 restrictions to take advantage of lulls in defender environmental enforcement and engagement. With COVID restrictions rendering defenders less mobile, political actors intensified the red-tagging and political censure of activists, amped up the exploitation of timber and coastal resources, and further expanded mining tenements as part of the country's post-COVID "recovery strategy."

Although NGOs, activists, and the government body, the Palawan Council for Sustainable Development (PCSD)—charged with regulating resource access and use within and beyond the province's Environmental Critical Areas Network (ECAN) zones—have long been at odds with one another, the political contestations intensified under COVID-19 restrictions. In particular, a historical political feud between the fiery activist leader of the Palawan NGO Network Incorporated (PNNI), attorney Bobby Chan, and the PCSD, Provincial Board, and the former governor (and logging baron) spilled over in dramatic fashion.

During the July 2020 lockdown, the PNNI and PCSD strategically used social media to accuse one another of not pursuing sufficient environmental monitoring and defending due to COVID restrictions. PNNI and other NGOs pointed out that with staff under quarantine and enforcement being curbed, there were significant increases in mangrove and timber deforestation in northern and southern portions of Palawan (Fabro 2020), particularly in the higher elevation (>800 m asl) "core zones" under the PCSD's ECAN jurisdiction. As the smear campaigns accelerated, the Provincial Board drafted a formal resolution declaring attorney Chan "persona non grata"—broadly equivalent to red-tagging—for slandering the work of the PCSD and provincial government in a Vimeo cast two years earlier for a defender's funding campaign (Laririt and Magdayao 2021).[7]

As illegal resource exploitation continued across upland forests, coastal areas, and oceans, the PCSD and the DENR responded to Duterte's push to lift a nine-year moratorium on granting new mining permits in the Philippines as part of the country's pandemic recovery strategy. Signed into force on April 14, 2021, Executive Order 130 was meant to revive the country's ailing economy by reinvigorating nickel mining, particularly on Palawan's southern mountains (Chavez 2021). With new mineral agreements on the table, the PCSD announced plans to review the criteria by which the ECAN's core and restricted zones are designated, to "reduce the restraints on many industries from operating in Palawan."[8] PNNI's Chan and other defenders quickly pointed out that the PCSD aimed to modify the designation of "no-touch" core zones (meant for strict forest conservation and watershed protection) into controlled or multiple-use zones, allowing for timber clearing and the expansion of mining activities (see also the Environmental Legal Assistance Center's [ELAC] Facebook page).[9]

Not long after the Palawan-based NGOs began their social media campaign against the lifting of the mining moratorium, another act of illegal timber clearing took place at Pyramid Hill Mining's concession, which overlaps with the ancestral lands of the Indigenous Pala'wan. Amidst the protests against the sustained deforestation in upland areas, Jean Feliciano, the anti-mining activist mayor of Brookes Point town in southern Palawan, was censured and suspended from mayoral duties by the Office of the Ombudsman due to protests against the illegal clearing of 25,000 ha of trees by Ipilan Nickel Corporation two years earlier. The fact that she was suspended from office for a year without pay just as Duterte's office signed Executive Order 130 was no coincidence. The suspension was designed to instill fear into the hearts and minds of defenders resisting the plunder of the island's forests and oceans (Ocampo and Miranda 2021).

Under Duterte's regime, informal and formal censures further criminalized defenders like Chan, Feliciano, PNNI, and partner NGOs, and ultimately legitimized their harassment, intimidation, and murder. In such ways, slow violence emerged as fast and deadly violence against defenders who worked in an entanglement of viral restrictions, political oppression, and mining dust subsuming grassroots activism.

Discussion

Building on a long history of authoritarian rule in the Philippines, President Duterte's coercive populism reinforced earlier political economies of violence to embolden the military, police, and hitmen to unleash violence across the countryside. In the twilight of his six-year term, Duterte directly enabled and intensified the violent red-tagging of Filipino defenders as leftist "anti-capitalists" and presumed sympathizers of the CPP-NPA. Endured by defenders like Chan and Feliciano, red-tagging and similar censures are now entrenched in the country as a system of surveillance and intimidation that drives the harassment, intimidation, and, ultimately, the murder of activists. Activism has become increasingly synonymous with terrorism in the country. In this violent atmosphere, the government's new Anti-Terrorism Act (RA no. 11479) has deliberately (and now legally) conflated terrorism and activism in practice and intensified the ongoing suppression of citizen rights and freedoms. Since 2016, the corrosive atmosphere of impunity has allowed enforcement agencies, politicians, and others to red-tag almost anyone with activist inclinations as a potential terrorist, legitimatizing harassment and murder. Amidst the country's preexisting violent political economy, Duterte's coercive governance reflected a definitive conjunctural moment involving toxic ideology, rhetoric, and patron-client relations that drive violence against human rights, the environment, and their protectors in rural and urban areas (see Theriault 2020).

Since March 2020, defenders' struggles during Duterte's coercive rule intersected with the violent atmospheres of COVID-19 and the drive for mineral extraction (Aspinwall 2020c). Affected by sustained emergency quarantines, the already dangerous work of defender activists was subjected to intensified monitoring, restrictions, and violence across the country. Those enabling Duterte's agenda used the viral spread of COVID-19 and quarantine laws to intensify the suppression of activism, unleashing spatially concentrated forms of harassment, arrests, and murder (Nixon 2011). Using COVID-19 health checkpoints and lockdown rules (e.g., home quarantine, curfews, etc.), state authorities stopped, contained, and arrested activists suspected of aligning with the CPP-NPA or protesting against mega-infrastructure that threatened vulnerable livelihoods. This mix of authoritarian clampdowns and pandemic lockdowns instilled growing fear and resentment in civil society and deepened anxiety among the poor, who often rely upon NGOs for livelihood support during periods of crisis. As the rural and urban poor found food supply lines being cut due to government checkpoints curbing food deliveries or by having their mobility curtailed, they were also criminalized for alleged leftist activist behaviors. The resulting levels of social, economic, and physical precarity have been profound (*Mongabay* 2020; Marquez and Gascon 2020). Given such local uncertainty, the fear and fallout of such violent atmospheres will only intensify.

On Palawan Island, state authorities, civil society, and defenders found themselves in a deepening political imbroglio involving censure, violence, and accelerating extractive plunder under COVID-19. With repressive lockdown measures in place, defenders could not protect the social and environmental safeguards—such as the ECAN zoning system—that have maintained forest cover, biodiversity, and

Indigenous livelihoods for decades, as state and private sector actors attempted to deregulate and accelerate the mining sector under the guise of economic recovery. As the harassment of defenders intensified on Palawan amid state actors flouting their own laws and accruing wealth from lands and largesse, the future of the island and those who protect it appears increasingly grim at the nexus of the viral containment of activism and expansion of extractive development.

In sum, authoritarian rule and violence against defenders was dramatically amplified as the right to movement and protest was quarantined. As the pandemic articulated with the violent political economy of Duterte's administration, many defenders across the country found themselves in an increasingly uncertain and vulnerable state, where constitutionally enshrined civil liberties afforded them few, if any, protections and redress. As the COVID-19 pandemic lingered, and vaccinations were given slowly and unevenly, the activists who fought for poor people's right to secure livelihoods and dignity have continued to suffer from the harassments and murders that began in 2020. The question remains: From where will redress and justice come?

Notes

1. As in the past, the brand of authoritarian populism emerging in the region aims to "construct around itself an active popular consent" (Hall 1979, 15) that legitimates economic expansion, political control, and securitization through the violent oppression of those defenders resisting dominant state ideals.

2. Duterte first imposed a state of emergency in Mindanao in September 2016, and it remained in place as of October 22, 2020 (Aspinwall 2020b).

3. Various NGOs and UN agencies have framed the term "defender" in a relatively open manner. Global Witness (2014, 23) uses the term "environmental and land defender" to mean "people who take peaceful action to protect environmental or land rights, whether in their own personal capacity or professionally." The UN uses the broader term "environmental human rights defenders" to refer to "individuals and groups who, in their personal or professional capacity and in a peaceful manner, strive to protect and promote human rights relating to the environment, including water, air, land, flora and fauna" (UNE 2018). This media review and analysis drew on a similarly broad definition of environmental and human rights defenders: all those (e.g., NGO staff, lawyers, Indigenous farmers and fishers, park rangers, local politicians, mothers, and brothers) who work in different capacities to protect and promote human rights and the environment in the context of suppression under authoritarian rule, or otherwise. I use the term "defenders" as shorthand for "environmental and human rights defenders."

4. Palm oil development has existed in Mindanao since the 1960s–1970s (see Villanueva 2011; Miller 2017).

5. Under President Arroyo, the NGO Karapatan (2018) noted 194 and 235 extrajudicial killings in 2005 and 2006, respectively. These deaths include activists and insurgents whose politics and actions are sometimes blurred in practice or deliberately criminalized by the Philippine National Police, Armed Forces of the Philippines, and other right-wing militia.

6. In other cases, community quarantine measures made it increasingly difficult for thousands of poor urban and rural dwellers to rely on collective labor across different locations to sustain typically diverse livelihoods and income sources, thereby forcing many to violate curfews, overexploit natural resources, and be fined or imprisoned as a result.

7. See "Defenders of Palawan, the Philippines' Last Environmental Frontier," GoGetFunding, https://gogetfunding.com/defenders-of-the-philippines-last-ecological-frontier/.

8. See Palawan Council for Sustainable Development, Facebook, April 14, 2021, https://www.facebook.com/pcsd7611/photos/a.355182424691142/1593722484170457/?type=3.

9. See Environmental Legal Assistance Center, Inc.—ELAC, Facebook, April 15, 2021, https://www.facebook.com/453671728086434/posts/3835102959943277/?d=n.

References

Arsel, Murat, Fikret Adaman, and Alfredo Saad-Filho. 2021. "Authoritarian Developmentalism: The Latest Stage of Neoliberalism?" *Geoforum* 124:261–266. https://doi.org/10.1016/j.geoforum.2021.05.003.

Aspinwall, Nick. 2020a. "Mindanao after Martial Law." *The Diplomat*, March 10, 2020. https://thediplomat.com/2020/03/mindanao-after-martial-law/.

Aspinwall, Nick. 2020b. "Philippine Court Asked to Annul Anti-Terror Law amid Concerns It Will Target Dissidents." *The Diplomat*, July 10, 2020. https://thediplomat.com/202+0/07/philippine-court-asked-to-annul-anti-terror-law-amid-concerns-it-will-target-dissidents/.

Aspinwall, Nick. 2020c. "The Philippines' Coronavirus Lockdown Is Becoming a Crackdown." *The Diplomat*, April 3, 2020. https://thediplomat.com/2020/04/the-philippines-coronavirus-lockdown-is-becoming-a-crackdown/.

Aspinwall, Nick. 2020d. "The Killings in the Philippines Grow More Brazen." *The Interpreter*, August 25, 2020. https://www.lowyinstitute.org/the-interpreter/killings-philippines-grow-more-brazen.

Aspinwall, Nick. 2020e. "Manila's New China-Backed Airport Bogged Down by Land Reclamation Controversy." *China Dialogue*, October 30, 2020. https://chinadialogue.net/en/cities/manilas-new-airport-land-reclamation-controversey/.

Batac, Marc. 2020. "The Philippines' Anti-Terror Bill Is Poised to Cause More Terror." *Al Jazeera*, June 25, 2020. https://www.aljazeera.com/opinions/2020/6/25/the-philippines-anti-terror-bill-is-poised-to-cause-more-terror.

Beban, Alice, Laura Schoenberger, and Vanessa Lamb. 2020. "Pockets of Liberal Media in Authoritarian Regimes: What the Crackdown on Emancipatory Spaces Means for Rural Social Movements in Cambodia." *Journal of Peasant Studies* 47 (1): 95–115. https://doi.org/10.1080/03066150.2019.1672664.

Bello, Walden. 2019. *Counterrevolution: The Global Rise of the Far Right*. Halifax: Fernwood Publishing.

Bello, Walden, Herbert Docena, Marissa de Guzman, and Mary Lou Malig. 2004. *The Anti-Development State. The Political Economy of Permanent Crisis in the Philippines*. London: Zed Books.

Borras, Saturnino M., Jr. 2008. *Competing Views and Strategies on Agrarian Reform*. Vol. 1, *International Perspective*. Quezon City: Ateneo de Manila University Press.

Borras, Saturnino M., Jr., and Jennifer C. Franco. 2005. "Struggles for Land and Livelihood: Redistributive Reform in Agribusiness Plantations in the Philippines." *Critical Asian Studies* 37 (3): 331–361.

Bugaric, Bojan. 2019. "The Two Faces of Populism: Between Authoritarian and Democratic Populism." *German Law Journal* 20:390–400. https://doi.org/10.1017/glj.2019.20.

Canovan, Margaret. 2004. "Populism for Political Theorists?" *Journal of Political Ideologies* 9 (3): 241–252.

Chavez, Chito. 2020. "Local Officials Voluntarily Back Anti-Terrorism Bill." *Manila Bulletin,* June 17, 2020. https://mb.com.ph/2020/06/17/local-officials-voluntarily-back-anti-terrorism-bill-dilg/.

Chavez, Leilani. 2021. "'Complete Turnaround': Philippines' Duterte Lifts Ban on New Mining Permits." *Mongabay,* April 15, 2021. https://news.mongabay.com/2021/04/complete-turnaround-philippines-duterte-lifts-ban-on-new-mining-permits/.

Clarke, Gerard. 1998. *The Politics of NGOs in South-East Asia: Participation and Protest in the Philippines.* London: Routledge.

Conde, Mavic. 2020. "Ex-Anakpawis Congressman, Relief Drive Volunteers Charged with Sedition. Rappler News." *Rappler,* April 21, 2020. https://www.rappler.com/nation/ex-anakpawis-congressman-relief-drive-volunteers-charged-sedition-april-2020.

Curato, Nicole. 2016. "Politics of Anxiety, Politics of Hope: Penal Populism and Duterte's Rise to Power." *Journal of Current Southeast Asian Affairs* 35 (3): 91–109. https://doi.org/10.1177/186810341603500305.

Delina, Laurence L. 2020. "Indigenous Environmental Defenders and the Legacy of Macli-Ing Dulag: Anti-Dam Dissent, Assassinations, and Protests in the Making of Philippine Energyscape." *Energy Research and Social Science* 65:101463. https://doi.org/10.1016/j.erss.2020.101463.

Dressler, Wolfram H. 2009. *Old Thoughts in New Ideas: State Conservation Measures, Livelihood and Development on Palawan Island, the Philippines.* Quezon City: Ateneo de Manila University Press.

Dressler, Wolfram H. 2017. "Contesting Moral Capital in the Economy of Expectations of an Extractive Frontier." *Annals of the American Association of Geographers* 107 (3): 647–665. https://doi.org/10.1080/24694452.2016.1261684.

Dressler, Wolfram H. 2021. "Defending Lands and Forests: NGO Histories, Everyday Struggles, and Extraordinary Violence in the Philippines." *Critical Asian Studies* 53 (3): 380–411. https://doi.org/10.1080/14672715.2021.1899834.

Dressler, Wolfram H., and Eulalio Rueda Guieb III. 2015. "Violent Enclosures, Violated Livelihoods: Environmental and Military Territoriality in a Philippine Frontier." *Journal of Peasant Studies* 42 (2): 323–345.

Esguerra, Darryl John. 2020. "Duterte Warns Left, Troublemakers vs Challenging Gov't amid COVID-19 Crisis: I Will Order You Shot." *Philippine Daily Inquirer,* April 1, 2020. https://newsinfo.inquirer.net/1252557/duterte-warns-left-vs-challenging-govt-amid-covid-19-crisis-i-will-order-you-detained.

Fabro, Keith Anthony S. 2020. "Illegal Logging Continues in MIMAROPE despite Luzon Lockdown." *Rappler,* April 3, 2020. https://www.rappler.com/nation/illegal-logging-continues-mimaropa-despite-luzon-lockdown.

Fegan, Brian. 2002. "Entrepreneurs in Votes and Violence: Three Generations of a Peasant Political Family." In *An Anarchy of Families: State and Family in the Philippines,* edited by Alfred W. McCoy, 33–107. Quezon: Ateneo de Manila University Press.

Global Witness. 2014. "Deadly Environment: The Dramatic Rise in Killings of Environmental and Land Defenders." *Global Witness,* April 15, 2014. https://www.globalwitness.org/en/campaigns/environmental-activists/deadly-environment/.

Hall, Stuart. 1979. "The Great Moving Right Show." *Marxism Today* (January): 14–20.

Hall, Stuart. 2011. "The Neo-liberal Revolution." *Cultural Studies* 25 (6): 705–728.

Hall, Stuart, and Doreen Massey. 2012. "Interpreting the Crisis." In *The Neoliberal Crisis,* edited by Jonathan Rutherford and Sally Davison, 55–70. London: Lawrence and Wishart.

Harvey, D. 2017. "The 'New' Imperialism: Accumulation by Dispossession." In *Karl Marx,* edited by Kevin Anderson and Bertell Ollman, 213–237. London: Routledge.

Heydarian, Richard. 2017. "Tragedy of Small Power Politics: Duterte and the Shifting Sands of Philippine Foreign Policy." *Asian Security* 13 (3): 220–236.

Holden, William, Kathleen Nadeau, and R. Daniel Jacobson. 2011. "Exemplifying Accumulation by Dispossession: Mining and Indigenous Peoples in the Philippines." *Geografiska Annaler: Series B, Human Geography* 93 (2): 141–161. https://doi.org/10.1111/j.1468-0467.2011.00366.x.

Jayasuriya, Kanishka. 2020. "The Rise of the Right: Populism and Authoritarianism in Southeast Asian Politics." *Southeast Asian Affairs* 2020 (1): 43–55.

Jennings, Ralph. 2020. "Philippines Denies Claim of Increase Police Drug-related Killings." Voice of America, September 18, 2020. https://www.voanews.com/east-asia-pacific/philippines-denies-claim-increased-police-drug-related-killings.

Kimura, Masataka. 2006. "The Federation of Free Farmers and its Significance in the History of the Philippine Peasant Movement." *Japanese Journal of Southeast Asian Studies* 44 (1): 3–30.

KPNE. 2019. *Kalikasan People's Network for the Environment Report on Human Rights and Environment Defenders and Climate Change: Taking Lands, Taking Lives.* Quezon City: KPNE.

Laririt, Patricia, and Aira Genesa Magdayao. 2021. "Palawan Environmental NGO Leader Declared 'Persona Non Grata' by Province." *Palawan News,* January 12, 2021. https://palawan-news.com/palawan-environmental-ngo-leader-declared-persona-non-grata-by-province/.

Lewis, Simon. 2016. "Duterte Says Journalists in the Philippines Are 'Not Exempted from Assassinations.'" *Time Magazine,* June 1, 2016. https://time.com/4353279/duterte-philippines-journalists-assassination/.

Lowe, Celia. 2010. "Viral Clouds: Becoming H5N1 in Indonesia." *Cultural Anthropology* 25 (4): 625–649.

Luna, Franco. 2020. "'Critical but Not Seditious,' Journalists, Artists Say of Papers in Halted Bulacan Relief Drive." *PhilStar.* April 21, 2020. https://www.philstar.com/headlines/2020/04/21/2008760/critical-not-seditious-journalist-artists-say-papers-halted-bulacan-relief-drive.

Marquez, Consuelo, and Melvin Gascon. 2020. "DILG: Dismantle all Checkpoints." *INQUIRER.NET,* April 1, 2020. https://newsinfo.inquirer.net/1252003/dilg-dismantle-all-checkpoints.

McCarthy, John F. 2019. "Authoritarianism, Populism, and the Environment: Comparative Experiences, Insights, and Perspectives." *Annals of the American Association of Geographers* 109 (2): 301–313. https://doi.org/10.1080/24694452.2018.1554393.

McCoy, Alfred W., ed. 2002. *An Anarchy of Families: State and Family in the Philippines.* Quezon: Ateneo de Manila University Press.

McCoy, Alfred W. 2017a. "Philippine Populism: Local Violence and Global Context in the Rise of a Filipino Strongman." *Surveillance and Society* 15 (3/4): 514–522.

McCoy, Alfred W. 2017b. "Global Populism: A Lineage of Filipino Strongmen from Quezon to Marcos and Duterte." *Kasarinlan: Philippine Journal of Third World Studies* 32 (1–2): 7–54.

Middeldorp, Nick, and Phillipe Le Billon. 2019. "Deadly Environmental Governance: Authoritarianism, Eco-populism, and the Repression of Environmental and Land Defenders." *Annals of the American Association of Geographers* 109 (2): 324–337. https://doi.org/10.1080/24694452.2018.1530586.

Miller, Brad. 2017. "Philippine Palm Oil Plan 'Equals Corruption and Land-Grabbing' Critics Say." *Mongabay Series: Global Palm Oil,* August 31, 2017. https://news.mongabay.com/2017/08/philippine-palm-oil-plan-equals-corruption-and-land-grabbing-critics-say/.

Moffitt, Benjamin, and Simon Tormey. 2014. "Rethinking Populism: Politics, Mediatisation and Political Style." *Political Studies* 62 (2): 381–397.

Mongabay. 2020. "Deaths, Arrests and Protests as Philippines Remerges from Lockdown." *Mongabay Series: Endangered Environmentalists,* May 21, 2020. https://news.mongabay.com/2020/05/deaths-arrests-and-protests-as-philippines-re-emerges-from-lockdown/.

Montefrio, Marvin Joseph F. 2014. "Growing Low-Carbon Commodities in Upland Philippines: Integration of Smallholders in Biofuels and Rubber Production Regimes." PhD diss., State University of New York.

Montefrio, Marvin Joseph F., and Wolfram H. Dressler. 2016. "The Green Economy and Constructions of the 'Idle' and 'Unproductive' Uplands in the Philippines." *World Development* 79:114–126.

Moore, Jason W. 2000. "Sugar and the Expansion of the Early Modern World-Economy: Commodity Frontiers, Ecological Transformation, and Industrialization." *Review (Fernand Braudel Center)* 23 (3): 409–433.

Neimark, Benjamin, John Childs, Andrea J. Nightingale, Connor Joseph Cavanagh, Sian Sullivan, Tor A. Benjaminsen, Simon Batterbury, Stasja Koot, and Wendy Harcourt. 2019. "Speaking Power to 'Post-Truth': Critical Political Ecology and the New Authoritarianism." *Annals of the American Association of Geographers* 109 (2): 613–623. https://doi.org/10.1080/24694452.2018.1547567.

Nixon, Rob. 2011. *Slow Violence and the Environmentalism of the Poor.* Cambridge, MA: Harvard University Press.

Ocampo, Karl R., and Romar Miranda. 2021. "Mayor vs Mining 'Guilty of Oppression.'" *Philippine Daily Inquirer,* June 19, 2021. https://newsinfo.inquirer.net/1448063/mayor-vs-mining-guilty-of-oppression.

OHCHR. 2020. "Report of the United Nations High Commissioner for Human Rights on the Situation of Human Rights in the Philippines." Human Rights Council, Annual report of the United Nations High Commissioner for Human Rights and reports of the Office of the High Commissioner and the Secretary-General. Geneva: United Nations.

Palo, Anton Simon M., Mercedita A. Rosetes, and Donna P. Cariño. 2020. "COVID-19 and Food Systems in the Philippines." In *COVID-19 and Food Systems in the Indo-Pacific: An Assessment of Vulnerability, Impacts and Opportunities for Action*, 165–195. ACIAR Technical Report 96. Canberra: Australian Centre for International Agricultural Research.

Putzel, James. 1992. *A Captive Land: The Politics of Agrarian Reform in the Philippines*. New York: Monthly Review Press.

Putzel, James. 2020. "The 'Populist' Right Challenge to Neoliberalism: Social Policy between a Rock and a Hard Place." *Development and Change* 51 (2): 418–441.

Ramos, Charmaine G. 2021. "The Return of Strongman Rule in the Philippines: Neoliberal Roots and Developmental Implications." *Geoforum* 124:310–319. https://doi.org/10.1016/j.geoforum.2021.04.001.

Rappler. 2020a. "Iloilo Cops Arrest 40 Activists Protesting Murder of Bayan Muna Coordinator." *Rappler,* May 1 2020. https://newsinfo.inquirer.net/1252557/duterte-warns-left-vs-challenging-govt-amid-covid-19-crisis-i-will-order-you-detained.

Rappler. 2020b. "They Shot My Tatay Nine Times." *Rappler,* April 30, 2020. https://www.rappler.com/nation/they-shot-my-tatay-nine-times-jory-porquia.

Rutten, Roseanne, ed. 2008. *Brokering a Revolution: Cadres in a Philippine Insurgency.* Quezon City: Ateneo de Manila University Press.

San Juan, Ratziel. 2020. "Lumad Students Reported Missing Are in Military Camp—Report." *Philstar.com,* June 18, 2020. https://www.philstar.com/nation/2020/06/18/2021759/lumad-students-reported-missing-are-military-camp-report.

Scoones, Ian, Marc Edelman, Saturnino M. Borras, Ruth Hall, Wendy Wolford, and Ben White. 2018. "Emancipatory Rural Politics: Confronting Authoritarian Populism." *Journal of Peasant Studies* 45 (1): 1–20.

Singh, Jojo Nem, and Alvin A. Camba. 2016. "Neoliberalism, Resource Governance and the Everyday Politics of Protests in the Philippines." *Everyday Political Economy of Southeast Asia* 3:49–71.

Theriault, Noah. 2019. "Unravelling the Strings Attached: Philippine Indigeneity in Law and Practice." *Journal of Southeast Asian Studies* 50 (1): 107–128.

Theriault, Noah. 2020. "Euphemisms We Die By: On Eco-Anxiety, Necropolitics, and Green Authoritarianism in the Philippines." In *Beyond Populism: Angry Politics and the Twilight of Neoliberalism,* edited by Jeff Maskovsky and Sophie Bjork-James, 182–205. Morgantown: West Virginia University Press.

UNE. 2018. *Who Are Environmental Defenders?* Geneva: UN Environment. https://www.unenvironment.org/fr/node/21162.

Villanueva, J. 2011. "Oil Palm Expansion in the Philippines: Analysis of Land Rights, Environment and Food Security Issues." In *Oil Palm Expansion in South East Asia: Trends and Implications for Local Communities and Indigenous Peoples,* edited by Marcus Colchester and Sophie Chao, 110–216. RECOFT Forest Peoples Programme, Perkumpulan Sawit Watch, Samdhana Institute.

Vitug, Marites Dañguilan. 1993. *Power from the Forest: The Politics of Logging.* Manila: Philippine Center for Investigative Journalism.

Wright, Sarah L. 2019. "Towards an Affective Politics of Hope: Learning from Land Struggles in the Philippines." *Environment and Planning E: Nature and Space* 6 (3): 1501–1522. https://doi.org/10.1177/2514848619867613.

SECTION II

Dams and Displacement

Figure B. Stung Treng, Cambodia: aerial view of the old Kabal Romeas, one of the villages submerged in water after the gates of the Lower Sesan 2 dam were closed in 2017. (Photo credit: © Thomas Cristofoletti/Roum)

CHAPTER 4

Violent Displacement and Volumetric Change

KIMBERLEY ANH THOMAS, LISA C. KELLEY,
AND ANNIE SHATTUCK

Migration has been an enduring feature of social life, with evidence of the earliest migrations of modern humans dating back more than 200,000 years (Harvati et al. 2019). Despite this, or perhaps because of it, questions about *who* moves *where, when,* and *why* have sustained critical inquiry for centuries. Such questions are not uniformly applied, however. For the world's elite, physical mobility is assumed and even celebrated, while for others it is often viewed as the result of something that has gone awry. Regardless of the actual drivers involved, the impetus to migrate is increasingly attributed to climate change.

In his 2020 article for the *New York Times Magazine* titled "The Great Climate Migration," the journalist Abrahm Lustgarten speculated about the nearly one billion people who live in what would be "barely livable" hot zones of the world by 2070, asking, "Where will *they* go?" (emphasis added). Lustgarten's analysis of forced migration was unquestionably situated in the present-future tense, engaged as it was with both the reality and the specter of escalating climate change. At the same time, the resulting account had as much to do with the past as it did with the future, reflecting and reproducing many of the same racialized neo-Malthusian imaginaries and reductionisms that have long characterized media, state, and institutional work on the themes of environmental security, violence, and displacement. In this regard, Lustgarten's argument was perhaps most notable not because it was unique, but because it exemplified how old tropes are being repackaged with a view to climate.

Indeed, whereas earlier work on environmental security posited the inevitability of resource scarcity in developing countries leading to violent conflict (Baechler 1998; Homer-Dixon 1999; Kaplan 1994), more recent iterations have situated climate change as a "threat multiplier" that intensifies the risk of conflict in already destabilized regions (Scheffran and Battaglini 2010). Such perspectives suggest climate change will render certain environments uninhabitable by triggering competitions over space and resources and by bringing regions of the world that already struggle with political instability or weak governance to the point of collapse. As the authors of a report by the NGO International Alert put it: "It is safe to predict that the consequences of climate change will combine with other factors to put additional strain on already fragile social and political systems. These are the conditions in which conflicts flourish and cannot be resolved without violence because governments are arbitrary, inept and corrupt" (Smith and Vivikenanda 2007, 9).

Related work also commonly situates climate change as an "ecological threat" that is likely to "force" entire populations to relocate (e.g., Myers 2002). One highly cited 2018 World Bank report predicts that climate change will "force" more than 143 million people to relocate internally from South Asia, sub-Saharan Africa, and Latin America (Rigaud et al. 2018, xiv), while the Institute for Economics and Peace notes that extreme ecological shocks may displace up to 1.2 billion people globally by 2050 (IEP 2020, 4).

Clearly, such presentations leave much to be desired—a point repeatedly and convincingly made by more than two decades of critical geographical work on these themes. Foundational work on violent environments as early as 2001, for instance, questioned overly teleological takes on the linkages between resource scarcity and violence by emphasizing the historical and political economic processes that shape how environmental change engenders violence, the role of states in enacting violence, the relationships between resource abundance and conflict, and the commonality of unspectacular, mundane acts of violence (Peluso and Watts 2001). Copious research since has built on this work by emphasizing the complex interplay between resource narratives and protection, uneven development, accumulation, and violence (Le Billon 2008; Peluso and Vandergeest 2011; Woods and Naimark 2020), as well as the need to understand resulting displacements as a *process,* one informed by broader political economies and the ways capitalism exploits social difference, as well as local histories, livelihoods, and everyday aspirations. Our goal in this chapter is thus to "speak back" to contemporary claims surrounding probable climate violence and displacement by situating them within the kind of relational and historical processes carefully pulled into frame by such work. Equally, it is to contribute to this literature by emphasizing the accretive effects of historical violences that give rise to the so-called climate impacts and displaced climate refugees of today. These are volumetric questions, reflecting the convergence of terrestrial and atmospheric relations that reconfigure the surface and subsurface flows of water and their composition, altering localized climates, hydrology, and agroecology.

The violences wrought by a changing climate—mundane as well as extreme— are increasingly undeniable in the agrarian regions of Southeast Asia in which we work (figure 4.1). Despite decades of industrialization, the number of smallholders has held steady or increased across the region even as farming itself contributes less to household income and as average farm sizes decrease (Rigg et al. 2018). Climatic impacts on these households are reflected in long-term shifts in precipitation, temperatures, and sea levels, and in the form of droughts, floods, and the salinization of previously productive farmland—changes that take the shape of both catastrophic and slow violences of the kind described by Ian G. Baird in Laos (see chapter 5 in this volume). To read such dynamics and their ramifications as novel, however, would be to obscure other slow violences at play, including the ways climate change works in and through at least the past century of colonial, state, and neoliberal developments, from those that forcibly sedentarized mobile agrarian peoples in the name of development to those that have subsidized agribusiness expansion and the theft and degradation of village lands. As we argue, such histories have not only set the stage for the climate impacts playing out today, but they have also preconditioned mobility (including mobility that is inappropriately read as permanent displacement) as an integral and often-necessary response to violent change.

Below, we begin by more fully contextualizing the perspectives from recent work on displacement and violence that informs our approach, including those that have expanded beyond traditional and more static two-dimensional analysis toward thinking in terms of volumes, flows, and sedimented change (Grundy-Warr, Sithirith, and Li 2015). The research we present is based on published work as well as ongoing mixed-methods data collection in each location (see figure 4.1).

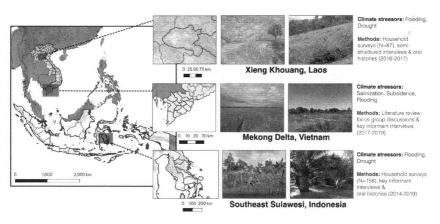

Figure 4.1. The three study areas in regional and commodity-climate context. Photos, top to bottom, depict maize production and erosion in Laos, irrigation in a triple rice cropping area and shrimp ponds with aerators in Vietnam, and the flooding of vegetable lands and newly planted oil palm in Indonesia. (Source: Lisa C. Kelly, Annie Shattuck, and Kimberly Anh Thomas)

Ethnographic fieldwork entailed household surveys and oral histories with smallholders in Xieng Khouang, Laos (2016–2017) and Southeast Sulawesi, Indonesia (2014–2019), as well as focus group discussions with residents and key informant interviews with local officials in the Vietnamese Mekong Delta (2017–2019). These qualitative accounts were supplemented by remote sensing analysis (Indonesia), statistical analysis of census data (Vietnam), and government policy analysis (all sites).

After briefly sketching the complex existing dynamics of mobility in agrarian Southeast Asia that complicate claims of so-called climate displacement, we then turn to an empirical treatment of why climate impacts and resulting mobilities are best understood as one among many interactive and accreted violences now playing out. We conclude by making a case for how such perspectives can help to decenter climate as a focal point of either security or adaptation policy while recentering the multiple non-climatic dimensions of the (unequal, unstable, and unjust) socio-environmental configurations that we believe lie at the heart of a more radical and transformative approach to climate policy.

Displacement and the Volumetric

Agrarian landscapes across the world have long contended with violences, be they quiet (Hartmann and Boyce 1983), silent (Watts 2013), swift or slow (Nixon 2011; Thomas 2021). While climate change has tended to overshadow these other forms of socio-ecological rupture and destabilization, they persist and, we argue, demand renewed attention. In documenting historical and ongoing violences, we focus on displacement, which has garnered significant attention in climate security debates and popular media. Such accounts tend to frame climate-related migration as both involuntary and unprecedented. These often-alarmist projections imply an ideal of keeping things as they are, suggesting that migration itself is the problem, rather than the systems within which it occurs (Bettini 2017). As Bettini (2017) also highlights, alternative development logics simultaneously reframe the figure of the climate refugee fleeing untenable conditions as pursuing a "legitimate adaptation strategy." Within this neoliberal governmentality of climate adaptation, mobility is conceptualized as an important element of individual preparedness, while the structures and institutions most responsible for producing violent global economic and environmental changes are obscured from view (Bettini 2017).

This chapter focuses instead on the socio-environmental and volumetric configurations that, despite facing climate threats, are more suitable as targets of transformative change than protective measures. Our arguments in this regard are informed closely by scholarship from political ecology and critical geography that engages displacement not as a full or final exodus (see Gray et al. 2014) but as a complex relational and historical process (Doshi 2015; Werner 2015), one informed by shock events and disasters, but also by the way such stressors interact with the slower processes of agrarian change, ecological unraveling, social difference, and state policy (Tacoli 2009). As Billé (see the afterword in this volume) puts it, displacement does not represent "a transformation from benign to violent, but a lateral slippage revealing the violence that was there all along." Our work is also informed by Simon Dalby's (2013, 38) suggestion that "a material sensibility is necessary to think about security and geography but one that is not linked to traditional determinist formulations." This approach highlights the equal need to attend to the *nonclimatic* environmental changes often sidelined in both anthropocentric debates on rural displacements and climate doomsday scenarios. Importantly, however, our approach goes beyond traditional political ecologies that have overwhelmingly emphasized the non-climatic to attend to the kinds of imbrications and entanglements that make climate and other forms of long-term environmental change inseparable. Mobile labor relations disrupt the terrestrial boundaries of the "agrarian." Simultaneously, atmospheric and terrestrial forces converge to shape atmospheric or hydrological mobilities (see chapter 8 in this volume, by Varkkey, Copeland, and Shaiful) that unevenly undercut prospects for production and reproduction within more normative agrarian spaces.

Such perspectives are relevant to understanding apparent climate displacements and violences in Southeast Asia, particularly given that the complex and durable histories of mobility complicate a determination of when so-called climate displacement may be taking place. As past work illustrates, such mobilities are shaped not only by shifting gendered and generational relations (Lam and Yeoh 2018) or aspirations for "modernity" (Hertzman 2014) but by long-standing patterns of dispossession and agrarian inequality that occupy little space in media, corporate, and state framings of climate displacement. It is now well understood, for instance, that flows of people have increased in both relative and absolute numbers in agrarian Southeast Asia vis-à-vis myriad stressors, including state and corporate land grabs and green grabs; diverse environmental changes (e.g., soil erosion, groundwater extraction, and the loss of crop diversity); and the deterioration of smallholder farming prospects resulting from market liberalization and the erosion of state support (Kelly 2011; Rigg et al. 2018; Kelley et al. 2020).

Attention to this complexity—and indeed, the blurriness between voluntary and involuntary mobilities—also reveals the circumstances under which migration can also *counteract* uneven developments. Indeed, Rigg and colleagues (2018, 327) argue that "one of the enduring agrarian puzzles of the development era has been the persistence of the Asian smallholder"—a dynamic sustained in part (paradoxically) by recent increases in domestic and transnational labor migration. Remittances associated with migration have enabled new agrarian investments, even in highly constrained tenurial circumstances (McKay 2005; Peluso and Purwanto 2018) and can improve individual and collective "access to adaptation" (McDowell and Hess 2012)—albeit indeterminately and in ways that are often circumscribed by the diverse rights abuses and personal and financial violences migrant workers experience (Silvey 2006; Peou 2016).

Southeast Asian Case Studies

Below, we focus on the climatic and environmental—as well as cultural, political, financial, and linguistic—volumes, fluxes, and flows that contribute to the accreted violences and mobility responses that are often too simplistically read as either "climate impacts" or "climate displacement." We welcome the invitation to attend to volumes, a compelling alternative to earlier geographical scholarship that invoked flat-world ontologies and containerized notions of space (see critique by Rosière and Jones 2012). In doing so, we also foreground the need to account for both the material (atmospheric and otherwise) and the social composition of these volumes to understand how violence shapes and is shaped by diverse socionatures. One way to conduct such an accounting, as we discuss below, is to envision volumetric space (aerial, terrestrial, and subterranean) as sedimented layers of, inter alia, people, nonhuman nature, land-use practices, knowledge, and regional and local climates, as well as the historical and ongoing violences that shape the socio-spatial and volumetric relations of the present. Such volumetric engagements, in our view, provide powerful traction in overcoming the ontological and political impasses engendered by prevailing narratives that collapse climate migration/displacement/violence into convenient but misleading binaries of either successful or failed adaptation.

Maize and Migration in Northeastern Laos

Northeastern Laos is currently undergoing a dramatic agrarian transformation, of which rising migration, especially by youth, is an integral part. In 2006, a boom in maize production to meet agribusiness demand for livestock feed in neighboring countries transformed forests and village life. By 2017, yields were declining, and soil erosion was a significant concern for many farmers. In a survey of eighty-six households, incomes had plummeted to less than US$1 per person per day, and land was no longer available to clear. While not known as a migrant-sending region, the province was seeing more young people leaving for off-farm work. Localized drought in 2012 was often mentioned as the onset of the bust, but it had its origins in decades of social and ecological change.

Government efforts to end shifting cultivation and relocate ethnic minorities closer to municipal centers have increased land pressures. In the 1990s and early 2000s, forced resettlement crowded minority communities onto inadequate land prone to erosion, often taking grazing areas from majority villages. At the same time, demographic pressure from low-lying communities sent landless young people to the nearby uplands to pioneer forest areas. In 2003, the government began enforcing a limit on swidden rotations; the long fallows that had kept upland production sustainable in the past were no longer possible. Demand for lumber and non-timber forest products provided farmers with a source of modest cash income, but by the mid-2000s, surrounding forests were emptied of valuable species. Opium production, another source of cash, was shut down in large part by 2006, leaving upland farmers with few opportunities for cash income. At the same time, demand for cash increased as hospitals, motorbikes, rural schools, cell phones, and other modern essentials became the social standard. While few people from this part of the country were migrating internationally, domestic migration had become a fact of life alongside larger social and ecological changes. Forms of labor migration, and what it paid, were highly uneven. In one better-connected village, 33 percent of surveyed households included someone working outside the province, though only half of those households received any remittances. In a more remote village with mixed ethnic groups, 17 percent of households included a migrant worker, but none earned enough to send money home.

The maize monoculture system and the erosion and land clearing it requires is significantly more vulnerable to drought and flooding than the upland rice, forest, and fallow systems that came before it, but ecological changes have ensured there is no return to that system. Therefore, the displacement and climate vulnerability that were beginning to be apparent in the late 2010s need to be read in terms of these longer histories of ecological extraction, forced resettlement, and restricted mobilities.

Agriculture and the State in Southern Vietnam

The net outmigration of one million people in recent years from the Vietnamese Mekong Delta (VMD), in conjunction with severe flooding, drought, and salinity intrusion events appears to corroborate projections of climate-induced displacement from low-lying deltas (Oanh and Truong 2017; Berlemann and Tran 2020). However, to attribute such relocation solely or even primarily to climate change would require the gross omission of decades of agrarian change in the VMD that has significantly altered the delta's biophysical dynamics and, in turn, livelihood possibilities and prospects.

Vietnam is the world's third-largest exporter of rice, but this has not always been the case. The country periodically faced acute food shortages during the twentieth century and was a net importer of rice as recently as 1985. Much of this dramatic shift in food security can be accounted for by looking to the Mekong Delta, where 90 percent of Vietnam's rice exports are sourced. Here, rich deposits of alluvial soil are highly conducive to agriculture, but their benefits were limited by the six-month monsoon season, during which the region receives over 90 percent of its annual rainfall and surface water, and severe floods can reach depths of up to three meters. In addition to contending with extreme seasonality, farmers are also strongly influenced by political economic factors. Rice yields were particularly low under state-led attempts at collectivization, which started in the North in the 1960s and then in the South after reunification in 1975 (Raymond 2008). Against a backdrop of chronic grain shortfalls and pervasive malnutrition, the central government implemented sweeping economic reforms in the late 1980s, including land and water management practices geared toward optimizing rice production.

This national "rice first" food security policy entailed the widespread adoption of high-yield rice varieties and agrochemicals in conjunction with physical engineering of the hydrological regime to regulate fresh and saltwater flows to support these modern rice varieties (Tran and Kajisa 2006). Water management schemes were modeled on Dutch polders: swaths of land encircled by earthen embankments for flood protection. Such structures had been introduced to the Mekong Delta in the 1930s as part of French colonial experiments in flood control, but they were not developed in earnest until the late 1980s reform period (Biggs 2011). The drive to increase rice production for domestic and international markets encountered significant challenges in the upper delta, where naturally deep floodwaters were not conducive to high-yield rice varieties that had short stems compared to the "floating rice" typical of the region. Engineers and planners therefore implemented a vast network of embankments across the upper delta to exclude floodwaters from the paddy fields.

From 2001 to 2011, local authorities introduced high dikes to An Giang and Dong Thap provinces to regulate floods and facilitate multi-cropping, successfully boosting rice yields in subsequent years (GSO 2020). However, the water infrastructure simultaneously disadvantaged poor households by diminishing their access to informal farm work and access to wild capture fisheries (Tran 2019). The decline in on-farm employment opportunities is significant given the centrality of agrarian livelihoods in the VMD, where two-thirds of the land area is dedicated to agriculture and an equivalent proportion of the workforce is employed in agriculture, forestry, or fisheries (Le et al. 2018). Moreover, national policies aimed at boosting rice and shrimp production have inadvertently increased farmers' vulnerability to water hazards and crop losses and led to greater inequalities among wealthy and poor households (Gorman 2019). Shrimp is a lucrative export commodity that has experienced explosive growth in Vietnam, largely facilitated by the conversion of over 500,000 hectares of land for aquaculture over the past three decades (GSO 2020). Farmers seeking to join the sector often take out loans to overcome the steep costs of converting from rice to shrimp cultivation, but it is difficult to recover financial losses resulting from disease outbreaks, which are common (Käkönen 2008). Shrimp farmers also regulate pond salinity levels through unregulated groundwater extraction that is driving parts of the VMD to subside at rates up to ten times that of absolute sea level rise, thereby accelerating risk of coastal inundation (Minderhoud et al. 2017). Such factors have contributed to greater household insecurity and workforce precarity, with important implications for mobility in the VMD.

While the persistence of smallholders in the midst of prolonged agrarian change is remarkable (Rigg et al. 2018; Nguyen, Gillen, and Rigg 2020), it should be highlighted that land accumulation has been proceeding apace since the mid-1990s, despite size limits on cropland acquisition established by the 1993, 2003, and 2013 land laws (Tran 2018). The consolidation of landholdings is consistent with two decades of government policies aimed at accelerating agricultural and rural industrialization and modernization, boosting commodity export production, and downsizing the agricultural labor force since 2001 (GOV 2001). Thus, temporary and long-term migration out of the VMD more clearly becomes a function not only of climate-driven environmental change, but also of the top-down reorientation of agriculture toward increasingly mechanized and low-labor cultivation.

Dispossession, Development, and Climate Change in Southeast Sulawesi, Indonesia

Historically and into the present, the Konawe'eha River and lowland floodplains, peatland swamps, and smaller marshes of Southeast Sulawesi, Indonesia, have been a key site of trade and mobility as well as a vital source of subsistence and biocultural salience for the Indigenous Tolaki people—a fact reflected in some of the earliest clan names from the region, which include Andolaki ("brave people of the river"), Tolaiwoi ("people of the river"), Toiwoiesi ("people of the small river"), and Toepe ("people of the swamp") (de Jong 2011, 38).

Though information on historical flood regimes is limited, severe lowland floods do not appear to have been common through the latter nineteenth century to mid-twentieth century—in part given the flood-attenuating presence of historically extensive wetlands. However, while only three severe lowland floods occurred between 1950 and 2010, there have been four in the decade since (Kelley and Prabowo 2019; *Antara* 2020), a dynamic that aligns with the predictions of climate models and which has precipitated apparent climate displacements.[1] In 2020, for instance, floods left forty-nine villages underwater and forced thousands of people to evacuate homes and fields (*Antara* 2020). While atmospheric and terrestrial convergences undeniably inform recent intensifications in flood severity and frequency, such violences are inextricable from those under colonial, state, and neoliberal development regimes, which have reconfigured the relations between land, water, and climate in ways that set the stage for intense flood events and precondition migration as a response.

In 1906, for instance, Dutch colonial officers and engineers began a multi-decade road construction initiative to facilitate forest product extraction in the uplands and access to coastal port cities. Given the difficulties of building roads in the uplands, reinforced roads were often constructed directly through wetlands and peat swamps instead, initiating the first recorded wetland drainage schemes and the installation of culverts and reticulated water systems (de Jong 2011). Dutch military troops and colonial officers subsequently traveled roads to relocate mobile Tolaki swidden settlements into permanent villages along the roads newly adjoining the river. Localized inundation events, high malarial loads, and recurrent epidemics in these floodplains resulted in massive loss of life and cattle wealth and led to further attempts to stabilize and fix the boundaries between land and water, as through road reinforcement and reconstruction.

Suharto's New Order regime (1965–1997/8) doubled down on these trajectories, in part by establishing state claims over all lands deemed to be un/underused (Peluso and Vandergeest 2011), which encompassed 70.5 percent of Southeast Sulawesi's land area and 96 percent of remaining forests as of 2018 (Kelley 2018). Such lands were used as the basis for diverse "improvement" schemes intended to sedentarize agrarian populations, quell revolutionary resistances, and increase the economic and agronomic productivity of smallholder land. From the 1970s onward, state-claimed lands provided the basis for timber extraction in the uplands and smallholder tree cropping block grants, irrigation, and relocation schemes in the lowlands. These initiatives were associated with the state-sponsored in-migration of extensive transmigrant communities and the establishment of permanent cropping on land in and around the Konawe'eha's floodplains—lands once used by Tolaki people as seasonal hunting, fishing, and grazing lands (Departemen Tenaga Kerja dan Transmigrasi 2015).

Neoliberal and post-liberalization developments have inverted these logics while otherwise offering much of the same. Specifically, they suggest a shift from a focus on sedentarizing mobile swidden farmers to a focus on incentivizing the mobility of corporate capital, albeit in ways that further amplify lowland flooding risks and the necessity of mobility as a response. Such developments include those linked to the more than 300 concessions granted in the province since 2009, primarily for nickel (199), gold (36), asphalt (36), and oil palm (20). These concessions are implicated in roughly a quarter of provincial tree cover loss since 2000, landslides and silting that increasingly affect upstream passage points previously less vulnerable to flooding, and the further conversion and pollution of swamps and rivers (Morse 2019; Kelley 2020).

These are among the multiple and cumulative socionatural violences that force a rereading of apparent "climate displacements" like the ones that occurred in 2016, when several large trucks of people left the village in search of work after three months of heavy rainfall inundated croplands and houses and led managers to temporarily lay off three hundred people from a nearby oil palm plantation. Such departures speak to the interplay of hydroclimatic change and the contradictions of capital borne of changes within plantation labor regimes. More centrally, however, they reflect the cumulative and accreted effects of those historical epidemics, land enclosures, wetland drainage schemes, and upland extractivism that render anomalous rains disastrous. In this case, as others, re-emplacements also inform a deepening dependence on out-migration as a coping response when disaster inevitably strikes. Indeed, as many individuals returned from distant worksites several months after their initial departure, they found newly constructed plantation barracks populated with recruited in-migrants from elsewhere in eastern Indonesia (Kelley and Prabowo 2019).

Taken together, the key dimensions of cumulative socionatural displacement we identify here include histories of dispossession via state territorialization, long-term deterioration of smallholder agro-ecologies, recent intensifications in export-oriented commodity production, recent increases in labor migration, and increasingly apparent climate impacts (see table 4.1).

Policy Implications

Much has been made of the political foot dragging and grandstanding that has impeded international climate negotiations and policy for the past three decades. However, focusing on the limited gains of multilateralism risks missing significant developments in climate policy at other scales. As noted above, deterministic and neo-Malthusian logics within environmental security studies have carried neatly over to the climate change arena, where they underpin widely circulated ideas about climate change fomenting territorial and resource conflicts (e.g., Yayboke et al. 2020). Just as expectations of environmental degradation and civil unrest shaped national security strategy in the 1990s (Peluso and Watts 2001), so too are they informing climate imaginaries and responses to them (Paprocki 2018). Thus, simplistic narratives about environmental violence that have spurred so much rhetoric about water wars and other clashes over resources are also reproduced in a wide range of climate policies, with equally troubling implications.

Table 4.1. Drivers of cumulative socionatural displacements in three sites of agrarian Southeast Asia

Drivers of cumulative socionatural displacement	Xieng Khouang, Laos	Mekong Delta, Vietnam	Southeast Sulawesi, Indonesia
Long-standing processes of dispossession	State limits on shifting cultivation; involuntary resettlement of ethnic minorities; loss of legal land access for young people; demographic pressure; accelerating debts.	Livelihood and property dispossession through interlocking processes of debt, mechanization, and land accumulation.	State forest establishment and criminalization of swidden agriculture; in-migration for land; agricultural intensification and associated debt, ecological change, and land consolidation.
Long-term ecological change	Logging; NTFP (non-timber forest product) overharvesting; soil erosion from shortened fallow cycle; intense soil erosion from maize monocropping on steep slopes.	Canalization of waterways; land subsidence; riverbank and coastal erosion; mangrove deforestation.	Soil erosion; landscape homogenization and associated pest and pathogen challenges; montane and swamp forest clearance; water pollution.
Export commodity production	Maize boom for export on former forest and fallows following collapse of opium and forest products economy.	Vietnam is the third-largest exporter of rice and shrimp in the world, with most production sourced from the VMD.	Sulawesi is the third-largest exporter of cacao globally and increasingly a site of oil palm, gold, and nickel production.
Agribusiness investment	Smallholder-driven maize production for Thai and Vietnamese agribusinesses.	Agricultural mechanization and intensification for export commodity production.	Agribusiness investments in over 300 concessions since 2009 within the province.

Drivers of cumulative socionatural displacement	Xieng Khouang, Laos	Mekong Delta, Vietnam	Southeast Sulawesi, Indonesia
State policy	Promotion of maize and export agriculture; involuntary relocation; prohibition on swidden agriculture; enforced opium ban.	Promotion of agribusiness industrialization and export commodity production; construction of flood management and irrigation networks for agricultural intensification.	Promotion of sedentary and export-oriented agricultural production; villagization and resettlement, colonization via *transmigrasi* schemes; agribusiness promotion.
Circular labor migration	~32% of households have a family member working outside the province; wealthier families send children to work in Thailand; poorer families become casual laborers in primary industries.	40% of surveyed households in Ben Tre and Tra Vinh have a family member working outside the province; adults seek work in urban areas and industrial zones, leaving grandparents to care for children.	52% of 311 surveyed adults had migrated from one particularly flood-prone village in Southeast Sulawesi, including 36% between 2018 and 2019; most migration is circular and for work sites within Indonesia or Malaysia.
Climate change impacts	Increased vulnerability to minor drought (2012) and floods (2014) due to altered hydrology, soil organic matter. Connected to migration decisions.	Extreme droughts and record spatial and temporal extent of seawater intrusion (2016, 2019, 2020) decimated rice crops and freshwater fisheries.	Extreme floods in 2013, 2019, and 2020 disrupted access to local employment opportunities and subsistence and market production. Recurrent droughts contribute to flooding impacts.

At one level, individuals, households, and communities have become the primary targets of resilience efforts aimed at bolstering their capacity to anticipate, prepare for, withstand, and recover from environmental shocks. This broad and ambitious strategy has received widespread support from such diverse entities as environmental policy think tanks (e.g., RAND Corporation, Center for Climate and Energy Solutions), multilateral development banks (e.g., Asian Development Bank), multilateral organizations (e.g., United Nations Environment Programme), and numerous governmental agencies. Despite such powerful backing, critical scholars and grassroots groups have questioned why people should strive to maintain the very systems of exploitation and extraction that have made them vulnerable to climatic disruptions in the first place (Mikulewicz 2019). In practice, resilience programs do little to address underlying drivers of socio-ecological instability, effectively serving instead to maintain the social, political, and economic status quo while devolving responsibility onto impacted groups for their own survival (Cretney 2014; Vilcan 2017). The result is that, should people find themselves in untenable circumstances and having to relocate, resilience thinking would interpret such outcomes as a failure of the person or group to adapt rather than emanating from broader processes of uneven development and underinvestment.

Projections of large-scale displacement and climate-induced conflict have shaped national level policymaking as well, particularly in the form of hardening state borders and discouraging would-be migrants. In the spring and summer of 2021, the Biden-Harris administration sent an unambiguous message to Haitians, Cubans, and Central Americans to "not come" to the United States (see figure 4.2). While the US Department of Homeland Security asserts that this directive is based on concern for migrant safety during a treacherous journey (DHS 2021b), this same agency has identified greater migration flows associated with climate change as posing national security risks. Its Climate Change Adaptation Roadmap, for instance, states that "more severe droughts and tropical storms, especially in Mexico, Central America, and the Caribbean, could increase population movements (both legal and illegal) across the US border, *leading to potential increases in drug trafficking, human smuggling, and transnational criminal organization activity*" (DHS 2012, emphasis added; see also DHS 2021b). Viewing climate-vulnerable populations as a *source* of risk thus leads to exclusionary border policies like migrant interdiction rather than measures that address the root causes of displacement (Thomas and Warner 2019).

Our work argues for such displacement to be placed squarely within its historical, political economic, and socio-ecological context. Reconceptualizing climate-driven migration as just one form of a diverse suite of cumulative socionatural displacements becomes essential for locating the variegated factors that shape

Figure 4.2. In May 2021, the US Embassy in Haiti delivered a stark message, translated into Creole, to prospective migrants seeking refuge in the United States.

human mobility. In documenting decades-long agrarian transformations in Southeast Asia, we question the premise that people can or should be expected to "adapt" to socio-ecological destabilizations instigated by state and corporate actors at scales far exceeding the influence of most individuals. We also show why these decades-long transformations are powerfully ecological, making previous forms of agrarian life difficult if not impossible.

Together, our cases employ a volumetric analysis, with a twist. The volumetric turn in geography was one that compelled a collective reckoning with the three-dimensionality of various planetary volumes as a corrective to prevailing conceptions of space as flat, static, and surficial (Billé 2019). Accordingly, much of the research animated by Elden's (2013) agenda-setting intervention has focused on the materiality of biophysical and atmospheric flows across multiple spatial scales to challenge the presumed fixity of space. We invoke and expand upon this work by adding a spatiotemporal lens of *accretion* to apprehend the additive effects of volumetric change. This approach demonstrates how biophysical and political economic transformations do not supplant existing socio-ecological arrangements but may instead accumulate in sedimentary fashion to produce new volumetric configurations, with all their attendant ramifications for social life.

This three-dimensional scope takes a comprehensive look at multiple scales, lifeforms, and temporalities (see the afterword in this volume) and at the violences—slow and fast—that build up over time. Climate policies must attend to these deep, historical transformations in ecological and social space that condition displacements in the present.

From this perspective, seeing climate-linked migrations as a question of cumulative socionatural displacements does not diminish either their significance to people's lives or the significance of addressing climate changes in agrarian regions. Rather, it can encourage us to broaden our sense of what constitutes good climate policy, decentering a predominant emphasis on "climate-smart" farming, improved disaster control, and other techno fixes and reiterating the importance of (among other things) land reform, migrant justice, and stronger controls on agribusiness investment.

> The twentieth century as an "age of extremes," as Eric Hobsbawm (1994) calls it, has drawn to a close, but it casts a long shadow over the new millennium.
>
> —*Peluso and Watts 2001, 38*

Over twenty years ago, *Violent Environments* (Peluso and Watts 2001) turned a critical gaze toward the burgeoning field of environmental security and raised unflinching challenges to its key premise that resource scarcity in developing countries was inevitable and would ultimately lead to violent conflict. Despite this groundbreaking work and subsequent research building on it, the intervening decades have been characterized by the re-entrenchment rather than abolishment of the more teleological, apolitical, and Malthusian overtones of early work in environmental security studies as concerns with climate change become more prominent.

Mainstream climate-conflict studies appear to follow the same playbook as their environmental security predecessors. They gloss over the precise mechanisms by which particular shifts in climate contribute to social strife, omit the historical and political economic factors that lay the groundwork for unrest, and focus on overt, conspicuous forms of conflict. While we join others in arguing against such practices, we also challenge the implicit treatment of violence as an outcome of climate change. Rather, our cases demonstrate that diverse forms of violence, ranging from the quotidian to the dramatic, are *antecedent* to the symptoms of climate impacts, such as displacement. Whereas so much environmental security research frames migration as a potential driver of violent conflict, we locate violences as being prior to displacement. We took it as our task in this essay to trace some of the violences that constitute the long shadow of the twentieth century over the present millennium.

Cases from Southeast Asia show these violences to be both slow and fast, leading people to move in circular, permanent, and episodic ways. Such movements are also long-standing features of agrarian life, with the maintenance of rural systems being partly contingent on remittances and migration flows. Attention to the dialectical relationship between biophysical processes and social (re)production prompted our engagement with an expansive notion of volumes as more than just compartments of atmospheric, terrestrial, or subterranean space. We envision volumes as sedimented layers of gases, soils, plants, and water, as well as land uses, infrastructures, cultural practices, kin relations, political economic systems, and accumulated ecological knowledge that also profoundly shape volumetric form and composition. That such volumes and their constituents have become targets for climate interventions crucially overlooks the fact that many contemporary socio-ecological arrangements are themselves the product of earlier violent transformations wrought during periods of colonialism, state making, and neoliberalism (Thomas 2020). The most radical and necessary "climate" policy will therefore move beyond popular techno-managerial and financialized solutions and attend instead to the resource and land theft, marginalization, and indebtedness of agrarian communities that script their vulnerability.

Note

1. Hirabayashi et al. (2013), for instance, analyze eleven different atmospheric-ocean general circulation models, finding that all eleven suggest an increase in annual precipitation, annual runoff, heavy precipitation periods, annual river discharge, and major flood events in Sulawesi. Wood et al. (2021) find that precipitation variability will also likely increase over the Pacific intertropical convergence zone as extreme precipitation increases.

References

Antara. 2020. "Floods Swamp Thousands of Homes in Konawe, SE Sulawesi." July 19, 2020. https://en.antaranews.com/news/152654/floods-swamp-thousands-of-homes-in-konawe-se-sulawesi.

Baechler, Günther. 1998. "Why Environmental Transformation Causes Violence: A Synthesis." *Environmental Change and Security Project Report,* Spring (4): 24–44.

Berlemann, Michael, and Thi Xuyen Tran. 2020. "Climate-Related Hazards and Internal Migration: Empirical Evidence for Rural Vietnam." *Economics of Disasters and Climate Change* 4 (2): 385–409.

Bettini, Giovanni. 2017. "Where Next? Climate Change, Migration, and the (Bio)politics of Adaptation." *Global Policy* 8 (4): 33–39. http://doi.org/10.1111/1758-5899.12404.

Biggs, David. 2011. "Fixing the Delta: History and the Politics of Hydraulic Infrastructure Development and Conservation in the Mekong Delta." In *Environmental Change and Agricultural Sustainability in the Mekong Delta,* edited by Mart A. Stewart and Peter A. Coclanis, 35–44. Dordrecht: Springer Netherlands.

Billé, Franck. 2019. "Volumetric Sovereignty Part 1: Cartography vs. Volumes." *Society and Space* March 4, 2019. https://www.societyandspace.org/articles/volumetric-sovereignty-part-1-cartography-vs-volumes.

Cretney, Raven. 2014. "Resilience for Whom? Emerging Critical Geographies of Socio-ecological Resilience." *Geography Compass* 8 (9): 627–640. http://doi.org/10.1111/gec3.12154.

Dalby, Simon. 2013. "The Geopolitics of Climate Change." *Political Geography* 37:38–47. http://doi.org/10.1016/j.polgeo.2013.09.004.

de Jong, C. G. F. 2011. *Nieuwe hoofden Nieuwe goden. Geschiedenis van de Tolaki en Tomoronene, twee volkeren in Zuidoost-Celebes (Indonesië), tot ca. 1950*. [New chiefs, new beliefs: A history of the Tolaki and the Tomoronene, two nations in Southeast Celebes (Indonesia) until ca. 1950]. London: LAP Lambert Academic Publishing.

Departemen Tenaga Kerja dan Transmigrasi. 2015. Unpublished data obtained in Kendari, Sulawesi Tenggara, Indonesia, March 30, 2015.

DHS (Department of Homeland Security). 2012. "Department of Homeland Security Climate Change Adaptation Roadmap." Department of Homeland Security, June 2012. https://www.dhs.gov/sites/default/files/publications/Appendix%20A%20DHS%20FY2012%20Climate%20Change%20Adaptation%20Plan_0.pdf.

DHS (Department of Homeland Security). 2021a. "Secretary Mayorkas Overviews U.S. Maritime Migrant Interdiction Operations." Press release, July 13, 2021. https://www.dhs.gov/news/2021/07/13/secretary-mayorkas-overviews-us-maritime-migrant-interdiction-operations.

DHS (Department of Homeland Security). 2021b. "Department of Homeland Security Climate Action Plan." Department of Homeland Security, September 2021. https://www.dhs.gov/sites/default/files/publications/21_1007_opa_climate-action-plan.pdf.

Doshi, Sapana. 2015. "Rethinking Gentrification in India: Displacement, Dispossession and the Spectre of Development." In *Global Gentrifications: Uneven Development and Displacement*, edited by Loretta Lees, Hyun Bang Shin, and Ernesto López-Morales, 101–120. Bristol: Bristol University Press.

Elden, S. 2013. "Secure the Volume: Vertical Geopolitics and the Depth of Power." *Political Geography*, 34, 35–51.

Gorman, Timothy. 2019. "From Food Crisis to Agrarian Crisis? Food Security Strategy and Rural Livelihoods in Vietnam." In *Food Anxiety in Globalising Vietnam*, edited by Judith Ehlert and Nora Katharina Faltmann, 235–266. Singapore: Palgrave Macmillan.

GOV (Government of Vietnam). 2001. *Strategy for Socio-Economic Development 2001–2010*. Hanoi.

Gray, Clark, Elizabeth Frankenberg, Thomas Gillespie, Cecep Sumantri, and Duncan Thomas. 2014. "Studying Displacement after a Disaster Using Large-Scale Survey Methods: Sumatra after the 2004 Tsunami." *Annals of the American Association of Geographers* 104 (3): 594–612.

Grundy-Warr, Carl, Mak Sithirith, and Yong Ming Li. 2015. "Volumes, Fluidity and Flows: Rethinking the 'Nature' of Political Geography." *Political Geography* 45:93–95. http://doi.org/10.1016/j.polgeo.2014.03.002.

GSO (General Statistics Office of Vietnam). 2020. "Economy: Agriculture, Forestry and Fishery." Accessed May 1, 2020. https://www.gso.gov.vn/en/homepage/.

Hartmann, Betsy, and James K. Boyce. 1983. *A Quiet Violence: View from a Bangladesh Village*. London: Zed Books.

Harvati, Katerina, Carolin Röding, Abel M. Bosman, Fotios A. Karakostis, Rainer Grün, Chris Stringer, Panagiotis Karkanas, Nicholas C. Thompson, Vassilis Koutoulidis, Lia A. Moulopoulos, Vassilis G. Gorgoulis, and Mirsini Kouloukoussa. 2019. "Apidima Cave Fossils Provide Earliest Evidence of *Homo sapiens* in Eurasia." *Nature* 571:500–504. https://doi.org/10.1038/s41586-019-1376-z.

Hertzman, Emily. 2014. "Returning to the Kampung Halaman: Limitations of Cosmopolitan Transnational Aspirations among Hakka Chinese Indonesians Overseas." *Austrian Journal of South-East Asian Studies* 7 (2): 147–164.

Hirabayashi, Yukiko, Roobavannan Mahendran, Sujan Koirala, Lisako Konoshima, Dai Yamazaki, Satoshi Watanabe, Hyungjun Kim, and Shinjiro Kanae. 2013. "Global Flood Risk under Climate Change." *Nature Climate Change* 3 (9): 816–821.

Homer-Dixon, Thomas. 1999. *Environment, Scarcity and Violence*. Princeton, NJ: Princeton University Press.

IEP (Institute for Economics and Peace). 2020. "Ecological Threat Register 2020: Understanding Ecological Threats, Resilience and Peace." Sydney: Institute for Economics and Peace. http://visionofhumanity.org/reports.

Käkönen, Mira. 2008. "Mekong Delta at the Crossroads: More Control or Adaptation?" *Ambio* 37 (3): 205–212.

Kaplan, Robert D. 1994. "The Coming Anarchy: How Scarcity, Crime, Overpopulation, and Disease Are Rapidly Destroying the Social Fabric of Our Planet." *Atlantic Monthly*, February 1, 1994. https://www.theatlantic.com/magazine/archive/1994/02/the-coming-anarchy/304670/.

Kelley, L. C. 2018. "The Politics of Uneven Smallholder Cacao Expansion: A Critical Physical Geography of Agricultural Transformation in Southeast Sulawesi, Indonesia." *Geoforum* 97:22–34.

Kelley, Lisa C. 2020. "Explaining the Limitations of Agricultural Intensification Initiatives in Sulawesi, Indonesia." *Frontiers in Sustainable Food Systems* 4:204.

Kelley, Lisa C., Nancy Lee Peluso, Kimberly M. Carlson, and Suraya Afiff. 2020. "Circular Labor Migration and Land-Livelihood Dynamics in Southeast Asia's Concession Landscapes." *Journal of Rural Studies* 73:21–33.

Kelley, Lisa C., and Agung Prabowo. 2019. "Flooding and Land Use Change in Southeast Sulawesi, Indonesia." *Land* 8 (9): 139.

Kelly, P. F. 2011. "Migration, Agrarian Transition, and Rural Change in Southeast Asia." *Critical Asian Studies* 43 (4): 479–506.

Lam, Theodora, and Brenda S. A. Yeoh. 2018. "Migrant Mothers, Left-Behind Fathers: The Negotiation of Gender Subjectivities in Indonesia and the Philippines." *Gender, Place and Culture* 25 (1): 104–117. https://doi.org/10.1080/0966369X.2016.1249349.

Le, Thuy Ngan, Arnold K. Bregt, Gerardo E. van Halsema, Petra J. G. J. Hellegers, and Lam-Dao Nguyen. 2018. "Interplay between Land-Use Dynamics and Changes in Hydrological Regime in the Vietnamese Mekong Delta." *Land Use Policy* 73:269–280.

Le Billon, Phillipe. 2008. "Diamond Wars? Conflict Diamonds and Geographies of Resource Wars." *Annals of the Association of American Geographers* 98 (2): 345–372.

Lustgarten, Abrahm. 2020. "The Great Climate Migration." *New York Times Magazine*, July 23, 2020. https://www.nytimes.com/interactive/2020/07/23/magazine/climate-migration.html.

McDowell, Julia Z., and Jeremy J. Hess. 2012. "Accessing Adaptation: Multiple Stressors on Livelihoods in the Bolivian Highlands under a Changing Climate." *Global Environmental Change* 22 (2): 342–52. https://doi.org/10.1016/j.gloenvcha.2011.11.002.

McKay, Deirdre. 2005. "Reading Remittance Landscapes: Female Migration and Agricultural Transition in the Philippines." *Geografisk Tidsskrift-Danish Journal of Geography* 105 (1): 89–99.

Mikulewicz, Michael. 2019. "Thwarting Adaptation's Potential? A Critique of Resilience and Climate-Resilient Development." *Geoforum* 104:267–282. http://doi.org/10.1016/j.geoforum.2019.05.010.

Minderhoud, Phillip S. J., Gilles Erkens, V. Hung Pham, V. T. Bui, L. Erban, H. Kooi, and E. Stouthamer. 2017. "Impacts of 25 Years of Groundwater Extraction on Subsidence in the Mekong Delta, Vietnam." *Environmental Research Letters* 12 (6): 064006.

Morse, Ian. 2019. "Indonesian Flooding Disaster Bears the Hallmarks of Agriculture and Mining Impacts." *Mongabay*, August 7, 2019. https://news.mongabay.com/2019/08/in-sulawesi-floods-bear-the-hallmarks-of-agriculture-and-mining-impacts/.

Myers, Norman. 2002. "Environmental Refugees: A Growing Phenomenon of the 21st Century." *Philosophical Transactions of the Royal Society of London. Series B: Biological Sciences* 357 (1420): 609–613. https://doi.org/10.1098/rstb.2001.0953.

Nguyen, Tuan Anh, Jamie Gillen, and Jonathan Rigg. 2020. "Economic Transition without Agrarian Transformation: The Pivotal Place of Smallholder Rice Farming in Vietnam's Modernization." *Journal of Rural Studies* 74:86–95.

Nixon, Rob. 2011. *Slow Violence and the Environmentalism of the Poor*. Cambridge, MA: Harvard University Press.

Oanh Le Thi Kim and Truong Le Minh. 2017. "Correlation between Climate Change Impacts and Migration Decisions in Vietnamese Mekong Delta." *International Journal of Innovative Science, Engineering and Technology* 4 (8): 111–118.

Paprocki, Kasia. 2018. "All That Is Solid Melts into the Bay: Anticipatory Ruination and Climate Change Adaptation." *Antipode* 51 (1): 295–315. http://doi.org/10.1111/anti.12421.

Peluso, Nancy Lee, and Agus Budi Purwanto. 2018. "The Remittance Forest: Turning Mobile Labor into Agrarian Capital." *Singapore Journal of Tropical Geography* 39 (1): 6–36. https://doi.org/10.1111/sjtg.12225.

Peluso, Nancy Lee, and Peter Vandergeest. 2011. "Political Ecologies of War and Forests: Counterinsurgencies and the Making of National Natures." *Annals of the Association of American Geographers* 101 (3): 587–608. https://doi.org/10.1080/00045608.2011.560064.

Peluso, Nancy Lee, and Michael Watts, eds. 2001. *Violent Environments*. Ithaca, NY: Cornell University Press.

Peou, C. 2016. "Negotiating Rural-Urban Transformation and Life Course Fluidity: Rural Young People and Urban Sojourn in Contemporary Cambodia." *Journal of Rural Studies,* 44, 177–186.

Raymond, Chad. 2008. "'No Responsibility and No Rice': The Rise and Fall of Agricultural Collectivization in Vietnam." *Agricultural History* 82 (1): 43–61. http://doi.org/10.3098/ah.2008.82.1.43.

Rigaud, Kanta Kumari, Alex de Sherbinin, Bryan Jones, Jonas Bergmann, Viviane Clement, Kayly Ober, Jacob Schewe, Susana Adamo, Brent McCusker, Silke Heuser, and Amelia Midgley. 2018. *Groundswell: Preparing for Internal Climate Migration.* Washington, DC: World Bank.

Rigg, Jonathon, Albert Salamanca, Monchai Phongsiri, and Mattara Sripun. 2018. "More Farmers, Less Farming? Understanding the Truncated Agrarian Transition in Thailand." *World Development* 107:327–337.

Rosière, Stéphane, and Reece Jones. 2012. "Teichopolitics: Re-considering Globalisation through the Role of Walls and Fences." *Geopolitics* 17 (1): 217–234. https://doi.org/10.1080/14650045.2011.574653.

Scheffran, Jürgen, and Battaglini, Antonella. 2010. "Climate and Conflicts: The Security Risks of Global Warming." *Regional Environmental Change* 11 (S1): 27–39. http://doi.org/10.1007/s10113-010-0175-8.

Silvey, Rachel. 2006. "Geographies of Gender and Migration: Spatializing Social Difference." *International Migration Review* 40 (1): 64–81.

Smith, Dan, and Janani Vivekananda. 2007. *A Climate of Conflict: The Links between Climate Change, Peace and War.* London: International Alert.

Tacoli, Cecelia. 2009. "Crisis or Adaptation? Migration and Climate Change in a Context of High Mobility." *Environment and Urbanization* 21 (2): 513–525.

Thomas, Kimberley Anh. 2020. "Shifting Baselines of Disaster Mitigation." *Climate and Development* 12 (2): 147–150. https://doi.org/10.1080/17565529.2019.1605875.

Thomas, Kimberley Anh. 2021. "Enduring Infrastructure." In *A Research Agenda for Geographies of Slow Violence: Making Social and Environmental Injustice Visible,* edited by Susan O'Lear, 107–122. Cheltenham: Edward Elgar Publishing.

Thomas, Kimberley Anh, and Benjamin P. Warner. 2019. "Weaponizing Vulnerability to Climate Change." *Global Environmental Change* 57:1–11. https://doi.org/10.1016/j.gloenvcha.2019.101928.

Tran Hữu Quang. 2018. "Land Accumulation in the Mekong Delta of Vietnam: A Question Revisited." *Canadian Journal of Development Studies/Revue Canadienne D'études Du Développement* 39 (2): 199–214.

Tran, Thong Anh. 2019. "Land Use Change Driven Out-Migration: Evidence from Three Flood-Prone Communities in the Vietnamese Mekong Delta." *Land Use Policy* 88:104157.

Tran, Ut, and Kei Kajisa. 2006. "The Impact of Green Revolution on Rice Production in Vietnam." *Developing Economies* 44 (2): 167–189.

Vilcan, Tudorel. 2017. "Articulating Resilience in Practice: Chains of Responsibilisation, Failure Points and Political Contestation." *Resilience* 5 (1): 29–43. http://doi.org/10.1080/21693293.2016.1228157.

Watts, Michael. 2013. *Silent Violence: Food, Famine, and Peasantry in Northern Nigeria: With a New Introduction*. Athens: University of Georgia Press.
Werner, Marion. 2015. *Global Displacements: The Making of Uneven Development in the Caribbean*. Hoboken, NJ: John Wiley and Sons.
Wood, Raul R., Flavio Lehner, Angeline G. Pendergrass, and Sarah Schlunegger. 2021. "Changes in Precipitation Variability across Time Scales in Multiple Global Climate Model Large Ensembles." *Environmental Research Letters* 16 (8): 084022.
Woods, Kevin M., and Jared Naimark. 2020. "Conservation as Counterinsurgency: A Case of Ceasefire in a Rebel Forest in Southeast Myanmar." *Political Geography* 83 (November): 102251. https://doi.org/10.1016/j.polgeo.2020.102251.
Yayboke, Erol, Trevor Houser, Janina Staguhn, and Tani Salma. 2020. "A New Framework for U.S. Leadership on Climate Migration." *CSIS Briefs*. Washington, DC: Center for Strategic and International Studies.

CHAPTER 5

The Catastrophic and Slow Violence of the Xe Pian Xe Namnoy Dam in Southern Laos

IAN G. BAIRD

On July 23, 2018, up to 500 million cubic meters of water gushed from the reservoir of the Xe Pian Xe Namnoy dam in Champasak Province, southern Laos, after a breach of "saddle" or auxiliary dam D. The people in the path of the massive deluge of water in downstream Attapeu Province had little or no advance warning of the impending disaster (*Vientiane Times* 2018h). It was the biggest catastrophic event ever to occur in Laos in relation to a hydropower dam. However, well before the dam broke, it was already causing considerable but less-visible social and environmental impacts that constitute slow violence. In the case of the dam, catastrophic and slow violence were not separate entities. Rather, catastrophic violence variously shifted into becoming slow violence and vice versa; in many respects, the two were intertwined. This chapter considers the Xe Pian Xe Namnoy dam and the ways that catastrophic violence is depicted and treated differently by the media, as well as other actors, compared to the social and environmental impacts caused by slow violence associated with the development of the Xe Pian Xe Namnoy dam. I emphasize the importance of thinking about how the impacts of violence play out, especially under circumstances when large development projects are prioritized over social and environmental justice.

Long investigated by political ecologists, temporality is conceived of in this chapter as central to understanding how problems associated with certain types of development projects such as the Xe Pian Xe Namnoy dam breach coproduce violent atmospheres. The need to adopt a volumetric perspective is also emphasized, as temporalities and volumes of water are clearly critical here. As I show, such violence co-emerges through mistakes made by state and especially non-state actors in the pursuit of accumulating as much capital as possible, and at the expense of villagers not benefiting from the project.

This study draws on media reports and my own fieldwork and observations over twenty-five years of monitoring this particular hydropower project in ethnic Heuny (Nha Heun) areas of the Bolaven Plateau in Paksong District, Champasak Province.

In May and July 2019, I also visited impacted villages in Sanamxay District, Attapeu Province, where I interviewed, in Lao language, over sixty ethnic Lao, Oi, and Jrou Dak (Sou) people variously impacted by the project.

Different kinds of violence are perpetrated through large hydropower dams, and catastrophic events involving large volumes of water often morph into slow violence related to much smaller quantities of water or no water at all, thus making the binary between catastrophic violence and slow violence insufficient for understanding the complex ways the impacts of hydropower dams frequently unfold. I consider how the impacts of violence play out, especially under circumstances where modernized large development projects are prioritized over social and environmental justice. Rob Nixon's (2011, 8) emphasis on the importance of temporality is crucial: "Violence, above all environmental violence, needs to be seen—and deeply considered—as a contest not only over space, or bodies, or labor, or resources, but also over time" (see also Cecire 2015). Given the importance of temporality, I argue that there is a need to understand how the different temporalities and quantities of water associated with slow violence and catastrophic violence are interwoven and play out over time.

The next section provides a brief overview of the dam breach. I then consider the concept of catastrophic events, which I follow up by exploring the concept of slow violence. After the history of the Xe Pian Xe Namnoy dam is briefly explained, the catastrophic impacts of the dam collapse are considered, before I examine some of the slow violence that the Xe Pian Xe Namnoy dam has inflicted in the project's reservoir area, and also downstream in the Xe Pian River Basin. I then consider how catastrophic violence can emerge as slow violence. The chapter concludes with some thoughts about the relationship between catastrophic and slow violence, and the importance of considering temporality in relation to violence.

Immediate Impacts of the Dam Collapse

Because such a large quantity of water was released from the dam over such a short period of time, the collapse of the Xe Pian Xe Namnoy dam caused immense damage, obliterating much of what was in its path, including homes, domestic animals, and people. The official death count stands at seventy-one (*Vientiane Times* 2019b). More than 14,440 people living in 19 villages were impacted, with 7,095 people in six of those villages who were forced to relocate being particularly hard hit (*Vientiane Times* 2018g, 2018e) (see figure 5.1). People's rice crops were wiped out and forests were negatively impacted by the deluge of water (*Vientiane Times* 2018c; Humphrey 2018). A large amount of silt and debris was washed down with the five billion cubic meters of water and deposited on rice farms, making farming difficult and impacting livelihoods. This is one way that volume and time are critical over the long term.

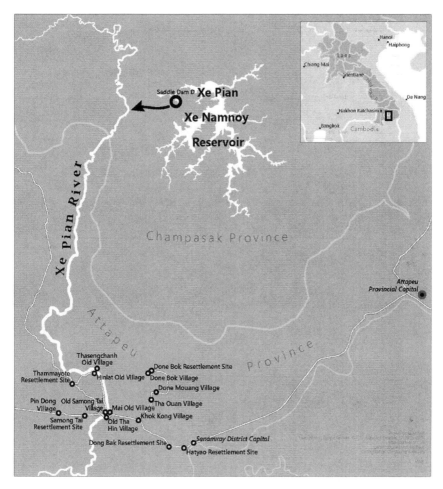

Figure 5.1. Map of Xe Pian Xe Namnoy dam showing downstream villages most impacted in Sanamxay District, Attapeu Province, Laos. (Source: Jerald Archuleta)

Over 100 km downstream, communities in the Siem Pang and Sekong districts and Stung Treng Province of northeastern Cambodia were also inundated with water, which led to serious impacts on rice crops, which the owners of the Xe Pian Xe Namnoy dam have refused to take responsibility for (VOA 2018). Some parts of northeastern Cambodia were initially inundated with 11.5–12 meters of water, and some 5,000 people were displaced (Sassoon 2018; VOA 2018) (figure 5.2).

The international team brought in by the Lao government to investigate has since concluded that the collapse was not due to a force majeure event but rather

Figure 5.2. The aftermath of the Xe Pian Xe Namnoy dam breach. (Source: Ian G. Baird)

poor-quality construction of the saddle dam that broke, thus laying full blame for the disaster on the South Korean and Thai companies that built the dam (Xinhua 2019). There is also strong evidence that the South Korean companies involved in the project sacrificed quality by reducing the height of the saddle dams by 6.5 meters in order to save US$19 million (Young-ji 2018), and that the companies were negligent in informing the people impacted in a timely fashion (RFA 2018b). However, these deficiencies also raise questions about the Lao government's will and ability to appropriately monitor and regulate project development to ensure the public good is not sacrificed.

Violence and Catastrophic Violence

In the introductory essay to *Violent Environments,* Peluso and Watts (2001, 5) consider violence to be a "site specific phenomenon rooted in local histories and social relations yet connected to larger processes of material transformation and power relations." Drawing on Dumont (1995), they also see violence as being a type of habitus, both structured and structuring—structured because of ideas about violence that emerge out of historical events and memories. Indeed, resource development is intended to naturalize structures of resource control, while at the same time keeping the violence hidden from view (Peluso and Watts 2001, 7).

According to Merriam-Webster's online dictionary, "catastrophe" can be defined as "a momentous tragic event ranging from extreme misfortune to utter overthrow or ruin," or "a violent and sudden change in a feature of the earth."[1] Thus, catastrophic violence can be considered a particular variety of violence that occurs rapidly and tends to cause more than normal destruction and/or loss of life or injury. Catastrophic violence is also hard to hide from view because of the speed and force with which it occurs.

Temporality is crucial for thinking about catastrophic violence, as are the volumes of water involved. The types of impacts that occur due to catastrophic events are experienced differently from those that occur over more extended periods, with regard to actual affects but also in relation to the ways that people respond (Slovic 2000). For example, there is considerable evidence that people are generally more fearful or anxious about the impacts of catastrophic events as compared to non-catastrophic ones, even when the latter is likely to cause more harm over the long term (Slovic 2000; Robbins, Hintz, and Moore 2014). In other words, temporality and volume are not only crucial, but they partially influence how the media responds to and reports on catastrophic events as opposed to how they deal with changes that play out gradually and over time. The first, involving a lot of water over a short period, is often considered newsworthy, whereas the latter is not generally elevated to the mainstream news media. It is crucial to understand these differences, as they greatly affect the ways we become exposed to and come to understand different temporalities of violence. This in turn influences the response of state and non-state actors.

Slow Violence

In *Slow Violence and the Environmentalism of the Poor,* Rob Nixon (2011, 2) argues for the importance of investigating slow violence, which he defines as "a violence that occurs gradually and out of sight, a violence of delayed destruction that is dispersed across time and space, an attritional violence that is typically not viewed as violence at all. Violence is customarily conceived as an event or action that is immediate in time, explosive and spectacular in space, and as erupting into instant sensational visibility." In addition, Nixon (2011, 2) appeals to his readers to consider temporality seriously and more thoroughly investigate slow violence as compared to catastrophic violence, writing that "we need, I believe, to engage a different kind of violence, a violence that is neither spectacular or instantaneous, but rather incremental and accretive, its calamitous repercussions playing out across a range of temporal scales. In doing so, we also need to engage the representational, narrative, and strategic challenges posed by the relative invisibility of slow violence." Nixon (2011) interprets slow violence as being linked to poverty-inducing policies, ones that are often hidden from public view, and typically accumulate slowly over time. Michael Watts (1983, 14) has similarly written about the rupture of a local system in his examination of capitalist incorporation and famine in northern Nigeria. In *Silent Violence,* Watts (1983) also explores temporality and the unrecognized structured violence that occurs over time.

However, my main argument here is that slow violence and catastrophic violence, despite being situated in different temporalities, and involving different volumes of water, are often intertwined, and that catastrophic violence can gradually morph into slow violence, and slow violence can be integrally linked with catastrophic violence.

A Brief History of the Xe Pian Xe Namnoy Dam

In 1996–1997, at a time when large-scale international investment in hydropower development was just beginning in Laos, Dong Ah, a South Korean company, started preparing to construct the Xe Pian Xe Namnoy dam, but was forced to give up on the project due to the Asian financial crisis. However, between 1996 and 2000, the government of Laos relocated over 2,700 ethnic Heuny Indigenous peoples from eleven villages in the watershed area of the Xe Pian Xe Namnoy auxiliary dams, moving them into an area of the Bolaven Plateau historically inhabited by their rivals, the ethnic Jrou (Laven) Indigenous peoples (Green and Baird 2016; Baird 2013; International Rivers 2008).

The premise for resettling the villages was always questionable given that some of the communities were not actually located within the reservoir areas of either dam. The government was determined to resettle the Heuny, at least partially to "stabilize" their swidden agriculture, and concentrate and modernize the people (see Evrard and Goudineau 2004). In the late 1990s, small houses were built for each family in different parts of the resettlement area, and initially three hectares of agricultural land—some good quality and some less so—were allocated to each family, regardless of family size. However, soon after resettlement was completed in the early 2000s, the Jrou communities living nearby reclaimed all but about 20 percent of the land allocated to the Heuny (Baird 2013), arguing that it was Jrou fallow swidden land and that it should not have been given to the resettled people. The Heuny were not in their traditional territory, so they did not explicitly resist. Local government officials were aware of what was happening, but they did not do much, as they did not agree with the original resettlement plan, and many agreed that Jrou land had been inappropriately given to the Heuny. The Heuny became "development refugees": people who have been forced to relocate due to development policies (see Vandergeest, Idahosa, and Bose 2007). Many Heuny were forced to take on daily farming work in the fields of the Jrou or others on the Bolaven Plateau (Baird 2013).

Before long, due to severe difficulties associated with staying in the resettlement villages, a large number of Heuny families started to defy the government and return to their old villages. Initially, they received permission to return to pick up rice that they had stored in barns from when they were living there before. Often, however, they would stay for days or weeks before returning to the resettlement villages with a small amount of rice. Within a few days, that rice would be eaten, and then they would again ask to return to their old villages to get more rice. Again, they would stay days or weeks in the old villages before returning to the resettlement villages, and gradually the periods of time that they spent in the old villages got longer and longer. Soon many families were living full-time in their old villages, and over the years the number of people who moved back gradually increased.

In 2006, the Lao government approved a two-year investigation of the Xe Pian Xe Namnoy dam, thus marking its possible revival, and in November 2008, a consortium of companies comprising SK Engineering and Construction (South Korea, 26 percent), Korea Western Power (South Korea, 25 percent), and Ratchaburi Electricity Generating Holding Public Company (Thailand, 25 percent) signed an agreement with the Ministry of Planning and Investment to develop the 390 MW dam, at an estimated cost of US$500 million. The Lao government would hold a 24 percent share of the project (*Vientiane Times* 2008). However, the project would not commence until several years later.

Once construction on the project began in February 2014, the company and the government started again resettling the Heuny people who had unofficially moved back to their former villages, much to their dismay. The plan was to move the Heuny back to the same resettlement sites that they were moved to in the second half of the 1990s, without resolving the land problem in the resettlement areas (Green and Baird 2016). Villagers were unhappy with the proposed plan, and in March 2017, many Heuny families protested—quite a rare event in Laos (RFA 2017). Many villagers refused to move until they were granted sufficiently good-quality land for agriculture. They have remained determined, and as of 2021, seventy-five families were still refusing to move into the resettlement areas. The dam was reportedly closed to gradually collect water and prepare to operate in December 2016, and on July 23, 2018, the day the saddle dam broke, the project was reportedly 80–90 percent complete (*Vientiane Times* 2018a).

The Catastrophic Impacts of the Xe Pian Xe Namnoy Dam Break

After the catastrophic collapse of the Xe Pian Xe Namnoy saddle dam D caused five billion cubic meters of water to plummet down to the communities, five camps were established in Sanamxay District (Rujivanarom 2019; *Vientiane Times* 2018d) (figure 5.1). The temporary housing in these camps was not completed until early 2019, with many complaints about delays. Various roads and bridges were also damaged by the floodwaters (*Vientiane Times* 2018b). The Attapeu Province Department of Agriculture reported that more than 1,700 hectares of agricultural land had been devastated. In addition, four irrigation systems were destroyed, 190 fishponds were damaged, and over 1,200 buffalo, 4,000 cattle, and a large number of poultry and pigs were lost (*Vientiane Times* 2018f). Many tractors, motorcycles, and other vehicles were destroyed (*Vientiane Times* 2018e).

The international media response to the dam break was unprecedented. While concerns regarding hydropower dam development in Laos have received considerable press coverage in recent years, the dam break attracted attention like never before. However, the media showed little interest in those impacted by the slow violence of the project. Temporality, the volume of water involved, and the catastrophic nature of the disaster explain the difference.

The breaking of the dam resulted in an influx of humanitarian aid from governments and private citizens, both in Laos and especially from abroad (*Vientiane Times* 2018a; Shim 2018; High 2019). The response of Lao citizens demonstrated much more concern compared to anything that has ever occurred in relation to slow violence and hydropower in Laos. Within a day or two of the disaster, people started posting and reposting messages in Lao language on social media stating that the minister of energy and mines, Khammany Inthirath, had resigned from his position in order to take responsibility for the disaster, which was assumed to have occurred due to insufficient government oversight. Within a few days, however, it became evident that the rumor that the minister had resigned had no basis in truth. There were also other rumors about the dam break spreading around Laos immediately after the event. Local perceptions were further influenced by the breaking of a smaller dam, the Nam Ao dam, in Laos's central Xaysomboun Province, in September 2017 (Hutt 2018).

Compensation for those impacted by the breaking of the dam is supposed to come from the dam consortium. Initially, each family of the forty people recognized to have been killed by the Xe Pian Xe Namnoy dam break received US$198 (1.7 million kip) (RFA 2018a). Later, on January 23, 2019, the families of seventy-one people who were by that time recognized as having been killed were each given US$10,000 (85.7 million kip) as compensation (*Vientiane Times* 2019a). However, in May 2019, villagers expressed dissatisfaction with the lives of their loved ones being valued so low. For those not killed in the disaster, the equivalent of US$60 (500,000 kip) in "pocket money" was provided to each family displaced by the breaking of the dam (RFA 2018a).

Since the dam burst, those impacted and resettled have been receiving only 250,000 kip—less than US$30 each—per month to live on in the temporary camps, along with 20 kg of rice per person (*Vientiane Times* 2019a). These payments, however, did not arrive in a timely fashion, and in May 2019, villagers reported that they had not received any money for two months. The rice arrived on time, but villagers complained bitterly about it. One woman said, "The rice is very low quality non-glutinous rice. It makes me sick when I eat it."[2] The rice came from the Association of Southeast Asian Nations (ASEAN) plus Three Emergency Rice Reserve (APTERR+3) (*Vientiane Times* 2019b). Villagers were ultimately dissatisfied with the compensation given.

Slow Violence: Moving from the Reservoir Area

The example of the Heuny mentioned above—who were resettled into difficult conditions, with insufficient agricultural land, to make way for the Xe Pian Xe Namnoy dam's reservoir—indicates how much less attention the protracted impacts of the project have received compared to the catastrophic impacts. The Heuny were resettled in the late 1990s and early 2000s to accommodate the Xe Pian Xe Namnoy dam, but most still do not have sufficient farmland. They were previously swidden cultivators who rotated their fields over a large area of forest. When they were relocated, they were allocated upland cropland to grow perennial crops, such as coffee. However, soon after they arrived, the land was allocated to the original landowners, and ethnic Jrou (Laven) people from adjacent villages reclaimed their previously fallowed land. This left the Heuny with insufficient farmland to support their livelihoods, a form of slow violence occurring over a longer period of time.

Slow Violence Preceding Catastrophic Violence: People Who Rely on the Xe Pian River

The Jrou Dak (Sou) and Oi Indigenous peoples and the ethnic Lao people who live downstream from the Xe Pian Xe Namnoy dam in Sanamxay District were also neglected before the dam broke. Villagers in these communities that were washed away were unaware that the dam was being built, and in July 2019 villagers were still unaware that the Xe Pian River had been dammed and that water was being diverted into the dam's reservoir, reducing the amount of water downstream that supports local fisheries and livelihoods. As predicted in a 1995 fish and fisheries impact study conducted for the dam developers, this dewatering can cause significant negative impacts on aquatic life, and the people who relied on fisheries to provide them with animal protein (Roberts and Baird 1995). Despite these impacts being predicted over twenty years ago, no efforts were made to mitigate them. This represents another form of slow violence, this time against downstream communities, including those who were impacted by the dam rupture.

The passage of time is crucial, combined with the volume of water. As time passes, the slow violence of water diversion converges with dam breaks as a powerful form of catastrophic violence.

Downstream Impacts

Although the Xe Pian River's downstream sections were already being negatively impacted by the Xe Pian Xe Namnoy dam, the dam's breach released a large quantity of water, carrying significant amounts of silt, sand, and debris. Rapids and deepwater pools were smothered with sand, which destroyed habitat and made the riverbed shallower. Villagers interviewed in May and July 2019 reported negative impacts on aquatic life and the possibility of future flood risks as the riverbed held less water than previously. While the river may eventually be flushed out, it will probably take years, and once-clear water will remain silty. As slow violence was initially perpetrated against people living downstream by diverting the water from their river, these same people were affected by the catastrophic breaking of the dam with dramatic, prolonged social and ecological consequences.

Unexploded Ordnances

After the dam broke, the large amount of fast-flowing water had unearthed and dislodged unexploded ordnances (UXOs) still buried since the US bombing of the area during the 1960s and early 1970s. Large quantities of cluster bombs were dropped from American airplanes during the Secret War in Laos, with the intent of inflicting catastrophic impacts on communist enemies. However, not all the bombs exploded and, upon being unearthed, they resulted in a form of slow violence for subsequent generations. The Lao Red Cross issued a warning regarding the increased danger of UXOs, including cluster bombs or "bombies," just a few days after the dam broke (ABC News 2018). This incident blurs the boundaries between catastrophic and slow violence, revealing the synergies of timing and volume.

Post-traumatic Stress Disorder

Catastrophic and slow violence also emerged through post-traumatic stress disorder (PTSD), generating both immediate and slower forms of violence. When the dam broke, and a huge amount of water poured down over a very short period, the impacts led to devastating long-term psychological trauma—a form of slow violence that manifests over longer periods of time. Since the late 1960s and early 1970s, various studies have shown that traumatic experiences associated with various types of disasters can result in serious psychological impacts (Green et al. 1990), including PTSD, anxiety and depression (Crombach and Siehl 2018), and sleep disorder impacts (Zhen, Quan, and Zhou 2018). These problems, which relate to both temporality and volume, can persist for years or decades. While psychological trauma tends to decrease over time, the impacts are experienced unevenly, making it difficult to predict what the individual impacts might be.

Many residents of impacted villages—not just those mentioned above—are having second thoughts about returning to live in their former villages due to the trauma they experienced from the worst hydropower dam disaster to hit the Mekong River Basin. One man injured during the disaster reported hearing the river's flow in his ears during his twenty-day hospital stay. He expressed fear about moving back to his village from Hat Nyao Camp. Moreover, the headman of Thasengchanh Village, the most affected area, told me that many village residents had been psychologically impacted: "You can hear people yelling out in the camp at night when people wake up having nightmares," he reported. Some are moving back to Mai, Samong Tai, and Tha Hin Villages, but will those who return be able to sleep well in the future, knowing that the dam is still upstream from them? Will they trust that the dam will not break again? Thitithamtada and Varasane (2019), from the Lao Red Cross, wrote that it is the fear of such future disasters that may be the most worrying aspect of the situation. Landscapes can be seen as "archives of memories" (Baird 2013), but in the case of the people impacted by the dam break, they may experience what resembles landscapes of nightmares.

The Heuny people who were resettled to make way for the Xe Pian Xe Namnoy dam have faced uncertainty over the years, which has emotionally affected families and communities, even if they have not been affected by PTSD. These examples show how important temporality is to understanding impacts, and how catastrophic and slow violence are deeply intertwined.

Restoring Lives

The restoration process for those impacted by the breaking of the dam is likely to take years to complete. The most problematic part of the restoration process to date has been the way that the dam developers and government have tried to restore agriculture for those displaced. In early 2019, displaced villagers were allocated land for farming, but they were told that they had to cultivate it following a particular system that would involve each family cultivating the allocated land with either cassava or sugar cane. Crucially, the farmers would have to follow the instructions of a private Vietnamese company brought in to oversee the project. The idea was that the company would advance money to pay for all initial expenses. The company would contribute expertise, inputs, and marketing. The farmers would contribute land and labor. Once the crops were harvested, the company would sell them at "market price" and give the farmers whatever profit remained, after they subtracted their expenses (and presumably profit) from the revenue generated. However, the villagers were immediately wary of the scheme, and not one family agreed to sign a contract to participate. As one farmer put it, "We don't want to work for the Vietnamese. We want to have our own land and plant on it whatever we want when we want. We don't believe that there will be any profit left for us once the Vietnamese subtract their expenses."[3] To make matters worse, villagers widely reported that corrupt government officials had taken a large amount of the funds allocated for helping them. One villager said, "Some people have gotten rich from this disaster, but none of those people were impacted by the dam." No wonder frustration has been building.

On April 26, 2019, ethnic Oi villagers in Ta Ouat Subvillage, including former communist veterans who fought against the Royal Lao Army in the 1960s and early 1970s, protested to receive a higher rice allocation. Veterans at Done Bok Camp claim that they may protest in the future if conditions do not improve.[4] Although much attention was given to those affected by the dam break, over time those who resettled as a result have been increasingly neglected. As one villager described, "At first, soon after the disaster, we were encouraged when we saw all the aid agencies coming to help us. But now, they have mainly forgotten us, and we are still suffering."[5]

As of 2021, the Xe Pian Xe Namnoy dam has been repaired and completed, and is selling energy. In the meantime, many of those impacted are still living in temporary accommodation, and problems related to agricultural land remain unresolved, indicating the continuing slow violence of the catastrophic breaking of the Xe Pian Xe Namnoy dam.

Temporality and volume of water crucially affect the ways that environmental violence is understood in different contexts. Catastrophic violence often involves a lot of water moving over a short period, thus causing certain types of impacts. These sorts of impacts also elicit particular types of responses. However, the responses to the slow violence that the same dam has been causing for over two decades to Heuny Indigenous peoples living on the Bolaven Plateau have been starkly different. The same holds for the responses to impacts caused downstream along the Xe Pian River due to water having been diverted into the reservoir and the silting of the river following the breaking of the dam. Governments, aid agencies, the media, and the public have all responded differently to them.

While thinking about the impacts of the Xe Pian Xe Namnoy dam in relation to catastrophic and slow violence is useful for better understanding the impacts of the dam, and why responses to different types of impacts have varied so much, the conceptual binaries between slow and catastrophic violence are less apparent as both are entangled in reality. Indeed, the boundaries are often blurred between the two, and are constantly shifting. When the Xe Pian Xe Namnoy dam broke, it immediately unleashed a large amount of water that inflicted catastrophic violence on thousands of people living downstream. It was initially considered by some to be a form of natural atmospheric violence, unusually heavy precipitation perhaps induced by climate change. However, it has ultimately been proven to have been due to neglect arising from decades of capital accumulation, rather than human-induced climate change. Moreover, the displacement and resettlement of Indigenous and other local peoples and other downstream impacts related to water diversion for the dam—varieties of slow violence—are very much related to the catastrophic breaking of the dam and the capitalist motivations associated with it.

What was catastrophic violence has now, in various ways, turned into slow violence as the result of several long-term impacts, such as PTSD, and the likelihood that it will take many years before villagers receive compensation for their losses. What they are likely to receive is far less compensation than they deserve. In other words, catastrophic violence has turned into slow violence, and ironically, the interventions designed to remedy the impacts of the catastrophic breaking of the dam are quite similar to the interventions introduced in Heuny communities on the Bolaven Plateau to address past slow violence.

The dam break unearthing and spreading UXOs has unleashed another form of slow violence that involves the fear of not knowing where the UXOs settled and the potentially catastrophic result of inadvertently stepping on UXOs submerged in mud. This underscores the need to recognize the intertwined nature of the temporalities and water volumes associated with different kinds of violence and how such violence sediments into complex and multifaceted locally specific circumstances.

The real value of thinking about catastrophic and slow violence in tandem is that they both reveal the importance of temporality and different volumes of water in affecting and transforming different kinds of violence, something that Nixon (2011) also emphasized, but in a different context. Thinking about temporality and volume can help us better characterize and understand when environmental violence may occur, and when it may receive insufficient attention. This finding of course suggests that we need to be particularly mindful of environmental violence that occurs over longer time frames and understand how catastrophic and slow violence are related and intertwined. Only through recognizing the structural issues—which are inherent in situations where slow and lower-profile impacts are occurring—can we expect to be able to appropriately address the serious challenges associated with different kinds of environmental violence.

Notes

1. Merriam-Webster, s.v. "catastrophe," https://www.merriam-webster.com/dictionary/catastrophe, accessed November 27, 2019.
2. Woman, Hat Nyao Camp, pers. comm., May 25, 2019.
3. Man, Hat Nyao Camp, pers. comm., July 7, 2019.
4. Man, Done Bok Camp, pers. comm., May 26, 2019.
5. Villager, Dong Bak Camp, pers. comm., May 26, 2019.

References

ABC News (Australian Broadcasting Corporation). 2018. "Laos Dam Collapse Survivors Warned of Unexploded Bombs Dislodged During Floods." July 30, 2018. https://www.abc.net.au/news/2018-07-30/laos-dam-collapse-survivors-warned-of-unexploded-ordinance/10052804.

Baird, Ian G. 2013. "Remembering Old Homes: The Houay Ho Dam, the Resettlement of the Heuny (Nya Heun), and the Struggle for Space." In *Interactions with a Violent Past: Reading Post-Conflict Landscapes in Cambodia, Laos, and Vietnam,* edited by Vatthana Pholsena and Oliver Tappe, 241–263. Singapore: University of Singapore Press.

Cecire, Natalia. 2015. "Environmental Innocence and Slow Violence." *Women's Studies Quarterly* 43 (1/2): 164–180.

Crombach, Anselm, and Sebastian Siehl. 2018. "Impact and Cultural Acceptance of the Narrative Exposure Therapy in the Aftermath of a Natural Disaster in Burundi." *BMC Psychiatry* 18:233. https://doi.org/10.1186/s12888-018-1799-3.

Dumont, Jean Paul. 1995. "Ideas on Philippine Violence: Assertions, Negations and Narrations." In *Discrepant Histories: Translocal Essays on Filipino Cultures,* edited by Vicente Rafael, 104–139. Philadelphia: Temple University Press.

Evrard, Olivier, and Yves Goudineau. 2004. "Planned Resettlement, Unexpected Migrations and Cultural Trauma in Laos." *Development and Change* 35 (5): 937–962.

Green, Bonnie L., Jacob D. Lindy, Mary C. Grace, Goldine C. Gleser, Anthony C. Leonard, Mindy Korol, and Carolyn Winget. 1990. "Buffalo Creek Survivors in the Second Decade: Stability of Stress Systems." *American Journal of Orthopsychiatry* 60 (1): 43–54.

Green, W. Nathan, and Ian G. Baird. 2016. "Capitalizing on Compensation: Hydropower Resettlement and the Commodification and Decommodification of Nature-Society

Relations in Southern Laos." *Annals of the American Association of Geographers* 106 (4): 853–873.
High, Holly. 2019. "The 2018 Dam Collapse in Attapeu Laos." *Anthropology Today* 35 (4): 26–28.
Humphrey, Chris. 2018. "Devastating Laos Dam Collapse Leads to Deforestation of Protected Forests." *Mongabay,* December 28, 2018. https://news.mongabay.com/2018/12/devastating-laos-dam-collapse-leads-to-deforestation-of-protected-forests/.
Hutt, David. 2018. "Lao Dam Disaster Points to Communist Party Failings." *Asia Times,* July 25, 2018. https://asiatimes.com/2018/07/lao-dam-disaster-points-to-communist-party-failings/.
International Rivers. 2008. *Power Surge: The Impacts of Rapid Hydropower Dam Development in Laos.* Berkeley, CA: International Rivers.
Nixon, Rob. 2011. *Slow Violence and the Environmentalism of the Poor.* Cambridge, MA: Harvard University Press.
Peluso, Nancy Lee, and Michael Watts. 2001. "Violent Environments." In *Violent Environments,* edited by Nancy Lee Peluso and Michael Watts, 3–38. Ithaca, NY: Cornell University Press.
RFA (Radio Free Asia). 2017. "Lao Villagers Face Eviction from Dam Sites after Refusing 'Unfair' Compensation." March 29, 2017. https://www.rfa.org/english/news/laos/eviction-03292017143705.html.
RFA (Radio Free Asia). 2018a. "Lao Government's Compensation for Villagers Affected by Dam Disaster 'Inappropriate.'" August 22, 2018. https://www.rfa.org/english/news/laos/lao-governments-compensation-inappropriate-08222018160745.html.
RFA (Radio Free Asia). 2018b. "Exclusive Report: Bureaucratic Chaos Rife in Hours before Laos Dam Burst." October 31, 2018. https://www.rfa.org/english/news/laos/pnpcdam exclusivereport-10312018135319.html.
Robbins, Paul, John Hintz, and Sarah A. Moore. 2014. *Environment and Society: A Critical Introduction.* 2nd ed. West Sussex: Wiley-Blackwell.
Roberts, T. R., and Ian G. Baird. 1995. "Rapid Assessment of Fish and Fisheries for the Xe Nam Noy-Xe Pian Hydroscheme in Southern Lao PDR." Unpublished report for the Wildlife Conservation Society, Vientiane, Lao PDR.
Rujivanarom, P. 2019. "Special Report: The Deadly Wave That Changed Everything for Some Laotians." *The Nation,* January 22, 2019. https://www.nationthailand.com/in-focus/30362746.
Sassoon, Alessandro Marazzi. 2018. "Thousands of Cambodians Evacuated as Floods Hit." *Al Jazeera,* July 26, 2018. https://www.aljazeera.com/news/2018/7/25/thousands-of-cambodians-evacuated-as-floods-hit.
Shim Sun-ah. 2018. "Korean Medical Team Arrives in Laos to Assist Flood Recovery." *Yonhap News Agency,* July 29, 2018. https://en.yna.co.kr/view/AEN20180729000755315.
Slovic, Paul. 2000. *The Perception of Risk.* London: Earthscan Publications.
Thitithamtada, Tiamkare, and Somphon Varasane. 2019. "Laos Villagers Rebuild Their Lives after Shocking Dam Collapse." International Federation of the Red Cross, February 20, 2019. https://www.ifrc.org/article/laos-villagers-rebuild-their-lives-after-shocking-dam-collapse.

Vandergeest, Peter, Pablo Idahosa, and Pablo S. Bose. 2007. *Development's Displacements: Economies, Ecologies, and Cultures at Risk*. Vancouver: University of British Columbia Press.

Vientiane Times. 2008. "New Hydropower Plant Set for Southern Laos." November 9, 2008.

Vientiane Times. 2018a. "Flood Impacts Deep, Widespread as Survivors Offer Survival Stories." July 27, 2018.

Vientiane Times. 2018b. "Attapeu to Spend 5.2 Billion Kip on Emergency Road Repairs." August 3, 2018.

Vientiane Times. 2018c. "Flood Victims to Have Temporary Housing within Two Months." August 2, 2018.

Vientiane Times. 2018d. "Make Sure All Sanamxay Flood Victims Get Cash Handouts: President." August 20, 2018.

Vientiane Times. 2018e. "Officials Evaluating Impact of Flood in Attapeu." August 18, 2018.

Vientiane Times. 2018f. "Sanamxay Counts the Cost of Flood Damage to Agriculture." September 3, 2018.

Vientiane Times. 2018g. "31 Missing Still as Sanamxay Search Ceases, DPM says." October 16, 2018.

Vientiane Times. 2018h. "Govt to Begin Dam Safety Checks Next Year." November 30, 2018.

Vientiane Times. 2019a. "Attapeu Continues Support for Dam Collapse Victims." February 19, 2019.

Vientiane Times. 2019b. "Attapeu Flood Victims to Receive 2,221 Tonnes of Rice." March 12, 2019.

VOA (Voice of America). 2018. "Laos Suspends New Dam Projects Following Catastrophe." August 8, 2018. https://www.voanews.com/a/laos-dam-project-on-pause/4518337.html.

Watts, Michael. 1983. *Silent Violence: Food, Famine, and Peasantry in Northern Nigeria: With a New Introduction*. Athens: University of Georgia Press.

Xinhua. 2019. "Attapeu Dam Collapse in Laos Not Force Majeure Event: Investigator." Xinhuanet, May 29, 2019. http://www.xinhuanet.com/english/2019-05/29/c_138099872.htm.

Young-ji, Seo. 2018. "SK E&C's Attempts to Cut Costs Led to Design Changes That Resulted in Collapse of Dam in Laos." *Hankyoreh*, October 15, 2018. https://english.hani.co.kr/arti/english_edition/e_international/865895.html.

Zhen, Rui, Lijuan Quan, and Xiao Zhou. 2018. "Fear, Negative Cognition, and Depression Mediate the Relationship between Traumatic Exposure and Sleep Problems among Flood Victims in China." *Psychological Trauma: Theory, Research, Practice, and Policy* 10 (5): 602–609.

CHAPTER 6

Dams, Flows, and Data
Volumetric Hydropolitics in the Mekong Basin

CARL GRUNDY-WARR AND CARL MIDDLETON

In the Mekong Basin, social life and household economies are strongly associated with living by freshwater bodies and living off aquatic resources. In different reaches of the basin, the rising and falling waters create their own multidimensional waterscapes. Along the tributaries and mainstem, any changes in water levels, whether associated with the timing and duration of the annual flood pulse, or more unpredictable diurnal and periodic water-level changes associated with water releases from hydropower operations, have implications for multiple river-connected activities (e.g., dry-season agriculture and riverbank gardens, and fishing practices [figure 6.1]).

Figure 6.1. Riverside gardens, such as these in Chiang Khong, northern Thailand, are a feature of the Mekong along much of its course. (Photo credit: Carl Grundy-Warr)

A Social Flood Pulse

Throughout the lower basin, people rely on the multiple ecological resources the rivers provide. A typical image is of a family enjoying eating snails from the Tonle Sap (or Great Lake of Cambodia), where their floating home is located (figure 6.2). Figure 6.3 is a drone image of one of numerous "floating villages" in the Tonle Sap taken in September, when water inundation is at its annual peak.

These images represent a microcosm of the biophysical and human landscapes of the lower Mekong Basin with its river systems, wetlands, lakes, and seasonal waterbodies, which act like blood vessels in an interconnected hydrological body spread over six countries (China, Myanmar, Laos, Thailand, Cambodia, and Vietnam). In many parts of the basin, the Mekong system has provided vital flows and nutrients that are central to the idea of the Mekong as a "river of life" from Southwest China to the Mekong Delta (Santasombat 2012). The annual "flood pulse" (Junk 1997), which is a key hydrological and ecological driver in the Mekong, is perhaps best seen as a "social" phenomenon—or at least a hydrosocial one (Linton and Budds 2014)—as it relates to multiple activities and ways of life, especially in Lower Mekong's densely populated wetlands and river systems (Grundy-Warr, Sithirith, and Yong 2015). To think of a biophysical driver as *(hydro)social* is central to understanding how and why large hydropower dams have profound implications for human landscapes, rhythms of life, and socio-ecological interrelations.

In this chapter, we focus on "topologies of power" (Allen 2016) relating to hydrological knowledge and data about river flows, including the flood pulse, that are being profoundly changed by hydropower dam operation. There is growing evidence that flows and volumes are becoming intensified objects of concern in transboundary hydropolitics and water diplomacy (Middleton 2022a). Through various international alignments, developmental regimes, and geopolitical relations within the Mekong Basin, there are power topologies at work, whereby metrics such as investment flows, revenue streams and profits, electricity trade and kilowatt hours, and various volumes—especially that of water both flowing and stored in reservoirs—take on growing significance relative to geographic issues of distance, proximity, and place. Cumulative impacts of hydropower are being felt on flows and volumes with various complex spatial-socio-temporal implications, particularly within the biodiverse and densely populated Lower Mekong Basin. While it matters to consider the issues of scale, position, and place, multiple hydropower developments mean that "topology parts company with topography" (Allen 2016, 151) as there are considerable decentered powers to control flows that lie with state-capital alliances controlling clusters and cascades of dams.

Figure 6.2. A family living in a floating village on the Tonle Sap tuck into a bowl of freshwater snails. (Photo credit: Carl Grundy-Warr)

Figure 6.3. A drone image of a floating community and flooded forests of an area in the southern end of the Tonle Sap Lake of Cambodia. (Photo credit: Carl Grundy-Warr)

State-capital alliances operating within capitalist logics have been reshaping the Mekong region unevenly for decades (Glassman 2010), whether through the Asian Development Bank–sponsored Greater Mekong Subregion program, or by political economic forces influencing the direction of claims for "sustainable development" taken by the Mekong River Commission (MRC), or through transnational investments and megaprojects under the more recent Beijing-led Lancang Mekong Cooperation (LMC) framework (Hirsch 2016). While there are undoubtedly many topographical power implications of the various intra- and extra-regional alliances, the topological dimension is that "distance as measured in miles or kilometers does not hinder powerful bodies from establishing a more-or-less direct presence; relationships can be made proximate or distant by drawing things closer or pushing them further apart" (Allen 2016, 155). The implication of these topologies of power is how these metrics are abstracted from the lived spaces and ecological character of the Mekong River Basin. Nowhere is this more apparent than in the progressive enclosure of the river by large hydropower dams that has ruptured preexisting biophysical processes and nature-society relations as capitalism has expanded and intensified in the region, with its internal contradictions and resource conflicts (Mahanty et al. 2018; Miller et al. 2021).

In this chapter, we argue that as hydropower expands, it produces new topologies and volumetric hydropolitics that tend to subsume the ecological and social dynamics of the flood pulse. Securing and managing the flows of the flood pulse has become a speculative scientific hydrological arena for "designing flows" (Sabo et al. 2017), and ongoing engineered mitigation (MRC 2019a, 2020a). The causes and consequences are commonly examined in terms of two-dimensional regional political economy and territorial sovereignty–centered geopolitics (with some exceptions, such as Hirsch [2016]). We propose a volumetric political ecology that connects the logics of "securing the volume" (Elden 2013) with "topologies of power" (Allen 2016). The relationship between large water infrastructure, political authority, and hydropolitics is well established (Obertreis et al. 2016), including in the Mekong Region (e.g., Hensengerth 2015). However, volumetric dimensions of hydropolitics have barely been considered. For example, the volumetric dimensions of intergovernmental agreements and the issue of hydrological data sharing have remained largely unproblematized, but over the last few years they have emerged as almost a defining trait of the region's hydropolitics (again with some notable exceptions, such as Fox and Sneddon [2005]). Thinking with topologies of power and a "volumetric political ecology" (Mostafanezhad and Dressler 2021) enables a way of connecting the atmospheric violence of climate change with hydropolitics, which we consider via the contested role of hydropower as a climate change mitigation technology in the Mekong Basin. Attention to topologies of power reveals the means by which structural processes of "slow violence" emerge and become embedded in hydropolitics through the planning, construction, operation, and institutionalization of large hydropower dams (Blake and Barney 2018; see also chapter 5 in this volume, by Baird).

We argue that basing volumetric hydropolitics on time-series hydrological data and other metrics, while relating to Mekong geographies, makes the socio-ecological consequences more remote. The hydropolitics of data have become more topological than topographical, literally about differing political interpretations of time-series hydrological data and flows of data. Our analysis considers volumetric politics as they relate to notions of "securing flows" and how and why hydropower architectures should be understood as political features of power-laden landscapes relating to dominant capital-state-technological assemblages of resource control. We critically reflect on an emerging volumetric logic in the region around hydropower mitigation technologies, hydropeaking, and designed flows and geo-engineered hydrology for managing ecological traits of the river, such as commercial and wild-capture fisheries. Before concluding, we also link our analysis of volumetric geopolitics to narratives of sustainable hydropower and climate change.

Thinking about Volumetric Politics and Architectures of Hydropower

Catalyzing the "volumetric turn" regarding territory and security (Billé 2019), Elden (2013, 35) asks: "How does thinking about volume, height and depth instead of surfaces, three dimensions instead of areas, change how we think about the politics of space?" He examines the political arithmetic of "securing the volume," which, as underscored by Bridge (2013), is intended for *particular ends*. Elden connects his work to Eyal Weizman's research on forensic architecture that reveals how buildings, infrastructure, and architecture contribute to the creation of new political realities on the ground and may contribute to forms of geopolitical violence (Weizman 2012). Significant to this chapter is that a material investigation into hydropower infrastructures and architectures must consider how they transform and are integral to a wider "force field that is shaped by but also shapes conflict" (Weizman 2014, 9), which leads to the consideration of material things as part of "a multi-layered political practice" (Weizman 2014, 18). Each hydropower dam produces its own three-dimensional political geography by transforming a part of the river into a partially enclosed entity. Multiple dams in hydropower cascades, taken together, have enormous socio-ecological and cumulative implications for river systems and riparian communities, producing a progressively anthropogenic waterscape.

The idea that three-dimensional territories and topographies are continually being transformed by architecture and infrastructure for national, state, security, and political economic motives is far from new. Canals, dikes, ditches, irrigation channels, diversions, and hydraulic transformations constituting contested socio-ecological waterscapes are part of the environmental and political histories of the Mekong region (Biggs 2010). What is novel is the scale, depth, breadth, and temporal implications of multiple hydropower architectures along the mainstem and major tributary systems. Until the early 1990s, much of the Mekong River was largely free-flowing. As of 2019, there were eighty-nine medium and large dams in the lower Mekong Basin (Cambodia, Laos, Thailand, and Vietnam), with a further fourteen dams under construction and thirty at a planning stage (MRC 2022). In China, eleven medium and large hydropower dams have been constructed on the mainstem, with another eleven planned, while ninety-five more dams have been built on the tributaries (Eyler 2020).

Hydropower technologies are part and parcel of varying forms of political hydraulic control over territories and waterscapes (Sneddon 2015). Thinking this way about hydropower links ideas about volumetric regimes and architectures to the force field of geopolitical economic power shaped by powerful political-financial-technological assemblages.

Topologies of Power of Impact Assessment Studies

According to Adamson et al. (2009, 54), "the most remarkable feature of the [Mekong] river's hydrology is the consistency of the size and duration of [its] wet-season peak, and the regularity of its onset." The regular pattern of the annual monsoonal flood pulse has shaped the vegetation, fisheries productivity, aquatic resources, and aquatic-based agriculture across the Lower Mekong Basin (Arias et al. 2013; Baran and Myschowoda 2009). Figures 6.1 to 6.3 reveal the ways that the flood pulse also shapes social life.

Multiple hydropower dams in the Mekong Basin are causing significant hydrological alterations (Arias et al. 2014). These unseasonal, irregular, and unpredictable changes in water levels have multiple implications for the Mekong's "pulsing ecosystems" (Grundy-Warr and Lin 2020). The MRC's own *Hydropower Mitigation Guidelines* reveal that engineered efforts cannot prevent "the loss of migratory (fish) species (biomass and biodiversity)" (MRC 2020a, xiii). As Everard (2013, 42) notes, there is "no 'one size fits all'" solution when it comes to complex ecosystems and connected complex social relations. In the Mekong Region, while environmental impact assessments are formally required in decision-making processes, in practice they have numerous shortcomings (Middleton 2022a). It is rare, for example, that they consider the more-difficult-to-measure—but readily anticipated—cumulative and long-term temporal biophysical and social impacts (Soukhaphon, Baird, and Hogan 2021). Yet, cumulative impacts are known through various studies, such as the strategic environmental assessment study on Mekong mainstream dams commissioned by the MRC (ICEM 2010), in various MRC "integrated water resource management" guided basin planning studies, as well as in the recently completed "council" study (MRC 2017).

Thus, even with this knowledge, or in spite of it, a power topology based around transnational political economic alliances and technological-capitalist assemblages is changing the flood pulse, radically altering ecosystems as the river's hydrology becomes more engineered and regulated. While local topographies, place, and scale continue to matter immensely in terms of precise hydrological changes and impacts, riparian social lives, flora, and fauna are abstracted from the levers of decision-making and control.

Hydropeaking, and How Project Development Life Cycles Displace Ecological Cycles

In addition to the changing flood pulse, short-term and abrupt variations in river flow—termed "hydropeaking"—are also disrupting aquatic ecology and wild-capture fisheries (e.g., Lamberts 2008) and have become a common and troublesome phenomenon affecting riparian and floodplain communities. Hydropeaking is caused by the daily operations of hydropower projects as they open their turbines to generate electricity, responding to fluctuations in peak energy demands in distant load centers.

In Laos, at the Nam Theun 2 (NT2) dam for example, Baird, Shoemaker, and Manorom (2015) show how the project's operation has resulted in downstream impacts for many communities along the Xe Bang Fai River. These impacts in part relate to hydropeaking, including riverbank erosion, loss of sandbars and rapids, impacts on fisheries and aquatic plant species, and a decline in riverbank gardening. In another paper, Baird and Quastel (2015) connect the operation of the NT2 dam and hydropeaking on the Xe Bang Fai River to Thailand's peak electricity demand, shaped, for example, by air conditioner use. They demonstrate how technical and commercial "modes of ordering" emerged as the project was negotiated between the Thai and Lao governments, with the involvement of the project backers, including the construction companies, project owners, and the World Bank, and other financial institutions. Here, the topologies of electricity trade, investment flows, revenues, and profits are maximized through the management of NT2's water volumes, restructuring local nature-society relations in the process.

Hydropeaking has tended to be handled as an apolitical outcome of hydropower development, yet it is another element in the volumetric geopolitical arena between the dam operators, relevant state agencies, and myriad livelihoods dependent upon the river's ecological services, as well as regional organizations such as the

MRC and LMC. There are operational protocols that reduce hydropeaking and some of its impacts, although they tend to be geographically constrained and often bypass the cumulative impacts of multiple projects (Almeida et al. 2020).

In the MRC's technical reports, there is explicit recognition that the Mekong Basin is intensively developed by the hydropower industry, so that "sustainability" becomes basin-wide planning in support of "immediate project development requirements" (MRC 2019a, 1). Environmental harms are normalized within a technical language of bettering engineered mitigation efforts, which over time become ever more complex as more hydropower dams come on stream. For example, the MRC's *Hydropower Mitigation Guidelines* state that they "provide a clear process and detailed technical guidance to address a range of known risks and impacts in all phases of the Project Development Lifecycle" (MRC 2019a, 2). They cover a broad range of issues, including "hydrology and flows, geomorphology and sedimentation, water quality, fisheries and aquatic ecology, environmental flows, biodiversity and natural resources, ecosystem services as well as engineering response to environmental risks, impacts and vulnerabilities" (MRC 2019a, 3). What these technical documents and their associated practices reveal, however, is that volumetric governance relating to flows and fugitive mobile resources within flows are dynamic and require endless and multiple mitigation measures. Furthermore, it evidences that the priority is less on preserving rich, biodiverse ecosystems and the ecological services that they provide than upon ensuring the continuity of the project development cycle and ultimately the construction of more hydropower projects.

Transboundary Water Data Politics and Their Volumetric Abstractions

Over the past decade, the Mekong River has experienced seasonal low river flows that are among the most severe in living memory, most recently in 2019–2021. The low flows have caused significant hardship for riparian communities, including low sediment suspensions that resulted in the river taking an aquamarine hue in some areas and rapid algae growth, as well as reduced wild-capture fisheries (MRC 2019b). There has been heated geopolitical, academic, and media debate about the relative contribution of regional drought, El Niños, and climate change—versus the now-extensive operation of hydropower across the basin—to these low flows (Middleton 2022a, 2022b). Attention was directed toward China's twelve dams on the upper Mekong (Lancang), as well as the Xayaburi Dam on the Mekong River mainstream in Northern Laos, commissioned in 2019.

Water data politics have been at the center of the debate, given the ambiguity about the extent of existing water storage and operation schedules of existing hydropower dams, especially during the dry season (Grünwald, Feng, and Wang 2021; Keovilignavong, Nguyen, and Hirsch 2023). During the 2019–2020 low flows, heightened geopolitical tension between China and the US further intensified, particularly with the publication of a United States–funded report in April 2020 by the research consultancy Eyes on the Earth that presented a statistical model on the impact of China's mainstream dams on downstream areas of northern Thailand (Basist and Williams 2020). The report was widely disseminated in the media (see *New York Times* 2020), as it was amplified by several civil society groups as well as US government representatives to claim that China was responsible for the severity of the low flows. The Eyes on the Earth study, as it is now known, introduced a new verticality to the region's existing hydropolitics as it used historical and current satellite data as a basis for its statistical model to create a "wetness index" to estimate the amount of water in the catchment, and then related this to monthly measurements of water levels at the gauging station in Chiang Saen in northern Thailand. Subsequently, the Stimson Center launched a Mekong Dam Monitor that uses the Eyes on the Earth satellite data system to report water levels and releases from twenty-six "virtual gauges" located at dam sites on the mainstem and tributaries, rendering their water releases and operation more visible. The study also catalyzed volumetric debate among researchers as to whether the satellite data could be credibly converted to water volumes stored behind dams (Ketelsen, Räsänen, and Sawdon 2020; Basist and Williams 2020; Kallio and Fallon 2020; MRC 2020b), as well as on the politicization of volumetric water data in public discussion in general (Grünwald, Feng, and Wang 2021; Keovilignavong, Nguyen, and Hirsch 2023).

The issue of intergovernmental water data sharing has long been a point of negotiation both between the member states of the MRC and with China. Water data sharing is central to the "Agreement on the Cooperation for the Sustainable Development of the Mekong River Basin" that guides the MRC and subsequent procedures. This includes data on water quantity and quality, inter- and intra-basin water use, on maintaining minimum dry-season flows (including to ensure the Tonle Sap "reverse flow"), and on the systems that monitor, manage, share, and make water data publicly available. The MRC's data sharing focuses primarily on physical water levels and volumes, with other data sharing progressively included, such as on water quality, sediment, wild-capture fisheries ecology, and social impacts. China began limited water data sharing in 2002 from two monitoring stations (one on the mainstem and one on a tributary) in the lower river section during the dry season, consisting of river level and rainfall data (Wouters, Daza-Clark, and Devlaeminck 2024). Following the intense (satellite) scrutiny—and volumetric politics—on China's dams in 2020, year-round data sharing between China and the

MRC was announced in October that year. China also occasionally announces "emergency water releases" when exceptional hydropeaking is planned.

The focus on intergovernmental water data sharing emphasizes "quanta-based flows" (cf. Bridge 2013), which has been a focus of intergovernmental "water diplomacy" through the MRC and LMC. They connect to "quanta-based rights" stated in the Mekong Agreement, for example, in terms of maintaining minimum flows in the mainstem in the dry season, which reveals how the Mekong Agreement is very much a *volumetric* international agreement. Regarding the relationship between China and the downstream countries, quanta-based rights are at the heart of "securing the flow" in relation to the operation of China's Lancang dam cascade. In both cases, however, the emphasis of intergovernmental cooperation is on the basin-wide optimization of hydropower cascade management, and fundamentally toward instrumental ends of securing the flow for hydroelectricity generation and profit.

Elden (2013, 49) emphasizes "geo-metrics," namely, the (politics of) measurement in volumes as a "means of comprehending and compelling, organising and ordering." What is measured—and what is not measured—matters. The current abstract water data shared between governments remains disconnected from lived experiences on the river. In northern Thailand, for example, downstream of Lancang cascade, the impacts of hydropeaking and the overall regulated river regime are apparent on river ecosystems, fishing, and riverbank farming livelihoods practices (Santasombat 2012; Yong 2020), and the use of sandbars, reefs, and rocks in the river (Lin and Grundy-Warr 2020). Yet, the abundant riparian community experience and knowledge of the changing river conditions and its consequences have few avenues to seriously influence the river basins transboundary management, despite the various participatory mechanisms that exist (Middleton 2022a, 2022b).

Designed Flows and Geo-engineered Hydrology

Within some hydrology and hydrological modelling literature on the Mekong Basin, a school of thought has emerged hypothesizing that "fisheries yields are driven by measurable attributes of hydrologic variability, and that these relationships can be used to design and implement future flow regimes that improve fisheries yield through control of impending hydropower operations" (Sabo et al. 2017, 1). After three decades of hydropower expansion across the basin, there now exist accumulated time-series hydrological and fishery datasets to explore ideas about "designing flow." The logic here is that data-supported regulation of flows is an answer to a natural flood pulse irreversibly altered by capital working relentlessly through nature.

This hydrological science on designing flows requires volumetric reasoning, as it relies upon metrics about flow regimes and specific commercial fishery operations.

Sabo et al. (2017, 1) state: "The method for design that we propose leverages a highly flexible and well-understood spectral toolbox that would have direct, transferable applicability to systems engineers who operate dams. In short, the design provides a potential tool for managing mainstem hydrology for fisheries as new dams come on line." Here, science would provide data-driven models to enable geo-engineering in support of hydropower, implying also that a weakened natural flood pulse may be mitigated through "designed flows" and volumetric international regimes could incorporate geo-engineering into their complex mitigation plans. Sabo et al.'s hypothesis was challenged by other scientists, who questioned its ecological, political, and economic assumptions, with Williams (2018) arguing that if the designed flow proceeded as planned, it would "devastate the fishery" (see also Halls and Moyle 2019). In response, Holtgrieve et al. (2018, 2) confidently argued: "There is now means for formal trade-off evaluation useful to policymakers and a potential path toward mitigating some of the impacts that dam development will have on lower Mekong fisheries. Exactly how designed flow regimes might be implemented in the real world will require substantial additional research and stakeholder engagement." The question is who are the stakeholders to be engaged in such processes? There are no guarantees that riparian communities whose food security is threatened would be officially included within stakeholder engagements. The Dai fisheries used for fishery data (Sabo et al. 2017) to design flows are commercial operations, but what about smaller wild-capture fisheries that rely upon migratory fisheries?

In response to Sabo et al. (2017), Hogan et al. (2018, 1) argue that "Mekong fish require more than designed flows" as dams have had negative impacts on fish habitat, connectivity, and biodiversity. They warn against "ignoring the power objectives of dam operations," in that electricity generation and trade is the primary objective of project operations, and there is no precedent to date that dam operators will regulate flows to enhance commercial fish production, let alone broader wild-capture fisheries. These "power objectives" have other essential underpinnings, which remain unchallenged, as they are integral to the powerful political-economic assemblages that support the MRC's volumetric international regimes and the continued expansion of hydropower, with or without designed flows.

"Sustainable Hydropower" and the Atmospheric Violence of Climate Change

At the United Nations Framework Convention on Climate Change (UNFCCC) COP26 in Glasgow in November 2021, among the many differences of opinion revealed was whether hydropower should be considered as a mitigation technology for reducing greenhouse gas emissions. The International Hydropower Association

(IHA), which represents the interests of the industry, issued a statement to COP26 claiming that "sustainable hydropower will play a vital role in international efforts to achieve net zero emissions targets, delivering a clean, reliable source of back-up energy to support rapidly growing wind and solar energy" (IHA 2021a). They called on governments to "urgently scale up investment in hydropower." However, a civil society statement endorsed by 340 organizations from 78 countries demanded that hydropower be excluded from UN climate finance mechanisms (Declaration 2021). They cited human rights and climate impacts from hydropower dams and argued the benefits of healthy rivers and other energy options.

Flows of financial and investment capital support hydropower in an era of climate change. A global illustration of this is the Climate Bonds Initiative, which is an international, investor-focused nonprofit aiming to support the development of the Climate Bonds Standard and Certification Scheme. A stated goal of the Climate Bonds Certification Scheme is "to accelerate investment in a global transition to a low-carbon, climate-resilient future" in which hydropower features prominently "in the global push to decarbonize, due to its potential scale, low GHG emissions, important role in grid support and energy storage capability" (Climate Bonds Initiative 2021, 7). In addition to the view of hydropower as a means to a "climate-resilient future," the same report enthusiastically sees drought mitigation and flood management as further reasons to support sustainable hydropower expansion.

The role of climate finance in influencing hydropower design, construction, and operation is relatively little researched in the Mekong Basin. Some studies on financing via the Kyoto Protocol's Clean Development Mechanism in Vietnam and Cambodia identified that it had limited influence on the design, operation, and economic viability of projects (Smits and Middleton 2014; Baird and Green 2020). Käkönen and Try (2019) also demonstrate how CDM financing in Cambodia contributed to "the vulnerabilisation of local fisher communities, incarceral labour practices on the dams' construction sites and accelerated logging in the conservation zone."

This "sustainable hydropower" discourse has many proponents in the energy industry and among its financial backers of the Mekong region. Overall, the hydropower industry lobbies from an elevated pedestal of its projects being considered favorable to climate adaptability, supported by key international agencies, including the World Bank, the Asian Development Bank, the Commission Internationale des Grands Barrages (International Commission on Large Dams), and powerful alliances of state, corporate, and financial backers, making it easier to pin the prefix "sustainable" to hydropower projects. The "sustainable hydropower" discourse is rooted in a legitimacy crisis for the industry in the 1990s that cumulated in the publication of the World Commission on Dams report in 2000, and the need for the industry to reinvent itself as contributing to "development" (Middleton 2022b). Globally, the discourse has since been furthered by the IHA, which has prepared its own Hydropower Sustainability Assessment Protocol and has gone so far as to even declare October 11, 2022, as Global Hydropower Day.[1]

In the Mekong region, the MRC launched an Initiative on Sustainable Hydropower in 2009 and approved a Sustainable Hydropower Development Strategy in 2021. The MRC's website states: "Development of hydropower brings synergies with other water related sectors as well, including expanding irrigation that is key to food security, provides access to electricity that is key to poverty reduction, contributes to navigation that enhances regional trade, and provides flood management and drought relief that is an important part of adapting to climate change" (MRC 2022). Here, hydropower's socio-ecological impacts at the basin and sub-basin scales have become subsumed by broader volumetric, flow regulation, and geo-engineering discourses. These claims to sustainability, however, are certainly contested, even on the count of significantly reduced greenhouse emissions (Räsänen et al. 2018).

Topologies, Volumes, and Flows of Life

Over the past twenty-five years, the Mekong River has been transformed by powerful capital-state-technological assemblages from largely free-flowing, with reasonably predictable flows of ecosystem services that supported lives and livelihoods across the basin, into a system geared to the project life cycles of hydropower. Thus, like the Arctic, in the Mekong "there are plenty of volumetric inequalities to attend to" (Dodds 2021, 1142). This includes the ways in which flows are becoming more regulated by hydropower dam operations, and consequently how seasonal flows and daily variations are less predictable than in the past, as well as concerns about a weakening annual flood pulse. Less visible than "catastrophic dam disasters," the weakening of the flood pulse is indeed a slow structural violence on preexisting riparian livelihoods and nonhuman ecologies across the basin. "Securing flows" has required technology and infrastructure, including dams, roads, and electricity lines, which create new geographical distributions of energy and materials (Sneddon 2015). Many of these technological developments are designed to partially enclose selective bits of nature. While a hydropower dam is not mobile, it has profound implications for nonhuman mobility (larvae, sediment, migratory fishes) by impacting volume and flow patterns and forming blockages on rivers, channels, and tributaries (Grundy-Warr and Lin 2020). It is important to explore not only the impacts of multiple dams on flows through territory, but also the 3D implications relating to hydrological characteristics, monsoonal seasonality, and pluri-temporal impacts from short-term hydropeaking to cumulative impacts on the annual flood pulse and related pulsing ecosystems.

As this chapter shows, volumetric geopolitics relates to the political-economic assemblages that operate in the basin and the politics of big-data control and flows; hydrological calculation and models; transparency, secrecy, and sharing of data; and applying the metrics that matter in energy-water resource decision-making. These volumetric geopolitics have increasingly turned complex watersheds into energy- and water-sharing units of control, abstracted from the myriad socio-ecological and spatiotemporal complexities that exist even as the river basin has become increasingly regulated by water infrastructure. The volumetric datasets generated and utilized define common measurement denominators that act in a similar way to monetary valuations. As David Harvey (1996, 151) argues, comparability of ecological projects requires a "universal yardstick of values," which reduces "the wondrous multidimensional ecosystem world of use values" to "common objective" denominators that "everyone can understand." While Harvey is referring to monetary values, the same idea of common denominators may apply to hydrological data measurements used in water governance when the nitty-gritty grounded implications of the data and what lies beneath it are brushed over.

The connections between atmospheric processes and hydrological processes are also subject to a range of datasets, especially the growing consideration of climate change and the anticipated impacts, including on rainfall patterns and temperature, river hydrology, and floods and droughts. As we have discussed above, these climate change impacts have been discursively woven into legitimations for—and institutionalization of—large dams as "sustainable hydropower": a form of climate change mitigation technology and an adaptation measure to "regulate" a "more uncertain" river system. Yet these projects and their operation generate impacts, risks, and uncertainties for riparian communities. It is here that the atmospheric violence of climate change intersects with the slow violence of hydrological change due to large dam infrastructure.

As more and more hydropower plants are activated in the Mekong Basin, complex mitigation plans and geo-engineered solutions are seen as ways to counter serious environmental harms and changes to natural flow patterns. These solutions are part of the high-level water diplomacy within and between international regimes, particularly the LMC and the MRC, and are founded on the growing extent of hydrological data sharing. However, the data that counts in these official processes is abstracted from the lived spaces and ecological character of the river basin. This is a trait of the volumetric international agreements that regulate the intergovernmental institutions, and which enable a particular form of hydrological expertise to lead the management of the river basin for large dams and downplay the social and ecological consequences. The interpretation of this data, however, is also subject to differing political narratives. Here, we suggest, that both the expert-driven analysis and the political narratives exemplify topological forms of power in transnational water governance that legitimize top-down discussions on designing flows that seem removed from deliberative and participatory forms of governance. Rather, under the increasingly established volumetric international regime in the Mekong Basin, sustaining "sustainable hydropower" project life cycles has risen in priority relative to protecting the *social* flood pulse and socio-ecosystem connectivity and vitality.

Notes

1. "Global Hydropower Day," IHA, https://www.hydropower.org/global-hydropower-day (accessed December 17, 2021).

References

Adamson, Peter T., Ian D. Rutherford, Murray C. Peel, and Iwona A. Conlan. 2009. "The Hydrology of the Mekong River." In *The Mekong: Biophysical Environment of an International River Basin,* edited by Ian C. Campbell, 53–76. New York: Elsevier Academic Press.

Allen, John. 2016. *Topologies of Power: Beyond Territory and Networks.* Abingdon: Routledge.

Almeida, Rafael M., Stephen K. Hamilton, Emma J. Rosi, Nathan Barros, Carolina R. C. Doria, Alexander S. Flecker, Ayan S. Fleischmann, Alexander J. Reisinger, and Fábio Roland. 2020. "Hydropeaking Operations of Two Run-of-River Mega-Dams Alter Downstream Hydrology of the Largest Amazon Tributary." *Frontiers in Environmental Science* 8:120. https://doi.org/10.3389/fenvs.2020.00120.

Arias, Mauricio E., Thomas A. Cochrane, David Norton, Timothy J. Killeen, and Puthea Khon. 2013. "The Flood Pulse as the Underlying Driver of Vegetation in the Largest Wetland and Fishery of the Mekong Basin." *Ambio* 42 (7): 864–876.

Arias, Mauricio E., Thanapon Piman, Hannu Lauri, Thomas Cochrane, and Matti Kummu. 2014. "Dams on the Mekong Tributaries as Significant Contributors of Hydrological Alterations to the Tonle Sap Floodplain in Cambodia." *Hydrological Earth Systems Science* 18:5303–5315.

Baird, Ian G., and W. Nathan Green. 2020. "The Clean Development Mechanism and Large Dam Development: Contradictions Associated with Climate Financing in Cambodia." *Climatic Change* 161 (2): 365–383.

Baird, Ian G., and Noah Quastel. 2015. "Rescaling and Reordering Nature–Society Relations: The Nam Theun 2 Hydropower Dam and Laos–Thailand Electricity Networks." *Annals of the Association of American Geographers* 105 (6): 1221–1239.

Baird, Ian G., Bruce Shoemaker, and Kanokwan Manorom. 2015. "The People and Their River, the World Bank and Its Dam: Revisiting the Xe Bang Fai River in Laos." *Development and Change* 46 (5): 1080–1105.

Baran, Eric, and C. Myschowoda. 2009. "Dams and Fisheries in the Mekong Basin." *Aquatic Ecosystem Health and Management* 12 (3): 227–234.

Basist, Alan, and Claude Williams. 2020. *Monitoring the Quantity of Water Flowing through the Mekong Basin through Natural (Unimpeded) Conditions.* Bangkok: Sustainable Infrastructure Partnership.

Biggs, David. 2010. *Quagmire: Nation-Building and Nature in the Mekong Delta.* Chiang Mai: Silkworm Books.

Billé, Franck. 2019. "Volumetric Sovereignty." *Environment and Planning D: Society and Space,* March 3, 2019. https://www.societyandspace.org/forums/volumetric-sovereignty.

Blake, David J. H., and Keith Barney. 2018. "Structural Injustice, Slow Violence? The Political Ecology of a 'Best Practice' Hydropower Dam in Lao PDR." *Journal of Contemporary Asia* 48 (5): 808–834. https://doi.org/10.1080/00472336.2018.1482560.

Boyé, Henri, and Michel de Vivo. 2016. "The Environmental and Social Acceptability of Dams." *Field Action Science Reports,* special issue 14. http://journals.openedition.org/factsreports/4055.

Bridge, Gavin. 2013. "Territory, Now in 3D!" *Political Geography* 34:55–57.

Climate Bonds Initiative. 2021. "Hydropower Criteria: Development of Eligibility Criteria for the Climate Bonds Standard and Certification Scheme." Background paper, March 2021. https://www.climatebonds.net/files/files/Hydro-Background-Paper-Mar%202021-release3%281%29.pdf.

"A Declaration: Climate Mitigation Efforts Must Reject So-Called 'Sustainable Hydropower' as a Solution to Combat Climate Change." November 9, 2021. Retrieved from https://www.internationalrivers.org/wp-content/uploads/sites/86/2021/11/Rivers-For-Climate-Declaration.pdf.

Dodds, Klaus. 2021. "Geopolitics and Ice Humanities: Elemental, Metaphorical and Volumetric Reverberations." *Geopolitics* 26 (4): 1121–1149.

Elden, Stuart. 2013. "Secure the Volume: Vertical Geopolitics and the Depth of Power." *Political Geography* 34:35–51.

Everard, Mark. 2013. *The Hydro-Politics of Dams: Engineering or Ecosystems?* London: Zed Books.

Eyler, Brian. 2020. "Mekong Reservoirs in Yunnan Province, China." *Stimson,* July 7, 2020. https://www.stimson.org/2020/mekong-reservoirs-in-yunnan-province-china/.

Fox, Coleen, and Chris Sneddon. 2005. "Flood Pulses, International Watercourse Law, and Common Pool Resources: A Case Study of the Mekong Lowlands." WIDER Research Paper, UNU-WIDER.

Glassman, Jim. 2010. *Bounding the Mekong. The Asian Development Bank, China, and Thailand.* Honolulu: University of Hawai'i Press.

Grundy-Warr, C., M. Sithirith, and M. L. Yong. 2015. "Volumes, Fluidity, and Flows: Rethinking the 'Nature' of Political Geography." *Political Geography* 45:93–95.

Grundy-Warr, Carl, and Shaun Lin. 2020. "The Unseen Transboundary Commons That Matter for Cambodia's Inland Fisheries: Changing Sediment Flows in the Mekong Hydrological Flood Pulse." *Asia Pacific Viewpoint* 62 (2): 249–265.

Grünwald, R., Yan Feng, and Wenling Wang. 2021. "Politicization of Science in the Lancang–Mekong Basin: The Eyes on Earth Study." *International Journal of Water Resources Development,* October 29, 2021. https://doi.org/10.1080/07900627.2021.1990025.

Halls, Ashley S., and Peter B. Moyle. 2019. "Comment on 'Designing River Flows to Improve Food Security Futures in the Lower Mekong Basin.'" *Science* 361 (6398): eaat1989.

Harvey, David. 1996. *Justice, Nature and the Geography of Difference*. Oxford: Blackwell Publishing.
Hensengerth, Oliver. 2015. "Where Is the Power? Transnational Networks, Authority and the Dispute over the Xayaburi Dam on the Lower Mekong Mainstream." *Water International* 40 (5–6): 911–928.
Hirsch, Philip. 2016. "The Shifting Regional Geopolitics of Mekong Dams." *Political Geography* 51:63–74.
Hogan, Zeb, Teresa Campbell, Peter J. Weisberg, Sarah E. Null, and Sundeep Chandra. 2018. "Mekong Fish Need More than Designed Flows." *Science,* April 2018. https://www.researchgate.net/publication/324721259_Mekong_fish_need_more_than_designed_flows.
Holtgrieve, G. W, M. E. Arias, A. Ruhi, V. Elliott, So Nam, Peng Bun Ngor, T. A. Räsänen, and J. L. Sabo. 2018. "Response to Comments on 'Designing River Flows to Improve Food Security Futures in the Lower Mekong Basin.'" *Science* 361 (6398). https://doi.org/10.1126/science.aat1477.
ICEM (International Center for Environmental Management). 2010. *Strategic Environmental Assessment of Hydropower on the Mekong Mainstream*. ICEM Australia for the Mekong River Commission, Hanoi, Vietnam.
IHA (International Hydropower Association). 2021a. "IHA to COP26: Sustainable Hydropower Is Essential for Net Zero Emissions." October 28, 2021. https://www.hydropower.org/news/press-release-iha-to-cop26-sustainable-hydropower-is-essential-for-net-zero-emissions.
IHA (International Hydropower Association). 2021b. "International Leaders Back Bold New Blueprint for Sustainable Hydropower." September 24, 2021. https://www.hydropower.org/news/international-leaders-back-bold-new-blueprint-for-sustainable-hydropower.
Junk, Wolfgang J., ed. 1997. *The Central Amazon Floodplain: Ecology of a Pulsing System*. Berlin: Springer-Verlag.
Käkönen, Mira, and Try Thuon. 2019. "Overlapping Zones of Exclusion: Carbon Markets, Corporate Hydropower Enclaves and Timber Extraction in Cambodia." *Journal of Peasant Studies* 46 (6): 1192–1218. https://doi.org/10.1080/03066150.2018.1474875.
Kallio, Marko, and Amy Fallon. 2020. *Critical Nature: Are China's Dams on the Mekong Causing Downstream Drought? The Importance of Scientific Debate*. Centre for Social Development Studies, Chulalongkorn University, April 28, 2020. https://www.csds-chula.org/publications/2020/4/28/critical-nature-are-chinas-dams-on-the-mekong-causing-downstream-drought-the-importance-of-scientific-debate.
Keovilignavong, Oulavanh, Tuong Huy Nguyen, and Philip Hirsch. 2023. "Reviewing the Causes of Mekong Drought before and during 2019–20." *International Journal of Water Resources Development* 39 (1): 155–175.
Ketelsen, Tarek, Timo Räsänen, and John Sawdon. 2020. "Did China Turn Off the Lower Mekong? Why Data Matters for Cooperation." Southeast Asia Globe.com, May 13, 2020. https://southeastasiaglobe.com/china-mekong-river-flow/.
Lamberts, Dirk. 2008. "Little Impact, Much Damage: The Consequences of Mekong River Flow Alterations for the Tonle Sap Ecosystem." In *Modern Myths of the Mekong: A Critical Review*

of Water and Development Concepts, Principles and Policies, edited by Matti Kummu, Marko Keskinen, and Olli Varis, 3–18. Helsinki: Helsinki University of Technology.

Lin, Shaun, and Carl Grundy-Warr. 2020. "Navigating Sino-Thai 'Rocky' Bilateral Ties: The Geopolitics of Riverine Trade in the Greater Mekong Subregion." *Environment and Planning C: Politics and Space* 8:826–833.

Linton, Jamie, and Jessica Budds. 2014. "The Hydrosocial Cycle: Defining and Mobilizing a Relational-Dialectical Approach to Water." *Geoforum* 57:170–180.

Mahanty, Sango, Sarah Milne, Phuc Xuan To, Keith Barney, and Philip Hirsch. 2018. "Introducing 'Rupture: Nature–Society Transformation in Mainland Southeast Asia.'" *New Mandala,* September 17, 2018. https://www.newmandala.org/introducing-rupture/.

Middleton, Carl. 2022a "The Political Ecology of Large Hydropower Dams in the Mekong Basin: A Comprehensive Review." *Water Alternatives* 15 (2): 251–289.

Middleton, Carl. 2022b. "Moving beyond 'Sustainable Hydropower' in the Mekong Basin." The Water Dissensus—A *Water Alternatives* Forum, June 15, 2022. https://www.water-alternatives.org/index.php/blog/mekong.

Miller, Michelle, Alfajri, Rini Astuti, Carl Grundy-Warr, Carl Middleton, Zu Dienle Tan, and David M. Taylor. 2021. "Hydrosocial Rupture: Causes and Consequences for Transboundary Governance." *Ecology and Society* 26 (3): 21. https://doi.org/10.5751/ES-12545-260321.

Mostafanezhad, Mary, and Wolfram H. Dressler. 2021. "Violent Atmospheres: Political Ecologies of Livelihoods and Crises in Southeast Asia." *Geoforum* 124:343–347.

MRC (Mekong River Commission). 2015. "MRC Initiative for Sustainable Hydropower. Final Report. ISH01 Pilot Testing in the Sre Pok Sub-Basin on the Identification of Ecologically Sensitive Sub-Basins for Sustainable Development of Hydropower on Tributaries." Vientiane: MRC Secretariat.

MRC (Mekong River Commission). 2017. "The Study on Sustainable Management and Development of the Mekong Including Impacts of Mainstream Hydropower Projects." Accessed December 17, 2021. https://www.mrcmekong.org/highlights/the-council-study-reports/the-study-on-sustainable-management-and-development-of-the-mekong-river-including-impacts-of-mainstream-hydropower-projects/.

MRC (Mekong River Commission). 2019a. *The MRC Hydropower Mitigation Guidelines. Guidelines for Hydropower Environmental Impact Mitigation and Risk Management in the Lower Mekong Mainstream and Tributaries*. MRC Technical Guideline Series, vol. 1. Vientiane: MRC Secretariat.

MRC (Mekong River Commission). 2019b. "Mekong River's Aquamarine Hue Likely to Occur Elsewhere due to Low Flows, Bringing Possible Risks." Vientiane: MRC Secretariat.

MRC (Mekong River Commission). 2020a. *The MRC Hydropower Mitigation Guidelines. Guidelines for Hydropower Environmental Impact Mitigation and Risk Management in the Lower Mekong Mainstream and Tributaries*. Vol. 3. Vientiane: MRC Secretariat.

MRC (Mekong River Commission). 2020b. "Understanding the Mekong River's Hydrological Conditions: A Brief Commentary Note on the 'Monitoring the Quantity of Water

Flowing through the Upper Mekong Basin under Natural (Unimpeded) Conditions' Study by Alan Basist and Claude Williams (2020)." Vientiane: MRC Secretariat.
MRC (Mekong River Commission). 2022. "Hydropower." Accessed December 17, 2021. https://www.mrcmekong.org/hydropower.
New York Times. 2020. "China Limited the Mekong's Flow. Other Countries Suffered a Drought." https://www.nytimes.com/2020/04/13/world/asia/china-mekong-drought.html.
Obertreis, Julia, Tim Moss, Peter Mollinga, and Christine Bichsel. 2016. "Water, Infrastructure and Political Rule: Introduction to the Special Issue." *Water Alternatives* 9 (2): 168–181.
Räsänen, Timo A., Olli Varis, Laura Scherer, and Matti Kummu. 2018. "Greenhouse Gas Emissions of Hydropower in the Mekong River Basin." *Environmental Research Letters* 13 (3): 034030. http://dx.doi.org/10.1088/1748-9326/aaa817.
Sabo, John L., Albert Ruhi, G. W. Holtgrieve, Vittoria Elliott, Mauricio Arias, Pen Bung Ngor, Timo A. Räsänen, and Nam So. 2017. "Designing River Flows to Improve Food Security Futures in the Lower Mekong Basin." *Science* 358 (6368). https://doi.org/10.1126/science.aao1053.
Santasombat, Yos. 2012. *The River of Life: Changing Ecosystems of the Mekong River.* Chiang Mai: Silkworm Books.
Smits, M., and Carl Middleton. 2014. "New Arenas of Engagement at the Water Governance-Climate Finance Nexus? An Analysis of the Boom and Bust of Hydropower CDM Projects in Vietnam." *Water Alternatives* 7 (3): 561–583.
Sneddon, Christopher. 2015. *Concrete Revolution: Large Dams, Cold War Geopolitics, and the US Bureau of Reclamation.* Chicago: University of Chicago Press.
Soukhaphon, Akarath, Ian G. Baird, and Zeb S. Hogan. 2021. "The Impacts of Hydropower Dams in the Mekong River Basin: A Review." *Water* 13 (3): 265. https://doi.org/10.3390/w13030265.
Weizman, Eyal. 2012. *Forensic Architecture: Notes from Fields and Forums.* English-German ed. Kassel: dOCUMENTA.
Weizman, Eyal. 2014. "Introduction: Forensis." In *Forensis: The Architecture of Public Truth,* 9–32. London: Sternberg Press and Forensic Architecture.
Williams, J. M. 2020. "The Hydropower Myth." *Environmental Science and Pollution Research* 27 (12): 12882–12888.
Williams, John G. 2018. "Comment on 'Designing River Flows to Improve Food Security Futures in the Lower Mekong Basin.'" *Science* 361 (6398). https://doi.org/10.1126/science.aat1225.
Wouters, Patricia, Ana Maria Daza-Clark, and David J. Devlaeminck. 2024. "China's Transboundary Hydropower Development at Home and Abroad: Exploring the Regulatory Interface between International Water Law and International Economic Law." *Frontiers in Climate* 5. https://doi.org/10.3389/fclim.2023.1302103.
Yong, M. L. 2020. "Reclaiming Community Spaces in the Mekong River Transboundary Commons: Shifting Territorialities in Chiang Khong, Thailand." *Asia Pacific Viewpoint* 61 (2): 203–218.

SECTION III

Aerial Entanglements

ure C. Student mural on a school wall: the aerial entanglement against COVID-19 in the Philippines. (Photo dit: Wolfram Dressler)

CHAPTER 7

The Volumetric Territory of Indonesia's Peat Fires

JENNY E. GOLDSTEIN

Indonesia's land is often on fire. In addition to blanketing parts of rural Sumatra and Indonesian Borneo with noxious smoke, airborne pollution from the forest and peatland fires—innocuously known as "haze"—strays into Singapore and peninsular Malaysia, sparking near-annual tension between Indonesia and its neighbors in what has become referred to as a regional "transboundary haze" crisis. While nearly all of this burning land lies within territorial zones of state-designated and controlled forest—Indonesia's forest estate—what burns are not simply trees; the most noxious air pollution originates from smoldering peat soil rather than incinerating plants. Peat is a carbon-dense mixture of partially decomposed vegetation that is typically waterlogged, but when it is drained for commercial oil palm or pulpwood products, it becomes dry and flammable. During particularly severe fire seasons, such as in 2015, villagers, local government officials, agribusiness companies, and state ministers from Indonesia and Singapore blame each other for igniting the fires while largely absolving themselves of responsibility for any underlying causes. Enabled by large-scale forest conversion to agricultural plantations and exacerbated by climate change, these Indonesian fires are a dramatic example of how forests' materiality has undergone rapid transformation since Vandergeest and Peluso first conceptualized "political forests" as spaces of state rule and resistance (1995). Analyzing how states make territorial claims to forests is helpful for understanding how forests are created, maintained, and controlled. But territory's typically flat spatial dimensions, theorized through existing formations of the political forest as circumscribed two-dimensional areas on maps, does not fully capture the expansive material and conceptual nature of the contemporary political forest. As the Southeast Asian haze crises demonstrate, Indonesia's forest politics unfold beyond forests' circumscribed land surfaces: the atmospheric dimension of these fires extends into airspace that falls beyond a single nation-state's territory. Furthermore, the fires' tendency to spread into and through the peatlands' subsurface invites a rethinking of the political forest not as a flat plane as it often appears on maps but inclusive of the space below, above, and beyond the forested land itself. Such a spatial conceptualization reveals the ways in which state, non-state, and extra-state actors must now contend with such multidimensional forest materiality and therefore find new ways to strategically surveil and control the atmospheric and subterranean spaces associated with forests.

Territoriality, or the use of territory for economic and/or political objectives (Agnew 2005), shapes how states control use and access of natural resources within specified geographical areas (Vandergeest and Peluso 1995, 388). In a genealogy of twentieth-century political forests marked by three indistinct conjunctures of state power, resistance, and territorial practices, forest territoriality was first enacted by colonial states throughout the tropics in the first decades of the century. These practices continued through postcolonial state-led development programs following World War II, and finally through Cold War–era counterinsurgencies that pitted guerrilla resistance against state actors (Peluso and Vandergeest 2001). Literature drawing on this lineage equates forest territory with state-delineated and controlled forest area (Kosek 2006; Vandergeest and Peluso 2015) or with indigenous-led resistance to state territorialization but nonetheless assumes forest territoriality as a de facto state process in which states claim, control, and commodify forests and the people inhabiting them for natural resource extraction and/or political objectives, such as identity or citizenship formation (Anthias 2017; Peluso 1995).

In a departure from earlier conjunctures of political forests in which forest territorialization pivoted around the state, political forest-making in the twenty-first century is underscored by what Devine and Baca (2020) describe as the era of neoliberal conservation. Political forest-making now involves non-state actors such as transnational nongovernmental organizations (NGOs), corporations, scientists, foreign donors, and financiers that operate across scales and spaces (Byrne, Nightingale, and Korf 2016; Corson 2011; Goldstein 2016). Despite territorializing practices enacted by non-state actors, such land often remains owned by states, if not directly controlled by them. These arrangements create new configurations of state and non-state actors with a stake in forest politics and new objectives surrounding forest control in ways that do not necessarily pit non-state actors in binary opposition to states. Throughout the tropics, international NGOs, domestic civil society groups, and external state aid organizations cordon off forests for wildlife habitat, biodiversity preservation, carbon conservation, and/or indigenous reserves in collaboration with, but not necessarily in ways imposed by, the state. Simultaneously, as multinational companies convert tropical forests to oil palm, soybean, and pulpwood plantations, state actors at various levels of government do the bureaucratic work of making forest land available for commercial plantation licenses yet no longer finance forest conversion directly (Arshad 2016; McCarthy, Vel, and *Afiff* 2012).

Such seemingly contradictory practices—sparing certain forest landscapes while sacrificing others—are part of the neoliberal conservation strategy, as deforestation in certain areas justifies conservation in others and vice versa.[1]

The contemporary conjuncture of political forests is further complicated by the increased role of satellite-based geospatial technology in forest surveillance and territoriality. What new territorial dynamics emerge from the capacity of a multiplicity of actors to access geospatial data on political forests and conduct forest surveillance remotely? How do the politics of ground truthing this remotely collected data play out on the ground, and what is at stake? While state mapping and monitoring of forests is not a new phenomenon, it was once conducted exclusively on foot or through static aerial photographs (Vandergeest and Peluso 2015). As Cold War–era satellite technology was reapportioned for nonmilitary use in the late 1970s, states began to use remotely detected satellite data, or remote sensing, to monitor deforestation within their borders (Rajão and Vurdubakis 2013). Access to remote sensing data and the capacity to analyze it was once limited to states and scientists (Edwards 2010), but since the early 2010s, NGOs and open government software platforms have made information about forest-cover change, fire location, and other geospatial data free and legible to nonexperts (Showstack 2014; see also Global Forest Watch n.d.). Near-real-time remote sensing draws new extra-state and non-state actors into forest politics, enabling anyone with a stable internet connection to "see" like a state (Li 2005; cf. Scott 1998), even those who may never set foot in the forest in question since remote sensing is—by definition—monitoring at a distance (Monteiro and Rajão 2017). Simultaneously, internet access has penetrated many previously disconnected regions in the rural tropics. Inhabitants of villages within forested areas without road access, for instance, can now download deforestation and fire hotspot data to their smartphones at a low cost. This technological intervention enables a range of actors with different objectives to surveil forests from afar and to inhabit these spaces with unprecedented access to environmental data, creating new power dynamics and alliances.

Such seismic shifts in material forest transformation, the assemblages of actors involved in this present conjuncture of political forests, and the technologies by which forests are surveilled and represented invite new ways of thinking about the territorialization and spatial politics of contemporary forests. Cross-border forest phenomena—such as fire-related air pollution and carbon emissions—as well as multinational and private sector financial investment that underpins much forest territorialization in the twenty-first century expand the spatial dynamics of forest access and control beyond the formally demarcated area of the forest itself. As Indonesia's peat fires penetrate the land's subsurface and smoke travels upward into the atmosphere and across political borders, the causes and the consequences of the fires complicate bordered conceptions of forest territory and territoriality. This chapter thus takes up the provocation from Elden (2013) and Adey (2015) to consider territory's vertical and volumetric dimensions. I argue that state and non-state actors assume new modes and configurations of control by operating strategically within political forests' vertical and volumetric dimensions of territory. As forests materially fill the subterranean and the atmosphere beyond the enclosed, bounded surfaces and areas that have traditionally rendered forests political through territorialization, analyzing the vertical and volumetric dimensions of forest territory reveals how political forest making occurs not only through territorialization of land but through strategic control of the expansive space above, below, and beyond forests themselves. Doing so better acknowledges the increasingly volatile material and atmospheric dimensions of forests but also the resulting politics of contemporary forest territory in which state, extra-state, and non-state actors respond to forest-based crises. The claims made by state and non-state actors within volumetric territories are not only traditional territorializing strategies of claiming resources for economic and/or political ends but contestations of blame and responsibility for environmental destabilization within atmospheric and subterranean spaces. The use of legal mechanisms and mapped representations that rely on satellite-based surveillance technology are the primary means by which territorialization is enacted in volumetric space in this case.

This chapter proceeds as follows: After discussion of existing conceptualizations of territory in scholarship on political forests, I introduce the relevance of vertical and volumetric perspectives from work in political geography to understanding contemporary forest territorialization beyond "areal expression where resources are imagined as fixed territory" (Bridge 2013, 57). I suggest that conceptualizing political forest territory as volumetric is better suited to analyze the rapidly changing materiality of forests and the proliferation of actors beyond the state who are now engaged in forest territoriality in ways that do not necessarily correspond with political borders. I then explore the concept of volumetric territory vis-à-vis Indonesia's burning peatlands in two ways. First, I show that the creation of incendiary landscapes, such as Indonesia's burning peatlands, where peat fire expands unnaturally into subsurface soils and regional airspace, is the result of peatlands' peculiar materiality and relatively new configurations of state and non-state actors particular to the current neoliberal era of political forests. Second, I suggest that representational practices—in particular, remote sensing of fires and plantation concession mapping—that seek to ascribe culpability for fires strategically obscure actors' economic and political territorial strategies by failing to account for the three-dimensional material dynamics of the fires themselves, thereby enabling a smokescreen of blame for environmental crisis.[2]

Political Forest Territoriality and the Three-Dimensional Shift

Modern states' notions of forest territoriality have long been predicated on abstract space that can be divided into discrete but homogenous units and mapped accordingly (Vandergeest and Peluso 1995). Forest enclosure—enacted on the ground and as represented in two-dimensional mapping strategies—has been integral to the process of forest territorialization. Colonial and modern states have drawn lines around forests to clearly demarcate states' rights to rule natural and social resources. This designation of calculable space is, as Rose-Redwood notes, "a condition of possibility that has enabled the modern notion of territory to emerge as a political category in its contemporary form" (2012, 301). Now used prolifically by state and non-state actors alike, remote sensing–based forest surveillance (apolitically called "monitoring") is a "high-technology" extension of land surveys and forest maps that states have used as a tool of territorialization for centuries (Scott 1998; Winichakul 1994). However, while geospatial technology offers a roster of techniques to create new forms and permutations of calculable space by mapping forest change through points, lines, areas, and surfaces, conceptions of territory as a political category have remained static. Consequently, forest territories are reinforced as two-dimensional closed areas (Crampton 2010) and as an expression of state sovereignty. To be sure, Indigenous and other forest-based inhabitants have pushed back against hegemonic state-led mapping strategies through participatory mapping and counter-mapping practices to represent their version of community forests (Harris and Hazen 2005). Nevertheless, from these earlier conjunctures of twentieth-century political forests through to the contemporary moment, the spatial politics of forest territory and territorialization have remained centered around the state and its opposition and fixed to two-dimensional, enclosed mapped representations and corresponding enclosures on the ground.

As powerful as mapping technologies—and resistance to these constructions—have been in rendering forests political, recent work in political geography has sought to rethink territory's two-dimensional spatiality. Such territories remain, as Elden describes, stuck as geographic areas, "bordered, divided, and demarcated, but not understood in terms of height and depth" (2013, 35). Political geographers, however, have long decoupled the notion of territory from an emphasis on nation-state boundaries. If land is fundamentally "a relation of property, a finite resource that is distributed, allocated and owned, a political-economic question" (Elden 2010, 805), territory is the relation between the state and socio-space but not inherently the socio-space of the nation-state. Thinking through the various relations that territory encompasses breaks apart the "territorial trap" of seeing nation-states in relation to their spatial containers or borders (Agnew 1994). Agnew argued that the territorial trap in international geopolitics inaccurately fixed political boundaries around sovereign states, subsequently leading to a "fixation on the 'national' economy as the fundamental geographical entity in international political economy" (1994, 59). Elden (2013), meanwhile, calls for a further rethinking of the politics of space through three-dimensional volume rather than relying on traditional notions of political territory, which are tied to surface area, rendered in two-dimensions. He offers a reading of the politics of territory through the vertical dimensions of the Israeli-Palestinian conflict, in which tunnels, submarine battles, hilltops, and airspace are as fundamental to the conflict as land and terrain itself (Elden 2013, 37). In connecting volumetric territory to environmental politics, Bridge (2013, 57) notes that power "increasingly centers on the calculative and technical-legal practices for inventorying, securing, and anticipating volumes in space," demanding analysis of both how material environmental politics unfold within volumes and also how the "technologies of calculation, visualization, and manipulation" are enacted between and within political borders in ways that do not necessarily align with the boundaries of the nation-state.

Consideration of spaces above and below the earth's surface as sites of inquiry for environmental politics is not entirely new for critical nature-society scholars. Braun showed how the emergence of geologic science "rendered the space of the Canadian state vertical" (2000, 28), leading to new forms of governmentality while advancing capital accumulation. More recently, scholars have attended to how state-based territorial claims shape subsurface resource extraction of minerals, oil, and gas (Appel, Mason, and Watts 2015; Bebbington and Bury 2013). Subterranean resources challenge nation-state–based conceptions of planar territory, as states often attempt to reinforce national sovereignty through territorial claims to subterranean resources while simultaneously encouraging foreign capital investment in those resources (see, for instance, chapter 1 in this volume, by Toumbourou et al.). The significance of the subterranean to state sovereignty and capital flows engages with a politics of verticality that demonstrates how "the departure from a planar division of a territory to the creation of three-dimensional boundaries across sovereign bulks redefines the relationship between sovereignty and space" (Weizman 2002, 2).

Yet subterranean resources and the territorial strategies they engender are, by nature, fixed in place. As such, discussion of their material properties vis-à-vis legal and sovereign space engages a politics of verticality but not necessarily a politics of volume. As Steinberg and Peters (2015) argue, materiality within recent accounts of vertical territory tend to conceive of matter as static rather than as constantly shifting, three-dimensional forms. Steinberg and Peters take up Bridge's (2013) provocation to value matter "not just through recognition of a substance's location in space but through the ways in which it persists, seeps into cracks, and transforms itself" (2015, 258; see also Jones and Clark 2017; Dittmer 2014). Following this, I advance here a means of thinking about territorialization of forests *through* their volatile environmental materiality as it unfolds broadly in volumetric space as fire and particulate matter, infiltrating the subsurface layers and atmospheric spaces not typically included in analyses of political forests. State and non-state actors strategically confront these material conditions as they play out underground and in the atmosphere by claiming, contesting, and disavowing such materiality. Considering the vertical and volumetric dimensions of forest territorialization thus reveals strategies of forest control particular to the contemporary era as states attempt reifying territorial strategies in the face of material environmental destabilization *and* neoliberalization that draws extra-state and non-state actors into forest politics.

Fire and Smoke as Volumetric Forest Territory

Forest fire politics in an era of neoliberal conservation and increasing ecological volatility break down the longstanding binary of the state and its resistance in assigning blame and responsibility for fire. As an incendiary landscape, Indonesia's peat fires have furthermore taken on spatial dynamics that are not bound by the land's surface but spread three-dimensionally into the subterranean and into regional airspace, thereby enrolling new and more remote actors with a stake in fire—and forest—politics. Fire's presence in forests globally has traditionally been a menace to state officials and inhabitants, who see uncontrolled orange flames as a threat to civilized, urban societies. Yet underlying normative fire-as-emergency discourses are territorializing strategies in which fire is wielded to claim land, resist state governance, and manage natural resources (Kull 2002). In the tropics, states have long maligned fire as unproductive in agricultural landscapes by repressing swidden practitioners who use fire cyclically to clear trees and generate nutrients for crops (Dove 1985; Harwell 2000). Fire in inhabited landscapes can be more complex, however, as states criminalize it as a means of societal control, while peasants often use fire to resist the state directly but anonymously (Kull 2004; Mathews 2005). While this literature provides critical insight into how fire shapes socio-state relations, the state—as with political forests more generally—has remained central to controlling fire or the failure to do so. Non-state actors' response to or use of fire, meanwhile, is cast as resistance to the state, with an emphasis on individual fires and the actors who ignite them as a strategy of forest territorialization for political objectives. Emphasizing individuals associated with fire ignitions that spread to a landscape scale, however, shifts emphasis away from systemic causes of fires and the ways in which broader political economic dynamics cultivate landscape vulnerability to fire. Yet it is precisely the ambiguity surrounding the obsession with finding a single culprit responsible for a particular fire, whether a supposed arsonist or accidental fire setter, that obscures the strategies of material accumulation that create incendiary landscapes. Furthermore, discourses on changing climatic conditions, such as increased drought risk, help maintain depoliticized causal connections between landscape fires and the actors ultimately responsible *not* for igniting fires but for creating the conditions that enable them (Harwell 2000; Simon 2017).

Indonesia's landscape-scale peat fires have grown more frequent and expansive in the past twenty years within the context of shifts in neoliberal forest politics more generally. Under Indonesia's Basic Agrarian Law dating to 1960, the state owns all forested land—over three-quarters of Indonesia's land mass—and has the right to designate it as protection forest, production forest for commercial logging, or conversion forest for conversion of degraded forests to agriculture. Despite the steep reduction in forest cover since the 1980s, the Ministry of Forestry (MoF, currently called the Ministry of Environment and Forestry) still claims over 70 percent of state forest within its jurisdiction, an amount of land that has remained largely unchanged since the MoF territorialized the country's forests from the 1960s to 1980s as a resource for timber exports in collaboration with Suharto-era cronies (Brockhaus et al. 2012). Since democratic decentralization in the early 2000s, however, large-scale land enclosures for oil palm and pulpwood accelerated in Indonesia's outer islands, particularly Sumatra and Indonesian Borneo (Kalimantan), including peatland areas, as foreign investors took advantage of unclear land rights at local levels and the ability of district-level leaders to provide final authority on whether an area can be developed for plantation agriculture (McCarthy, Vel, and *Afiff* 2012). Since 2000, over 60 percent of oil palm concessions have been on peatlands in Sumatra and Indonesian Borneo, a result of their perceived low population concentrations and proximity to coastlines, despite the capital-intensive infrastructure necessary to convert these swamps to drained agricultural land (Carlson et al. 2012; Goldstein 2016).

In Indonesia's peatlands, while much blame for fire ignition has focused on individuals or typologies of actors—pyromaniac peasants, greedy land grabbers, reckless corporate managers—these discourses around ignition belie the fact that subterranean peat fires are only possible in peatlands that have been drained through extensive canal construction. The actors responsible for such practices, and thus for catalyzing landscape-scale fires, are primarily corporations overseeing agribusiness plantations in a chain of command stretching from overseas investors to plantation managers. Whereas fire in political forests was, throughout the twentieth century, largely an act of state resistance by smallholders and Indigenous communities, fire causality and culpability in the contemporary era of forest politics have become less clear as relations between state and non-state actors are increasingly muddled.

The Politics of Indonesian Peatland Burning

The ecological properties in most existing analyses of fire's political dynamics are taken largely at face value: wild flames that are ignited and extinguished on the land in question. Yet Indonesia's peatland-based fires differ from existing empirical examples of fire in political forests in several ways. While the fires discussed in this chapter occur in Indonesia's state-designated forest estate, they are not always, ecologically speaking, forest fires.[3] Unlike fires that burn through forests of North America, Europe, and Australia (see, for example, Kosek 2006; Simon 2017), fires in Indonesian peatlands frequently occur in the absence of trees and without visible orange flames. While rapidly spreading flames can and do burn through vegetation, this constitutes a peatland *surface* fire. Peat fire, meanwhile, burns through buried, decaying vegetation matter—the soil itself—at low temperatures and emits copious white smoke but few visible flames. Furthermore, because tropical peatland is waterlogged under historically normal conditions, peat soil does not burn unless systematically drained over a large hydrological area as it is for agribusiness plantations (Cattau et al. 2016; Page et al. 2009). Burning vegetation, or fire "fuel"—shrubs, dry leaves, felled logs—on the surface of the peatland can ignite dry peat soil, leaving it smoldering for up to several months at a time, until prolonged rainfall raises the groundwater level enough to extinguish fire in the soil (Cochrane 2010). Such fires can spread through the soil relatively undetected and then reignite dry leaves or logs on the peatland surface several hundred meters from the original fire. This secondary surface fire obscures the role of human agency in fire ignition, as fire spreads unpredictably across and *through* the subterranean landscape over prolonged periods of time, making it difficult if not impossible to trace a landscape-scale peatland fire to a single spatial and temporal origin. The timing and extent of a fire's spread across the landscape surface and through the soil is dependent on wind speed and direction, soil moisture content, and the size and moisture content of fire fuels, making biophysical dynamics as significant as socio-state relations in determining the proximate cause of a peat fire.

Political-Legal Territorial Strategies: Blame and Responsibility

Although states have long sought hegemony over forests through practices of enclosure, forest inhabitants and other actors who also lay claim to and enact change in political forests rarely obey state borders. Similarly, few environmental crises remain embedded within the land itself or stay within political lines on maps but spread through various reaches of the atmosphere, watersheds, oceans, and geologic subsoil. In particular, greenhouse gasses and particulate-laden air pollution originate not only in sites of fossil fuel–based industry but in forests and land use–based change. Methods and politics of accounting for airborne pollution have begun to recognize the unique challenge in responding to such transboundary environmental problems (Jones and Hameiri 2015). As international climate change negotiations have demonstrated, tracking and curbing greenhouse gas emissions has highlighted the enduring role of the nation-state as the primary actor—and territorial container—through which responsibility for mitigation is ascribed. But the socio-spatial complexity of such environmental crises is better captured by understanding territory as three-dimensional, in order to see beyond the ways in which forest territorialization is driven by the nation-state.

During successive Southeast Asian fire crises, the term "haze" is used euphemistically, referring to dispersed airborne particulates without a clear origin, obscuring fire's intentionality and agency and thus the politics embedded in the smoke itself (Forsyth 2014; Harwell 2000; Jones and Hameiri 2015). However, haze from Indonesia's peat fires is borne out of forest territorialization strategies and catalyzes geopolitical tensions in response. As voluminous airborne particulates expand into the regional atmosphere and cross into the airspace of other nation-states, the Indonesian state becomes just one of many actors engaging territorial strategies that both precipitate and respond to the fires. This dynamic atmospheric process, as Mahony (2014, 120) argues in relation to climate change, "poses distinct challenges to the territorial logic of the modern nation-state," whose claims of sovereignty rely on imagined and material manifestations of enclosed space. A further challenge comes from the increasing number and diversity of actors who stake territorial claims. In showing how the fires burning through this political forest expand territory beyond the typical reach of the nation-state, I do not, however, suggest that the nation-state has become irrelevant with respect to claims of forest territoriality within its political boundaries. Rather, new collaborations between state, extra-state, and non-state actors have formed to enact territorial strategies that do not pivot solely around the nation-state, nor around marginalized groups' resistance to the state (cf. Kull 2002).

As peat fire smolders, it emits particulate material that transcends spaces traditionally considered by conceptualizations of the political forest. The complexity of this phenomenon, unmoored as it is from the land itself, pushes the spatial and analytical boundaries of territory into the regional atmosphere, crossing into airspace as far away as Thailand and the Philippines, depending on wind direction. Scholars writing on air pollution have pointed out that the effects of such pollutants are highly differential across populations (Whitehead 2009; Véron 2006). Though originating in rural areas, the fire-based air pollution only becomes a "crisis" for the state when the pollution descends upon major urban centers, such as Singapore and Kuala Lumpur, and provincial capitals in Sumatra to a lesser extent. For instance, the areas with some of the highest population densities in the region, Singapore and South Sumatra, are far more likely to be affected by smoke from fires in Sumatra than in Kalimantan. The worst year for fire-driven atmospheric emissions in Southeast Asia (including particulates, ozone, aerosols, and carbon dioxide) since NASA's Earth Observing System satellites began tracking troposphere pollution in the early 2000s was 2015. A large plume of carbon dioxide lingered over the Indian Ocean west of Indonesia through September and October 2015, until monsoon rains arrived in November (Field et al. 2016). Landscape fire occurrence in Southeast Asia correlates strongly with El Niño Southern Oscillation (ENSO) atmospheric cycles, but there is no indication that the arrival of ENSO causes fires directly (Marlier et al. 2012). However, ENSO cycles enable dry conditions and generate atmospheric inversion, which suspends particulate matter over Southeast Asia for longer periods of time, when it would normally be quickly dispersed over the Indian Ocean (Murdiyarso et al. 2004). This indicates that not only does El Niño exacerbate conditions leading to fire but also that inhabitants of Singapore and peninsular Malaysia *experience* poor air quality more than they would during a non–El Niño year. The fires' particulate matter thus fills the regional airspace of Southeast Asia volumetrically, in ways that are dependent on atmospheric dynamics far from the fires themselves. Moreover, the experiences of living with the particulate matter on the ground are vastly uneven across and within communities and countries.

Between August and November 2015, an estimated 2.6 million hectares of rural Indonesian land burned, affecting roughly 45 million people across Southeast Asia and costing Indonesia's national economy US$16 billion as regional transportation slowed (Glauber et al. 2016). International media captured images of urban commuters with face masks as the Singaporean media reported the daily air pollution index alongside grim reminders to curb outdoor activity. On the ground, the Pollution Standards Index (PSI) peaked in Singapore in September 2015 at an all-time local record of 322, above the 300 "hazardous" level set by the World Health Organization (Lin, Wijedasa, and Chisholm 2017). Yet in Palangkaraya, the capital of Central Kalimantan Province in Indonesia, the PSI exceeded 2,200 in October 2015, a nearly unprecedented event globally (Chan 2015). Smallholders across Indonesia lost a season's worth of food crops as the sun was dimmed for weeks by the smoke. Government officials, at a loss to stop the haze crisis once it started, encouraged the elderly and parents with small children to evacuate, despite the financial and logistical impossibility of doing so: even for those who could afford to travel, there were few places with clear air to escape to.

Though Singapore experienced less-severe localized air pollution than Indonesia, the Singaporean government advanced more punitive legislation in response to the haze. Singapore's Transboundary Haze Pollution Act (THPA), passed in 2014, created a protocol for determining culpability for haze that reaches Singapore's airspace.[4] The law allows the Singaporean state to use NASA's fire hotspot maps coupled with meteorological wind maps to make inferences about whether a specific fire occurring on Indonesian land caused air pollution that drifted in the direction of Singapore within twenty-four hours of burning (Leong 2014). This evidence can then be used to arrest and fine anyone associated with the land where the fire occurred when they enter Singapore. The Singaporean Ministry of Environment and Water Resources, which is responsible for enforcing the law, maintains that the law targets both Singaporean and foreign companies and not state officials of any nationality or the Indonesian state itself. But such an "equal opportunity" legal tool extends Singapore's judicial reach to prosecute corporate entities such as Malaysian-held companies operating through Indonesian subsidiaries in addition to companies and plantation managers with ties to or based in Singapore.

Prior to and after implementation of the THPA, Indonesia repeatedly turned down the requests of the Singaporean Ministry of Environment and Water Resources for data on concession ownership and mapped concession boundaries, which were needed to assign fire culpability, leading Singapore to include a section in the THPA that allows for "presumptions" of land ownership and causal linkages to haze. In 2016, Indonesia's vice president, Jusuf Kalla, and the ministry of environment and forestry, Siti Nurbaya Bakar, resisted such requests through claims to the sovereignty of Indonesian law and the protection of its own citizens from prosecution under Singaporean law (Soeriaatmadja 2015). Singapore countered such claims by stating that the law did not seek to prosecute on the basis of citizenship or nationality and therefore was not an issue of sovereignty but only aimed to "deter and prosecute entities that are responsible for transboundary haze pollution in Singapore, whether Singaporean or foreign" (Reuters 2016). Singapore's strategy of leveraging extraterritorial environmental regulation against entities with potential ties to Singaporeans via plantation company investors or subsidiary holdings operating within Indonesia's political forest enables Singapore to disavow the haze pollution in response to its citizens' concerns. It also attempts to punitively respond to activities occurring in another state's political forest by enacting a form of legal territorialization—controlling activity within political forests through legal means—that emerges out of new material dynamics unfolding in volumetric space. Because the THPA is punitive and not preventative, Singapore does little to hinder the *economic* territorialization of Indonesia's forest estate by extra-state and non-state actors, however, even though it is in coordination with the Indonesian state through the issuance of plantation concession licenses. Nevertheless, Singapore's use of the regional atmosphere as a site to advance legal measures against activities undertaken on Indonesian land represents a new frontier of forest control, and a territorialization strategy enacted not merely on terrain but in volumetric airspace.

Despite the increased accessibility of satellite technology that enables a broad range of non-state and extra-state actors to see the geo-locational data of fires, the idiosyncrasies of peat fire's three-dimensional behavior, and thus ambiguity when it comes to attributing fire causality through fire hotspot mapping, enables actors—from powerful corporations to lone villagers clearing land—to evade responsibility for fires. In doing so, state and non-state actors use the ambiguities in peat fire attribution and ensuing responsibility for haze pollution to strategically enact territoriality in Indonesia's burning peatlands. The Indonesian state retains the appearance of rule over its political forests, while non-state actors, particularly plantation companies and their investors, maintain capital-intensive production as a form of enacting forest territoriality through economic means.

This chapter has aimed to expand and sharpen the contemporary instantiation of "political forests" by making visible the power relations increasingly playing out through the subterranean and atmospheric dimensions of forests. In particular, I have drawn on conversations in political geography to suggest that considering the spatial dimensions of forest territory as volumetric better reveals the politics playing out through, and as a consequence of, volatile materiality across biophysical and political scales. Analyzing forest territory volumetrically also reflects the continued exploration of the forest estate for economic gains in multiple countries and a shift toward multinational, extraterritorial governance. While Indonesia continues to resist extraterritorial judicial strategies, it remains unclear whether maintaining claims of state rule within its national borders will endure, as international law becomes increasingly significant through regulation of other transboundary phenomena such as intellectual property, electronic data, and even human migration. The effects of a changing climate are also pushing forest ecosystems into increasingly unpredictable forms: these volatile landscapes invite a rethinking of political forest territoriality precisely *because* they sometimes lack tree cover that typically corresponds to forest territory demarcated by the state. Political forests are furthermore now apt to be materially altered over highly compressed time periods as a result of the scale of foreign capital-driven exploitation of forests and the search for minerals and fossil fuels in forest areas that were previously inaccessible, in part as a result of widely available advanced surveillance technologies.

All of these material changes to contemporary political forests have resulted in a proliferation of non-state and extra-state actors involved in forest territoriality, in ways that bolster, undermine, and/or maintain states' roles in territoriality. While earlier moments in political forest conceptualization relied heavily on the ways in which state institutions—and their adversaries—shaped forest politics, contemporary forests are shaped as much by non-state actors, extraterritorial states, and private/public configurations as they are by states themselves. This does not, however, indicate that the state has retreated from forest territoriality, leaving behind a vacuum for non-state actors, such as corporations, to seize control. States continue to wield control over their national land through non-state and extra-state interlocutors, and through economic territorialization by extra-state and non-state actors that benefits the state through agribusiness expansion. This requires states to evolve strategically, operating across and through three-dimensional, volumetric territory. Instances of volumetric forest spaces, like Indonesia's burning peatlands, reveal the ways in which the state is no longer at the center of forest territory, as other actors strategically control forests by enacting territoriality in airspace and the underground.

Notes

A more comprehensive version of this chapter was previously published as Goldstein, J. E. 2020. "The Volumetric Political Forest: Territory, Satellite Fire Mapping, and Indonesia's Burning Peatland." *Antipode* 52 (4): 1060–1082.

1. In a re-exploration of the political forest concept, Vandergeest and Peluso (2015) point out that forests are made political through their territorial designation as state legislated forest, often despite a lack of tree cover at a given point in time.
2. This chapter draws on interviews and ethnographic fieldwork conducted in 2014 and 2016 in Central Kalimantan Province, Indonesia.
3. Fires occur in standing forests in non-peatland areas throughout Indonesia as well, particularly during drought years.
4. The wording of the Singapore Transboundary Haze Pollution Act 2014 (2020 revised edition) is available at https://sso.agc.gov.sg/Act/THP014.

References

Adey, Peter. 2015. "Air's Affinities: Geopolitics, Chemical Affect and the Force of the Elemental." *Dialogues in Human Geography* 5 (1): 54–75.
Agnew, John. 1994. "The Territorial Trap: The Geographical Assumptions of International Relations Theory." *Review of International Political Economy* 1 (1): 53–80.
Agnew, John. 2005. "Sovereignty Regimes: Territoriality and State Authority in Contemporary World Politics." *Annals of the Association of American Geographers* 95 (2): 437–461.
Anthias, Penelope. 2017. "Ch'ixi Landscapes: Indigeneity and Capitalism in the Bolivian Chaco." *Geoforum* 82:268–275.
Appel, Hannah, Arthur Mason, and Michael Watts. 2015. *Subterranean Estates: Life Worlds of Oil and Gas*. Ithaca, NY: Cornell University Press.

Arshad, Arlina. 2016. "Data Submitted by Indonesia's Asia Pulp and Paper on Land Concessions Incomplete: Peatland Restoration Agency." *Straits Times,* June 15, 2016. https://www.straitstimes.com/asia/se-asia/data-submitted-by-indonesias-asia-pulp-and-paper-on-land-concessions-incomplete.

Bebbington, Anthony, and Jeffrey Bury. 2013. *Subterranean Struggles: New Dynamics of Mining, Oil, and Gas in Latin America.* Austin: University of Texas Press.

Braun, Bruce. 2000. "Producing Vertical Territory: Geology and Governmentality in Late Victorian Canada." *Ecumene* 7 (1): 7–46.

Bridge, Gavin. 2013. "Territory, Now in 3D!" *Political Geography,* no. 34, 55–57.

Brockhaus, M., K. Obidzinski, A. Dermawan, Y. Laumonier, and C. Luttrell. 2012. "An Overview of Forest and Land Allocation Policies in Indonesia: Is the Current Framework Sufficient to Meet the Needs of REDD+?" *Forest Policy and Economics* 18:30–37.

Byrne, Sarah, Andrea J. Nightingale, and Benedikt Korf. 2016. "Making Territory: War, Post-War, and the Entangled Scales of Contested Forest Governance in Mid-Western Nepal." *Development and Change* 47 (6): 1269–1293.

Carlson, K. M., L. M. Curran, G. P. Asner, A. M. Pittman, S. N. Trigg, and J. M. Adeney. 2012. "Carbon Emissions from Forest Conversion by Kalimantan Oil Palm Plantations." *Nature Climate Change* 2 (10): 1–5.

Cattau, M. E., M. E. Harrison, I. Shinyo, S. Tungau, M. Uriarte, and R. DeFries. 2016. "Sources of Anthropogenic Fire Ignitions on the Peat-Swamp Landscape in Kalimantan, Indonesia." *Global Environmental Change* 39:205–219.

Chan, Francis. 2015. "Indonesia Set to Evacuate Kids in Worst Haze Hit Areas." *Straits Times,* October 24, 2015. https://www.straitstimes.com/asia/se-asia/indonesia-set-to-evacuate-kids-in-worst-haze-hit-areas.

Cochrane, Mark A. 2010. *Tropical Fire Ecology.* Berlin: Springer Science & Business Media.

Corson, Catherine. 2011. "Territorialization, Enclosure and Neoliberalism: Non-State Influence in Struggles over Madagascar's Forests." *Journal of Peasant Studies* 38 (4): 703–726. https://doi.org/10.1080/03066150.2011.607696.

Crampton, Jeremy W. 2010. "Cartographic Calculations of Territory." *Progress in Human Geography* 35 (1): 92–103.

Devine, Jennifer A., and Jenny A. Baca. 2020. "Political Forests in an Era of Green Multiculturalism." *Antipode* 52 (4): 911–927.

Dittmer, Jason. 2014. "Geopolitical Assemblages and Complexity." *Progress in Human Geography* 38 (3): 385–401.

Dove, M. R. 1985. "The Agroecological Mythology of the Javanese and the Political Economy of Indonesia." *Indonesia* 39:1–36.

Edwards, Paul N. 2010. *A Vast Machine: Computer Models, Climate Data, and the Politics of Global Warming.* Cambridge, MA: MIT Press.

Elden, Stuart. 2010. "Land, Terrain, Territory." *Progress in Human Geography* 34 (6): 799–817.

Elden, Stuart. 2013. "Secure the Volume: Vertical Geopolitics and the Depth Of Power." *Political Geography* 34:35–51.

Field, Robert D., Guido R. van der Werf, Thierry Fanin, Eric J. Fetzer, Ryan Fuller, Hiren Jethva, Robert Levy, Nathaniel J. Livesey, Ming Luo, Omar Torres, and Helen

M. Worden. 2016. "Indonesian Fire Activity and Smoke Pollution in 2015 Show Persistent Nonlinear Sensitivity to El Niño-Induced Drought." *Proceedings of the National Academy of Sciences* 113 (33): 9204–9209.

Forsyth, Tim. 2014. "Public Concerns about Transboundary Haze: A Comparison of Indonesia, Singapore, Malaysia." *Global Environmental Change* 25:76–86.

Glauber, Ann Jeannette, Sarah Moyer, Magda Adriani, and Iwan Gunawan. 2016. "The Cost of Fire: An Economic Analysis of Indonesia's 2015 Fire Crisis." Indonesia Sustainable Landscapes Knowledge Note no. 1. Jakarta: World Bank. https://openknowledge.worldbank.org/handle/10986/23840.

Global Forest Watch. n.d. "Forest Monitoring Designed for Action." Accessed December 30, 2018. https://www.globalforestwatch.org/.

Goldstein, Jenny E. 2016. "Knowing the Subterranean: Land Grabbing, Oil Palm, and Divergent Expertise in Indonesia's Peat Soil." *Environment and Planning A* 48 (4): 754–770.

Goldstein, Jenny E. 2020. "Lots of Smoke, But Where's the Fire? Contested Causality and Shifting Blame in the Southeast Asian Haze Crisis." In *Disastrous Times: Beyond Environmental Crisis in Asia,* edited by Eli Elinoff and Tyson Vaughn, 102–120. Philadelphia: University of Pennsylvania Press.

Harris, Leila M., and Helen D. Hazen. 2005. "Power of Maps: (Counter) Mapping for Conservation." *ACME: An International E-Journal for Critical Geographies* 4 (1): 99–130. https://acme-journal.org/index.php/acme/article/view/730.

Harwell, Emily. 2000. "Remote Sensibilities: Discourses of Technology and the Making of Indonesia's Natural Disaster." *Development and Change* 31:307–340.

Jones, Alun, and Julian Clark. 2017. "Assembling Geographies of Diplomacy under Neoliberalism." *Transactions of the Institute of British Geographers,* August 20, 2017. https://doi.org/10.1111/tran.12197.

Jones, Lee, and Shahar Hameiri. 2015. *Governing Borderless Threats: Non-Traditional Security and the Politics of State Transformation.* Cambridge: Cambridge University Press.

Kosek, Jake. 2006. *Understories: The Political Life of Forests in Northern New Mexico.* Durham, NC: Duke University Press.

Kull, Christian Arthur. 2002. "Madagascar Aflame: Landscape Burning as Peasant Protest, Resistance, or a Resource Management Tool?" *Political Geography* 21:927–953.

Kull, Christian Arthur. 2004. *Isle of Fire: The Political Ecology of Landscape Burning in Madagascar.* Chicago: University of Chicago Press.

Leong, G. 2014. "Government Proposes Law to Fight Transboundary Haze Pollution." *Business Times,* February 20, 2014. https://www.businesstimes.com.sg/govt-proposes-law-fight-transboundary-haze-pollution.

Li, Tania Murray. 2005. "Beyond 'the State' and Failed Schemes." *American Anthropologist* 107:383–394.

Lin, Yuan, Lahiru S. Wijedasa, and Ryan A. Chisholm. 2017. "Singapore's Willingness to Pay for Mitigation of Transboundary Forest-Fire Haze from Indonesia." *Environmental Research Letters* 12 (2): 024017.

Mahony, Martin. 2014. "The Predictive State: Science, Territory and the Future of the Indian Climate." *Social Studies of Science* 44 (1): 109–133.

Marlier, Miriam E., Ruth S. DeFries, Apostolos Voulgarakis, Patrick L. Kinney, James T. Randerson, Drew T. Shindell, Yang Chen, and Greg Faluvegi. 2012. "El Niño and Health Risks from Landscape Fire Emissions in Southeast Asia." *Nature Climate Change* 3:131–136.

Mathews, Andrew S. 2005. "Power/Knowledge, Power/Ignorance: Forest Fires and the State in Mexico." *Human Ecology* 33 (6): 795–820.

McCarthy, John F., Jacqueline A. C. Vel, and Suraya Afiff. 2012. "Trajectories of Land Acquisition and Enclosure: Development Schemes, Virtual Land Grabs, and Green Acquisitions in Indonesia's Outer Islands." *Geoforum* 39 (2): 521–549.

Monteiro, Marko, and Raoni Rajão. 2017. "Scientists as Citizens and Knowers in the Detection of Deforestation in the Amazon." *Social Studies of Science* 47 (4): 466–484.

Murdiyarso, Daniel, Louis Lebel, A. N. Gintings, S. M. H. Tampubolon, Angelika Heil, and Merillyn Wasson. 2004. "Policy Responses to Complex Environmental Problems: Insights from a Science–Policy Activity on Transboundary Haze from Vegetation Fires in Southeast Asia." *Agriculture, Ecosystems and Environment* 104 (1): 47–56.

Page, S., A. Hoscilo, A. Langner, and K. Tansey. 2009. "Tropical Peatland Fires in Southeast Asia." In *Tropical Fire Ecology*, edited by M. Cochrane, 263–289. New York: Springer.

Peluso, Nancy Lee. 1995. "Whose Woods Are These? Counter-Mapping Forest Territories in Kalimantan, Indonesia." *Antipode* 27 (4): 383–406.

Peluso, Nancy Lee, and Peter Vandergeest. 2001. "Genealogies of the Political Forest and Customary Rights in Indonesia, Malaysia, and Thailand." *Journal of Asian Studies* 60 (3): 761–812.

Rajão, Raoni, and Theodore Vurdubakis. 2013. "On the Pragmatics of Inscription: Detecting Deforestation in the Brazilian Amazon." *Theory, Culture, and Society* 30 (4): 151–177.

Reuters. 2016. "Singapore Calls on Indonesia for Information on Suspected Polluters." June 15, 2016. https://www.reuters.com/article/us-singapore-haze/singapore-calls-on-indonesia-for-information-on-suspected-polluters-idUSKCN0Z11GE.

Rose-Redwood, Reuben. 2012. "With Numbers in Place: Security, Territory, and the Production of Calculable Space." *Annals of the Association of American Geographers* 102 (2): 295–319.

Scott, James C. 1998. *Seeing like a State: How Certain Schemes to Improve the Human Condition Have Failed.* New Haven, CT: Yale University Press.

Showstack, Randy. 2014. "Global Forest Watch Initiatives Provides Opportunity for Worldwide Monitoring." *Eos* 95 (9): 77–78.

Simon, Gregory L. 2017. *Flame and Fortune in the American West: Urban Development, Environmental Change, and the Great Oakland Hills Fire.* Berkeley: University of California Press.

Soeriaatmadja, Wahyudi. 2015. "Ministers Agree to Share Hot Spot Info." *Straits Times*, July 29, 2015. https://www.straitstimes.com/asia/se-asia/ministers-agree-to-share-hot-spot-info.

Steinberg, Philip, and Kimberley Peters. 2015. "Wet Ontologies, Fluid Spaces: Giving Depth to Volume through Oceanic Thinking." *Environment and Planning D: Society and Space* 33 (2): 247–264.

Vandergeest, Peter, and Nancy Lee Peluso. 1995. "Territorialization and State Power in Thailand." *Theory and Society* 24:385–426.

Vandergeest, Peter, and Nancy Lee Peluso. 2015. "Political Forests." In *The International Handbook of Political Ecology,* edited by Raymond L. Bryant, 160–175. Cheltenham: Edward Elgar Publishing.

Véron, René. 2006. "Remaking Urban Environments: The Political Ecology of Air Pollution in Delhi." *Environment and Planning A* 38 (11): 2093–2109.

Weizman, Eyal. 2002. "Introduction to the Politics of Verticality." *Open Democracy: Free Thinking for the World,* April 23, 2002. https://www.opendemocracy.net/ecology-politicsverticality/article_801.jsp.

Whitehead, Mark. 2009. *State, Science and the Skies: Governmentalities of the British Atmosphere.* Malden, MA: Wiley-Blackwell.

Winichakul, Thongchai. 1994. *Siam Mapped: A History of the Geo-Body of a Nation.* Honolulu: University of Hawai'i Press.

CHAPTER 8

The Violence of Transboundary Haze
The Wealth/Health Paradox in Southeast Asia

HELENA VARKKEY, ALISON COPELAND, AND ALYA SHAIFUL

The regional Association of Southeast Asian Nations (ASEAN) defines "haze" as "sufficient smoke, dust, moisture, and vapor suspended in the air to impair visibility" (ASEAN Secretariat 2013). The seasonal haze that has increasingly afflicted several countries in Southeast Asia originates from forest and peatland fires, mainly on Sumatra and Kalimantan in Indonesia. For those living close to the haze-producing fires, this atmospheric crisis is categorically violent. Locals face raging fires and billowing smoke—an apocalyptic atmosphere—and local and central authorities struggle to keep the sick alive in emergency makeshift "oxygen houses" as medical facilities surpass capacity (Antara 2019). These effects can be both severe and long-term: a study on prenatal and infant children living close to the epicenter of the 1997 fires in Indonesia found that these children were on average 3.3 cm shorter than their contemporaries (Tan-Soo and Pattanayak 2019). This violent atmosphere was especially poignant in 2019, when the sky over the burning Jambi Province in central Sumatra was tinted red.

However, the haze is also a trans-scalar crisis. Due to the persistence of fine particles in the atmosphere and the ability of particles to move over large areas, the effects of haze are usually regional in scale (Latif et al. 2018). Haze pollution is transboundary when "its density and extent is so great at the source that it remains at measurable levels after crossing into another country's airspace" (ASEAN Secretariat 2013). One of the earliest records of transboundary haze in the Southeast Asian region was in 1982; this phenomenon has since developed into an almost-annual occurrence in the region (Varkkey 2016). During especially severe episodes, haze can reach up to eight Southeast Asian countries, with the most severely affected usually being Malaysia and Singapore due to their proximity to the fires. For decades, these neighbors have remained in a low-level, protracted state of diplomatic conflict with each other and Indonesia over haze.

This chapter considers the scaled political-ecological conflict unfolding due to the escalating regional haze crisis. Even though the local violence (in the form of fires) takes place primarily in Indonesia, the politics of the conflict unfold across regional atmospheres. In this context, violence is not only seen as the brutal (localized) physical outcome of an escalating conflict but also as a situated and multidimensional process taking many forms across vast areas. Adopting a trans-scalar analytical approach to haze therefore helps us to critically document and understand the diversity of actors, narratives, relationships, processes, and practices involved (Peluso and Watts 2001).

Fires and haze in Indonesia are the violent visible expression of a protracted resource-related conflict. These fires often occur on peatlands that are cleared for lucrative commercial agriculture like palm oil and pulpwood. Apart from local companies, transnational companies, usually based in Malaysia and Singapore, are also involved in these activities. By recognizing the chronic and multi-scalar character of this resource- and capital-linked environmental conflict (Le Billon and Duffy 2018), a political ecology approach exposes the structural dimensions of peat fires. It also reveals the hidden responsibilities that contribute to haze, the most visible expression of its structural drivers. Accordingly, this chapter will draw out a more nuanced understanding of the wider context that drives haze, which involves uneven power relations and deep inequalities between the local and trans-scalar business elites and local and trans-scalar victims of haze (Østby et al. 2011), culminating in multiple manifestations of the wealth/health paradox.

This chapter is divided into four parts. The first section defines haze as an aerial, volumetrically shaped crisis. The second section elaborates on political ecology and geography concepts such as the "silent violence" of policy-induced famines (Watts 1983) and the "slow violence" of pollutants (Nixon 2011). We describe how haze can be considered "distanced violence" affecting the lives and livelihoods of the poor across the region—particularly those in rural settings. The third section describes how atmospheric violence is rooted in grounded resource conflicts over capital accumulation. The final section unpacks how structural inequalities between the victims (the poor across the region) and the drivers (powerful local and transnational economic actors) create an asymmetric conflict that has led to a failure of governance efforts to mitigate transboundary haze. The chapter argues that haze has become a "revelatory crisis" in which the structural contradictions of modes of production are revealed through interruptions to socioeconomic life that cannot be ignored (Watts 2018).

Haze as a Volumetrically Shaped Crisis

The concept of "volumetrics" has been used by scholars (Billé 2017, 2019; Elden 2013; Jackman and Squire 2021; Squire and Dodds 2020) to account for the three-dimensional sphere within which social and environmental phenomena take place.

These scholars are increasingly concerned with realms such as air, oceans, and even outer space and their social, political, and cultural reverberations. Soil, water, air, and ice are not only intermeshed environments; they leak, seep into each other, coalesce, fissure, and clot (Billé 2017). Hence, conversions of forests to plantations, fired fields to carbon, rivers to dams, and hills to mines volumetrically coproduce atmospheric violence that impacts society, politics, and culture in powerful ways (Baird and Barney 2017; Dressler 2017). In paying attention to the materiality of volumetric space and to the complex ways in which human and nonhuman animals, ecology, and climate are entangled in three-dimensional worlds, this "volumetric turn" probes the gap between the cartographic imagination and the lived realities of modern political space (Billé 2017).

As intensifying resource exploitation influences atmospheric space, Southeast Asia regularly experiences "volumetric" moments and periods of violent atmospheres, like dust tsunamis, landscape ruptures, and viral pandemics. Haze-producing fires, which are the focus of this chapter, are such an example of violent, volumetric moments in the Southeast Asian atmosphere. Although large-scale fires in Indonesia have occurred throughout history, their frequency before the 1960s was relatively rare. However, since the early 1960s, these events have occurred more frequently due to increased land-use activities in the country (Latif et al. 2018). The Great Fire of Borneo in 1982—the worst fires the region had seen at that time—destroyed 3.6 million hectares of forestland. However, the fire events of 1997–1998 massively surpassed the scale of the 1982 fires, burning an estimated ten million hectares around Indonesia, destroying forests and bushland, including conservation areas and national parks (Varkkey 2016).

Scientifically, haze can be defined as the existence of dry particles and smoke in the atmosphere when the relative humidity is considered lower than usual (less than 80 percent) and visibility is below 10 km. Haze occurs when a sufficient concentration of aerosols in the atmosphere scatters visible light, resulting in a measurable reduction in visual range. Haze formation is closely related to meteorological conditions, emissions of pollutants, and gas-to-particle conversion (Latif et al. 2018). There are many types of forest fires that can occur in Southeast Asia, and peatland fires constitute only around 40 percent of these fires (ASM Haze Task Force 2018). However, it was found that most of the transboundary haze in the region (conservative estimates suggest 60 percent, while others say up to 90 percent) is attributable to peatland fires (Heil 2016), as the partial combustion from peat fires produces more smoke, and the particles released from these fires take longer to settle.

Peatlands are naturally waterlogged; however, peatland drainage changes the water table in these areas. Drained and degraded peatlands expose semi-decomposed, carbon-rich organic matter, drying out quickly and becoming highly flammable.

The conversion processes of peatlands to agricultural sites often result in a volumetrically coproduced atmospheric violence in the form of peat fire. When peat burns, smoldering combustion (where the soil burns steadily without flames and slowly permeates the soil) will occur. Smoldering combustion can last for long periods, spanning from a week to a month under low temperatures, high moisture content, and low oxygen concentration conditions. Sometimes, peat fires cannot even be detected (a form of silent or invisible violence) when they smolder deep underground and can burn again during the next dry period, which makes them hard to extinguish. The smoldering combustion of peat soils emits high concentrations of gases and fine particulate matter (PM) into ambient air. These fine particles can be transported across borders from their main sources due to regional wind directions (Latif et al. 2018).

The El Niño Southern Oscillation (ENSO) atmospheric event primarily determines how this smoke haze travels across the region. ENSO describes the fluctuations in temperature between the ocean and atmosphere in the east-central Equatorial Pacific. The transport and extension of the haze are modulated by the ENSO variations that control the regional surface circulation and climatic condition. El Niño tends to cause prolonged drought episodes over these regions during the developing phase (June to November). A strong El Niño modulates regional circulation and leads to prolonged dry conditions in Southeast Asia, especially in Sumatra and Kalimantan. During severe El Niño years, drier conditions and stronger winds exacerbate the anthropogenic forest fires and cause widespread distribution of smoke over Southeast Asia (Latif et al. 2018).

In these ways, the volumetric connections between the subterranean peat soils, their terrestrial lives, and their aerial afterlives, occurring within a shared atmospheric container through which matter circulates and affects things, become obvious. This combination of anthropogenic activities and meteorological conditions has resulted in severe transboundary haze episodes in 1997–1998, 2005, 2006, 2009, 2013, 2015, and most recently in 2019. While there is no doubt that those living closest to the haze suffer its most severe effects, this volumetric property of the haze illuminates border processes that deploy beyond the two-dimensional (Billé 2017) to bear upon the lived realities of political space across Southeast Asia.

Asymmetric Impacts across the Region

Toxic haze inflicts "distanced violence" on the lives and livelihoods of the rural poor throughout Southeast Asia. It has differential health impacts on rural and urban populations in Malaysia and beyond (Bridge 2009). To quote (Billé 2017), "as we choke on the [haze], as our lungs struggle to fill with oxygen . . . we are continually confronted with the textured and voluminous presence of this space . . . [haze] blurs the line between earth and liquid as it is driven downwind . . . as a fugitive substance, it is a voluminous entity that surrounds, embraces, confuses, and potentially kills." The gases and fine PM that make up haze are especially toxic and represent a slower form of atmospheric violence. They include inorganic materials such as black carbon, potassium, chloride, sulfate, zinc, and silicon and organic materials such as dicarboxylic acids and dicarboxylate salts, tracer compounds (e.g., methyl halides, K, levoglucosan, and acetone), monosaccharide anhydrides (e.g., asosan, mannosan, and galactosan), and the highly carcinogenic polycyclic aromatic hydrocarbon (ASM Haze Task Force 2018).

These minute particles can be as small as 2.5 μ or less. While microphages can filter out larger particles, these smaller particles can easily penetrate the lung tissue of those exposed to the haze, settle deep in the lungs, and interfere with lung function after prolonged exposure (Amul 2013). They can also enter cells passively and often result in very (slow) violent health complications that can build up gradually and bring more serious effects over time: temporal exposure to high concentrations of PM2.5 increases the risk of myocardial infarction after a few hours in high-risk populations, and PM2.5 was found to have a direct correlation with upper respiratory tract infections during haze periods. PM2.5 has also been found to affect all-cause, cardiopulmonary, and lung cancer mortality (How and Ling 2006).

In 2016, a highly publicized study by scholars from Cambridge, Columbia, and Harvard universities (Koplitz et al. 2016) estimated that the serious regional haze in 2015 resulted in an estimated 100,300 excess deaths across Indonesia, Malaysia, and Singapore—more than double the excess deaths caused by the 2006 event. For Indonesia, the study reported an estimated additional 91,600 deaths, while for Malaysia and Singapore, the figures were around 6,500 and 2,200 respectively. Kiely et al. (2020) presented a more modest estimate of 44,040 deaths regionwide in 2015, with Sumatra in Indonesia accounting for around 38 percent of mortalities, Kalimantan for 23 percent, Malaysia for 18 percent, and Singapore for 4 percent. Hence, even though these populations are "distanced" from the source of the fires and haze, regional atmospheric processes bring the volumetric crisis close to home in the form of sickness, deaths, and interruptions to daily socioeconomic life (Watts 2018).

Both the urban and rural populations of source and neighboring countries are exposed to this slow and silent violence. However, while the urban, upper, and middle class of society can often educate themselves independently on the health risks of haze, afford medical treatment, or instigate preventive measures themselves, the more at-risk populations are the poor in these countries (Varkkey and Copeland 2020). As an illustration of the wealth/health gap in the haze context, N95 masks, which can filter out at least 95 percent of airborne particles larger than 0.3μ, including PM2.5, are prohibitively more expensive than regular surgical masks, which reduces the ability of the poor to protect themselves against haze effectively. In Indonesia, in contrast to the largely rural populations of Sumatra and Kalimantan, the urban populations of Jakarta and other big cities on Java are upwind from the fires, and thus virtually never experience haze. In Malaysia, in general, the rural poor have higher mortality and morbidity rates across age groups (Mariapun, Hairi, and Ng 2016). For haze, the elderly (over sixty-five years) and the very young are particularly vulnerable health-wise (Nazeer and Furuoka 2017); this is especially so in rural populations.

The generally lower levels of education in rural populations also affect their ability to protect themselves against the haze. A study by Vethanayagam and How (2017) in the Klang Valley in Greater Kuala Lumpur found that 70 percent of urban residents have an average level of knowledge about the health impacts of haze, and 21.5 percent have high knowledge. In contrast, 50 percent of rural residents have average knowledge, and 33 percent have low knowledge about haze. This has translated directly to preventative health practices: 88 percent of rural residents engage in poor or high-risk health practices during haze episodes, compared to 74.5 percent of urban residents. This knowledge deficit may also be linked to the limited internet coverage in rural areas (Ab Aziz and Mohamad Ali 2015) and the low number of rural health clinics (Thomas, Beh, and Nordin 2011), which narrows the reach of government health advisories.

More importantly, rural infrastructure, lifestyles, and livelihoods in Malaysia, especially those of the poor, are not conducive to protective and preventative health practices. In urban areas, especially among the upper and middle class, homes are usually equipped with airtight windows, air conditioning, and sometimes even air purifiers. However, in rural areas, most homes are made of wood, with traditional louvre window ventilation systems designed to allow a continuous flow of air (Hassan et al. 2020). This reduces the effectiveness of haze-related school closures for rural children living in such homes. Furthermore, jobs in rural areas are typically outdoors, manual, and agriculture based, with regular harvesting periods (compared to upper- and middle-class urban workers, who have access to air-conditioned offices and mandated days off). This means that rural populations have greater levels of exposure to haze pollution and may be unable to afford the suspension of these activities during haze episodes. Indeed, even within these urban/rural cleavages, the urban poor face heightened risk due to their unique work and living arrangements. However, the rural wealthy should have the resources to better insulate themselves from the worst effects of haze. Hence, studies confirm that even though they are some distance away from where the conflict (fire) originates, neighboring populations, such as in Malaysia, especially the rural poor, are not buffered from the violent processes unfolding at this broader scale. The social and economic structures that are outside of the control of rural populations, like the nature of work and lifestyle, the design of houses, and access to utilities and public services, result in situations where the rural poor of neighboring countries are subjected to "distanced" violence that asymmetrically and disproportionately affects their health and wellbeing, more so than those in wealthier, urban areas. Therefore, while violence in the context of haze occurs both in urban and rural areas, the rural poor are at heightened risk. This highlights environmental justice issues where environmental risk allocation and associated economic and health impacts disproportionately affect these marginalized communities and segments of society (Bullard 1994).

Burdens of Blame Concealing Resource Conflicts

The haze crisis has heightened urban-rural conflict and animosity, whereby state agencies, corporations, and—by extension (and influence)—urban dwellers often adopt discourses that blame environmental crises like the haze on the rural poor (Montefrio and Dressler 2016). For many years, fires and haze in Indonesia and elsewhere in the region have been blamed on poor rural farmers who use fire as part of their swidden agricultural practices. These swidden farmers, who have used traditional methods to clear and burn forests for centuries, are now blamed for "escape fires." However, while swidden agriculture may contribute marginally to forest fires, these traditional practices usually do not occur on peatlands and thus do not significantly contribute to haze (Varkkey 2016). Peat soil is acidic, low in inorganic ions and oxygen, high in carbon, and has high concentrations of humic acid (Phillips 1998). These are very infertile conditions that are unsuitable for most swidden farming crops.

The more serious cause of haze-producing fires is rooted in rapid commercial land-use change in the region's peatlands. Beginning in the 1960s, land pressure for agriculture began to drive large-scale development of Indonesian peatlands. The burgeoning need for land brought about by the oil palm boom in countries like Indonesia has encouraged the conversion of peatlands to plantations.

Despite their unsuitability for other crops, peatlands are quite suitable for the growth of oil palm and certain types of pulpwood when deeply drained. Research has shown that oil palm has a high tolerance for areas with fluctuating water tables, and oil palm grown on reclaimed peat soil has a particularly high fruit production. However, draining and preparation operations generate conditions that make peat more combustible and increase fire risk (Basiron 2007). Once valuable timber is removed to be sold, the peat is usually burned to remove any remaining vegetation

(Stone 2007), either by the company directly or by subcontractors. Burning peatlands is a fast way to clear unwanted weeds and grass in preparation for planting and reduces the risk of pests. Furthermore, using machinery is problematic and expensive on the soft peatlands, with the soggy soil hindering the use of bulldozers. The ash produced from burning can also replace expensive alkaline fertilizer, which is otherwise required to increase the acidity of peatlands to levels suited to oil palm growth (Zakaria, Thiele, and Khaimur 2007).

While these constraints make oil palm development on peat soil more expensive (with setting-up costs on peatlands almost double those on regular mineral soil), higher oil palm trading prices have made this economically viable (Varkkey 2016). Even for the companies that do not deliberately use fire and practice good water management on their concession, their activities can still generate fires in other parts of the dome. Peat scientists have found that the peat dome, which forms a single hydrological unit, is highly sensitive to disturbances in any part of the dome (Hooijer et al. 2010). Drainage in one part of the dome will also dry out peat in other areas (Parish et al. 2008). Drastic land conversion further degrades the natural landscape, so that future hotspots and accidental fires are liable to occur again and are likely to be more severe (Raman et al. 2008).

In Indonesia, peatlands are protected against clearance and degradation through a web of local and national laws and regulations, including an ongoing moratorium for permits on all Indonesian peatlands (Astuti, Varkkey, and Tan 2019). However, the persisting trend in the Indonesian business ecosystem of mutually reinforcing patron-client relationships between administrative and political elites ("patrons") and business elites ("clients"), weak state capacity, and a lack of bureaucratic oversight enables influential actors in the sector to obtain rights to these environmentally sensitive lands not normally released for conversion. As a result, an estimated 25 percent of all palm oil plantations in Indonesia are on peatlands (Silvius and Kaat 2010). These symbiotic relationships are further called upon when fires occur. Patrons in the government will carry out their responsibilities to their clients by shielding them against severe administrative or legal fallout from the fires. Because of this, powerful plantation companies with good patronage ties have no reason to fear punishment, which fosters a culture of impunity among well-connected elites in the sector (Varkkey 2016). This further highlights the unequal nature of haze-induced violence, where well-connected elites are able to shield themselves from the legal ramifications of their actions while the general public is left to suffer the violent consequences.

While Indonesian interests generally make up the bulk of these commercial plantations, a significant number of these concessionaires have been found to have foreign, especially Malaysian and, to a lesser extent, Singaporean, linkages. When the government of Indonesia opened up the oil palm sector to foreign investors during the early 1990s (McCarthy and Cramb 2009), governments in both the home country and host country were highly involved in facilitating the regionalization of these plantation companies. There has been considerable evidence of Malaysian and Singaporean companies, alongside Indonesian ones, being complicit in directly or indirectly causing peat fires through their commercial agricultural activities. For example, the Singaporean company Wilmar was the focus of several fire-related lawsuits in 2006 and 2007 (Varkkey 2016), and Malaysian companies were listed among the firms responsible for haze-producing fires released by the Indonesian government in 2019 (*The Star* 2019). However, patronage relations cultivated by these companies, both in Indonesia and the home country, have similarly also shielded them from any serious legal consequences (Varkkey 2016).

In all these ways, it becomes clear how the transboundary haze is a regional, multi-scalar resource and capital-linked environmental conflict. Hence, the atmospheric violence inflicted upon regional populations becomes a site-specific phenomenon rooted in the peatlands in Indonesia and embedded in localized histories and social relations, yet connected to larger material transformation processes and power relations across the region (Peluso and Watts 2001). For instance, authorities, corporations, and speculators adopted the narrative that smallholder farmers in Sumatra and Kalimantan were using "outdated" slash-and-burn techniques and mismanaging their own properties (Goldstein 2016) as a justification for the corporate acquisition of these lands, wherein they would ostensibly be better managed. The burden of blame placed upon swidden farmers can thus be seen as an effort to further conceal the deteriorating conditions and relations of production by diverting attention to the peripheral branches of the crisis itself (swidden farming fires) rather than its structural roots (corporate resource and capital accumulation) (Soloway 1994).

Fetishization processes, including the imaginative aspects of resource production and consumption, further affect power relations, conflicts, and associated forms of violence (Cavanagh and Benjaminsen 2014). Palm oil is the world's most widely consumed vegetable oil, and Indonesia and Malaysia are its first- and second-largest producers, respectively. In Indonesia and Malaysia, palm oil remains ideologically and functionally linked to national progress, poverty alleviation, and modernization. It is known as the "golden crop" and has been the subject of government-sponsored public relations campaigns like "Good Palm Oil" ("Sawit Baik") in Indonesia and "Palm Oil—God's Gift" ("Sawit Anugerah Tuhan") in Malaysia. It features beside Malaysia's father of independence, Tunku Abdul Rahman, on the latest RM50 note and the 1993 issue of the Indonesian IDR1,000 coin (O'Reilly et al. 2020). This fetishization process has increased the power differential between corporate plantations and the trans-scalar victims of haze and underlined the incompatible goals (wealth/health) of the two parties. Hence, the conflict becomes even more asymmetrical, where one party (corporate plantations) is not only more powerful and more well resourced (Ramsbotham, 2016), but also more influential and well-regarded than local farmers by the government and the public at large.

Neoliberal Challenges in Haze Governance

The remoteness of the locations in which this resource conflict is taking place has meant that the structural roots of this crisis, involving unsustainable land-use change driven by capital accumulation, would not have been widely recognized beyond the ground level in Indonesia if not for the visibly multi-scalar expression of its volumetric effects through haze traveling across borders. Indeed, as the haze continues to drastically disrupt socioeconomic life across the region, civil society pressure has slowly built up. The public and the media, especially in Malaysia and Singapore, have become increasingly vocal about their dissatisfaction at having to suffer haze year after year and have begun to demand action from their governments (Varkkey 2016). This has escalated the conflict beyond the national scale of rural versus urban populations, to that between neighboring sovereign states.

Spurred on by their citizens, episodes of finger-pointing have ensued between the "source" (Indonesia) and "victim" (Malaysia and Singapore) countries. Arguments have ranged from Malaysia and Singapore being "ungrateful" for the clean air that Indonesia's forests had provided them all year round outside the haze season to accusations that Malaysian and Singaporean companies were equally (or even more) to blame for the fires than Indonesian companies, which were quickly denied by both Malaysia and Singapore (Varkkey 2016). These arguments are repeatedly raised every time the haze extends to the region and have been the basis for the long-running, low-level diplomatic conflict between Malaysia, Singapore, and Indonesia. Eventually, this conflict became so protracted that member countries agreed to elevate haze as a regional issue at the ASEAN following the particularly severe 1997–1998 fire and haze season.

Environmental peace building, through things like cooperative environmental agreements, can have a positive impact on the relationship between conflicting states, where the environment can be a source of cooperation, conflict reduction, and the creation of peace (Ide 2018). It is anchored in the idea that areas of common environmental interest and the need for cooperation over transboundary environmental resources can foster peaceful relationships between neighboring states that previously engaged in (low- or high-level) conflict (Barquet, Lujala, and Rød 2014; Conca and Wallace 2013; Krampe 2017). However, environmental conflicts can also produce new forms of conflict and environmental struggles because of their neoliberal underpinnings (Le Billon and Duffy 2018). Indeed, this has been the case over transboundary haze.

Agriculture, and especially the palm oil sector, is critical for the economies of key ASEAN member states. While members agreed to cooperate to mitigate haze at the ASEAN level, the root causes of the crisis were not recognized. First, the term "haze" itself is euphemistic and thus inappropriate for describing such a human-made problem. Semantically, the term normally denotes a naturally occurring climatic condition in which visibility is affected (for example, "heat haze"), hence it downplays both the severity and the prolonged health impacts of the environmental crisis. The political and strategic choices of terms for mainstream representations of conflicts have been identified in the literature before, for example, using terms such as "riots" instead of "demonstrations" in an attempt to criminalize aggrieved victims of inequalities as "troublemakers" and delegitimize their struggles (Zalik 2011).

Secondly, in the spirit of the "ASEAN Way" (a set of agreed behavioral and procedural norms including consensus, sovereignty and noninterference, sensitivity and politeness, nonconfrontational and nonlegalistic procedures), issues that were deemed too "sensitive" were not discussed at the ASEAN level. Even though there was an unspoken understanding that commercial plantation burning was the primary source of haze, the issue of illegal burning by local and foreign plantation companies was never raised during discussions leading up to the landmark, legally binding ASEAN Agreement on Transboundary Haze Pollution (AATHP). This agreement was signed by member states on June 10, 2002, in Kuala Lumpur, Malaysia (ASEAN Secretariat 2002). The effects of the close patronage relationship between the government and (local and regional) business elites in the sector extended to the ASEAN level, where member states strategically used the ASEAN Way to favor arrangements that ensure domestic and regional political-economic stability and market access to these natural resources rather than incentivizing effective regional environmental conservation (Varkkey 2016). Hence, even at the ASEAN level, neoliberal underpinnings have trumped the collective interests of the ASEAN people—both rural and urban.

As a result, the AATHP was a highly watered-down document that continued to protect national economic interests, preserve state sovereignty, and deflect responsibility for seasonal peatland haze. Thus the treaty, although technically legally binding, was vague and lacking in various hard-law instruments such as strong dispute resolution and enforcement mechanisms. Important provisions, including those for developing preventive measures (both legislative and administrative) and national emergency response, were left to member parties to interpret and apply. Furthermore, no provision was made for disputes to be settled by recourse to international courts or arbitration tribunals, unlike other relevant treaty regimes. As a result, the AATHP was useful in generating a massive amount of information on the haze but not much in terms of effective implementation of haze mitigation activities (Varkkey 2016). While haze continues to remain on the ASEAN agenda, the implementation of the AATHP is still stuck on basic processes, such as the establishment of an ASEAN Coordinating Centre for Transboundary Haze Pollution Control. Likewise, more recent arrangements within the regional haze framework have been met with low levels of buy-in.

Far from being a source of conflict reduction, ASEAN's weak attempts to govern and mitigate this trans-scalar, violent atmospheric conflict have only succeeded in further politicizing it (Martinez-Alier 2009). As per its neoliberal motivations, ASEAN has continued to prioritize (elite) development over environmental matters at the regional level while providing a visible platform for rhetoric and policy pronouncements to appease civil society, with little emphasis on effective haze mitigation. Although the haze has exposed the trans-scalar wealth/health contradictions in the modes of palm oil production in Indonesia's peatlands, the ASEAN governance process has further reinforced old structural inequalities and asymmetries between those ultimately responsible for and those impacted by this environmental crisis.

This chapter has described how fires and haze in Indonesia are the violent visible expression of an essentially resource-related trans-scalar conflict. Peatlands, which are usually nonflammable, become violently flammable through the process of degrading land-use change for lucrative commercial agriculture. Even at the local level, these peatlands, which are supposed to be protected through a web of laws and regulations, fall victim to opaque policies enabled by patrons engaged in symbiotic relationships with elite business owners. In this way, local and regional business elites are rarely held accountable for fires directly or indirectly caused by their capital and resource accumulation. The enabling structural dimensions of these weak regulatory systems and hidden responsibilities of patronage networks in the Indonesian peatlands have been, over the years, more obviously revealed and exposed as a form of slow and silent violence not only through localized fires but through transboundary haze.

Failed attempts at governing this trans-scalar conflict have trickled upward to the regional (ASEAN) level, where even though member states acknowledged that the haze was a legitimate area of common environmental interests, their material interests in addressing it through ASEAN arose from the importance of domestic economic progress—to maintain the availability of and access to natural resources, in this case, land for oil palm. Motivated by the close relationships between political elites and prominent plantation owners in the region, ASEAN member states were encouraged to ensure outcomes that privileged the interests of these economic actors and allies. To do this, member states leveraged the "ASEAN Way" principles. This has resulted in highly watered-down plans and documents that continue to protect national economic interests, preserve state sovereignty, and deflect responsibility on the haze issue. This is the regional manifestation of patronage, where governments are obligated to disregard the long-term health interests of their citizens, focusing instead on helping their clients maximize profitability in the oil palm plantation sector.

Suboptimal environmental governance outcomes like this are often rooted in a range of socio-material paradoxes: value/intensity, wealth/poverty, and intimacy/ignorance that comprise the social and drive the material basis of violent atmospheres (Bridge 2009). This chapter has highlighted the wealth/health paradox in two ways: Firstly, it highlights how affluent and typically urban communities across the region can better shield themselves from the worst effects of transboundary haze, as compared to poorer, rural communities due to socioeconomic structures that are beyond their control. Secondly, it shows how (wealthier) business elites play a significant role in the persistence of transboundary haze but are indemnified by their political patrons, who have historically directed blame at local farmers and other marginalized groups. In all these ways, haze manifests itself as a slow and unequal form of violence: wealthier, more well-connected individuals are able to shield themselves not only from the legal ramifications of their actions but also from the physical effects of the violent fire and haze by living outside the haze zone (in Jakarta), having better access to protective measures (masks, medical care), and/or being able to afford to flee for fresher pastures when necessary. On the other hand, poorer groups, particularly those in rural areas, are both physically positioned more closely to the violent fires and less able to protect themselves effectively against them.

The term "conflict" is broadly understood as a contested incompatibility: the interaction of parties that perceive their goals as incompatible and engage with each other through persuasion, arbitration, or coercion (Folger, Poole, and Stutman 1996). The asymmetrical nature of the relations between powerful, well-resourced, influential, and well-regarded elites and the marginalized rural poor highlights the incompatibility of the interests of these groups: one continues to accumulate (capital and resource) wealth, while the other slowly but surely faces increasingly violent risks to their health. Through civil society across the region, marginalized groups have pushed their governments to engage with the more influential party on their behalf. However, this chapter demonstrates how structural dimensions—and the mutual benefits—of the relationship between governments and business elites can hinder constructive engagement. For change to occur, what is necessary is the widespread transformation of a range of highly unequal power relationships upon which the present system is based (Bryant and Bailey 1997; Holifield 2015).

Note

This chapter was developed with the financial support of a Newton Fund Impact Scheme (NFIS) and Malaysian Industry-Government Group for High Technology (MIGHT) grant IF021–2020 on "Using Public Engagement to Enhance the Effectiveness of Local Health Advisories for Environmental Pollution and Transboundary Haze."

References

Ab Aziz, Nur Fadilah, and Noor Azian Mohamad Ali. 2015. "4G Coverage in Malaysia." *International Journal of Science and Research* 4 (1): 1817–1823.

Amul, Gayle G. 2013. "Haze and Air Pollution: The Potential Health Crisis." *RSIS Commentaries*, 67906982.

Antara. 2019. "Pontianak sediakan tujuh rumah oksigen antisipasi warga terpapar-asap" [Pontianak has provided seven oxygen houses to prevent residents from being exposed to smoke]. September 16, 2019. https://www.antaranews.com/berita/1065734/pontianak-sediakan-tujuh-rumah-oksigen-antisipasi-warga-terpapar-asap.

ASEAN Secretariat. 2002. "ASEAN Agreement on Transboundary Haze Pollution." https://asean.org/wp-content/uploads/2021/01/ASEANAgreementonTransboundaryHazePollution-1.pdf.

ASEAN Secretariat. 2013. "Information on Fire and Haze." Haze Action Online, June 3, 2013. http://haze.asean.org/about-us/information-on-fire-and-haze/.

ASM Haze Task Force. 2018. *ASM Local and Trasnbundary Haze Report*. Edited by Helena Varkkey. Kuala Lumpur: Academy of Sciences Malaysia.

Astuti, Rini, Helena Varkkey, and Zu Dienle Tan. 2019. "Three Things Jokowi Could Do Better to Stop Forest Fires and Haze in Indonesia." *The Conversation*, August 2, 2019. https://theconversation.com/three-things-jokowi-could-do-better-to-stop-forest-fires-and-haze-in-indonesia-120497.

Atteridge, Aaron, May Thazin Aung, and Agus Nugroho. 2018. *Contemporary Coal Dynamics in Indonesia*. Stockholm: Stockholm Environment Institute. https://www.sei.org/wp-content/uploads/2018/06/contemporary-coal-dynamics-in-indonesia.pdf.

Baird, Ian. G., and Keith Barney. 2017. "The Political Ecology of Cross-Sectoral Cumulative Impacts: Modern Landscapes, Large Hydropower Dams and Industrial Tree Plantations in Laos and Cambodia." *Journal of Peasant Studies* 44 (4): 769–795.

Barquet, Karina, Päivi Lujala, and Jan Ketil Rød. 2014. "Transboundary Conservation and Militarized Interstate Disputes. *Political Geography* 42:1–11. https://doi.org/10.1016/j.polgeo.2014.05.003.

Basiron, Yusof. 2007. "Palm Oil Production through Sustainable Plantations." *European Journal of Lipid Science and Technology* 109:289–295.

Beban, Alice, Laura Schoenberger, and Vanessa Lamb. 2020. "Pockets of Liberal Media in Authoritarian Regimes: What the Crackdown on Emancipatory Spaces Means for Rural Social Movements in Cambodia." *Journal of Peasant Studies* 47 (1): 95–115. https://doi.org/10.1080/03066150.2019.1672664.

Bersihkan Indonesia. 2020. "Omnibus Law: Oligarch's Legal Holy Book; Mining Businessmen and Dirty Energy behind Omnibus Law: Their Roles, Conflicts of Interests, and Track Record." Bersihkan Indonesia and Fraksi Rakyat Indonesia. https://drive.google.com/file/u/0/d/1zpBmvXcemwQj5kyKE0GWyBg1g3qg-Atz/view.

Billé, Franck. 2017. "Introduction: Speaking Volumes." Theorizing the Contemporary, *Fieldsights*, October 24, 2017. https://culanth.org/fieldsights/introduction-speaking-volumes.

Billé, Franck. 2019. "Volumetric Sovereignty." *Environment and Planning D: Society and Space*, March 3, 2019. https://www.societyandspace.org/forums/volumetric-sovereignty.

Bridge, Gavin. 2009. "Material Worlds: Natural Resources, Resource Geography and the Material Economy." *Geography Compass* 3 (3): 1217–1244.

Bryant, Raymond L., and Sinéad Bailey. 1997. *Third World Political Ecology*. London: Routledge.

Bullard, Robert D., ed. 1994. *Unequal Protection: Environmental Justice and Communities of Color*. San Francisco: Sierra Club Books.

Cavanagh, Connor, and Tor A. Benjaminsen. 2014. "Virtual Nature, Violent Accumulation: The 'Spectacular Failure' of Carbon Offsetting at a Ugandan National Park." *Geoforum* 56:55–65. https://doi.org/10.1016/j.geoforum.2014.06.013.

Conca, Ken, and Jennifer Wallace. 2013. "Environment and Peacebuilding in War-Torn Societies: Lessons from the UN Environment Programme's Experience with Post-Conflict Assessment." In *Assessing and Restoring Natural Resources in Post-Conflict Peacebuilding*, edited by David Jensen and Stephen Lonergan, 63–84. London: Routledge.

Dressler, Wolfram H. 2017. "Contesting Moral Capital in the Economy of Expectations of an Extractive Frontier." *Annals of the American Association of Geographers* 107 (3): 647–665. https://doi.org/10.1080/24694452.2016.1261684.

Elden, Stuart. 2013. "Secure the Volume: Vertical Geopolitics and the Depth of Power." *Political Geography* 34:35–51.

Folger, Joseph P., Marshall Scott Poole, and Randall K. Stutman. 1996. *Working through Conflict: Strategies for Relationships, Groups, and Organizations*. New York: Routledge.

Goldstein, Jenny E. 2016. "Knowing the Subterranean: Land Grabbing, Oil Palm, and Divergent Expertise in Indonesia's Peat Soil." *Environment and Planning A* 48 (4): 754–770.

Graham, Stephen, and Lucy Hewitt. 2013. "Getting off the Ground: On the Politics of Urban Verticality." *Progress in Human Geography* 37 (1): 72–92. https://doi.org/10.1177/0309132512443147.

Hassan, Jalees, Rosli Mohamad zin, Muhd. Zaim Abd Majid, Saeed Balubaid, and Mohd Rosli Hainin. 2014. "Building Energy Consumption in Malaysia: An Overview." *Jurnal Teknologi* 70 (7): 33–38.

Heil, Angelika. 2007. "Indonesian Forest and Peat Fires: Emissions, Air Quality, and Human Health." (January). Max-Plank Institute for Meteorology. Reports on Earth System Science.

Holifield, Ryan. 2015. "Environmental Justice and Political Ecology." In *The Routledge Handbook of Political Ecology*, edited by Tom Perreault, Gavin Bridge, and James McCarthy, 585–597. London: Routledge.

Hooijer, Aljosja, Susan Page, J. Canadell, Marcel Silvius, Jaap Kwadijk, H. Wösten, and Jyrk Jauhiainen. 2010. "Current and Future CO_2 Emissions from Drained Peatlands in Southeast Asia." *Biogeosciences* 7 (5): 1505–1514. https://doi.org/10.5194/bg-7-1505-2010.

How, Chooi Yong, and Yong Ee Ling. 2006. "The Influence of PM 2.5 and PM 10 on Air Pollution Index (API)." Faculty of Civil Engineering, Universiti Teknologi Malaysia, Kuala Lumpur. https://civil.utm.my/wp-content/uploads/2016/12/The-Influence-of-PM2.5-and-PM10-on-Air-Pollution-Index-API.pdf.

Humphreys Bebbington, Denise, and Celina Grisi Huber. 2017. "Political Settlements, Natural Resource Extraction, and Inclusion in Bolivia." Effective States and Inclusive Development Working Paper no. 77. University of Manchester. https://justice-project.org/wp-content/uploads/2017/08/esid_wp_77_humphreys_bebbington_grisi_huber.pdf.

Ide, Tobias. 2018. "Does Environmental Peacemaking between States Work? Insights on Cooperative Environmental Agreements and Reconciliation in International Rivalries." *Journal of Peace Research* 55 (3): 351–365. https://doi.org/10.1177/0022343317750216.

Jackman, Anna, and Rachael Squire. 2021. "Forging Volumetric Methods." *Area* 53 (3): 492–500. https://doi.org/10.1111/area.12712.

Kiely, Laura, Dominick V. Spracklen, Christine Wiedinmyer, Luke Conibear, Carly L. Reddington, Stephen R. Arnold, Christoph Knote, Md Firoz Khan, Mohd Talib Latif, Lailan Syaufina, and Hari A. Adrianto. 2020. "Air Quality and Health Impacts of Vegetation and Peat Fires in Equatorial Asia during 2004–2015." *Environmental Research Letters* 15 (9): 094054. https://doi.org/10.1088/1748-9326/ab9a6c.

Koplitz, Shannon N., Loretta J. Mickley, Miriam E. Marlier, Jonathan J. Buonocore, Patrick S. Kim, Tianjia Liu, Melissa P. Sulprizio, Ruth S. DeFries, Daniel J. Jacob, Joel Schwartz, Montira Pongsiri, and Samuel S. Myers. 2016. "Public Health Impacts of the Severe Haze in Equatorial Asia in September–October 2015: Demonstration of a New Framework for Informing Fire Management Strategies to Reduce Downwind Smoke Exposure." *Environmental Research Letters* 11 (9): 094023. https://doi.org/10.1088/1748-9326/11/9/094023.

Krampe, Florian. 2017. "Towards a Sustainable Peace: A New Research Agenda for Post-Conflict Natural Resource Management." *Global Environmental Politics* 14 (4): 1–4. https://doi.org/10.1162/GLEP.

Latif, Mohd Talib, Murnira Othman, Nurfathehah Idris, Liew Juneng, Ahmad Makmom Abdullah, Wan Portia Hamzah, Md Firoz Khan, Nik Meriam Nik Sulaiman, Jegalakshimi Jewaratnam, Nasrin Aghamohammadi, Mazrura Sahani, Chung Jing Xiang, Fatimah Ahamad, Norhaniza Amil, Mashitah Darus, Helena Varkkey, Fredolin Tangang, and Abu Bakar Jaafar. 2018. "Impact of Regional Haze towards Air Quality in Malaysia: A Review." *Atmospheric Environment* 177 (January): 28–44. https://doi.org/10.1016/j.atmosenv.2018.01.002.

Le Billon, Philippe, and Rosaleen V. Duffy. 2018. "Conflict Ecologies: Connecting Political Ecology and Peace and Conflict Studies." *Journal of Political Ecology* 25 (1): 239–260.

Mariapun, Jeevitha Mariapun, Noran N. Hairi, and Chiu-Wan Ng. 2016. "Are the Poor Dying Younger in Malaysia? An Examination of the Socioeconomic Gradient in Mortality." *PLoS ONE* 1334:1–12. https://doi.org/10.1371/journal.pone.0158685.

Martinez-Alier, Joan. 2009. "Social Metabolism, Ecological Distribution Conflicts, and Languages of Valuation." *Capitalism, Nature, Socialism* 20 (1): 58–87. https://doi.org/10.1080/10455750902727378.

McCarthy, John F., and Rob A. Cramb. 2009. "Policy Narratives, Landholder Engagement, and Oil Palm Expansion on the Malaysian and Indonesian Frontiers." *Geographical Journal* 175 (2): 112–123. https://doi.org/10.1111/j.1475-4959.2009.00322.x.

Montefrio, Marvin Joseph F., and Wolfram H. Dressler. 2016. "The Green Economy and Constructions of the 'Idle' and 'Unproductive' Uplands in the Philippines." *World Development* 79:114–126.

Nazeer, Nazia, and Fumitaka Furuoka. 2017. "Overview of ASEAN Environment, Transboundary Haze Pollution Agreement." *International Journal of Asia Pacific Studies* 13 (1): 73–94.

Nixon, Rob. 2011. *Slow Violence and the Environmentalism of the Poor*. Cambridge, MA: Harvard University Press.

O'Reilly, Patrick, Helena Varkkey, Shofwan Al Banna Choiruzzad, and Rory Padfield. 2020. "The Value(s) of Palm Oil." *Fulcrum: Analysis on Southeast Asia*, December 24, 2020. https://fulcrum.sg/the-values-of-palm-oil/.

Østby, Gudrun, Henrik Urdal, Mohammad Zulfan Tadjoeddin, S. Mansoob Murshed, and Håvard Strand. 2011. "Population Pressure, Horizontal Inequality and Political Violence: A Disaggregated Study of Indonesian Provinces, 1990–2003." *Journal of Development Studies* 47 (3): 377–398. https://doi.org/10.1080/00220388.2010.506911.

Parish, F., A. Sirin, D. Charman, H. Joosten, T. Minayeva, M. Silvius, and L. Stringer. 2008. "Assessment on Peatlands, Biodiversity and Climate Change: Main Report." Global Environment Centre, Kuala Lumpur, and Wetlands International, Wageningen.

Peluso, Nancy Lee, and Michael Watts, eds. 2001. *Violent Environments*. Ithaca, NY: Cornell University Press.

Phillips, Victor D. 1998. "Peatswamp Ecology and Sustainable Development in Borneo." *Biodiversity and Conservation* 7 (5): 651–671. https://doi.org/10.1023/A:1008808519096.

Raman, Meenakshi, Anne Van Schaik, Kenneth Richter, and Paul De Clerck. 2008. "Malaysian Palm Oil: Green Gold or Green Wash? A Commentary on the Sustainability Claims of Malaysia's Palm Oil Lobby, with a Special Focus on the State of Sarawak." Friends of the Earth International, no. 114 (October). https://www.foei.org/wp-content/uploads/2020/12/04-foei-sarawak-8p-lr.pdf.

Ramsbotham, Oliver, Tom Woodhouse, and Hugh Miall. 2016. *Contemporary Conflict Resolution*. 4th ed. Cambridge: Polity Press.

Silvius, Marcel, and Alex Kaat. 2010. *Peat Swamp Forests and Palm Oil*. Slide Player. https://slideplayer.com/slide/3400752/.

Soloway, Jacqueline S. 1994. "Drought as a Revelatory Crisis: An Exploration of Shifting Entitlements and Hierarchies in the Kalahari, Botswana." *Development and Change* 25 (3): 471–495.

Squire, Rachael, and Klaus Dodds. 2020. "Introduction to the Special Issue: Subterranean Geopolitics." *Geopolitics* 25 (1): 4–16. https://doi.org/10.1080/14650045.2019.1609453.

The Star. 2019. "Indonesia Claims Four Malaysian Firms behind Open Burning." *The Star,* September 14, 2019. https://www.thestar.com.my/news/nation/2019/09/14/indonesia-claims-four-malaysian-firms-behind-open-burning.

Stone, Richard. 2007. "Can Palm Oil Plantations Come Clean?" *Science* 317 (5844): 1491. https://doi.org/10.1126/science.317.5844.1491.

Tan-Soo, Jie-Sheng, and Subhrendu K. Pattanayak. 2019. "Seeking Natural Capital Projects: Forest Fires, Haze, and Early-Life Exposure in Indonesia." *Proceedings of the National Academy of Sciences of the United States of America* 116 (12): 5239–5245. https://doi.org/10.1073/pnas.1802876116.

Thomas, Susan, LooSee Beh, and Rusli Bin Nordin. 2011. "Health Care Delivery in Malaysia: Changes, Challenges and Champions Health Care System in Malaysia." *Journal of Public Health in Africa* 2:93–97. https://doi.org/10.4081/jphia.2011.e23.

Varkkey, Helena. 2016. *The Haze Problem in Southeast Asia: Palm Oil and Patronage.* London: Routledge.

Varkkey, Helena, and A. Copeland. 2020. "Exchanging Health for Economic Growth? Haze in the Context of Public Health and Political Economy in Malaysia." *Journal of Social Health* 3 (1): 1–13.

Vethanayagam, J. N., and V. How. 2017. "Urban and Rural Inequality in Knowledge, Attitude and Practice on Haze Pollution Episode in Klang Valley, Malaysia." *Malaysian Journal of Public Health Medicine* 17 (1): 157–162.

Watts, Michael. 1983. "Hazards and Crises: A Political Economy of Drought and Famine in Northern Nigeria." *Antipode* 15 (1): 24–34. https://doi.org/10.1111/j.1467-8330.1983.tb00320.x.

Watts, Michael. 2018. "Frontiers: Authority, Precarity, and Insurgency at the Edge of the State." *World Development* 101:477–488. https://doi.org/10.1016/j.worlddev.2017.03.024.

Zakaria, Adriani, Claudia Theile, and Lely Khaimur. 2007. "Policy, Practice, Pride and Prejudice: Review of Legal, Environmental and Social Practices of Oil Palm Plantation Companies of the Wilmar Group in Sambas District, West Kalimantan (Indonesia)." Amsterdam: Friends of the Earth Netherlands, Lembaga Gemawan, and KONTAK Rakyat Borneo. https://www.foeeurope.org/sites/default/files/publications/foee_wilmar_palm_oil_environmental_social_impact_0707.pdf.

Zalik, Anna. 2011. "Protest-as-Violence in Oil Fields: The Contested Representation of Profiteering in Two Extractive Sites." In *Accumulating Insecurity: Violence and Dispossession in the Making of Everyday Life,* edited by Shelley Feldman, Charles Geisler, and Gayatri A. Menon, 261–284. Athens: University of Georgia Press.

CHAPTER 9

Carbon Bureaucracy and Violence in Cambodia

SARAH MILNE AND SANGO MAHANTY

Efforts to curb emissions or sequester carbon in natural ecosystems often involve fraught encounters between atmospheric processes and local material realities. In tropical countries of the Global South, like Cambodia, these encounters typically occur through the techno-bureaucratic production of carbon credits by agents from the Global North, who are seeking cost-effective climate mitigation. Where forest cover is high, these carbon credits are usually generated through REDD+ activities that aim to conserve forests—or, more specifically, to "avoid deforestation" that is projected in future land-use scenarios.[1] Arcane calculations and myriad assumptions then convert avoided deforestation outcomes into emissions credits for global consumption. Carbon credits are therefore a volumetric construct, fashioned into a virtual commodity, but they have tenuous, coproductive, and still relatively unmapped relationships to their material and social underpinnings (Asiyanbi 2017; Bracking 2015; Mahanty et al. 2013). In this chapter, we consider how carbon credits emerge from the contested domain of forested land in Cambodia, which is steeped in an atmosphere of violence that is at once political, material, structural, and symbolic (Mahanty 2022; Menton, Navas, and Le Billon 2021; Milne 2022). The carbon bureaucracy, we demonstrate, can extend and deepen these underlying forms of violence.

Like many products and services within the green economy, the REDD+ mechanism involves extensive technical and bureaucratic work to produce carbon credits, a new commodity. To achieve this, REDD+ uses a veritable labyrinth of globally applicable rules, technical guidance, certification standards, validation and verification systems, and social safeguards—all of which seek to demonstrate to buyers the supposed *reality* and *quality* of the carbon credits on offer. Indeed, the market value of REDD+ credits emerges from the sum of these things: the demonstrated apparent existence of carbon sequestered, and the wider socio-environmental qualities of the credits (Cavanagh and Benjaminsen 2014; Milne and Mahanty 2019). Below, we critically address the local and material processes mobilized by REDD+, which

199

attempt to secure the "permanence," "additionality," and "co-benefits" of carbon credits: all technical concepts that are used to prove the real, physical existence of sequestered carbon, and its supposed positive side effects for communities and biodiversity.

To understand how concern over atmospheric carbon interacts with local materialities, we investigate REDD+ as a "commodity chain" (Mahanty, Bradley, and Milne 2015). This perspective reveals how forest carbon becomes a commodity and acquires value through institutional assemblages and bureaucratic constructs. To assure buyers that they are purchasing "trusted and fungible" units of nature or tons of CO_2 (Turnhout, Neves, and De Lijster 2014, 582), the commodity chain involves *validation* and *verification* exercises.[2] Through these, project proponents and auditors demonstrate that a given REDD+ project complies with international standards, like the Verified Carbon Standard (VCS, known as Verra) and/or the Climate, Community, and Biodiversity (CCB) Standard. We argue that achieving compliance with these standards requires intricate bureaucratic rituals and routines to construct "representational fabrications" (Ball 2000, 11). The emergence and value of forest carbon as a commodity thus relies on mundane bureaucratic performance (Cavanagh and Benjaminsen 2014; Bracking 2015; Milne and Mahanty 2019).

To illustrate, we use the case of the Seima REDD+ project in northeast Cambodia, where global biodiversity values and Indigenous populations coexist in a vast forested landscape. Under preparation since 2008, this project has served as a pilot offering important lessons for both national and international actors (Mahanty, Bradley, and Milne 2015). In 2016, the project's carbon credits were sold to the Disney Foundation for US$2.6 million, reflecting years of labor, skill, and negotiation on the part of the implementing NGO and its government partners (Phak and Kotoski 2016). We gathered ethnographic data on REDD+ project processes in the area from 2012 to 2015, including the implementation of Free Prior and Informed Consent (FPIC) with local and Indigenous communities under the CCB standard. Our findings illustrate the exigencies and risks of implementing REDD+ international standards in practice: project proponents must comply with complex and rapidly evolving bureaucratic standards, which have the capacity to mask and accentuate underlying forms of violence that in this case included Indigenous dispossession, illegal logging, and forest clearing by a range of actors for land markets and commodity production (Mahanty 2022; Milne 2015). Ultimately, we use the term "bureaucratic violence" to describe how the mundane and procedural aspects of carbon commodification can systematically conceal or even extend these local processes of violence in Cambodia. In this way, a global volumetric construct, commonly known as "tons of CO_2 equivalent," is implicated in more pervasive and multi-scalar atmospheres of violence (see also chapter 10, in this volume, by McGregor and Miller).

Bureaucracy and Violence as Integral Parts of the Green Economy

Foundationally, the green economy involves attempts to commodify nature, so that new goods and services can be transacted for profit (Castree 2010; Büscher, Dressler, and Fletcher 2014). This principle of "selling nature to save it" (McAfee 1999) is enacted through constructs like carbon credits, which require new governance logics and metrics, including technical standards (Turnhout, Neves, and De Lijster 2014; Corson, MacDonald, and Neimark 2013; Robertson 2012). Importantly, these new "socio-natural commodities" (Peluso 2012) disguise the underlying conditions of production (Kosoy and Corbera 2010). For this reason, mechanisms like REDD+ are criticized for their capacity to extend or reproduce endemic violence in forested landscapes (Pasgaard 2015; Howson 2018; Milne et al. 2019). In short, commodification deftly conceals underlying processes of violence.

In addition to carbon commodification, the co-benefits and representations of forest carbon are also sometimes commodified—leading to a "double act" of fetishization (Igoe 2010, after Richey and Ponte 2008). This occurs when a carbon credit's ethical, social, or biodiversity-related qualities are marketed too, as signaled through compliance with standards like the CCB. Carbon offsetting therefore relies heavily upon "the circulation of virtual representations" (Cavanagh and Benjaminsen 2014, 62), including representations of project success, rigorous calculation, healthy forests, and happy local communities. Key to this process is "performativity," especially that of "evaluative calculation," which appears to produce value "purely on its own account" (Bracking 2015, 2349). The carbon market is therefore upheld through constant measurement, verification, certification, and accounting by project managers (Ascui and Lovell 2011). The result is a carbon "audit culture" (Strathern 2000), in which systematic practices and rituals of assessment are deployed to demonstrate or *perform* accountability. These practices and representations of compliance aim to secure public trust and market value.

With this emerging carbon audit culture in play, there is potential for new technologies of governance to shape how carbon-rich landscapes are managed. For example, Shore and Wright (2015, 430) speak of a "new type of governmentality based upon financial calculus" in which governance is "by numbers . . . and *through* numbers." This can lead to "symbolic violence" (Bourdieu 1979) through the necessary gap between the numbers and local lived realities. Bureaucratic performance can therefore mask underlying inequalities and complexities, as we explore in the Cambodian case.

Studying REDD+ Implementation

This chapter draws on ethnographic field research into the Seima REDD+ project in Cambodia conducted over three years (2012–2015), as well as more recent analyses of publicly available documents associated with the project, published mainly by Verra (formerly the Voluntary Carbon Standard). Our "project ethnography" studied the practices and discourses of the REDD+ project, taking inspiration from exemplary studies of development and conservation (e.g., Mosse 2005; West 2006). Access to the field was gained through negotiation with the leading NGO involved in implementing REDD+, with both authors mobilizing prior relationships and external research funding to gather data. Additionally, Milne gained privileged access to some project processes through her brief role as a technical consultant in 2012. What she witnessed through this work has informed some aspects of this chapter.

With insider access to the REDD+ project in its preparatory phase, we observed some important early moments in project implementation (2012–2013). We also spent extended periods in the field interviewing villagers and local stakeholders about their livelihoods and their experiences with the REDD+ project. As the authors' fieldwork continued (2014–2015), however, the atmosphere of violence in the Cambodian context became more pronounced: villagers that had consented to REDD+ under FPIC were still waiting for project benefits to materialize; meanwhile, they had to face off threats like escalating illegal logging, land alienation, and forced displacement due to new economic land concessions in the project area (Dara and Chen 2018; Mahanty and Milne 2016; Milne 2015). These circumstances prompted us to examine the wide gap between REDD+'s early promises and actual lived experiences.

Our critical approach to REDD+ is not intended to discredit any of the project implementers. Rather, we observe how individuals in the REDD+ project, including government and NGO staff, were simply doing what the system demanded of them. On the one hand, they needed to ensure project survival in the increasingly hostile political environment of Cambodia. On the other hand, they needed to produce documentation that met the stringent demands of international carbon-auditing processes. In many cases project staff somehow had to implement or, indeed, *perform* the impossible to achieve this. For this reason, our analysis focuses on the bureaucratic practices and auditing constructs that shaped possibilities for forest conservation action within tight political constraints.

The Violence of Compliance with REDD+ Standards in Cambodia

The production of forest carbon in Seima occurred through the implementation of a range of bureaucratic processes. In particular, the international carbon standards of VCS and CCB demanded specific actions and evidence from the project team, which led to performative displays of apparent compliance in the face of violent local realities of forests being stripped and Indigenous people left sidelined and dispossessed. We unpack this below, by illustrating: 1) the bureaucratic architecture of REDD+ schemes; 2) the FPIC process in this case, and how it was orchestrated and performed in spite of dissonant local realities; and 3) the final moments of validation and verification, which were accomplished through technical maneuvering that had structurally violent effects.

Bureaucratic Architecture

The production of "trusted and fungible" carbon credits relies upon a highly evolved, yet ever-changing carbon bureaucracy. Key to the production of tradeable credits is compliance with the VCS (now Verra) standard. For added-value credits that promise desirable qualities and lower risk, there are optional measures to comply with the CCB Standards. These two sets of standards comprise the main bureaucratic architecture of the international voluntary carbon market.

Verra has a dizzying array of rules and requirements that must be met by projects so that they can first register with the scheme, and then be issued with tradeable units of carbon known as verified carbon units (VCUs). According to guidance online, key stages in registration include the presentation of project documents to the Verra Registry; a period of public comment; project visits by VCS-certified auditors to validate and then verify the project; and, if the project is deemed compliant, registration and VCU issuance. These terms, like "validation" and "verification," are now keywords in the bureaucratic vocabulary of carbon certification. Project proponents and independent auditors must adhere to a frequently updated and technically complex set of guidance documents. Verra warns that these documents are changeable and must be checked regularly, as the website states: "Documents are updated periodically. Please check this page to be sure you are using the latest version of a given document."[3]

The high level of specialization, effort, and knowledge required to engage in this process has spawned a side industry—one that is tightly controlled by those who maintain the carbon standards. For example, the independent auditors who conduct validation and verification processes must come from a formally trained and Verra-approved validation and verification body or VVB. Yet becoming and remaining a VVB is not straightforward. Verra explains that "VVBs are qualified, independent third parties which are approved to perform validation and verification. This independent assessment process is critical to ensuring the integrity of the projects registered with the VCS Program."[4] In 2018, the website listed twenty-three "active" or certified VVBs, and twenty-seven "inactive" VVBs who had either lost their accreditation or had it suspended.[5] Thus, the industry places great emphasis on the appearance of quality control and accountability—the very processes that underpin value generation.

For those seeking to increase market value and direct sales of carbon credits, meeting the CCB standards has become imperative. The Verra standards set out a requirement for "no net harm" in relation to environmental and social impacts, which should be achieved through local stakeholder consultation and periods of public comment.[6] However, the CCB standards go further, specifying stringent requirements to demonstrate environmental and social benefits. A notable example is that the CCB standards require FPIC to be implemented in affected communities. For social justice advocates, this requirement represents due recognition of Indigenous rights (Mahanty and McDermott 2013), a prominent sentiment in the REDD+ safeguards under the United Nation's Framework Convention on Climate Change.[7] However, in the voluntary carbon market, FPIC implementation is arguably more about risk minimization than Indigenous or community rights.

This emphasis on risk aversion is evident in Verra's validation reporting framework, in which community engagement forms part of the so-called non-permanence risk analysis for a given project. Here, the underlying assumption is that community noncompliance or resistance could damage the "permanence" of emissions reductions. The add-on CCB certification is similarly pitched to buyers for its risk-management benefits, with its ability to "identify high-quality projects that are unlikely to become implicated in controversy" (VCS 2017d, 4). During the early stages of the carbon market, sellers came to CCB enticed by the possibility of value addition, or the chance to gain a premium price on their carbon units. However, over time, this price differential has eased. CCB certification now represents a less risky form of carbon credit and remains an essential feature of the voluntary carbon market, with around half of the carbon traded being CCB certified.[8] The implication of this market share being tied to FPIC is that it too becomes part of the CCB brand—or another rubber stamp among many, to reassure investors. However, whether FPIC serves the interests of local communities is unclear.

The Seima REDD+ project undertook VCS and CCB certification over a period of about eight years, as outlined in table 9.1. To highlight how some of these bureaucratic processes unfolded, we now provide an ethnographic description of how FPIC implementation was achieved from 2011 to 2013.

Table 9.1. Project development timeline for the Cambodian case

Year/s	Carbon production steps	Key actions
2008	Government endorsement of REDD+ project	Council of Ministers endorses "carbon conservation" at the project site, and creation of the Seima Protection Forest (WCS 2009).
2010– ongoing	Clarification of tenure arrangements	Local resource rights mapped (2003 onward) and applications for Indigenous Communal Land Title secured or underway in many communities (2010 onward), with ongoing tenure clarification foreshadowed in REDD+ plans.
2011– 2013	Community consultations (VCS) plus FPIC (for CCB)	FPIC process run by the Wildlife Conservation Society–Forestry Administration team, with third-party community legal advisors and Indigenous language translators.
2013	Submission of project documents and deeds	Project development commenced 2008; final project design document (PD) submitted 2013.
2013– 2017	VCS and CCB validation	VCS validation commences November 2013; final report December 2014; "VCS Verification Deed" by SCS Global Services submitted to VCS March 2017. CCB validation undertaken in parallel with VCS validation; final report November 2015.
2016– ongoing	Implementation of PD measures	Increase forest protection, e.g., through stronger Forest Law enforcement.
2016	Credits sale	Agreement for sale of carbon credits to Disney Corporation (WCS 2016).
2017	VCS and CCB verification	VCS and CCB verification (for period January 1, 2010–December 31, 2015) covered in one final report and statement of CCB standards compliance issued (April 2017).
2017	VCS and CCB registration	Approval to CCB gold level November 2017 (VCS 2018).
2016– ongoing	Project maintenance	Credits sold to over six buyers (including offset brokers, and a French luxury lifestyle group, Kering). Project claims "17.4 million tons CO_2-e emissions avoided in next 10 years" (WCS 2021).

Sources: Adapted from Mahanty, Bradley, and Milne (2015), with updates from WCS (2021)

Performative Implementation of FPIC

FPIC was essential to the Seima REDD+ project's CCB compliance and, as a national REDD+ demonstration project, also piloted international best practice. The process was developed and conducted with the support of various donors, Khmer project managers, and foreign advisors (including Milne in late 2012). The first step, in 2011, involved a thorough review and synthesis of international FPIC principles and guidance from UN-REDD, the CCB Standards, and the Regional Community Forestry Training Centre. This guidance was then adapted to the Cambodian context.

Adapting the FPIC tool to Seima presented several design challenges, which had to be addressed ahead of community consultations. A key issue was that of inter- and intra-community heterogeneity. Target villages were identified because they were either located in the project area or they used resources from it. In 2010, this amounted to over 2,600 families, or 20 villages, scattered across a 300,000-hectare landscape. Those living in remote, forested areas tended to be of Bunong ethnicity, leading largely subsistence livelihoods, although recent years have brought increasing market integration (Mahanty 2022). Those living closer to the buffer zones, with good road access, faced rapid Khmer in-migration and the embrace of new markets for land and cash crops (Mahanty and Milne 2016). The idea of a "village" or "community" in these areas was fast changing and contested. Village coherence was also affected by the presence of powerful, absentee landowners, who exerted influence over local leaders (Milne 2013).

To address CCB requirements within this social complexity, the project managers decided to implement FPIC through a series of village-level agreements. Nominated or elected village leaders were to sign an agreement with the Forestry Administration consenting to REDD+ on behalf of all households in their village, for a total of twenty agreements for the project area. This was a pragmatic decision, but it left now-familiar questions about community representation in FPIC unanswered (Mahanty and McDermott 2013; Szablowski 2010). These included how village representatives would be legitimately chosen and the extent to which they might be beholden to elite interests, as is common in Cambodia (Milne and Mahanty 2019).

Other design problems similarly required techno-bureaucratic maneuvering around local contextual issues. Some questions were hard to answer, for example: What is "free" and "prior" in the context of a long-standing conservation project in which REDD+ financing will simply augment existing project activities? What is "consent" when the project's legal basis relies on the notion of state public land, which in Cambodia is known to override customary rights in violent ways (Springer 2013)?

Lastly, how can meaningful written agreements be established with Bunong people, whose mother tongue is not a written language and whose Khmer literacy skills are limited? Plausible technical answers to these questions were developed by project staff (see Kim 2012), in effect building a project narrative for staff to adhere to and a technical fix for the task of having to implement a policy tool that did not fit the Cambodian context well.

FPIC then proceeded as follows: local awareness raising about REDD+ and a REDD+ social impact assessment in 2010; drafting of the FPIC village agreement text, which included seeking community feedback and independent legal advice in 2011; and finalization of the agreement text in 2012, with the eventual signing of agreements by the Forestry Administration and village representatives in early 2013. Having observed the final stages of this process, we now examine how dissonance emerged between the FPIC ideal and project realities. To accommodate this dissonance, the performance of bureaucratic processes and FPIC policy prescriptions was required.

The first instance of dissonance concerned the text for the village-level agreement. A draft agreement was developed after exhaustive consultation with villagers and independent lawyers in 2011. But by mid-2012, its finalization was still subject to legal review and government approval, after months of delay and deliberation within the Cambodian Forestry Administration. With donor deadlines for FPIC completion looming, the NGO needed to take swift and decisive action, so it facilitated expedited legal reviews of the agreement text and then secured a meeting at the Forestry Administration to seek final approval of the text. This meeting involved line-by-line examination of the agreement, in Khmer and English, *and* editing at the discretion of government officials. A key decision on carbon ownership was made at this meeting without much discussion: that the government would hold the carbon rights, even if Indigenous people secured communal title to forested lands in the future.[9] This decision was treated by those in the room as just another technicality to be resolved later, once REDD+ was implemented. But it carries symbolic importance: for all the care taken to craft the agreement text in consultation with local communities, and for all the international commentary on Indigenous rights and carbon ownership (see Sikor et al. 2010), the final agreement text was decided upon unilaterally without carbon rights being granted to communities.

This departure from original intentions was also enabled because the agreement text had become a mundane technical object. Somehow no one owned it anymore, after all of the NGO advisors' comments, the legal amendments, and the time spent waiting for the Forestry Administration to respond. Even after the Forestry Administration's approval of the agreement, the final version was temporarily misplaced, given the numerous annotated versions of the agreement text in circulation and turnover of key staff. In addition, project staff tasked with implementing FPIC harbored a high degree of cynicism about the policy processes underway. As one expatriate staffer said: "We don't even know what REDD+ is, so how can communities consent to it?" But FPIC was a blanket requirement for CCB validation, so it had to be completed, without questions.

The second instance of dissonance emerged when it came to getting the agreements signed. Debates within the project ensued over *who* was signing on behalf of villagers, and *how* consent should be given. For the NGO staff involved, it was deemed appropriate for the community committees to provide consent. But this was at odds with the view of the Forestry Administration staff, who were more concerned with "making it legal," as they wanted a consent-giving process that used government structures and processes.[10] This led to the Forestry Administration insisting that each village chief secure thumbprints from every household, to signal individual-level consent, as well as a rubber stamp from the Commune Council. Thus, NGO-backed processes were bypassed, and a new governmental requirement for FPIC completion was introduced. This was apparently to ensure that the consent process would be perceived as robust in the eyes of senior government officials, like the director general of the Forestry Administration. It also led to an FPIC process that mobilized Cambodian sources of authority, where thumbprints are often more important than signatures (see Hughes 2001).

With these new governmental requirements for FPIC in play, the NGO now faced an additional set of implementation challenges. It was the wet season, and household thumbprints from twenty villages had to be gathered as soon as possible, without a budget. Again, what ensued was masterful administrative and logistical creativity on the NGO's part. Paper consent forms were produced—one for each household—and a process for getting them thumbprinted was devised. It was deemed, after guidance from the government, that getting 70–80 percent of households in every village to complete the consent form would be acceptable. This would involve at least one thousand forms, wrapped in plastic bags, carried on motorbikes through the forest. Under time and budgetary constraints, the only way to achieve this was to piggyback onto other planned community engagement processes, namely the Indigenous communal titling that was underway in several villages. For the NGO team, dedicated to communal titling, this was a frustrating bureaucratic diversion. However, it probably suited government officials, who preferred to drag their feet on Indigenous land rights in the area (Milne 2013).

The thumbprinting went remarkably smoothly in most villages, as it followed Cambodian protocols. First, the NGO team called village representatives to a meeting, to remind villagers about REDD+ and the community agreement that they were soon to sign.[11] Village chiefs were asked to call "their people" to attend the thumbprinting sessions, at appointed times and places in the village. The consenting space was therefore the meeting between NGO and village representatives, while the subsequent thumbprinting by households was a procedural consequence of local hierarchies and protocols. There was no observed discussion or reading of the consent form during village thumbprinting sessions: these proceeded without discussion because villagers had been summoned by their chief. Nor were there any qualms about one household representative providing three or four thumbprints on one form, to cover for all the adults in their home. For Milne, the only foreign observer, these departures from the individual consent-giving ideal were striking. But the Khmer team was not worried: for them, thumbprinting was a familiar Khmer ritual procedure or performance.

Consent-giving issues did occur in two villages, however, provoking a problem-solving flurry among the NGO staff. Located in the project's buffer zone, the two ethnically mixed villages had seen rapid in-migration by Khmer farmers and elite land grabbing, which had disrupted local social cohesion and caused high forest loss (Mahanty and Milne 2016). As one NGO staff member explained: "These are broken villages . . . maybe we should remove them from the FPIC process?" Here, the problems with FPIC revolved around land conflicts and villagers' confusion about the REDD+ project and ongoing land-tenure interventions by the government. In one of the villages, where an Indigenous communal land titling process was underway, one quarter of the village initially boycotted the thumbprinting process because they thought it would preclude them from later securing individual land titles. Indeed, they had been egged on by powerful elites, who sought to disrupt NGO activities that would limit their land dealings (see Milne 2013). The NGO eventually resolved this issue by appealing to higher powers: the commune chief was engaged in the matter, and he instructed his villagers to comply with the thumbprinting. In the other village, about 50 percent of households boycotted the consent process because they wanted to clear forest land illegally to extend their agricultural practices and sell land. Or, as the Forestry Administration manager explained: "Those who are cutting forest will not provide consent. If we give them land, they'll consent." In this case, the dissenters were treated as potential lawbreakers, and dealing with them became a matter of law enforcement rather than consent seeking.

Despite these hiccups, a thousand household thumbprints were secured, and NGO staff efforts refocused on the signing of the twenty village-level agreements. The Khmer project team insisted that a ceremony would be required: a formal, public ritual, during which all parties to the agreements would display their consent and willingness to collaborate on the REDD+ project. What ensued was a uniquely Cambodian performance, held at the Provincial Forestry Office. Villagers sat in rows, like students or subjects, to watch senior officials on stage. Everyone had to wait for the arrival of the provincial governor, who was inexplicably late, before the highly scripted proceedings could begin. Every speech was written by the NGO, with nothing left to chance. Those who spoke were selected carefully: the provincial governor, the donor, one local village chief. Unfortunately, the one Bunong community representative who *should* have spoken was not given the opportunity to do so—apparently because he could not read. And so, any truly representative or potentially dissenting local voices were not given space. This was a moment of spectacular display, not a moment for further dialogue with villagers. To finish, after the agreement was read out loud, three model villages signed off in front of everyone, providing an essential photo opportunity for donors and project actors. The other seventeen agreements were to be signed after the busy officials had left.

Offstage, the NGO staff were left with a scramble of paperwork as they tried to coordinate the necessary signatures for all agreements. Village chiefs and committee chiefs had to be rounded up for all the twenty villages. The idea was that they would first sign the agreement, and then they could receive their per diem for attendance. But not everyone had attended the ceremony, and some had left immediately afterward for lunch, neglecting to sign their village agreement. At the end of the day, this left about half of the agreements without signatures. More than anything, these observations captured the performative nature of the FPIC ceremony. It was a key moment of political posturing that served project needs, just as much as it ensured CCB validation.

Validation and Verification Experiences

With all the requirements of Verra and CCB standards finally met, the project proponents moved to complete validation and verification. The contracted auditor commenced work in November 2013 and concluded in July 2017 (see table 9.1). Following usual practice, this involved the auditor's preparation of assessment reports on project compliance with the standards, after review of existing project documents, and a four-day site visit. The auditor recruited his own Cambodian translator for fieldwork, to avoid bias and to conduct one follow-up field visit. According to online documentation, the auditor's initial assessment identified several areas requiring explanation or remedial action by project proponents in order for validation and verification to proceed. Strikingly, these bureaucratic processes and exigencies deflected consideration of real, material problems that were affecting the project area, like Indigenous land alienation, forest clearing for land concessions and illicit land deals, and illegal logging by powerful tycoons (see Mahanty 2022; Mahanty and Milne 2016; Milne 2013, 2015). We shall now illustrate this phenomenon of bureaucratic violence using three examples from the case.

The first problem of bureaucratic deflection or distraction became evident through shifting requirements on community consultation, as the Verra and CCB rules were continually being updated. These apparently minor adjustments held substantive implications for project personnel. In Seima, this happened in relation to the CCB's community awareness and consultation requirements. The initial validation report observed that although village leadership appeared knowledgeable about the project, this was not so at a broader community level. Furthermore, the validator was concerned that there may have been limited local awareness about the CCB's public comment and grievance procedures. Therefore, broader REDD+ consultation and communication plans were requested for the project.[12]

This request generated a flurry of activity on the ground, as project personnel duly prepared communication plans and conducted community awareness-raising activities. For example, "grievance cards" containing information on the project's grievance mechanism were issued to villagers—often regardless of whether they understood them or not, as one staff member shared. Despite this effort, a subsequent reformulation of the CCB standards made the validator's original concerns moot, as the auditor later wrote that, "as the CCB Standards Third Edition no longer contained this requirement, the validation finding was formally withdrawn and was no longer applicable" (SCS Global Services 2015, 94). Thus, the requirement for more stringent community engagement—and the implementation efforts this entailed—was rendered unnecessary by a minor rule adjustment. All the while, Indigenous people continued to face intimidation by local predatory elites intent on grabbing land and forest resources, with no one to come to their aid.

A second problematic verification moment arose in relation to the place of Indigenous communal title (ICT) zones within the project area. From its early days, the Seima project incorporated practical support for Indigenous communal title claims under the Cambodian Land Law. For the project proponents, ICT was seen as a way of securing forests and supporting conservation-friendly land use in the project's buffer zone (Evans, Arpels, and Clements 2012). Although a promise of carbon revenues from communally titled lands was never made to communities, project support for ICT *was* framed as a key potential REDD+ project benefit. In this way, the distinction between ICT, REDD+, and FPIC activities became blurred—what's more, all were implemented by the same community engagement team in the field, at the same time.

From the perspective of the auditor, however, the presence of areas subject to Indigenous title claims presented a threat to project permanence, since communities could seek to use land in ways other than stated in the REDD+ project document. Or, in the language of validation, ICT was framed as a risk to the carbon credits, because it could mean the lack of an "enforceable and irrevocable agreement with the holder of the statutory, property or contractual right in the land . . . that generates GHG emission reductions or removals."[13] Once deciphered, this finding caused much anxiety for the NGO team over what had always been a central facet of the REDD+ project. Eventually, to comply with the standards, they saw little alternative than to excise the potential ICT areas from the core REDD+ zone, leaving behind only the state-owned protected area. Project staff worried about how this might impact their relationships with local communities.

The excision of ICT areas from the formal REDD+ project was acknowledged in a perfunctory comment by the validator: "The Client's response adequately addresses the finding." But major unanswered questions were left about the future of Indigenous rights in the Seima REDD+ project, not to mention Verra's inability to deal with situations of mixed tenure or contested tenure, as is the case for most state-held forests in Cambodia and the region. Furthermore, although compliant for the purposes of carbon production, the factoring out of Indigenous claims is inconsistent with REDD+'s greater promise to deliver co-benefits.[14] Over time, the implementing NGO has circumvented Verra by supporting ICT claims alongside the certified REDD+ project.[15]

A third problematic effect of carbon accounting emerged from the project's case for "additionality." All carbon projects must establish that their emissions reductions are additional to business-as-usual scenarios. In Seima, it was the government's weak enforcement of the Forestry Law that provided grounds for additionality in the validation report (SCS Global Services 2015). The report referred to a "variety of reasons" for weak enforcement that in practice include rent seeking by local officials, along with elite and military-backed illegal logging, timber trafficking, and land grabbing. These issues and their deleterious effects upon local livelihoods were well-known (e.g., Mahanty and Milne 2016; EIA 2017; Dara and Chen 2018; Mahanty 2022). Indeed, as far back as 2010, in the first REDD+ community consultations, villagers had repeatedly raised concerns over illegal logging, but their pleas were never acted upon.[16] Instead, for the purposes of validation, their voices were counted merely as evidence of the project's case for additionality, which assumed future forest loss and degradation. When questioned about this, project personnel explained that the illegal logging of luxury timber cited by villagers would "not affect the carbon stocks very much" because this was already "factored into the model." The project's readiness to accommodate selective, illegal logging was a tacit acknowledgment of the effectively untouchable political economy in which the REDD+ project was embedded—one in which government-backed tycoons could log with impunity, including removing the ancient resin trees upon which Indigenous livelihoods depended (Milne 2015).

In the end, the validator only needed proof that nonenforcement of the law was standard practice for "more than 30 percent of the project area" (SCS Global Services 2015). This was achieved with a letter from the Forestry Administration, confirming that weak law enforcement was not only the norm in over 30 percent of the Seima area, but it was also the case in over 30 percent of Cambodia's forests. The validator was satisfied with this, leading to his conclusion that "the evidence and information provided is sufficient as demonstration that the requirement of VT0001 has been fulfilled" (SCS Global Services 2015). Thus, the project's case for additionality was confirmed, without any discussion of the feasibility of future law enforcement in the project area, and little acknowledgment of the distinctions between deforestation for agriculture and degradation due to extensive illegal logging. Tragically, with REDD+ underway, three park rangers were murdered by illegal logging gangs in 2018 in the project area, one of whom was Indigenous (Associated Press 2018). This highlights the drastic assumptions and risks hidden behind the carbon standard's banal bureaucratic requirements.

Carbon Bureaucracy and Its Violent Effects

Our case study shows how carbon credits emerge from a very particular kind of bureaucracy—one that places stringent demands upon auditors and project proponents, while actively ignoring local processes of violence. Without the standards, carbon credits cannot be considered as "trusted and fungible," nor can they be marketed as "low risk." Those who implement the bureaucracy, therefore, are compelled to uphold its constructs—a compulsion that can lead to performative behavior by project proponents, who must demonstrate compliance with rules that do not necessarily fit the local context. Furthermore, validation and verification are power-laden exercises, practiced only by external vetted experts, in a system whose rules keep changing. This highly inaccessible techno-bureaucracy systematically fails to hear local voices and fails to see processes of material and structural violence at the forest frontier. By rendering local processes of violence invisible, carbon credits emerge as a clean technical fix for the deepening crises of climate and capitalism—a "false solution" (Figueroa Helland 2022). It is bureaucratic violence that equates carbon emissions "out there" with carbon sequestered in old-growth forests that for centuries have been cared for under Indigenous custodianship.

Overall, these arrangements give rise to forms of violence that are not necessarily physical, but symbolic and indirect in nature (Menton, Navas, and Le Billon 2021). That is, technically framed and quietly deployed rules can cause violence in the way that certain knowledges, voices, and experiences are discounted. A similar phenomenon is Herzfeld's "bureaucratic indifference" (1991), where systems established for accountability ultimately generate a detached and abstracted disinterest. Or Arendt's (1969) insights that instrumental organizational practices can take on the mantle of violence when used in the service of power. In our case study, "following the rules" of the carbon standard worked to legitimize and normalize a status quo of elite-backed forest destruction and Indigenous dispossession that was materially violent. This especially occurred through the *denial of dissonance* between policy and practice, including a lack of response to local pleas for help through official adherence to bureaucratic constructs.

We call this phenomenon bureaucratic violence, and we argue that it comprises two key dynamics. First is the performance of bureaucratic constructs and accountability, as seen in the project's implementation of FPIC. Here, the CCB validation requirements provided a script to follow in the face of fraught local realities like divided local communities and produced partial forms of consent to REDD+. Performance, therefore, helped to deflect attention away from these intractable problems. The second dynamic in bureaucratic violence is the way that carbon standards shaped what could be "seen" (Robertson 2006). In other words, what was factored in and out of documentation for VCS compliance mainly involved contorted efforts to measure forest carbon as potentially airborne in the future. Here, for example, illegal logging became mere evidence for "additionality," and Indigenous land claims were excised from the project area in the name of "permanence." Thus, the carbon standards demand evidence production that adheres to technical rules for carbon credits, rather than any process of listening or crafting of local strategies to tackle deforestation and dispossession.

Ultimately, this case highlights how the mundane is capable of doing violence. Put another way, the painstaking bureaucratic effort to produce trustworthy and valuable carbon credits is also the work of an elaborate construct or cover-up, which systematically ignores, conceals, and at times deepens local experiences of structural and material violence. This phenomenon is another dimension in the emerging notion of "green violence" that highlights the physical and politico-legal aspects of violent tactics to protect nature (Fletcher 2018; Büscher and Ramutsindela 2016; Fairhead, Leach, and Scoones 2012), and "carbon violence" that attends to wider processes of molecular and capital accumulation in the global carbon cycle (see chapter 10 in this volume, by McGregor and Miller). Bureaucratic violence is distinct because of its prosaic, technical processes, which inconspicuously conceal or dismiss critical voices while extending systemic injustices and dissolving human responsibility for the consequences.

Notes

1. REDD+ (Reducing Emissions from Deforestation and Forest Degradation) is a voluntary climate change mitigation approach, developed by Parties to the UN Framework Convention on Climate Change. See https://redd.unfccc.int/. The term is also applied to "voluntary carbon markets" that privately verify and trade avoided carbon emissions or "carbon credits," such as https://verra.org/programs/verified-carbon-standard.
2. The phrase "trusted and fungible" comes from the Verified Carbon Standard Program Guide (VCS 2017a).
3. See Verra's "Rules and Requirements" at http://verra.org/project/vcs-program/rules-and-requirements/ (accessed April 4, 2018).
4. See Verra's "Validation and Verification" at https://verra.org/project/vcs-program/validation-verification/ (accessed October 12, 2018).
5. Ibid.
6. See Section 3.17, "Safeguards," in VCS (7017b).
7. Adopted in Cancun in 2010, these safeguards urge developing countries to pay attention to the knowledge and rights of Indigenous and local communities, and to ensure their "full and effective" participation. See UN FCCC (2011).
8. See Donofrio et al. (2019).
9. More than anything, this was so that the agreement text would comply with Cambodia's recent legal framework on REDD+ benefit sharing (see Government Decision no. 699, May 2008; see Yeang et al. 2014).
10. Quote from the agreement text meeting attended by Sarah Milne.
11. One meeting per village was held. The village committee was either the Indigenous community committee (in fourteen villages) or a combination of the village development committee and commune council (in six villages).
12. See VCS (2018).
13. VCS Standard 3.4, current at the time. The current VCS Standard 3.7 no longer contains this language.
14. For example, see the UN-REDD website on the "multiple benefits of REDD+," the delivery of which is now a requirement through the Cancun safeguards (UN-REDD 2017).
15. See the KEO Seima REDD+ project website for details: https://seimaredd.wcs.org/.
16. See "Community Consultation Meetings on the Seima Protection Forest REDD+ Project Design Document," October 2014, accessed through the VCS online database: htttps://s3.amazonaws.com/CCBA/Projects/Reduced_Emissions_from_Deforestation_and_Degradation_in_Seima_Protection_Forest/CCBA_Community_Consultations_Meetings_01-30_Oct_2014_Final.pdf.

References

Arendt, Hannah. 1969. "A Special Supplement: Reflections on Violence." *New York Review of Books,* February 27, 1969.

Ascui, Fransisco, and Heather Lovell. 2011. "As Frames Collide: Making Sense of Carbon Accounting." *Accounting, Auditing and Accountability* 24 (8): 978–999. https://doi.org/10.1108/09513571111184724.

Asiyanbi, Adeniyi P. 2017. "Financialisation in the Green Economy: Material Connections, Markets-in-the-Making and Foucauldian Organising Actions." *Environment and Planning A: Economy and Space* 50 (3): 531–548.
Associated Press. 2018. "Cambodian Forest Defenders Killed after Confronting Illegal Loggers." *The Guardian,* January 31, 2018. https://www.theguardian.com/environ ment/2018/jan/31/cambodian-forest-defenders-killed-after-confronting-illegal-loggers.
Ball, Stephen J. 2000. "Performatives and Fabrications in the Education Economy: Towards the Performative Society?" *Australian Educational Researcher* 27 (2): 1–23.
Bourdieu, Pierre. 1979. "Symbolic power." *Critique of Anthropology* 4 (13–14): 77–85.
Bracking, Sarah. 2015. "Performativity in the Green Economy: How Far Does Climate Finance Create a Fictive Economy?" *Third World Quarterly* 36 (12): 2337–2357.
Büscher, Bram, Wolfram H. Dressler, and Robert Fletcher, eds. 2014. *Nature™ Inc.: Environmental Conservation in the Neoliberal Age.* Tucson: University of Arizona Press.
Büscher, Bram, and Maano Ramutsindela. 2016. "Green Violence: Rhino Poaching and the War to Save Southern Africa's Peace Parks." *African Affairs* 115 (458): 1–22.
Castree, Noel. 2010. "Neoliberalism and the Bio-Physical World 2: Theorising the Neoliberalisation of Nature." *Geography Compass* 4 (12): 1734–1746.
Cavanagh, Connor, and Tor A. Benjaminsen. 2014. "Virtual Nature, Violent Accumulation: The 'Spectacular Failure' of Carbon Offsetting at a Ugandan National Park." *Geoforum* 56:55–65. https://doi.org/10.1016/j.geoforum.2014.06.013.
Corson, Catherine, Kenneth MacDonald, and Benjamin Neimark. 2013. "Grabbing 'Green': Markets, Environmental Governance and the Materialization of Natural Capital." *Human Geography* 6 (1): 1–15.
Dara, Mech, and Daphne Chen. 2018. "As Logging Changes Mondulkiri, Ethnic Phnong Are Reaping Only Meagre Gains from Major Loss." *Phnom Penh Post,* March 23, 2018. https://www.phnompenhpost.com/national-post-depth/logging-changes-mondulkiri -ethnic-phnong-are-reaping-only-meagre-gains-major.
Donofrio, Stephen, Patrick Maguire, William Merry, and Steve Zwick. "State of the Voluntary Carbon Markets 2019: Market Direction." Forest Trends. https://www.forest-trends.org /publications/state-of-the-voluntary-carbon-markets-2019-market-direction/.
EIA (Environmental Investigation Agency). 2017. "Repeat Offender: Vietnam's Persistent Trade in Illegal Timber." London: EIA. https://drive.google.com/viewerng/viewer ?url=https://eia-international.org/wp-content/uploads/Repeat-Offender.pdf.
Evans, Tom D., Marisa Arpels, and Tom Clements. 2012. "Pilot REDD Activities in Cambodia Are Expected to Improve Access to Forest Resource Use Rights and Land Tenure for Local Communities." In *Lessons about Land Tenure, Forest Governance and REDD+: Case Studies from Africa, Asia and Latin America,* edited by Lisa Naughton- Treves and Cathy Day, 73–82. Madison: University of Wisconsin-Madison Land Tenure Center.
Fairhead, James, Melissa Leach, and Ian Scoones. 2012. "Green Grabbing: A New Appropriation of Nature?" *Journal of Peasant Studies* 39 (2): 237–261.
Figueroa Helland, Leonardo E. 2022. "Indigenous Pathways beyond the 'Anthropocene': Biocultural Climate Justice through Decolonization and Land Rematriation." *New York University Environmental Law Journal* 30 (3): 347–412.

Fletcher, Robert. 2018. "License to Kill: Contesting the Legitimacy of Green Violence." *Conservation and Society* 16 (2): 147–156.

Herzfeld, Michael. 1991. *The Social Production of Indifference: Exploring the Symbolic Roots of Western Bureaucracy*. New York: Berg.

Howson, Peter. 2018. "Slippery Violence in the REDD+ Forests of Central Kalimantan, Indonesia." *Conservation and Society* 16 (2): 136–146.

Hughes, Caroline. 2001. "Mystics and Militants: Democratic Reform in Cambodia." *International Politics* 38:47–64.

Igoe, Jim. 2010. "The Spectacle of Nature in the Global Economy of Appearances: Anthropological Engagements with the Spectacular Mediations of Transnational Conservation." *Critique of Anthropology* 30 (4): 375–397.

Kim, Narong. 2012. *Obtaining FPIC at the Seima REDD+ Demonstration Site, Cambodia*. Wildlife Conservation Society Cambodia Program. Presentation given at the Regional REDD+ Information Exchange Meeting: Free, Prior and Informed Consent. Bogor, Indonesia, April 19–20, 2012.

Kosoy, Nicolás, and Esteve Corbera. 2010. "Payments for Ecosystem Services as Commodity Fetishism." *Ecological Economics* 69 (6): 1228–1236.

Mahanty, Sango. 2022. *Unsettled Frontiers: Market Formation in the Cambodia-Vietnam Borderlands*. Ithaca, NY: Cornell University Press.

Mahanty, Sango, Amanda Bradley, and Sarah Milne. 2015. "The Forest Carbon Commodity Chain in Cambodia's Voluntary Carbon Market." In *Conservation and Development in Cambodia: Exploring Frontiers of Change in Nature, State and Society*, edited by Sarah Milne and Sango Mahanty, 177–200. London: Routledge.

Mahanty, Sango, Wolfram H. Dressler, Sarah Milne, and Colin Filer. 2013. "Unravelling Property Relations around Forest Carbon." *Singapore Journal of Tropical Geography* 34:188–205.

Mahanty, Sango, and Constance L. McDermott. 2013. "How Does 'Free, Prior and Informed Consent' (FPIC) Impact Social Equity? Lessons from Mining and Forestry and Their Implications for REDD+." *Land Use Policy* 35:406–416.

Mahanty, Sango, and Sarah Milne. 2016. "Anatomy of a Boom: Cassava as a 'Gateway' Crop in Cambodia's North Eastern Borderland." *Asia Pacific Viewpoint* 57 (2): 180–193.

McAfee, Kathleen. 1999. "Selling Nature to Save It? Biodiversity and Green Developmentalism." *Environment and Planning D: Society and Space* 17 (2): 133–154. https://doi.org/10.1068/d170133.

Menton, Mary, Grettel Navas, and Philippe Le Billon. 2021. "Atmospheres of Violence: On Defenders' Intersecting Experiences of Violence." In *Environmental Defenders: Deadly Struggles for Life and Territory*, edited by Mary Menton and Philippe Le Billon, 51–63. London: Routledge.

Milne, Sarah. 2013. "Under the Leopard's Skin: Land Commodification and the Dilemmas of Indigenous Communal Title in Upland Cambodia." *Asia Pacific Viewpoint* 54 (3): 323–339.

Milne, Sarah. 2015. "Cambodia's Unofficial Regime of Extraction: Illicit Logging in the Shadow of Transnational Governance and Investment." *Critical Asian Studies* 47 (2): 200–228.

Milne, Sarah. 2022. *Corporate Nature: An Insider's Ethnography of Global Conservation.* Tucson: University of Arizona Press.

Milne, Sarah, and Sango Mahanty. 2019. "Value and Bureaucratic Violence in the Green Economy." *Geoforum* 98 (January): 133–143.

Milne, Sarah, Sango Mahanty, Phuc Xuan To, Wolfram H. Dressler, Peter Kanowski, and Maylee Thawat. 2019. "Learning from 'Actually Existing' REDD+: A Review of Ethnographic Findings." *Conservation and Society* 17 (1): 84–95.

Mosse, David. 2005. *Cultivating Development: An Ethnography of Aid Policy and Practice.* London: Pluto Press.

Pasgaard, Maya. 2015. "Lost in Translation? How Project Actors Shape REDD+ Policy Outcomes in Cambodia." *Asia Pacific Viewpoint* 56 (1): 111–127.

Peluso, Nancy Lee. 2012. "What's Nature Got to Do with It? A Situated Historical Perspective on Socio-Natural Commodities." *Development and Change* 43 (1): 70–104.

Phak, Seangly, and Kali Kotoski. 2016. "Disney Buys Up Carbon Credits in Mondulkiri." *Phnom Penh Post,* July 25, 2016. https://www.phnompenhpost.com/national/disney-buys-carbon-credits-mondulkiri.

Richey, Lisa Ann, and Stefano Ponte. 2008. "Better (Red)™ than Dead? Celebrities, Consumption and International Aid." *Third World Quarterly* 29 (4): 711–729.

Robertson, Morgan M. 2006. "The Nature That Capital Can See: Science, State and the Market in the Commodification of Ecosystem Services." *Environment and Planning D: Society and Space* 24 (3): 367–387.

Robertson, Morgan M. 2012. "Measurement and Alienation: Making a World of Ecosystem Services." *Transactions of the Institute of British Geographers (New Series)* 37 (3): 386–401.

SCS Global Services. 2015. "Final Validation Report: 'Reduced Emissions from Deforestation and Degradation in Seima Protection Forest.'" Available at the Verra Registry: http://vcsprojectdatabase.org/#/project_details/1650.

Shore, Cris, and Susan Wright. 2015. "Audit Culture Revisited: Rankings, Ratings, and the Reassembling of Society." *Current Anthropology* 56 (3): 421–444.

Sikor, Thomas, Johannes Stahl, Thomas Enters, Jesse C. Ribot, Neera Singh, William D. Sunderlin, and Lini Wollenberg Stahl. 2010. "REDD-Plus, Forest People's Rights and Nested Climate Governance." *Global Environmental Change* 20 (3): 423–425.

Springer, Simon. 2013. "Illegal Evictions? Overwriting Possession and Orality with Law's Violence in Cambodia." *Journal of Agrarian Change* 13 (4): 520–546.

Strathern, Marilyn, ed. 2000. *Audit Cultures: Anthropological Studies in Accountability, Ethics and the Academy.* London: Routledge.

Szablowski, David. 2010. "Operationalizing Free, Prior, and Informed Consent in the Extractive Industry Sector? Examining the Challenges of a Negotiated Model of Justice." *Canadian Journal of Development Studies* 30 (1): 111–130.

Turnhout, Esther, Katja Neves, and Elisa De Lijster. 2014. "'Measurementality' in Biodiversity Governance: Knowledge, Transparency, and the Intergovernmental Science-Policy Platform on Biodiversity and Ecosystem Services (IPBES)." *Environment and Planning A: Economy and Space* 46 (3): 581–597.

UN FCCC (Framework Convention on Climate Change). 2011. "Report of the Conference of the Parties on Its Sixteenth Session, Held in Cancun from 29 November to 10 December 2010." https://unfccc.int/resource/docs/2010/cop16/eng/07a01.pdf.

UN-REDD. 2012. "Free, Prior, and Informed Consent for REDD+ in the Asia-Pacific Region: Lessons Learned." https://www.un-redd.org/sites/default/files/2021-09/FPIC%20Lessons%20Learned_Final_En%20%28694915%29.pdf.

UN-REDD. 2017. "The Fantastic Multiple Benefits of REDD+ . . . and How to Get Them!" Blog, September 8, 2017. https://www.un-redd.org/news/fantastic-multiple-benefits-redd-and-how-get-them.

VCS. 2017a. "VCS Program Guide: VCS Version 3 Requirements Document, 21 June 2017, v3.7." Verra. Accessed April 12, 2018. https://verra.org/wp-content/uploads/PREVIOUS-VERSION-VCS-Program-Guide-v3.7.pdf.

VCS. 2017b. "VCS Standards: VCS Version 3 Requirements Document, 21 June 2017, v3.7." Verra. Accessed April 12, 2018.

VCS. 2017c. "VCS Registration and Issuance Process: VCS Version 3 Procedural Document, 21 June 2017, v3.7." Verra. Accessed April 12, 2018. https://verra.org/programs/verified-carbon-standard/vcs-version-3-rules-and-requirements/.

VCS. 2017d. "VCS Climate, Community and Biodiversity Standards, Third Edition, v3.1, 21 June 2017." Verra. Accessed April 12, 2018. http://verra.org/wp-content/uploads/2017/12/CCB-Standards-v3.1_ENG.pdf.

VCS. 2018. "Verra Project Database: Reduced Emissions from Deforestation and Degradation in Keo Seima Wildlife Sanctuary." Verra. Accessed April 11, 2018. https://registry.verra.org/app/projectDetail/CCB/1650.

WCS (Wildlife Conservation Society). 2009. "Cambodia Creates First Park to Protect Carbon and Wildlife." WCS Newsroom, October 22, 2009. https://programs.wcs.org/newsroom/News-Releases/articleType/ArticleView/articleId/4825/categoryId/127/Cambodia-Creates-First-Park-to-Protect-Carbon-and-Wildlife.aspx.

WCS (Wildlife Conservation Society). 2016. "Cambodia's Keo Seima Wildlife Sanctuary Sells First Carbon Credits." WCS Newsroom, July 22, 2016. https://newsroom.wcs.org/News-Releases/articleType/ArticleView/articleId/9125/Cambodias-Keo-Seima-Wildlife-Sanctuary-Sells-First-Carbon-Credits.aspx.

WCS (Wildlife Conservation Society). 2021. "The Keo Seima Wildlife Sanctuary REDD+ Project." WCS Cambodia. Accessed August 15, 2021. https://seimaredd.wcs.org/.

West, Paige. 2006. *Conservation Is Our Government Now: The Politics of Ecology in Papua New Guinea*. Durham, NC: Duke University Press.

Yeang Donal, Kirtiman Sherchan, Joe Heffernan, Sophie May Chapman, Beth Dooley, and Gretchen Engbring. 2014. "Policy Brief: Carbon Rights and Benefit-Sharing in Cambodia." REDD+ Asia-Pacific Community Carbon Pools Programme. https://www.ecologic.eu/sites/files/publication/2014/carbon-rights-and-benefit-sharing-in-cambodia-vers2–2014-dooley.pdf.

CHAPTER 10

Carbon Crises
Molecular Violence across and beyond Southeast Asia

ANDREW MCGREGOR AND FIONA MILLER

Carbon violence is volumetric. It follows the movement and material transformations of carbon molecules across space and time and through underground spaces, waters, surfaces, and atmospheres. When coal is mined and burned, cattle grazed, forests razed, or oceans heated, carbon is transformed, and places are forcibly changed. Livelihoods and habitats in those places are lost and replaced with new socio-ecological systems that privatize and profit from the agencies of carbon. However, carbon violence spreads much further as atoms circulate across borders, through the atmosphere, and into seas, trapping heat and contributing to a myriad of climate-related carbon crises. Thus, carbon violence is experienced across volumetric space, both proximate and dispersed.

Much political ecology work focuses on the immediate sites of violence, exposing the devastating localized socio-ecological impacts of carbon-intensive industries (Eldridge 2015; Watts 2016). Drivers of violence are commonly traced to broader scales of influence—usually national and global—where policies, politics, economies, and powerful actors shape local events and processes. However, case studies are often examined in isolation, focusing more on the scaled structures governing human-environment relations in that place, and less on the social or material flows that connect those processes to other places. Opportunities to build understandings and solidarities across distinct but connected sites can be missed.

In contrast, the volumetric approach of climate science focuses almost exclusively on metrics, calculating carbon atoms through processes of abstraction and quantification. There is almost no mention of place, nor the social relations bound up in flows of carbon. Instead, the focus is on disruptions to global carbon cycles (see figure 10.1). The specter of a generalized planetary violence is present but unspecified, hovering in the shadows of the "endless algebra" (Lohmann 2011) of climate change negotiations and project interventions. Places dissolve into generic spaces of carbon, either sources or sinks, and are fed into formulas to model possible futures. The carbon molecules at the center of these calculations are mere numbers, abstracted as if they have no materiality, volume, history, or geography, existing only in an ever-circulating system.

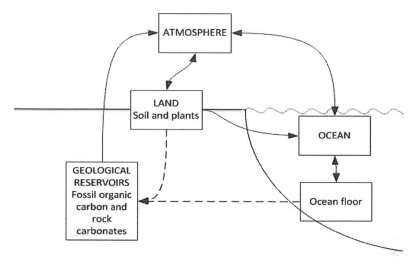

Figure 10.1. The biophysical carbon cycle. (Source: Sean Dunne, 2023)

In this chapter we develop a means of bringing these disparate bodies of knowledge together by focusing on the circulation of carbon through and between Southeast Asia and Australia, and the particular sites of violence that propel and are propelled by that circulation. In doing so, we emphasize that the abstract sources and sinks within the biophysical carbon cycle refer to unique and complex places where lives, livelihoods, economies, and ecologies are inseparably entwined with the agencies of carbon, through what McGregor et al. (2019) refer to as a "sociocarbon cycle." Similarly, we stress that carbon atoms transitioning through the biophysical carbon cycle materially connect sites of violence through more-than-human underground, surface, oceanic, and atmospheric networks that are often obscured by political ecology's more hierarchical, scalar, and human-focused approach.

In bringing these research trajectories into conversation, we seek to contribute novel approaches for a "world regional" political ecology (Miller and McGregor 2019). A regional lens provides a means of making connections between and within countries, so that the violence of coal extraction and combustion in Australia can be rendered visible and considerable at the same time as policies to sequester carbon in Indonesia or strategies of planned retreat from sea level rise in Vietnam. Through a world regional political ecology approach, we connect proximate and distant sites of carbon violence and generate stories and data that can inform questions concerned with regional responsibilities and justice in a climate-changing world.

Researching Carbon Violence

Violence, as a concept, has proved surprisingly difficult to define (Springer and Le Billon 2016; Pavoni and Tulumello 2018), and is instead commonly approached through three different descriptive forms. Direct violence refers to instances of immediate physical or mental harm; structural violence is associated with slow forms of violence that cause ongoing harm through oppressive or failing economic, political, social, or physical systems; and cultural violence refers to the symbols, mythologies, and ideologies that are used to legitimize direct and structural violence. These include the silencing, erasure, and othering associated with epistemic violence (Galtung 1969, 1990; Pavoni and Tulumello 2018; Spivak 1992).

Human geographers have explored the spaces of violence (e.g., Eldridge 2015; Pavoni and Tulumello 2018) and their underlying causes (Tyner and Inwood 2014) to position violence as a "processual and unfolding moment, rather than an 'act' or an 'outcome'" (Springer and Le Billon 2016, 2). Work in political ecology and science and technology studies has emphasized how changing biophysical conditions, such as those linked to climate change or access to natural resources, along with the production and dissemination of scientific knowledge, can also contribute to forms of violence (Barnett and Adger 2007; O'Lear 2016). While some of this work is critiqued for rekindling a version of environmental determinism, it also emphasizes the volumetric and temporal dimensions of violence. Bonds (2016), for example, analyzes the structural violence carbon industries inflict on others through climate change, something that requires thinking through the temporal and spatial disconnection between the causes and expression of violence. Rob Nixon (2011, 11) explains: "The explicitly temporal emphasis of slow violence allows us to keep front and centre the representational challenges and imaginative dilemmas posed not just by imperceptible violence but by imperceptible change whereby violence is decoupled from its original causes by the workings of time." Violence is both fast and slow, as well as proximate and distanced. As climate change and biodiversity loss spread across the planet, it is also clear that violence is more-than-human.

Theorists of violence acknowledge that violence against nonhumans exists (e.g., Galtung 1990) but is frequently hidden within analyses (Peluso and Watts 2001, 6). In contrast, recent work on infrastructural violence is increasingly advocating a more-than-human lens, recognizing that infrastructure projects inflict violence against humans and nonhumans, including "natural" infrastructures like rivers, forests, and landscapes (Enns and Sneyd 2020; Eldridge 2015). Rather than position nonhumans or nature as an inert backdrop upon which human violence occurs, a more-than-human approach recognizes that nonhumans can both cause and be affected by violence (e.g., Tsing 2005; Latour 2004). Further, violence against nonhumans is often inseparably entangled with violence against humans (Davis and Todd 2017; Whyte 2018). When more-than-human relations are violently altered, all those entities, including humans, who are reliant upon existing relations to flourish are affected. Adopting a more-than-human lens enables a much fuller appreciation of the extent of violence, including the slower forms of violence that occur through gradual degradation of socio-ecological systems over time and space.

As well as tracing and explaining the causes and effects of violence, theorists have sought to identify pathways to move beyond violence. Galtung (1969), for example, makes a distinction between negative and positive peace, with positive peace being not just the absence of violence (negative peace) but the presence of harmony and the active cultivation of the conditions of peace through an orientation to equity, reciprocity, and justice. A more-than-human consideration of violence can constructively contribute to not only the minimization of violence, but also opportunities to move toward the conditions of peace. Just as violence is always "processual and unfolding," so too is nonviolence, and so are the acts of care and repair required in the world to practice peace.

In what follows, we adopt this more-than-human lens to analyze sites of violence within the carbon cycle. We approach spaces of carbon in much the same way as Steinberg and Peters (2015) approach the oceans through their "wet ontology" that stresses "fluidity, volume, emergence, depth and liquidity." Carbon atoms, like water molecules, cycle through multiple material forms and volumetric spaces, inhabiting undergrounds, surfaces, seas, bodies, and atmospheres. The form carbon takes dictates the types of politics and violence that can emerge—from the wars surrounding fossil carbon, the clear-felling of forest carbon, and the global warming politics and impacts of atmospheric carbon. It also determines the fluidity, mobility, and governability of carbon, with fossilized carbon being claimed by states, extracted by corporations, and traded internationally, while atmospheric and oceanic carbon is largely ungovernable, slipping across geopolitical boundaries and creating fluid and shifting molecular connections between places. Our approach centers the transformation, fluidity, and flows of carbon to better understand how and why carbon violence occurs and how it might be avoided.

When carbon transforms into new states, the more-than-human relations reliant upon the initial state of carbon are also transformed. This need not be a negative transformation. For example, carbon sequestration by soils and forests increases the capacity for life. However, very often when humans forcibly transform carbon into new states, it is to accumulate value by capturing the economic benefits enabled through that transformation. Here we focus upon processes of extraction, combustion, sequestration, digestion, eructation, and molecular accumulation. We track these processes at four points in the biophysical carbon cycle:

mineral carbon, organic carbon 1 (cattle), organic carbon 2 (forests), and atmospheric and oceanic carbon. We then link each point with the practices of dispossession, privatization, and economic accumulation that characterize late-stage, neoliberal carbon capitalism.

To do so, we adopt a light-touch storytelling approach. Storytelling has become an important tool in environmental justice research, where it provides a means to give a voice to those suffering injustice while also providing a form in which narratives of injustice can be voiced and connected, prior to or in place of more conventional research techniques (Houston 2013; Pascoe, Dressler, and Minnegal 2019). Storytelling can creatively generate narratives that further understanding. Here we use storytelling as a method for centering research on the carbon cycle, reimagining the connections between proximate and distant sites of violence by following the journey of a carbon atom through a variety of material and molecular forms. We name this carbon atom based on the places and forms through which it passes to emphasize the materiality of carbon and that it has a history and geography. Our geographical focus is on Southeast Asia and some of the key carbon relations that connect it with Australia.

Mineral Carbon: Accumulation through Dispossession

*Through the process of **fossilization**, organic carbon—which starts as dense plant life—is converted into mineral carbon in the form of coal beneath Awabakal Country, now known in Australian settler colonial society as the Hunter Valley, located approximately 250 km north of Sydney. A Hunter Valley Coal carbon atom (HVC) lies untouched for millennia until a particular constellation of technology, ideology, and economic practices drives the displacement of people and the destruction of surface ecosystems to enable its **extraction**. Once dug from the ground, HVC is transported by train to the Port of Newcastle, before being loaded onto a massive bulk carrier—just one of the thousands of ships that form the extensive material flow of mineral carbon from Australia to countries in East, Southeast, and South Asia. HVC is loaded onto a ship that travels northward on the Pacific Ocean to a port in southern Thailand. Later, through the process of **combustion** in a Thai power plant, HVC creates electricity and is released into the atmosphere in the molecular form of CO_2.*

Long before the Anthropocene (Crutzen 2006), in the Paleozoic Era, volcanic and fluvial sedimentary rocks began to form in the Hunter River Valley. Deep, slow time resulted in the fossilization of ancient life to form large deposits of mineral carbon underground. The carbon lay undisturbed beneath the surface for millions of years and throughout the period of Aboriginal occupation, when the Awabakal, Darkinung, Geawegal, Gomeroi/Kamilaroi, Wiradjuri, and Wonnarua peoples cared for these lands and waters for millennia. An Awabakal creation story (Evans 2008) describes coal as "a combination of both darkness and light in the world," and, fearing the harm it could potentially cause, Awabakal ancestors kept it buried and hidden, trampling it underfoot for generations.

The origins of the Anthropocene are colonial (Davis and Todd 2017). British settler colonial expansion into the Hunter Valley was marked by the extraction of timber (forest carbon) and coal (mineral carbon) and the violent dispossession and displacement of Aboriginal peoples. When Australia was invaded and occupied by the British in 1788, a convict camp was established at the mouth of the Hunter River following the "discovery" of coal near what has become the present-day regional urban center of Newcastle (Evans 2008). The first exports of coal from Australia began in 1801, with 150 tons of Newcastle coal being sent elsewhere in the British Empire, to India (Huleatt 1981). Since that time, coal has shaped the settler colonial economy and presence in the Hunter Valley region and devastated ecological and human health. This has resulted in the loss of more than 99 percent of the vegetation of the central and lower valley and contributed to high levels of air and water pollution. The Hunter Valley has the highest human cancer fatality rates in the state of New South Wales (Evans 2008).

Few precautions have been taken regarding the potential human and more-than-human harm associated with coal. The extraction of mineral carbon from beneath stolen Aboriginal land has progressively intensified in recent decades, enabling a small set of mining corporations and their shareholders to capture value and accumulate immeasurable wealth, transforming the Hunter Valley into a key node in the global circuitry of coal. Each ton of coal from the Hunter Valley generates 2.7 tons of greenhouse gases, making "the burning of Hunter Valley coal the largest single direct and indirect contribution of the Australian economy to global warming" (Evans 2008, 6).

Much of this violence is driven by demand from Southeast, East, and South Asian countries (leading to localized forms of everyday violence—see chapter 2 in this volume, by Roberts and Mai), with Australia being the world's largest exporter of gas and coal (Moss 2021). Coal is extracted and sent through Newcastle, the world's largest coal port, to Southeast Asian power generators in Thailand, Indonesia, and Vietnam to generate electricity through processes of combustion. While the calculation of Australia's carbon emissions may stop at the nation's territorial border, the flows of carbon do not, with Australia's exported emissions (so-called Scope 3 emissions) now exceeding domestic/territorial (Scope 1 and 2) emissions (Moss 2021). The settler colonial ideology of extractivism and associated policies, infrastructure, and networks of actors have enabled and accelerated this immense material flow of mineral carbon around the globe, contributing to carbon-related violence near and far from sites of extraction. The combustion of this energy-dense matter and subsequent release of carbon dioxide into the atmosphere have resulted in disrupted and devastated underground, surface, and atmospheric ecologies.

In the neighboring country of Timor-Leste, huge oil and gas deposits lying beneath the Timor Sea are more likely to be associated with hope and possibilities. The wealth enabled by the extraction of this mineral carbon has the potential to enable newly independent Timor-Leste to rebuild after more than 270 years of Portuguese colonial rule and 26 years of Indonesian occupation, through investment in the much-needed human development of the Timorese people. The Australian government, however, sought to claim a disproportionate share of the oil and gas fields in negotiations concerning the Timor Gap Treaty, in contradiction of international maritime conventions (White 2017), and went so far as to approve spying operations to gain an unfair advantage in negotiations (Knaus 2019). An alliance between state and fossil fuel interests has sought to divert some of the flow of mineral carbon and associated wealth from deep below the Timor Sea to Australia. The enclosure of this mineral carbon wealth by Australia, if only partially, has the potential to reinforce regional inequalities and stymie Timor-Leste's efforts to bolster development through the agencies of carbon.

The extraction and combustion of mineral carbon in the form of coal, oil, and gas beneath the Hunter Valley and the Timor Sea is leading to the accumulation of extraordinary wealth for certain actors. It has also resulted in the intensification of material flows between Australia and the Asia Pacific region, the accumulation of the molecules of carbon dioxide in the atmosphere, and the associated intensification of global warming. It is evident that the mineral carbon industry's days are numbered. So, as attention turns to alternative sociocarbon futures for those tied to the mineral carbon industry, there are economic, physical, and social voids to be filled, restorative industries to be invested in, and reparations to be paid. Yet, the presence of mineral carbon in the atmosphere persists.

Organic Carbon 1: The Political Ecologies of Animal Protein

> *Released from coal via **combustion** within a Thai power plant, the HVC carbon atom drifts above Thailand, Malaysia, and Singapore, across the Indonesian archipelago and past Timor-Leste, before heading southeast toward Australia, traveling toward the place where it rested for so long. As it crosses the Northern Territory, it*

is ***sequestered*** *by gambia grass that has been introduced to feed the hundreds of thousands of cattle that are raised across the vast savannahs of northern Australia to feed Southeast Asian markets. The gambia grass converts CO_2 and light into plant carbohydrates via photosynthesis. After a few months, the gambia HVC atom is consumed by a cow. While most carbon molecules are converted via **digestion** into animal proteins, HVC is instead converted into methane that accumulates in the rumen of cattle. It is released into the atmosphere through **eructation** while on a massive boat exporting live cattle to Indonesia. The sequestration, digestion, and eructation processes transform HVC into HVC-NAC (Hunter Valley Coal— Northern Australian Cattle) and CO_2 into $CH4$, a much more potent and damaging atmospheric greenhouse gas.*

Organic carbon, in this case carbon inhabiting and sustaining cattle bodies, is a site of contestation. Historically, the carbon sequestration processes that infuse the sprawling savannahs of northern Australia have supported unique and diverse socio-ecological communities. Carbon becomes fixed into plants, enabling growth above and below the surface. When plants die and decompose, their roots degrade and enrich the soil with organic carbon, contributing to soil carbon sinks and providing nutrients for life. For millennia, Aboriginal Australians have cared for and sustained these processes through intimate understandings of place and practices of ecological and fire management.

For settler colonial society, savannahs are often seen as barriers to development. To create economic value, cattle have been introduced because their digestive processes can transform plant-based carbon into animal proteins much sought after domestically, and, more importantly, in growing Southeast Asian markets. While there are a variety of cattle stations in Australia's north, from small family-run farms and Aboriginal enterprises to huge corporate ventures, the beneficiaries of these industries are relatively few. Just 261 pastoral operations stretch across half the Northern Territory, with larger corporate entities disproportionately dominating the landscape (Neale and McDonald 2019). Massive cattle stations that run over millions of hectares are bought and sold for hundreds of millions of dollars to grow heat-tolerant Brahmin cattle, originally introduced from South Asia. Some of Australia's richest people, including those who have profited from carbon industries based on coal, as well as wealthy regional investors from Indonesia and Brunei and investors from further afield, like England and South Africa, profit from this transformative process.

The industry is enabled by legacies of violence, primarily being located on unceded Aboriginal land, and dotted with sites of frontier violence (Reynolds 2006; *The Guardian* 2019). Many conflicts were generated by the vast land claims made by colonialists to raise sheep and cattle, as well as reprisals for Aboriginal encounters with these "creatures of empire" (Anderson 2004). While Aboriginal cattle stations now exist, they were hard-fought, with the genesis of the Aboriginal Land Rights movement coming from the underpayment, mistreatment, and non-recognition of Gurindji people and their lands at the Wave Hill Station in the Northern Territory (Long 1996).

Contemporary violence takes many forms. There is the direct violence inflicted on cattle bodies as they are raised in hot climates to eventually be packed onto overcrowded ships and exported as "lively commodities" (Collard and Dempsey 2013) to Southeast Asian countries. Most end up in Indonesia, where they are fattened in feedlots before being slaughtered, dismembered, and sold. In the last decade, animal rights activists in Australia have occasionally exposed animal cruelty within the transport and slaughtering of live export animals, leading to nationalistic public protests in Australia and a temporary ban on live exports to Indonesia in 2014 (Munro 2014). Other forms of violence are less visible. To maximize profit, for example, woodlands are cleared if they are considered unproductive, causing widespread death, physical injuries, pain, and psychological distress to existing wildlife (Finn and Stephens 2017). Australia is a global deforestation hotspot, with the Wilderness Society (2019) estimating that 73 percent of all land clearing in Queensland and 93 percent in the Great Barrier Reef catchment is linked to cattle production. Some fifty million native animals are killed annually in Queensland and the neighboring state of New South Wales through land clearing (Finn and Stephens 2017).

Slower, structural forms of violence derive from the agencies of the organisms themselves. Biological processes of digestion and eructation convert plant carbohydrates into methane and release this rapidly accumulating and very potent greenhouse gas into the atmosphere. Despite decades of research, agricultural scientists have been unable to prevent the release of cattle methane (McGregor et al. 2021), the primary source of livestock industry emissions, which make up 14.5 percent of total anthropogenic greenhouse gas emissions (Gerber et al. 2013). In Australia, the introduction of exotic pasture such as fast-growing gambia grass to feed cattle has altered fire landscapes and contributed to decreases of species abundance in areas where it has escaped farm enclosures and invaded Aboriginal and ecological protected areas (Neale and MacDonald 2019). Despite the damage gambia grass is causing and its status as a declared weed by the Northern Territory government, pastoralists continue to grow and expand its range due to the profit that can be gained from growing cattle bodies faster (Neale and MacDonald 2019).

The cultural violence that normalizes these industries is not extremist ideologies but instead mainstream settler colonial assumptions that unceded land and more-than-human bodies are legitimate sites for economic accumulation, and that the "meatification"—or perhaps "beefication"—of Indonesian, Vietnamese, and broader regional diets is both desirable and unstoppable. Cattle exports have become bound up in discourses about feeding the world's seemingly insatiable need for animal protein by growing more beef, rather than addressing very uneven patterns of food consumption both among and within countries. While several high-profile reports have raised alarms about the impacts of animal agriculture on the carbon cycle and called for reductions in meat consumption (e.g., IPCC 2019; Springmann et al. 2018), they are likely to remain ineffectual while disconnected from the actual political ecologies of agricultural violence.

This is leading not only to local forms of more-than-human violences experienced by humans, cattle, and environments in Australia and Southeast Asia, but across the Asia Pacific, and much further afield as a consequence of global warming. Recognizing these connections—that gambia grass invasion, cattle welfare issues, biodiversity loss, and global warming are connected and enabled by globalizing settler colonial mentalities alongside the beefication of diets—provides opportunities to bring a much broader coalition of regional activists into conversation and action, including climate justice advocates, animal and land rights activists, and environmental campaigners. It also provides opportunities to extend the political scope for action from individualized dietary changes to structural reforms of land use.

Organic Carbon 2:
The Political Ecologies of Peat Forests

> Unlike most CH4 molecules that will eventually break down into other forms, the HVC-NAC molecule now circulates in the atmosphere as CH4 for ten years before it is absorbed by microscopic methanotrophs that inhabit the peat forests of Indonesia. In the province of Kalimantan, the methanotrophs convert it and release it as CO_2, which is again **sequestered**, this time by the ancient trees of a dense peat forest. For thousands of years, this sequestration process has supported the evolution of some of the most biodiverse landscapes on earth. However, forest carbon's **combustibility** results in the HVC-NAC atom being converted into HVC-NAC-KPF (Hunter Valley Coal—Northern Australian Cattle—Kalimantan Peat Forest) and it is released in searing heat as a CO_2 molecule once more when the peat forest is burned to make way for plantation agriculture.

The organic carbon stored in Indonesia's peat forests, like the savannahs stretching across northern Australia or the landscapes of the Hunter Valley, has value only to closely connected local communities, rather than external investors seeking quick profits. For investors, peat forests are an impediment to profit, often seen as underutilized wastelands in need of modernization. To that end, peat forests are being drained, and trees either harvested for their timber and/or burned to clear land for plantations, particularly oil palm plantations. Complex ecologies are violently ripped apart and local more-than-human communities forcibly dispossessed as chainsaws and fires combine to quickly devastate ancient socio-ecological systems. Astuti (2021, 382) writes that this form of both fast and slow violence "gradually renders the land uninhabitable, devoid of biodiversity, with the potential of displacing people who draw their livelihoods from peat ecosystems."

The more-than-human violence inflicted in peat forests comes from both smallholders who encroach upon forests as they establish small-scale agricultural plots and more extensive, often well-connected, agribusiness companies intent on setting up large-scale plantations, many of which are oil palm plantations (Austin et al. 2019). Denial of customary land rights, poverty, and a lack of alternative livelihood opportunities drive smallholder encroachment, while large plantation businesses are motivated by profit. Lack of land security and recognition for Indigenous and local forest communities, complex land use and concession systems that involve multiple ministries and layers of government, and close ties between forest and agricultural companies and government frustrate attempts by local and international civil society organizations interested in conservation, climate, and/or Indigenous rights to prevent deforestation. The combustibility, as well as malleability, of carbon in wooden forms (wood is made up of approximately 50 percent carbon atoms) makes them targets for timber harvesting and rapid clearance through fire. As is the case with mining and cattle production, the economic benefits of forest clearance are heavily skewed toward large agribusiness and forestry companies that can gain permits to clear large swathes of land (Austin et al. 2019).

Direct violence is experienced by the more-than-human communities endemic to Kalimantan, one of the most biodiverse places on earth. Peat forests are drained and then cleared, most often with fire, to create agricultural landscapes (see chapter 7 in this volume, by Goldstein). Perhaps the most notorious project was President Suharto's mega rice project that cleared one million hectares of peat forest on the island of Sumatra in 1996 to provide 2.5-hectare wet rice cultivation plots to 40,000 transmigrants from Java and Bali. Not only did the farmers struggle to establish these fields, but a drought in 1997 saw underground fires rip through the drained peat soils. Highly carbonized peat fires raged across Sumatra and Central Kalimantan in late 1997, generating a smoke haze and an associated health crisis across Sumatra, Singapore, and Malaysia (Goldstein 2016). Similarly devastating fires ripped through Indonesia in 2015 and again in 2019, causing upward of 100,000 premature deaths during each event. Structural violence is experienced by those forced off their traditional lands and through the rapid accumulation of carbon molecules released into the atmosphere through forest burning (see chapter 8 in this volume, by Varkkey et al.). The carbon dioxide emissions from the 1997 fires were estimated to have been the equivalent of between 13 percent and 40 percent of global annual carbon emissions from fossil fuels (Goldstein 2016).

Regular mass fire events have exposed the violence afflicting these shadow places to international communities and triggered a range of mechanisms aimed at slowing or reversing deforestation. These include timber and palm oil certification schemes that seek to prevent illegal deforestation and a high-profile financial mechanism, the REDD+ (Reducing Emissions from Deforestation and Forest Degradation) program. Countries or projects that can prove they have prevented deforestation through various verification mechanisms can apply for REDD+ carbon credits to sell to companies and countries seeking to offset their emissions. Indonesia, which has one of the highest rates of deforestation, and therefore potentially much to gain from reducing deforestation rates, has been an enthusiastic proponent of REDD+, attracting over a billion dollars of commitments from REDD+ supporters, some of whom, like Norway, have profited from the export of fossil carbon. The REDD+ program seeks to enable value formation from the carbon sequestration and storage capacities of forests, rather than the combustible properties of wood carbon.

While REDD+ has a certain compelling logic from the ecological modernization perspectives that pervade carbon cycle governance, putting a price on carbon sequestration to maintain the services of carbon sinks has been shown by many critical researchers to gloss over the complex political ecologies of deforestation (Corbera 2012; Milne et al. 2019; chapter 9 in this volume, by Milne and Mahanty). A range of problems have been identified, including technical issues of measurement, additionality, and permanence; complexity (Angelsen et al. 2012); uncertainty in funding streams (Dixon and Challies 2015); potential for the interests of large investors to override local concerns (McGregor 2010); poor community engagement and understanding (Howell 2015); and uncertainty around benefit flows, including jobs and income (Angelsen et al. 2012). This has led to global criticism of REDD+ from groups who are opposed to the commodification of nature, the ethics of offsetting, and green grabs and dispossession (Cabello and Gilbertson 2010). Local community opposition has also grown in many parts of Indonesia, including objections to a REDD+ afforestation project on the site of the failed mega rice project in Sumatra (Lounela 2015). While a handful of projects have been established in Indonesia, they have experienced delays and setbacks, and, somewhat ironically, given the economic logic that underpins them, their number and size represent very poor value for money given the enormous amounts of investment committed.

Some progress on environmental protection in Indonesia has been made, however, with a series of presidential decrees—beginning in 2011 and made permanent in 2019—placing a moratorium on draining and clearing new peat forest areas (Astuti 2021). While the decrees have been criticized for a range of reasons, there has nevertheless been a substantial decrease in the rate of deforestation in the protected areas (Samadhi 2019). A Peatland Restoration Agency has been established, with a grand mandate but limited resources and influence (Astuti 2021). Certainly, the political landscape governing peat forests in Indonesia appears to have shifted somewhat, raising the prospect that alternative sociocarbon cycles that are not based on the combustible properties of carbon but on its capacities for sequestration may yet be possible. Such a transformation is likely to be difficult and expensive and brings into view the responsibilities not only of Indonesian actors who have profited from the more-than-human violence of peat forest destruction, but of more distant governments and corporations, such as the Australian coal and cattle barons who are connected via the volumetric flow of carbon from underground spaces and cattle bodies into Indonesian atmospheres. Without action oriented at pursuing conditions of peace, the potential of the complex forest ecologies of Indonesia, together with other terrestrial and marine systems found throughout Southeast Asia, to effectively sequester carbon from the atmosphere and limit dangerous climate change will continue to be dramatically undermined.

Atmospheric and Oceanic Carbon: The Political Ecologies of Sea Level Rise

> *The burning of peat forests in Indonesia releases HVC-NAC-KPF in the form of a CO_2 molecule that **accumulates** in the atmosphere with other greenhouse gases. The warming of the atmosphere and oceans sets in motion slow onset changes, including sea level rise, as well as rapid onset events, such as floods. The CO_2 molecule circulates in the monsoon weather patterns that drive cycles of life and livelihoods across Asia. Eventually HVC-NAC-KPF becomes sequestered by the hotly contested and warming sea off the coast of Vietnam, variously known as the East Sea and South China Sea. HVC-NAC-KPF-ES (Hunter Valley Coal—Northern Australian Cattle—Kalimantan Peat Forest—East Sea) dissolves into seawater, becoming part of the rising tide of salt water that threatens the settlements, coastal forests, and rice fields of the "rice bowl" of the Mekong Delta.*

It is well known that the accumulation of CO_2, CH4 and other greenhouse gases (GHGs) in the atmosphere results in the warming of the atmosphere, the oceans, and the land, leading to both slow and rapid-onset environmental changes. Disruption of the carbon cycle affects atmospheric, maritime, and terrestrial systems globally, yet the manifestation of this disruption in various forms of slow or rapid violence is unevenly distributed across space.

Despite contributing little to global carbon emissions, Vietnam is subject to the manifestation of violence accompanying the accumulation of carbon in the atmosphere through its high vulnerability to climate risks, particularly sea level rise and environmental extremes (Dasgupta et al. 2009; Carew-Reid 2008). The geography of Vietnam situates it at the interface of the land and the sea, multiple rivers, and monsoon cycles. It therefore already deals with a significant humanitarian and economic toll from disasters. According to the Global Climate Risk Index, Vietnam is one of the most disaster-affected countries in the world (Eckstein et al. 2019). Sea level rise, coastal erosion, heatwaves, and drought, as well as more rapid-onset events such as storms and floods accompanying the accumulation of GHGs in the atmosphere, are likely to intensify carbon violence, leading to harmful direct impacts on human and nonhuman health, loss of life and ways of living, loss of livelihoods, and decline in the biodiversity of terrestrial, estuarine, and marine systems. A one-meter sea level rise, for instance, would be devastating for the complex coastal systems and settlements concentrated along Vietnam's long coastline and deltas, and is estimated to likely affect 12 percent of the country and inundate some 23 percent of the population, which is equivalent to 17 million people (ISPONRE 2009). Some 39 percent of the Mekong Delta would be at risk of severe flooding (MONRE 2016).

These changes have long been anticipated. The construction of defensive infrastructure in the form of sea walls and coastal dikes, the eviction of people from coastal forests for the purposes of maintaining natural defenses, and the forced resettlement of people from high-risk areas are leading to a reconfiguring of human and nonhuman relations within particular places (Miller 2020; Miller et al. 2022). These infrastructural and state-led resettlement schemes, though often justified on the basis of keeping people and places safe, can have their own harmful impacts on socio-ecologies (Miller et al. 2022). One clear expression of carbon violence is displacement.

Displacement of human and nonhuman populations for the purposes of extraction of fossil fuels and the clearance of land and forests for farm animals and plantations, as documented above, is associated with the processes that drive the molecular violence of climate change. Yet, displacement is also strongly evident with the deteriorating environmental and economic conditions resulting from climate risks, as well as some defensive infrastructural responses to these risks. Climate and other anthropogenic environmental changes have contributed significantly to the rapid rise in distress migration from the climate hotspot of the Mekong Delta in recent years, as have other slower forms of violence. For instance, a major World Bank–funded scheme (1999–2007) to protect coastal mangrove forests saw thousands of households forcibly resettled farther inland in the provinces of Ca Mau and Bac Lieu to establish forest conservation zones. Many of these households were subsequently unable to reestablish their livelihoods due to the deteriorating environmental conditions, including dramatically declining fisheries (Miller et al. 2022). Ca Mau province now has the highest out-migration rate in the delta (Nguyen et al. 2019). Coastal hazards, such as storms and erosion, floods, and droughts, are contributing to people abandoning agriculture, fishing, and aquaculture that had previously been well adapted to seasonal variations in temperature and rainfall. One of Southeast Asia's most intensive migration routes lies between the rice bowl of the Mekong Delta and the industrial zone of Ho Chi Minh City. In the five-year period up to 2009, some 714,000 people migrated from the delta to the region around Ho Chi Minh City (Entzinger and Scholten 2016). Slow violence is apparent in the way people's relations with familiar socio-ecologies are now being severed, with many migrants now forming a reservoir of cheap labor for energy-intensive industries on the edge of the coastal (soon to be mega-) city of Ho Chi Minh, with many forming a "surplus population" (Li 2010) unable to find dignified and meaningful employment.

Vietnam has experienced generations of violence wrought by French colonialism and the wars of independence from the French and against the United States and its allies. The violence of war scarred not only people's lives but also the landscape, with the term "ecocide" used to refer to the targeting of the environment with toxic chemicals, such as Agent Orange, by the US military (Zierler 2011). The war and its aftermath led to mass displacement, with over one and a half million people forced to leave their homeland in one of the biggest refugee crises of the last century. Now it is violence of a different kind that is driving displacement within Vietnam. Yet there are hopeful historical analogues that can be drawn on here. Just as the Herculean effort to replant mangroves damaged by defoliants in the war helped restore coastal socio-ecologies on a massive scale in the 1980s (Hong and San 1993), new reparative and regenerative efforts are not only possible but required as part of locally led adaptation efforts. The orientation of such actions should be to not only reduce harm and displacement but to build the conditions of peace through the creation of livelihoods premised on human and nonhuman flourishing. Yet, such efforts will be inconsequential if the drivers of carbon violence are not addressed. The recent construction of a coal-fired power plant and import terminal in the coastal district of Duyen Hai in the Mekong Delta, which will likely be fed by Australian coal, needs to be highlighted in this context, as regenerative and reparative efforts need to be pursued in parallel with decarbonization and regionally connected just transitions, or else carbon violence will persist.

In this chapter, we have sought to make connections between sites of carbon violence more visible. We do this for four reasons. First, we aim to politicize the carbon cycle. Climate science currently tracks the flow of carbon atoms through the carbon cycle as though the transformation of carbon from one state to another is a simple biophysical process. What we have emphasized here are the lives, places, socio-ecologies, and forms of violence caught up in the transformation of carbon from one state to another. While carbon does naturally transform from one state to another, often over much larger geological timescales (including the millions of years it takes for plant matter in the form of a peat forest to transform into coal), carbon economies have intensified this, making carbon transformation a rapid, socially produced, and contested process. In this formulation, the arrows that depict mineral, organic, or atmospheric carbon changing to another state within the carbon cycle represent processes and spaces of dispossession, accumulation, and violence (see figure 10.1). If the biophysical carbon cycle is seen as a sociocarbon cycle, a different politics of intervention becomes possible (McGregor et al. 2019).

Second, by placing sites of violence side by side, through the light storytelling approach we have adopted here, we make connections between places more visible. Through tracking the geography of an imaginary carbon atom—HVC-NAC-KPF-ES—we have shown that when carbon atoms shift state into new molecular forms, places often experience forms of more-than-human violence. Questions of responsibility within climate justice research have been hampered by the difficulties of associating blame with individual entities given that global heating is the outcome of cumulative actions over space and time. Australia's live export trade to Indonesia, for example, is insignificant at a global scale. However, we have shown that while climate change is the outcome of global capitalism, this manifests in particular place-based strategies of accumulation and dispossession. Clearly, Australian and Indonesian cattle barons, alongside plantation agribusinesses burning their way through Southeast Asian peatlands, as well as coal mining companies, coal-fired power generators, and the states captured by fossil fuel interests, are *more* responsible for Vietnamese experiences of sea level rise than many others. Our study demonstrates that the expanding carbon economies of Indonesia and Australia are directly linked to displacement and shrinking livelihood opportunities in Vietnam. In storying carbon transformations, the most influential and direct perpetrators of carbon violence can be made visible and held to account. As Bonds (2016, 15–17) argues, "responsibility for the structural violence of climate change is not shared evenly," and social scientists can play an essential role in "naming those organizations most responsible for global warming . . . [to] help advance political campaigns to reduce carbon emissions."

Third, when placed side by side, the similarities between sites and processes of violence become more apparent (see table 10.1). In the cases analyzed, powerful private interests profit from the agencies of carbon, accumulating wealth through transforming carbon from one state to another. Coal miners accumulate value through extraction and combustion, cattle barons through sequestration and digestion, plantation companies through sequestration and combustion. In each case, profits are concentrated among a relatively small group of externally based companies primarily operating on unceded lands where Indigenous and local communities have been dispossessed. Political ecology has traditionally focused on the direct violence inflicted on local socio-ecologies as ecosystems are destroyed, species and ecological communities lost, and people are either forced off their land and/or away from their livelihoods. Here we have also shown that local incidences of violence are connected to one another through the flows of carbon across volumetric spaces. Slower forms of structural violence dissipate through the atmosphere, in smoke haze, or through the multiple crises associated with the global accumulation of carbon atoms, such as sea level rise in Vietnam. In each case, it is the most vulnerable who are most impacted, and they are also excluded from the benefits, while those profiting from the destruction experience few negative impacts, if any at all. The cultural violence that enables such adverse outcomes is not only neocolonial but thoroughly neoliberal in ways that have sought to justify the privatization and utilization of socio-ecologies and land for short-term economic gain irrespective of the more-than-human costs.

Finally, we believe the first three points can inform regional responses to carbon crises in two ways. First, while global forums provide one route to pursue climate justice, we are hopeful that regional-scale analyses can also provide openings for a regional politics concentrating on responsibility and reparations. Our analysis reveals that many damaging industries work at regional scales, whether it is timber, oil palm, cattle, or coal, whereas many of the civil society organizations monitoring and contesting these industries are national in orientation. This means that coal and beef barons in Australia are less likely to be the focus of climate protests in Southeast Asia despite the linkages and responsibilities those Australian companies have to Vietnam and other vulnerable countries in Southeast Asia through volumetric carbon networks. Just as pressure has been placed on coal miners in Australia through the Pacific Climate Warrior campaigns that have developed regional strategies targeting Australian coal ports (Fair 2015; McNamara and Farbotko 2017), it is possible to imagine a regional Southeast Asian climate politics that seeks to leverage regional investment, commercial, trade, and diplomatic relations to pursue regional goals and responsibilities.

Table 10.1. Tracing the flows of carbon violence

States of carbon	Carbon agencies	Drivers of violence	Forms of violence	Strategies for peace
Mineral carbon	Fossilization; extraction; combustion.	Settler colonial and extractive economies; denial of Indigenous knowledges and relations with country; global capital networks enabling coal exports.	Displacement, dispossession; destruction of ecosystems; impacts on human health.	Regionally connected just transitions from fossil fuels; Indigenous land rights and reparations; repair and rehabilitation of mining voids; investment in alternative non-fossil fuel sources of energy.
Organic carbon 1: cattle	Sequestration; digestion; eructation.	Settler colonial land grabs; privatization of land and carbon; logics of economic accumulation; demand for cattle products.	Animal slaughter; deforestation; habitat and livelihood loss; land dispossession; invasive species; enhanced fire intensities; GHG emissions.	Land use change; alternative food systems; Indigenous land title; animal, biodiversity, climate, and Indigenous protest; sequestration economies.
Organic carbon 2: peat forests	Sequestration; combustion.	State and corporate land grabs; privatization of land and carbon; logics of economic accumulation; demand for plantation products.	Deforestation; habitat and livelihood loss; land dispossession; enhanced fire intensities; GHG emissions.	Land use change; Indigenous land title; conservation law and protection; restoration; sequestration economies.
Atmospheric and oceanic carbon	Accumulation.	GHG emissions leading to global warming as manifested in sea level change, meteorological and environmental extremes.	Displacement in the form of distress migration and forced resettlement; harm to human and nonhuman health; loss of life and ways of living; loss of livelihoods; decline in the biodiversity of terrestrial, estuarine, and marine systems.	Reparative, regenerative, and locally led adaptation efforts; decarbonization and regionally connected just transitions.

Following Galtung (1969), a second potential component of a regional response to carbon crises goes beyond preventing violence and seeking justice and reparations, to also pursuing the conditions for peace and more-than-human flourishing. This more generative approach asks what sort of carbon transformations are nurturing and desirable, and which ones improve societies, repair socio-ecologies, restore relations of care, and minimize violence. This will differ from place to place; even the extraction of fossil fuels may be used to reduce harm if used and distributed well, as many hope for the offshore Timorese gas and oil fields. Of the transformations we analyzed, however, it seemed carbon sequestration through forests and plants was the one that enabled diverse forms of life while also slowing the accumulation of carbon atoms in the atmosphere. Such regenerative processes will never be enough to address the multiple carbon crises associated with entrenched carbon industries, but they are potential sources of hope. While political ecologists have been quick to critique those that have sought to privatize the benefits of sequestration, there may be other pathways through which sequestration processes can be aided and supported in securing a less violent, more just, and more peaceful world.

References

Anderson, Virginia DeJohn. 2004. *Creatures of Empire: How Domestic Animals Transformed Early America*. Oxford: Oxford University Press.

Angelsen, Arild, Maria Brockhaus, William D. Sunderlin, and Louis V. Verchot, eds. 2012. *Analysing REDD+: Challenges and Choices*. Bogor: Centre for International Forestry Research.

Astuti, Rini. 2021. "Governing the Ungovernable: The Politics of Disciplining Pulpwood and Palm Oil Plantations in Indonesia's Tropical Peatland." *Geoforum* 124:381–391.

Austin, Kemen G., Amanda Schwantes, Yaofeng Gu, and Prasad S. Kasibhatla. 2019. "What Causes Deforestation in Indonesia?" *Environmental Research Letters* 14:024007.

Barnett, John, and W. Neil Adger. 2007. "Climate Change, Human Security and Violent Conflict." *Political Geography* 26:639–655.

Bonds, Eric. 2016. "Upending Climate Violence Research: Fossil Fuel Corporations and the Structural Violence of Climate Change." *Human Ecology Review* 22 (2): 3–24.

Cabello, Joanna, and Tamra Gilbertson, eds. 2010. *No REDD: A Reader*. Carbon Trade Watch and Indigenous Environmental Network.

Carew-Reid, Jeremy. 2008. *Rapid Assessment of the Extent and Impact of Sea Level Rise in Viet Nam*. Hanoi: ICEM.

Collard, Rosemary-Claire, and Jessica Dempsey. 2013. "Life for Sale? The Politics of Lively Commodities." *Environment and Planning A: Economy and Space* 45:2682–2699.

Corbera, Esteve. 2012. "Problematizing REDD+ as an Experiment in Payments for Ecosystem Services." *Current Opinion in Environmental Sustainability* 4 (6): 612–619. https://doi.org/10.1016/j.cosust.2012.09.010.

Crutzen, Paul J. 2006. "The 'Anthropocene.'" In *Earth System Science in the Anthropocene*, edited by Eckart Ehlers and Thomas Krafft, 13–18. Berlin: Springer.

Dasgupta, Susmita, Benoit Laplante, Craig Meisner, David Wheeler, and Jianping Yan. 2009. "The Impact of Sea Level Rise on Developing Countries: A Comparative Analysis." *Climatic Change* 93:379–388.

Davis, Heather, and Zoe Todd. 2017. "On the Importance of a Date, or Decolonizing the Anthropocene." *ACME: An International Journal for Critical Geographies* 16 (4): 761–780.

Dixon, Rowan, and Edward Challies. 2015. "Making REDD+ Pay: Shifting Rationales and Tactics of Private Finance and the Governance of Avoided Deforestation in Indonesia." *Asia Pacific Viewpoint* 56:6–20.

Eckstein, David, Vera Künzel, Laura Schäfer, and Maik Winges. 2019. "Global Climate Risk Index 2020: Who Suffers Most from Extreme Weather Events? Weather-Related Loss Events in 2018 and 1999 to 2018." Bonn: Germanwatch. https://www.germanwatch.org/sites/default/files/20-2-01e%20Global%20Climate%20Risk%20Index%202020_14.pdf.

Eldridge, Erin R. 2015. "The Continuum of Coal Violence and Post-Coal Possibilities in the Appalachian South." *Journal of Political Ecology* 22 (1): 279–298.

Enns, Charis, and Adam Sneyd. 2020. "More-than-Human Infrastructural Violence and Infrastructural Justice: A Case Study of the Chad–Cameroon Pipeline Project." *Annals of the American Association of Geographers* 111:481–497.

Entzinger Hans, and Peter Scholten. 2016. *Adapting to Climate Change through Migration: A Case Study of the Vietnamese Mekong River Delta*. Geneva: International Organization for Migration.

Evans, Geoff R. 2008. "Transformation from 'Carbon Valley' to a 'Post-Carbon Society' in a Climate Change Hot Spot: The Coalfields of the Hunter Valley, New South Wales, Australia." *Ecology and Society* 13 (1): 39.

Fair, Hannah. 2015. "Not Drowning but Fighting: Pacific Islands Activists." *Forced Migration Review* 49:58–59.

Finn, Hugh, and Nahiid S. Stephens. 2017. "The Invisible Harm: Land Clearing Is an Issue of Animal Welfare." *Wildlife Research* 44 (5): 377–391. https://doi.org/10.1071/WR17018.

Galtung, Johan. 1969. "Violence, Peace, and Peace Research." *Journal of Peace Research* 6 (3): 167–191.

Galtung, Johan. 1990. "Cultural Violence." *Journal of Peace Research* 27 (3): 291–305.

Gerber, P., H. Steinfeld, B. Henderson, A. Mottet, C. Opio, J. Dijkman, A. Falcucci, and G. Tempio. 2013. *Tackling Climate Change through Livestock: A Global Assessment of Emissions and Mitigation Opportunities*. Rome: Food and Agriculture Organisation.

Goldstein, Jenny E. 2016. "Carbon Bomb: Indonesia's Failed Mega Rice Project." *Arcadia* (Spring 2016), no. 6. https://doi.org/10.5282/rcc/7474.

The Guardian. 2019. "The Killing Times: A Massacre Map." November 18, 2019. https://www.theguardian.com/australia-news/ng-interactive/2019/mar/04/massacre-map-australia-the-killing-times-frontier-wars.

Hong Phan Nguyen and Ho'ang Thi San. 1993. *Mangroves of Vietnam*. Hanoi: IUCN.

Houston, Donna. 2013. "Environmental Justice Storytelling: Angels and Isotopes at Yucca Mountain, Nevada." *Antipode* 45 (2): 417–435.

Howell, Signe Lise. 2015. "Politics of Appearances: Some Reasons Why the UN-REDD Project in Central Sulawesi Failed to Unite the Various Stakeholders." *Asia Pacific Viewpoint* 56:37–47.

Huleatt, M. B. 1981. "Black Coal in Australia." Bureau of Mineral Resources, Geology and Geophysics. *Australian Mineral Industry Quarterly* 34. Archived in Australian Bureau of Statistics, *Year Book of Australia, 1982.* https://www.abs.gov.au/ausstats/abs@.nsf/featurearticlesbytitle/09E60850418239F6CA2570A80011A395.

IPCC (Intergovernmental Panel on Climate Change). 2019. *IPCC Special Report on Climate Change, Desertification, Land Degradation, Sustainable Land Management, Food Security, and Greenhouse Gas Fluxes in Terrestrial Ecosystems. Summary for Policymakers.* Geneva: IPCC.

ISPONRE. 2009. *Vietnam Assessment Report on Climate Change.* Hanoi: Institute of Strategy and Policy on Natural Resources and Environment. Viet Nam: ISPONRE.

Knaus, Christopher. 2019. "Witness K and the 'Outrageous' Spy Scandal That Failed to Shame Australia." *The Guardian,* August 10, 2019. https://www.theguardian.com/australia-news/2019/aug/10/witness-k-and-the-outrageous-spy-scandal-that-failed-to-shame-australia.

Latour, Bruno. 2004. *The Politics of Nature: How to Bring the Sciences into Democracy.* Cambridge, MA: Harvard University Press.

Li, Tania Murray. 2010. "To Make Live or Let Die? Rural Dispossession and the Protection of Surplus Populations." *Antipode* 41:66–93.

Lohmann, Larry. 2011. "The Endless Algebra of Climate Markets." *Capitalism, Nature Socialism* 22:93–116.

Long, Jeremy. 1996. "Frank Hardy and the 1966 Wave Hill Walk-Off." *Northern Perspective* 19:1–9.

Lounela, Anu. 2015. "Climate Change Disputes and Justice in Central Kalimantan, Indonesia." *Asia Pacific Viewpoint* 56:62–78.

McGregor, Andrew. 2010. "Green and REDD? Towards a Political Ecology of Deforestation in Aceh, Indonesia." *Human Geography* 3:21–34.

McGregor, Andrew, Edward Challies, Amanda Thomas, Rini Astuti, Pete Howson, Suraya Afiff, Sara Kindon, and Sophie Bond. 2019. "Sociocarbon Cycles: Assembling and Governing Forest Carbon in Indonesia." *Geoforum* 99:32–41.

McGregor, Andrew, Lauren Rickards, Donna Houston, Michael K. Goodman, and Milena Bojovic. 2021. "The Biopolitics of Cattle Methane Emissions Reduction: Governing Life in a Time of Climate Change." *Antipode* 53:1161–1185.

McNamara, Karen E., and Carol Farbotko. 2017. "Resisting a 'Doomed' Fate: An Analysis of the Pacific Climate Warriors." *Australian Geographer* 48 (1): 17–26.

Miller, Fiona. 2020. "Exploring the Consequences of Climate-Related Displacement for Just Resilience in Vietnam." *Urban Studies* 57 (7): 1570–1587.

Miller, Fiona, and Andrew McGregor. 2019. "Rescaling Political Ecology? World Regional Approaches to Climate Change in the Asia Pacific." *Progress in Human Geography* 44 (4): 663–682.

Miller, Fiona, Tran Thi Phung Ha, Huynh Van Da, Ngo Thi Thanh Thuy, and Boi Huyen Ngo. 2022. "Double Displacement—Interactions between Resettlement, Environmental Change and Migration." *Geoforum* 129:13–27.
Milne, Sarah, Sango Mahanty, Phuc Xuan To, Wolfram H. Dressler, Peter Kanowski, and Maylee Thawat. 2019. "Learning from 'Actually Existing' REDD+: A Review of Ethnographic Findings." *Conservation and Society* 17 (1): 84–95.
MONRE. 2016. *Climate Change and Sea Level Rise Scenarios for Viet Nam.* Hanoi: Ministry of Natural Resources and Environment.
Moss, Jeremy. 2020. "Australia: An Emissions Super-Power." Climate Transitions Series. Sydney: UNSW. https://apo.org.au/sites/default/files/resource-files/2020-07/apo-nid 306756.pdf.
Munro, Lyle. 2014. "The Live Animal Export Controversy in Australia: A Moral Crusade Made for the Mass Media." *Social Movement Studies* 14:214–229.
Neale, Timothy, and Jennifer Mairi Macdonald. 2019. "Permits to Burn: Weeds, Slow Violence, and the Extractive Future of Northern Australia." *Australian Geographer,* no. 50, 417–433.
Nguyen, Hung, Raymong Chiong, Manuel Chica, R. H. Middleton, and Sandeep Dhakal. 2019. "Agent-Based Modeling of Migration Dynamics in the Mekong Delta, Vietnam: Automated Calibration Using a Genetic Algorithm." In *2019 IEEE Congress on Evolutionary Computation (CEC),* 3372–3379. Wellington: IEEE.
Nixon, Rob. 2011. *Slow Violence and the Environmentalism of the Poor.* Cambridge, MA: Harvard University Press.
O'Lear, Shannon. 2016. "Climate Science and Slow Violence: A View from Political Geography and STS on Mobilizing Technoscientific Ontologies of Climate Change." *Political Geography* 52:4–13.
Pascoe, Sophie, Wolfram H. Dressler, and Monica Minnegal. 2019. "Storytelling Climate Change: Causality and Temporality in the REDD+ Regime in Papua New Guinea." *Geoforum* 124:360–370.
Pavoni, Andrea, and Simone Tulumello. 2018. "What Is Urban Violence?" *Progress in Human Geography* 44:49–76.
Peluso, Nancy Lee, and Michael Watts. 2001. "Violent Environments." In *Violent Environments,* edited by Nancy Lee Peluso and Michael Watts, 3–38. Ithaca, NY: Cornell University Press.
Reynolds, Henry. 2006. *The Other Side of the Frontier: Aboriginal Resistance to the European Invasion of Australia.* Sydney: UNSW Press.
Samadhi, Nirarta. 2019. "Three Benefits of Indonesia's Permanent Ban on Forest Clearance." *The Conversation,* August 15, 2019. https://theconversation.com/three-benefits-of-indonesias-permanent-ban-on-forest-clearance-121751.
Spivak, Gayatri Chakravorty. 1992. "Can the Subaltern Speak?" In *Colonial Discourse and Post-Colonial Theory,* edited by Patrick Williams and Laura Chrisman, 66–111. New York: Columbia University Press.
Springer, Simon, and Philippe Le Billon. 2016. "Violence and Space: An Introduction to the Geographies of Violence." *Political Geography* 52:1–3.
Springmann, Marco, Michael Clark, Daniel Mason-D'Croz, Keith Wiebe, Benjamin Leon Bodirsky, Luis Lassaletta, Wim de Vries, Sonja J. Vermeulen, Mario Herrero, Kimberly

M. Carlson, Malin Jonell, Max Troell, Fabrice DeClerck, Line J. Gordon, Rami Zurayk, Peter Scarborough, Mike Rayner, Brent Loken, Jess Fanzo, H. Charles J. Godfray, David Tilman, Johan Rockström, and Walter Willett. 2018. "Options for Keeping the Food System within Environmental Limits." *Nature* 562:519–525.

Steinberg, Philip, and Kimberley Peters. 2015. "Wet Ontologies, Fluid Spaces: Giving Depth to Volume through Oceanic Thinking." *Environment and Planning D: Society and Space* 33 (2): 247–264.

Tsing, Anna. 2005. *Friction: An Ethnography of Global Connection*. Princeton, NJ: Princeton University Press.

Tyner, J., and J. Inwood. 2014. "Violence as Fetish: Geography, Marxism, and Dialectics." *Progress in Human Geography* 38 (6): 771–784.

Watts, Michael. 2016. "The Political Ecology of Oil and Gas in West Africa's Gulf of Guinea: State, Petroleum, and Conflict in Nigeria." In *The Palgrave Handbook of the International Political Economy of Energy*, edited by Thijs Van de Graaf, Benjamin K. Sovacool, Arunabha Ghosh, Florian Kern, and Michael T. Klare, 559–584. London: Palgrave Macmillan.

White, Rob. 2017. "Corruption and the Securitisation of Nature." *International Journal for Crime, Justice and Social Democracy* 6 (4): 55–70.

Whyte, Kyle P. 2018. "Indigenous Science (Fiction) for the Anthropocene: Ancestral Dystopias and Fantasies of Climate Change Crises." *Environment and Planning E: Nature and Space* 1 (1–2): 224–242.

Wilderness Society. 2019. *Drivers of Deforestation and Land Clearing in Queensland*. Hobart: Wilderness Society.

Zierler, David. 2011. *The Invention of Ecocide: Agent Orange, Vietnam, and the Scientists Who Changed the Way We Think about the Environment*. Athens: University of Georgia Press.

Atmospheric
An Afterword

FRANCK BILLÉ

On September 9, 2020, the sun did not rise for the residents of Northern California's Bay Area. Instead, by 9 a.m. the darkness had gradually, reluctantly, turned an eerie shade of orange. Over the next twenty-four hours, news channels and social media published striking photographs and ran stories about apocalyptic Martian skies. As wildfires raged across the region, a haze had shrouded San Francisco and Oakland, blocking sunlight and tinging the skies an unprecedented color. But unlike the 2018 wildfires in the Napa Valley that had enveloped the Bay Area in acrid smoke, there was no perceptible smell on that day. Yet the orange haze was just as toxic—a combination of fog and smoke in the upper atmosphere scattering wavelengths of blue light, and letting only the warmer colors reach the Earth's surface—with noxious but imperceptible effects.

This extraordinary event connects with the suffocating haze crises in Southeast Asia and brings up three points of tension that echo core concerns in this book. I will develop these concerns in more depth below. It speaks, on the one hand, to the issue of visibility and invisibility that can belie the severity of atmospheric violence and environmental damage. As Dressler and Mostafanezhad highlight in their introduction and as is later exemplified in several chapters of the book (chapter 3, by Dressler; chapter 5, by Baird; chapter 8, by Varkkey, Copeland, and Shaiful), the violence of atmospheres often gains palpability through wars over resources, territories, and bodies. Like infrastructure, revealed only when it breaks down, the sudden perceptibility of air quality indexes a shift or trigger in the normal running of things. This is not a transformation from benign to violent, but a lateral slippage revealing the violence that was there all along.

A second aspect worth noting in the reporting of the orange skies of September 9, 2020, is the adjectives that were chosen: Martian, Mars-like, alien. But if this meteorological phenomenon was an outlier and certainly constituted a form of extreme weather, there was nothing extraterrestrial about it. Its occurrence denoted instead an acceleration: a different temporality rather than a different spatiality. This central issue is raised at several junctures in the collection, particularly in chapter 5 by Baird, chapter 6 by Grundy-Warr and Middleton, and chapter 10 by McGregor and Miller. Through the lens of different ethnographic contexts, they insist on the significance of slow, quotidian violence, which all too often is obscured by the rubric of the catastrophic yet imparts form and directionality to extreme weather events.

Where spatiality comes into view is in the intrinsic entanglements of the atmospheric, in the fact that ultimately all weather systems are planetary in nature. Analyses of atmospheric violence thus necessarily take us beyond the local, regional, and—more importantly, perhaps—the horizontal. The question of the volumetric is discussed in the introduction to the collection and reprised in several chapters, notably in chapter 1, by Toumbourou et al.; chapter 2, by Roberts and Mai; chapter 4, by Thomas, Kelly, and Shattuck; and chapter 7, by Goldstein. As I flesh out below, a three-dimensional scope allows for a more comprehensive view of entanglements across scales (local, regional, global), across life-forms (human and nonhuman animals, flora), and across the organic/nonorganic and animate/inert categories. A volumetric imagination thus helps ground ethnographic detail within a voluminous, decidedly material texture, away from flat cartographic representations (cf. Zee 2022).

Visible/Invisible

The COVID-19 lockdowns that shut down industries, took vehicles off the road, and saw cancellations of flights on a global scale led to a dramatic improvement in air quality, notably in places like China and India. In the northern Indian state of Punjab, for instance, people posted on social media photos of the Himalayan Mountain range, which had become visible again after three decades. While greater visibility did generally equate with better air quality—with a substantial decrease in air quality index (AQI) values being witnessed—the visibility/health equivalence is not always as straightforward. The particles in types of air pollution such as wildfire smoke come from a multitude of materials, both organic (like trees) and inorganic (like electronics and household materials). These particulates do not have the same size and weight and, as a result, do not have the same potential to travel. Heavier dust particles are among the first elements to descend, while finer dusts—which carry highly carcinogenic toxic material far more likely to be inhaled deeply—travel to more geographically distant locations. Dust plumes also contain microorganisms (bacteria, viruses, and fungi). Sediments and their tiny inhabitants, once airborne, can settle thousands of miles from their site of origin, impacting the health of human and nonhuman animals where they make landfall.

The chapters in this collection all speak to forms of environmental violence that address these entanglements across scales and lifeforms. Also foregrounded in many of the chapters is the relationship that violence bears with materiality, particularly through the digging of mines and the building of dams. In fact, very much running counter to the cliché that infrastructure should be—true to its name ("infra" meaning below)—invisible when running correctly, these chapters speak to forms of infrastructure that are hyper-visible, spectacular, and fetishized. Infrastructure, Michael Truscello reminds us (2020, 26), in fact spans an entire "range of visibilities that move from unseen to grand spectacles and everything in between." The Belt and Road Initiative, China's multi-trillion-dollar infrastructural project, would be, for instance, at the more spectacular end of that range, with the construction of railways, ports, roads, dams, pipelines, and industrial corridors across dozens of countries. Testament to the gargantuan nature of its endeavor, China has used, from 2011 to 2013, more cement than the United States in the entire twentieth century (Truscello 2020, 19). Such an impact on natural resources by a single state is unprecedented. The quantities of concrete being produced globally are in fact such that this has caused a shortage of sand—prompting geographer Mia Bennett (2022) to coin the term "Sinocene."

Equally vast, but lacking visibility, is the Internet. Frequently imagined as ethereal and airborne (think "the Cloud"), it is anything but. As Nicole Starosielski writes (2015, 1), fiber-optic cables (in part laid under the oceans) are critical infrastructures that support a global network, and it is "submarine systems, rather than satellites, that carry most of the Internet across the oceans." In reflection of these realities, Google has been described as a non-state and deterritorialized "actor operating with the force of a state" (Bratton 2015, 10)—one that is heavily reliant on real physical infrastructure and whose datacenters consume vast amounts of energy. Indeed, Greenpeace calculated that if the Cloud, constituted by all data centers, was a country, it would have the fifth largest footprint in the world in terms of electricity demand (Hu 2015, 79).

This misalignment between visibility and harmfulness is expertly deployed in Varkkey, Copeland, and Shaiful's analysis of the concept of "haze" (chapter 8). As they explain, "haze" usually denotes "a naturally occurring climatic condition in which visibility is affected." The euphemistic use of the term for what is essentially a human-made problem shifts responsibility to an undefined, natural agent—both conceptualizing the phenomenon as beyond resolution and downplaying its severity and prolonged health impacts. The ghostly presence of haze, on the cusp between visibility and invisibility, transparency and occlusion, finds an echo in temporalities that privilege the catastrophic over the quotidian—the latter frequently more elusive or below the threshold of detectability.

Slow/Fast

In chapter 5, Ian Baird draws attention to the different temporalities that inform slow and catastrophic violence. Even though everyday violent events are likely to cause more harm in the long run, people are generally more fearful or anxious about catastrophic events. Yet the distinction between slow and fast (and between benign and catastrophic) is somewhat artificial insofar as the two are frequently intertwined, inform one another, and coexist in a feedback loop. A seemingly insignificant difference of one degree Celsius in the context of climate change can thus trigger cataclysmic events with irreversible impacts.

Part of the failure in feeling (adequately) anxious about a single Celsius digit lies in the difficulty of conceptualizing temperatures on an averaged, global scale. It remains challenging to mentally model a concept such as climate given its planetary, multidimensional, and temporally extended nature—what philosopher Tim Morton calls a "hyperobject." In consequence, even people who acknowledge climate change as a genuine threat will tend to think of the climate as coextensive with the weather they experience on a daily basis. A similar conflation is seen with the doublet air/atmosphere. We generally conceptualize the latter as a broader entity: we speak of planet *atmospheres,* of noxious gases being released into the *atmosphere,* while it is *air* that we breathe. Here again, what we perceive is what enters our bodily world, and that is always a partial view.

In taking "atmosphere" as an analytical lens, the collection foregrounds entanglements between human lives and nonhuman animals and the wider environment, between local events and global phenomena, and is attentive to the ways in which violence is always more-than-human. In that sense, the chapters speak to what Sloterdijk (2009) has called "atmoterrorism"—an assault not on the body of the enemy, but on their environment. The collection is also in dialog with the work of Nicole Starosielski (2021) on the history of heat and cold as a means of communication, subjugation, and control, particularly in ways that reinforce racialized, colonial, gendered, and sexualized hierarchies.

In giving attention to slow and quotidian violence—rather than privileging the catastrophic—the chapters provide what one might term "envelopmental ethnographies" that give due credit to forms of violence that are incremental—yet not strictly linear in their outcomes. As discussed above, a one-degree shift in average global temperature can, in disrupting delicate equilibriums, cause abrupt changes, in turn leading to irreversible changes. Insofar as slow and fast violence exist in a feedback loop, the distinction between them may in fact be moot. What violent atmospheres in the twenty-first century reveal, instead, is a telescoping of temporalities.

Flat/Volumetric

Edwin A. Abbott's *Flatland: A Romance of Many Dimensions,* published in 1884, is a satirical novella about the fictional two-dimensional world of Flatland, where the inhabitants are unable to perceive the existence of three-dimensional shapes. As philosopher of science Tim Morton writes (2013, 70): "If an apple were to invade a two-dimensional world, first the stick people would see some dots as the bottom of the apple touched their universe, then a rapid succession of shapes that would appear like an expanding and contracting circular blob, diminishing to a tiny circle, possibly a point, and disappearing." *Flatland* was written as a critique of Victorian society and its lack of vision for a more socially complex world, notably gender equality. It is proving once again a useful parable today in the context of the volumetric turn in the social sciences.

The recent focus on volume is inherently tied to a (rather late) acknowledgment of the material, textured, and voluminous nature of space, which for too long had been theorized as a somewhat abstract and disembodied background to a human-centered "place." This recognition has been prompted in part by an extension of territorial sovereignty into spaces previously inaccessible to humans, such as the atmospheric, the maritime, and the subterranean. Increasingly integrated into the remit of the state through novel technologies (Billé 2019; Chambliss 2020), these spaces have revealed a critical breach between flat cartographic imaginaries and three-dimensional realities. Concurrent conversations within philosophy on the significance of entanglements and symbioses between lifeforms (Billé 2021) have helped congeal this shift into a broader reframing of the place of the human as a three-dimensional being embedded in, and reliant on, diverse species and microscopic lifeforms.

In spite of this important shift in the academic realm, it remains difficult to conceptualize more-than-human phenomena beyond the state. Thus, just like weather maps that tend to assume that meteorological events within the nation-state are more relevant than weather just across the border, the COVID-19 pandemic similarly framed safety and danger along national lines. In early 2020, as northern Italy was suddenly transforming into the principal site of infection in Europe—thus prompting several countries, including the United States, to issue advisory restrictions for the whole of Italy—countries bordering Italy were largely absent from news headlines. Italy was presented suspended in the air—virally tied to distant Wuhan and Iran yet wholly detached from its geographic context (Billé 2020).

As Wolfram Dressler writes in the context of the COVID-19 pandemic in the Philippines (chapter 3, this volume), both slow and fast violence coemerge volumetrically through atmospheric particles and uneven political economies to influence the bodies and lives of defenders in powerful ways. This attention to the volumetric nature of atmospheres, to the ways in which they are aerial yet "grounded" in terrestrial and subterranean material life—and also to their complex temporalities—is a crucial step to reconceptualize the vast, trans-scalar, and multimaterial character of violent atmospheres.

A further example of a volumetric hyperobject straddling the categories of presence/absence and transparency/opacity might be the so-called Great Pacific Garbage Patch—a plastic vortex of flotsam and jetsam whose contents and boundaries defy both spatial definition and visibility. It is described as larger than Texas—and sometimes as twice the size of the United States; evaluations of its size speak to the attempt (but ultimate impossibility) of comparing it to a landmass since the nature of the patch invalidates attempts at territorial referentiality. As the gyre churns vast quantities of discarded plastics, the material is broken down into ever smaller components. Most of the contents of the garbage patch are in fact so small that they are invisible to the naked eye, yet the impact of its overall mass—amounting to as much as a six-to-one ratio of plastic to zooplankton—is all too real. In suspension below the ocean's surface, these particles alter the usual transparency of the water, blocking sunlight in part or completely. Frequently imagined as a vast floating collection of refuse, the garbage patch is a ghostly presence reaching across scales both immense and minuscule (Te Punga Somerville 2017, 331).

Along similar lines, McGregor and Miller (chapter 10) note that "carbon violence spreads much further as atoms circulate across borders, through the atmosphere, and into seas, trapping heat and contributing to a myriad of climate-related carbon crises." As a result, they add, "carbon violence is experienced across volumetric space, both proximate and dispersed." Like Varkkey, Copeland, and Shaiful in their chapter on haze (chapter 8), they are especially attentive to how the cumulative effects of slow and local forms of violence can percolate into global and catastrophic events with uncertain long-term consequences.

In heeding the call of political geographers to think volumetrically about political space, the chapters in this collection make a valuable contribution to ethnography-based social science through a dual emphasis on local lives and broader phenomena. Keenly aware of the need to not remain imprisoned within the constraints of national boundaries while also recognizing the continued imprint of the state, the authors shed important light on the ways that "new collaborations between state, extra-state, and non-state actors have formed to enact territorial strategies that do not pivot solely around the nation-state, nor around marginalized groups' resistance to the state" (Goldstein, chapter 7). Finally, by focusing on the atmosphere's violent force on the body, the collection underscores the enmeshment of scales, both spatial and temporal, as well as the inherently "voluminous" nature of human and nonhuman bodies—dependent on land as they are on air, water, and soil.

References

Abbott, Edwin A. 1884. *Flatland: A Romance of Many Dimensions.* London: Seeley.
Bennett, Mia. 2022. "Rise of the Sinocene? China as a Geological Agent." In *Infrastructure and the Remaking of Asia,* edited by Max Hirsh and Till Mostowlansky, 19–41. Honolulu: University of Hawai'i Press.
Billé, Franck. 2019. "Murmuration." *Society and Space,* April 9, 2019. http://societyandspace.org/2019/04/09/murmuration.
Billé, Franck. 2020. "Containment." *Somatosphere,* April 6, 2020. http://somatosphere.net/forumpost/containment.
Billé, Franck. 2021. "Auratic Geographies: Buffers, Backyards, Entanglements." *Geopolitics* 29 (3). https://doi.org/10.1080/14650045.2021.1881490.
Bratton, Benjamin H. 2015. *The Stack: On Software and Sovereignty.* Cambridge, MA: MIT Press.
Chambliss, Wayne. 2020. "Spoofing: The Geophysics of Not Being Governed." In *Voluminous States: Sovereignty, Materiality, and the Territorial Imagination,* edited by Franck Billé, 64–77. Durham, NC: Duke University Press.
Hu, Tung-Hui. 2015. *A Prehistory of the Cloud.* Cambridge, MA: MIT Press.
Morton, Timothy. 2013. *Hyperobjects: Philosophy and Ecology after the End of the World.* Minneapolis: University of Minnesota Press.
Sloterdijk, Peter. 2009. *Terror from the Air.* Los Angeles: Semiotext(e).
Starosielski, Nicole. 2015. *The Undersea Network.* Durham, NC: Duke University Press.
Starosielski, Nicole. 2021. *Media Hot and Cold.* Durham, NC: Duke University Press.
Te Punga Somerville, Alice. 2017. "The Great Pacific Garbage Patch as Metaphor: The (American) Pacific You Can't See." In *Archipelagic American Studies,* edited by Brian Russell Roberts and Michelle Ann Stephens, 320–338. Durham, NC: Duke University Press.
Truscello, Michael. 2020. *Infrastructural Brutalism: Art and the Necropolitics of Infrastructure.* Cambridge: MIT Press.
Zee, Jerry C. 2022. *Continent in Dust: Experiments in a Chinese Weather System.* Oakland: University of California Press.

Contributors

Ian G. Baird is a professor of geography and Southeast Asian studies at the University of Wisconsin-Madison. As a political ecologist, he conducts research on various topics, mainly in Laos, Thailand, and Cambodia.

Anthony Bebbington's work has focused on extractive industries, natural resource governance, territorially based development, rural livelihoods, and civil society organizations. He is currently international director of the Natural Resources and Climate Change program at the Ford Foundation, having previously served at Clark University as director of the Graduate School of Geography and Milton P. and Alice C. Higgins Professor of Environment and Society. He is a member of the US National Academy of Sciences and the American Academy of Arts and Sciences.

Franck Billé is a cultural anthropologist/geographer based at the University of California, Berkeley, where he is program director for the Tang Center for Silk Road Studies. His core research focus is on borders, space, sovereignty, and materiality. More information about his current research is available at www.franckbille.com.

Alison Copeland is a lecturer in human geography specializing in quantitative methods and geographic information systems (GIS) at Newcastle University. Her research interests focus on health inequalities, specifically exploring access to health care for the population.

Wolfram Dressler is a professor of human geography at the School of Geography, Earth and Atmospheric Sciences, University of Melbourne. His research focuses on the politics of conservation, development, and agrarian change in the highlands of the Philippines and Indonesia.

Jenny E. Goldstein is an assistant professor at the Department of Global Development at Cornell University, an Atkinson Center for a Sustainable Future fellow, and a core faculty member of Cornell's Southeast Asian Studies Program.

She is interested in environmental conservation and development in the tropics, intersections of data infrastructure and environmental governance, human health impacts of ecological change, global food and agriculture systems, the financialization of land, and the role of scientific knowledge in climate change politics.

Carl Grundy-Warr is a senior lecturer at the Department of Geography, National University of Singapore. His current research interests include environmental geopolitics, natural resource politics, and political geographies of the Mekong Subregion and mainland Southeast Asia. He teaches geopolitics, geographies of war and peace, development and environment, and field studies courses in Southeast Asia.

Philip Hirsch is professor emeritus of human geography at the University of Sydney. He has published extensively on the environment, development, and agrarian change in the Mekong Subregion.

Lisa C. Kelley is an assistant professor of geography and environmental sciences at the University of Colorado, Denver. Her work is situated in the field of critical physical geography, and combines theories and methods from political ecology, critical agrarian studies, and remote sensing to understand ongoing land and livelihood transformations in Indonesia and Southeast Asia.

Sango Mahanty is a professor of resources, environment and development at the Australian National University's Crawford School of Public Policy. She studies the drivers and implications of nature-society transformation in rural landscapes of Cambodia and Vietnam.

Andrew McGregor is director of research and innovation and a professor of human geography at the School of Social Sciences at Macquarie University. His current research focuses upon food systems transitions and carbon forestry in Australia and Southeast Asia.

Carl Middleton is an assistant professor and deputy director of graduate studies in the International Development Studies Program, and director of the Center for Social Development Studies at the Faculty of Political Science of Chulalongkorn University, Thailand. His research interests focus on nature-society relations, the political ecology of water and energy, transboundary water governance, environmental change and mobility, and environmental justice in Southeast Asia.

Fiona Miller is an associate professor at the School of Social Sciences, Macquarie University. She is a human geographer who conducts research from a political ecology perspective on the social and equity dimensions of environmental change in the Asia Pacific, notably Vietnam and Cambodia, as well as in Australia.

Sarah Milne is an associate professor at the Resources, Environment and Development Group, Australia National University. Her research examines natural resource struggles and environmental intervention. She has conducted ethnographic studies of conservation, especially the use of tools like payments for environmental services (PES) and reducing emissions from deforestation and forest degradation (REDD+).

Mary Mostafanezhad is a professor in the Department of Geography and Environment at the University of Hawaiʻi at Mānoa. As a human geographer, she broadly focuses on development, tourism, and socio-environmental change in the Asia-Pacific Region. More information about her work is available at www.marymostafanezhad.com.

Muhamad Muhdar is a professor of environmental law at Universitas Mulawarman, Indonesia. His research is focused on extractives licensing and environmental justice issues in Indonesia.

K. B. Roberts is a PhD candidate at York University, Toronto, Canada. She is a political ecologist working on rural livelihood change, deforestation and forest degradation, and feminist research methods.

Alya Shaiful is a research assistant at Universiti Malaya, Malaysia. Her research focuses on international development at the nexus of public health, education, migration, and urban development. She currently works on projects related to foundational learning skills in primary and secondary schools in sub-Saharan Africa and South Asia and improving the physical spaces in public housing schemes in Malaysia.

Annie Shattuck is an assistant professor of geography at Indiana University, Bloomington. Her research looks at the political economy of agrarian change, food systems, rural health, and environmental transformation. She is a co-editor of the *Journal of Peasant Studies*.

Kimberley Anh Thomas is a political ecologist and assistant professor of human-environment geography at Temple University. Her research on vulnerability, international development, water infrastructure, and climate finance centers on environmental justice and power relations across multiple scales. More information about her work is available at kimberley.thomasresearch.org.

Tessa D. Toumbourou is a postdoctoral research fellow at the School of Agriculture, Food, and Ecosystem Sciences, University of Melbourne. Her research focuses on feminist political ecology, agro- and resource extractivism, and the (uneven dynamics of) livelihood change in Indonesia.

Helena Varkkey is an associate professor of Environmental Politics and Governance at Universiti Malaya, Malaysia. Her areas of expertise include transboundary haze governance in Southeast Asia, global palm oil politics, and climate politics and governance. Her monograph *The Haze Problem in Southeast Asia: Palm Oil and Politics* was published by Routledge in 2016.

Tim Werner is a senior lecturer and former ARC DECRA fellow at the School of Geography, Earth and Atmospheric Sciences, University of Melbourne. His research expertise encompasses geographical science, conservation biology, economic geology, and environmental engineering. His current focus revolves around examining land use change processes and their impacts in mining regions.

Index

Page numbers in **boldface** refer to illustrations.

AATHP (ASEAN Agreement on Transboundary Haze Pollution), 191–192
Aboriginal Australians. *See* Indigenous peoples
accretion, 104, 117
activism: criminalization of, 35, 80–82, 85, 87, 93; grassroots, 92; and harassment/intimidation, 42–43, 60, 79–81, 83, 85, 87–88, 91–94; suppression, 87; as terrorism, 80–81. *See also* defenders
adaptation: and displacement, 106; and hydropower, 154; local efforts, 237; strategies, 106
agrarian: Comprehensive Agrarian Reform Program (CARP), 86; displacement, 106–107; reform, 85–86
agribusiness, 86, 105, 114–115; demand for livestock, 108; investment, 118, 163; plantations, 170–171, 230, 235
agriculture: abandonment of, 234; animal, 227–229; commercial, 85; commodity production, 114, 115; concessions, 114; and fires, 189; intensification, 114, 115; mechanization, 114; smallholder, 107; in southern Vietnam, 109. *See also* swidden
air pollution, 65–67, 163, 165, 172–175, 176n4, 182–186, 191–192, 244; impacts of, 66–68, 70, 184–187. *See also* haze; particulates
Anthropocene, 224–225
Anti-Terrorism Act, Philippine, 80, 87–88, 93

Aquino, Benigno "Ninoy," 86
Aquino, Benigno "Noynoy" III, 86–87
Aquino, Cory, 86
Arroyo, Gloria Macapagal, 86–87, 94n5
ASEAN (Association of Southeast Asian Nations), 132–133, 190–192; Coordinating Centre for Transboundary Haze Pollution Control, 192
Asian Development Bank (ADB), 116, 144, 152
atmospheric: carbon, 226, 232, 237; crises, 15; flows, 117
audits: carbon, 199–213; clean and clear (CnC), 37, 38, 46n11; culture, 201; processes, 202
Australia, 221, 224–229, 235–236; cattle barons, 232, 235–236; deforestation hotspot, 228; export of cattle, 228; export of gas and coal, 225; Hunter Valley, 224–225, **227**; links to Vietnam, 235; Newcastle, 225
authoritarian/ism: and COVID-19, 83–84, 93, 94n1; developmentalism, 87; "enclaves," 86; in Myanmar, 61; populism, 83–84, 94n1; and Stuart Hall, 83; suppression of defenders, 94n3

Belt and Road Initiative, 15, 245
Biden, Joseph, 117
Biden-Harris administration: migration policy, 117. *See also* United States
biophysical: carbon cycle, 221–224, 235; dynamics, 109, 171; flows, 117; impacts,

255

147; landscapes, 142; processes, 119, 144, 235; properties of coal, 62; ruptures, 8; scales, 175; spheres, 8
Bolaven Plateau (Laos), 125, 130, 136–137
British: in Australia, 225; in Burma, 71n3; colonization by, 71, 225. *See also* colonialism
bureaucratic: diversion, 206, 208, 210–211; "indifference," 213; oversight, 188; practices, 199–204, 207–208, 210–211; violence, 13, 200, 210, 213–214

Cambodia, 142, 152, 199–215; Sekong district, 127; Siem Pang district, 127; Stung Treng province, **101**, 127; Tonle Sap, **143**
Camps. *See* resettlement
capitalism, 104, 144, 213; carbon, 224; global, 235; neoliberal, 224; predatory, 85, 104
carbon: audits, 201; capitalism, 224; and cattle, 227, 237; and displacement, 233–234; dioxide, 173; economies, 235; extraction, 224; flows, 225–226, 237; fossilization, 224; markets, 201, 203–204; materiality, 224; organic, 224, 227, 237; in peat forests, 237; plant-based, 213, 223, 227; subterranean, 224; transformations, 223, 235, 238; validation/verification, 203, 205, 210; wooden forms, 213, 223, 230, 238. *See also* carbon credits; carbon cycles; carbon sequestration/sinks; carbon violence
carbon credits, 199–205, 211, 213–214, 215n1, 231
carbon cycles, 221, 235; biophysical, 221, 223, 235; sociocarbon, 221–235
carbon sequestration/sinks, 199–200, 213, 220–221, 223, 227, 229–232, 236, 237, 238
carbon violence, 214, 220–238, 248
catastrophe: definition, 129; events, 125, 128–130, 131, 137; psychological impacts of, 129, 134; and temporality, 129–130; and violence, 105, 126, 128–130, 135, 136. *See also* emergency

cattle: barons, 232, 235, 236; Brahmin breed, 227; as carbon, 224; and colonialism, 227–229; as commodities, 228; and diet, 229; emissions, 227–228; exports of, 226–228; impact on the carbon cycle, 228–229; and violence, 228–229
Chan, Bobby, 91, 93
China: air quality, 244; Belt and Road initiative, 245; coal demand from, 25, 31–32, 35, 43, 45n6; financed projects, 56, 57, 80, 87, 90
clientelism, 30, 41–42, 93, 206. *See also* patronage
climate change: decentering, 106; and displacement/migration, 104, 106–107, 113, 116; as "ecological threat," 103–104; refugees, 104, 116; in South Sulawesi, 111
climate displacement. *See* displacement
climate violence, 12, 104
coal: Australian, 232, 234; emissions, 65; energy projects, 31; extraction, 26; mineral carbon, 225–226; mining, 27, 225–226; post-mining landscapes, 28–29; reclamation, 26; regulation, 26, 42. *See also* pit lakes
colonialism, 119; British in Australia, 225; British in Myanmar, 60, 62, 65–67, 70; Dutch in Indonesia, 29, 112; and forests, 167; French in Vietnam, 110, 234; Portuguese in Timor-Leste, 226. *See also* frontier
combustion, 183, 221, 223–224, 226, 236, 237; and coal, 221, 225–226; and fly ash, 66; and peat fires, 183–184. *See also* fire
commodification: carbon, 200–201; of nature, 231; socio-natural, 201
commodity frontiers, 80
commodities: carbon, 201; chain, 200; exports, 111; frontiers, 80; socio-natural, 201
communism, 80, 85, 89, 91, 136
compensation, 30, 62–63, 132–133; for dam breaks, 132–133, 137; for farmland, 62–63. *See also* reparations
Comprehensive Agrarian Reform Program (CARP), 86

concessions: asphalt, 112; gold, 112; nickel, 112; oil palm, 112; role in deforestation, 113
conflicts: resource, 113; territorial, 113
conservation, 86, 92, 152, 183, 191, 202, 206, 230; carbon, 164, 205; laws, 65, 68–69, 86; neoliberal, 164–165, 169; zones, 234
corn. *See* maize
COVID-19, 32–33, 79, 81–83, 85, 87, 161, 244, 247–248; economic slowdown, 32; lockdowns, 88; pandemic, 79–100; and violence against defenders, 88–89
crises, 166, 236; carbon, 220, 236, 238, 248; climate, 171–72, 187, 213; conjunctural, 84; fire, 172; haze, 163, 243; refugee, 234
critical geography, 106

dams, 126, 131–132, 145–146; impact of floods from, 127, 131–132; Nam Ao dam, Laos, 132; Nam Theun 2 dam (NT2), Laos, 147; ruptures, 12, 131–132; securing flows, 153; as "sustainable hydropower," 154; and violence, 126; Xayaburi Dam, Laos, 148; Xe Pian Xe Namnoy dam, Laos, 125–133, 136–137. *See also* hydropower
defenders, 79–83, 84, 85, 93–94, 94n3, 95n7. *See also* activism
deforestation, 35–36, 39, 231
DENR (Department of Environment and Natural Resources, Philippines), 90, 92
development: and hydropower, 153; refugees, 130–131; regimes, 112; sustainable, 60, 91, 95n8, 144, 148–149
DGWP (direct global warming potential), 65
diplomacy: water, 142, 150, 154. *See also* water
direct violence, 10, 222, 228, 230, 236; and political ecology, 236. *See also* violence
discourses, 170; cattle, 229; coal, 44; fire, 169; haze, 187; hydropower, 152–153; legal, 59; REDD+, 202; and volumes, 266
displacement, 58, 69, 104–109, 111–112, 135, 233, 237; climate, 103–104, 106–107, 113, 116; drivers of, 114–115; of Indigenous peoples, 111–112, 130–131; socionatural, 113–115. *See also* migration; mobility; resettlement
dispossession, 28–29, 114; and climate change, 111; and "green grabs," 231; of Indigenous peoples, 85–86, 236; processes of, 114–115; as violence, 237. *See also* displacement; migration; resettlement
drainage: acid mine, 36; peatlands, 183, 188, 232; wetlands, 112–113
droughts, 115; and migration, 115; mitigation, 152; and rice, 115
drownings: and mining, 36–37, **37**, 43–44, 47n20. *See also* pit lakes
Duterte, Rodrigo, 79–81, 83–84, 87–94

ECQ (enhanced community quarantine), Philippines, 81, 87–89
elites. *See* clientelism; patronage
El Niño, 148, 173, 184
emergency: and fire, 169; responses, 181, 191; rice reserves, 133; states of, 80–81, 94n2; water releases, 150. *See also* catastrophe
emissions: atmospheric, 173; Australian, 225; carbon, 31, 165, 173, 199, 213, 231; cattle, 228; credits, 199; from fossil fuels, 231; global, 65; and hydropower, 152–153; of pollutants, 183; reducing, 172, 204, 212, 215n1, 231, 236; targets, 152, 205. *See also* carbon; greenhouse gases; REDD+
energy companies: in Indonesia, 46n16; policy, 31–32, 43, 45n1; projects, 31, 57; Thai, 128, 131, 224, 225
ENSO (El Niño Southern Oscillation), 184. *See also* El Niño
erosion, 44, **105,** 107–108, 114, 147, 234; coastal, 114, 223; and maize, 109, 114; riverine, 147
ethnography, 59, 106, 202, 204, 244; and REDD+, 200
everyday violence, 56, 59, 60, 70–71. *See also* violence
exports: coal, 43, 46; commodities, 111; rice, 109–110, 115; shrimp, 110–111. *See also* illegal

extraction: carbon, 224; coal, 236; timber, 112
extractivism, 12, 15, 86–87, 113; neoliberal, 86; settler colonial, 225
extraterritoriality, 174–175. *See also* territoriality

farmers, 38, 62–63, 110, 136, 230; activist, 80, 94n3; and debt, 111; and erosion, 108; evictions, 62–63, 85; and fly ash, 67; and haze, 190, 193; Khmer, 209; landless, 86, 136; and opium, 109; shrimp, 111; swidden, 112, 187, 189; vulnerability, 110. *See also* agrarian; smallholders; swidden
Feliciano, Jean, 92–93
fetishization, 189, 201
finance, 152; foreign, 80; role in hydropower, 152. *See also* foreign investment
fire, 183; arson, 42; criminalization of, 169; discourses, 169; forest, 169; illegality of, 189; in Indonesia, 183; and peatlands, 188–189; politics of, 169, 171; subterranean, 171, 184; and territorialization, 169. *See also* peat forests
fisheries, 110, 133, 145, 148–149, 150–151; decline of, 234; and flood pulse, 146; freshwater, 115, 133; and hydropower, 151; wild-capture, 110, 145, 147, 149, 150–151; yields, 150–151
floods, 36, 44, 110–112, 126–127; compensation for, 126, 132–133; management, 115; psychological effects of, 129, 134–135, 137; pulses, 141–146, 151, 153; regimes, 111–112; risks, 133; in Southeast Sulawesi, 111–112, 115; in southern Vietnam, 109; and the Tolaki people, 111; and UXOs, 134. *See also* displacement
flows, 105, 108, 117, 142; of carbon, 220, 223, 225, 236–237; of data, 145; designed, 144, 150–151, 155; of everyday violence, 70; and hydropower, 145, 148, 153, 155; low, 148–149; material, 220, 226; minimum, 150; of money, 142, 147, 152, 168, 231; of people, 107, 116, 119; politics of, 154; seasonal, 153; of water, 36, 104, 110, 142, 145, 148–149, 150
forced relocation/resettlement. *See* displacement; migration; resettlement
foreign investment, 30, 34, 63, 170, 189; laws, 30. *See also* Korea-backed projects; Thai-backed projects
forest carbon, 200, 203, 214, 223, 225, 230; as commodity, 200–201; measuring, 214; producing, 203; timber as, 225. *See also* carbon; peat forest; wood
forest fires. *See* fire
forest products, 70, 81, 109, 114; non-timber, 81, 109, 114; and roads, 112. *See also* wood
forests, 166, 167; political, 164, 166–167, 175. *See also* peat forest, peatlands
fossil fuels, 65, 172, 175, 223, 226, 231, 233, 235, 237–238. *See also* carbon: fossilization; coal
fossilization, carbon, 224
freshwater. *See* rivers
frontier, 10, 80, 87, 95n7; violence, 58, 213, 227–228. *See also* colonialism; settler colonial

gambia grass, 227–229
geography, political. *See* political geography
gold, 112, 114
Golkar, 42, 46n18, 47n19
Great Pacific Garbage Patch, 248
green economy, 199, 201
green grabs, 107, 231
greenhouse gases (GHGs), 45, 65, 151–153, 172, 224, 228, 232–233, 237; as violence, 232–233. *See also* emissions
green violence, 214

hacienda, 86
harassment. *See* activism; defenders
haze, 172, 174, 181; as an aerial volumetric crisis, 182–183; definitions, 181–182, 183; health impacts, 185–186; in Indonesia, 182, 187; legislation, 174; and Malaysian companies, 189; mitigation, 192; from

peat fires, 172–173; and Singapore Transboundary Haze Pollution Act, 174; and territoriality, 174–175; transboundary, 163, 174, 184–194; and violence, 182, 184–185, 188. See also air pollution; particulates
health impacts, of haze, 185–186; relationship to education, 186
Ho Chi Minh City (Vietnam), 234
horizontality, 4, 8, 16n1, 28, 244. See also verticality
hot zones, 103
hydrology(ies), 36, 104, 115, 145–147, 150; designing flows of, 150–151; and fisheries, 150–151; of Mekong Basin, 142, 150; of peat domes, 188; of rivers, 151; and slow violence, 154
hydropeaking, 147–148, 150
hydropolitics, 12, 142, 144–145; volumetric, 144–145, 149
hydropower, 12–13, 125–126, 142, 144, 146; as climate mitigation technology, 144–145, 148, 151–152; dams, 126, 130, 144–146; and development, 153; in Laos, 125–126, 130, 132, 135; in the Mekong Basin, 141–155; in the Philippines, 80; sustainability of, 148, 151–155; and territoriality, 146. See also dams; power
hydrosociality, 142
hyperobjects, 246, 248

illegal: coal exports, 43; harvesting of natural resources, 81; land-clearing, 92; logging, 70, 200, 210, 212–213, 214, 231; of peat fires, 189; resource use, 61
impunity, 44, 79, 84, 87, 93, 188, 212; and clientelism, 189; and fires, 188
India, 31, 32, 43, 45n6, 59, 225, 244
Indigenous communal title (ICT) zone, 211–212
Indigenous peoples: Aboriginal Australians, 225, 227–228; Bunong people, 206–207, 210; Geawegall people, 225; Gomeroi/Kamilaroil people, 225; Gurindji people, 228; Heuny (Nha Heun), 125, 130–131, 133, 135, 136; Jrou (Laven), 130; Jrou Dak (Sou) people, 126, 133; laws, 86; Oi people, 126, 133, 136; Peoples' Rights Act (1997), 86; Toepe people, 111; Toiwoiesi people, 111; Tolaiwoi people, 111; Tolaki people, 111, 112; Wiradjuril people, 225; Wonnarua people, 225
Indonesia, 25–45, 163–176, 181–192; Central Kalimantan province, 173; East Kalimantan province, **23**, 25–27, 29–31, **32, 33**, 35–45, 45n5, 46n17, 47n19, 189; Konawe'eha River, 111–112; Samarinda, 12, 25, 36–37, 47n19; Southeast Sulawesi, 106, 114–115, 119n1
insurgents/cies, 61, 80–81, 85, 87, 94n5, 164
intergovernmental/international agreements. See transboundary
internet, 91, 132, 165, 186, 245
intimidation. See activism, defenders, red-tagging

Kalimantan, Indonesia: Central, 173; East, 25, 189; smallholders in, 189
Khammany Inthirath, 132
Korea-backed projects, 128, 130–131

labor: plantation, 113; migration, 113; and circular migration, 115
land: clearing, 228; grabs, 107, 212, 237; "green" grabs, 107, 231; Indigenous/tribal, 86
landscapes: agricultural, 106, 169, 230; as archives, 135; carbon-rich, 201; damaged, 26, 36, 43, 44; dangerous, 26; and fire, 166, 169–170, 228; human, 142; of nightmares, 135; post-coal mining, 27–29, 43; and power, 145; and violence, 45, 201; volatile, 175. See also forests
Lao: ethnic peoples of, 126, 133; government, 127, 128, 131, 147; language, 126, 132; Red Cross, 134–135; Royal Army, 136
Laos: Bolaven Plateau, Champasak Province, 125, 130, 136–137; Mai village, 135; Nam Ao dam, 132; outmigration from, 108–109; Samong Tai village, 135; Sanamxay District, 126, 132; Secret War

in, 133; Thasengchanh Village, 135; Tha Hin village, 135; UXOs in, 133; Xayaburi Dam, 148; Xe Pian Xe Namnoy Dam, 125; Xieng Khouang, 105, 114–115
leftists, 80, 87, 90–91, 93
liberalization: market, 107; post-, 112
logging: illegal, 200, 210, 212–213, 214, 231
lumber/timber products, 70, 109, 112

maize, 105; and crop monoculture, 108, 114; and erosion, 114; and migration, 108; smallholder production, 114
Malaysia, 115, 163, 173, 181, 184, 226, 230; companies, 182; and haze, 173, 181, 184–187, 191–192, 226; and palm oil, 189
Malthusianism (and neo-Malthusianism), 12, 103, 113, 118
mapping, 167; of fires, 175, 176n1; of forests, 165; of mining zones, 29; of plantations, 166. *See also* territoriality
Marcos, Bongbong, 80
Marcos, Ferdinand, 85
marine resources, 90
market liberalization, 107
markets, carbon, 201, 203–204
materiality(ies), 28, 168–169; of atmospheric and biophysical flows, 117; of carbon, 224; environmental, 169; of forests, 163–164, 166; of peatlands, 166; of volumetric space, 183
"meatification" of Southeast Asian diets, 227
mega rice projects, failed, 231; Suharto's, 230
Mekong: Basin, 141–149; Delta, 105–106, 109, 114–115, 234; outmigration from, 109; region, 144, 146, 152–153; River, 146, 148, 153; and Vietnam's rice exports, 110
Mekong Agreement, 150
Mekong River Commission (MRC), 144
migration, 103, 115; circular, 115; climate, 103, 108; illegal, 116–117; labor, 107–108, 113; and maize, 108–109; in the Mekong Delta, 234; and slow violence, 234. *See also* displacement; resettlement
Mindanao, Philippines, 80, 93, and palm oil development, 94
mineral carbon, 224–226, 237

mine voids, 25, 28–29, 36–37, 42–43, 46n17; refilling, 41. *See also* drownings; pit lakes
mining, coal, 26; "corridors," 38; in East Kalimantan, 25–27, 29–31, **32**, **33**, 35–45, 45n5, 46n17, 47n19, 189; illegal, 38, 42, 70, 81, 92, 114–115; laws, 64, 65; permits, 30–31, 40–41, 44, 46n12, 47n19, 92; in the Philippines, 92; unregulated, 26, 41, 70
mitigation: of climate change, 148, 151–152, 154, 172, 199; of haze, 192; and hydropower, 144–146, 148, 154; of floods, 144; and REDD+, 215n1. *See also* reparations
mobility: atmospheric, 107; and climate displacement, 105–107; hydrological, 107; nonhuman, 153. *See also* displacement
monsoon, 110, 146, 153, 173, 232–233
more-than-human: bodies, 229; communities, 230; costs, 236; flourishing, 234, 238; framing/lens, 222–223; phenomena, 247; practices and relations, 223; violence, 222–224, 229–230, 235, 246
Myanmar, 56–71; 2018 Mining Rules, 64; 2021 coup, 60, 69–70; coal in, 28, 56–71; energy companies, 56; Inle Lake, 58, 64; Mines Law of 1994, 65; Shan State, 56–71; states of, 71n4; Tatmadaw, 71n2; Tigyit, 56–70

Nam Ao dam, Laos, 132
Nam Theun 2 dam (NT2), Laos, 147; water volumes, 147
Ne Win, General, 61, 71n7
neglect, 59, 66, 136–137
neoliberalism, 112, 164, 191, 236; and carbon capitalism, 224; conservation, 164–165, 169; and forests, 170
New Order regime, 29–30, 112. *See also* Suharto
nickel, 81, 92, 114–115; concessions, 112; Ipilan Nickel Corporation, 92
Nixon, Rob, 129, 222

oceanic carbon, 223–224, 232–234, 237
oil and gas. See fossil fuels
oil palm. See palm oil
oligarchy: Indonesian, 26
opium, 109, 114, 115; ban on, 115
organic carbon, 229
ormas. See paramilitary groups

Pacific Climate Warrior campaign, 236
Palawan Times, 83
palm oil, 105, 189–190; concessions, 112; fetishization of, 189; in Indonesia, 105; and peatlands, 187–188; permits, 188; plantations, 80, 187–188, 230; in Sulawesi, 114
paramilitary groups (*ormas*), 28, 41–44; links to coal sector, 43; links to officials, 42
particulates, 7, 8, 10–11, 14–15, 65–66, 169, 172–173, 184, 244. See also haze
patronage, 188, 189, 191, 192, 193; "democracy," 41. See also clientelism
PCSD (Palawan Council for Sustainable Development), 91, 92
peat forests: and carbon sequestration, 229; domes, 188; fires, 163, 165–166, 169–171, 182, 230–231; governance of, 231–232; and haze, 172–173, 230; and more-than-human violence, 230, 232; and oil palm plantations, 230–231; and REDD+ carbon credits, 231
peatlands: Indonesian, 166, 170, 171, 175, 182, 187–188, 192, 229, 237; and oil palm development, 187–188; permits, 188
permits, 30–31, 40–41, 44, 46n12, 47n19, 92, 230; on peatlands, 188
Philippines: Bacoor, Pavite, 90; Communist Party of the, 80; COVID-19 pandemic in the, 81–83; DENR (Department of Environment and Natural Resources, Philippines), 90; Iloilo, Visayas, 89; Luzon, 87; Manila, 87; Mindanao, 80, 87; Palawan Island, 80, 87, 93; and palm oil development, 94
pit lakes, 25, 36–37, 43–44; drownings in, 36–37, 43–44, 47n20; as slow violence, 43–44. See also mine voids

plantation: labor, 113; licenses, 164. See also palm oil
PNNI (Palawan NGO Network Incorporated), 91, 92
polders (Dutch). See rice
political ecology, 2, 27–28, 106, 144, 182, 220, 222; studies, 27, 106; and violence, 57, 182, 220, 236; world regional, 221
political economy, 2, 26–27, 29–30, 41–42, 106, 212, 236; of coal mines, 29–30, 41, 43; international, 168; of peat forests, 229–231; regional, 144; of state repression, 87, 93–94
political forests, 164, 166–167; territoriality of, 167–169
political geography, 166, 167, 175; of dams, 145, 167
pollution. See air pollution; emissions; particulates
Pollution Standards Index (PSI), 173. See also air pollution; emissions; particulates
populism, authoritarian, 79, 82–84, 94n1; coercive, 92. See also authoritarianism
Porquia, Jory, 89
post-liberalization, 112
power: and space, 168; topologies of, 142–153. See also coal; hydropower
preman (mafia), 41–42
production: agrarian, 107, 109, 115; biofuel, 87; of carbon, 205, 212; of carbon credits, 203; of cattle, 228, 230; coal, 30–35, 38, 40, 45n6, 70; commercial fish, 151; commodity, 111, 113–115, 200; energy, 45, 66; and fly ash, 66; forest, 170; of forest carbon, 203; maize, **105**, 108, 114; mineral, 114; modes of, 182; opium, 109; palm oil, 80, 114, 192; and peat, 187; policies, 110; rice, 110. See also farmers; yields
PTSD, 129, 134, 135, 137

quarantines, 87–89, 93, 95n6

reclamation/remediation, 27, 36–37, 40–41; of coal pits, 25–26, 45n5
REDD+ (Reducing Emissions from Deforestation and Forest Degradation),

13, 199–215, 231; carbon credits, 231; definition, 215n1
red-tagging, 80, 87, 91, 93. *See also* activism; defenders; leftists
Reformasi, 30
refugees: climate, 104, 106, 234; development, 130. *See also* displacement; migration; resettlement
relocation/resettlement. *See* displacement; migration; resettlement
remittances, 107, 109, 119
remote sensing. *See* surveillance technologies
rents/rent seeking, 26, 31, 43, 212
reparations, 236. *See also* compensation; mitigation
resettlement: camps, 132–133; forcible, 62, 104, 109, 114–115, 130, 135, 234, 237; of Indigenous peoples, 45n3, 114, 131–133; return from, 131; as slow violence, 133. *See also* displacement; migration
resilience: climate, 45; disaster, 15; efforts, 116; programs, 116; thinking, 116
rice, 105; as compensation, 133; and droughts, 115; and Dutch polders, 110; failed mega projects, 231; and fisheries, 115; production, 109–110, 115; yields, 110
rivers: and hydropower, 133–134, 152–153; impacts of silting, 134; in the Mekong Basin, 141–142; Mekong River, 146, 148, 153; in Thailand, 141, 150
roads, 2, 80, 112, 132, 153, 245; damaged by floods, 132; and frontiers, 80; and wetland drainage, 112. *See also* Belt and Road Initiative

Samarinda Lawsuit Movement, 25
SARS-CoV-2. *See* COVID-19
satellite imagery, 29, 38, 149, 165–166, 173, 175. *See also* surveillanc technologies
savannahs, 227, 229
sea level rise, 111, 221, 232–233, 236
Secret War in Laos, 133
sedentarization, 105, 112
settler colonial: economies, 224–225, 237; ideology of extractivism, 225–226; land grabs, 237; mentality, 228–229, 237; society, 224–225, 227
Shan State, Myanmar, 56–71
shrimp: exports, 110, 114; farming, 110–111; ponds, **105**; in Vietnam, 114
silent violence, 106, 130, 182, 185, 192; of famines, 182; a la Michael Watts, 130
Singapore, 173–174; companies, 182; and haze impacts, 181, 185, 190, 226, 230; Transboundary Haze Pollution Act (STHPA), 174, 176n4
SLORC (State Law and Order Restoration Council), 61, 63, 71n2
slow violence, 6–7, 12–13, 44, 84–85, 92, 105, 126, 129–130, 132–133, 182, 234; and catastrophe, 125–126, 134–135, 137; and cattle, 228–229; and defenders, 92; and fast violence, 7, 246; and hydropower, 12–13, 131–136, 145; and Indigenous peoples, 133; of pollutants, 182; and resettlement, 133; a la Rob Nixon, 129; and UXOs, 134; and water, 126, 133, 154
smallholders, 105, 111, 173; displacement of, 113; impact of haze, 173; Indonesian, 173, 189; Kalimantan, 189; and peat forests, 230; persistence of Asian, 107; Sumatran, 189; Thai, 114; Vietnamese, 114. *See also* agrarian; farmers; production
smartphones. *See* internet
social media, 91, 132. *See also* internet
sociocarbon: cycles, 14, 221, 232, 235; definition, 221; futures, 226
socio-ecological displacement/migration, 116–117. *See also* dispossession; migration; resettlement
socio-ecologies, 230, 234, 236
socionatural, 107; commodities, 201; displacements and migrations, 114–116, 118; violence, 113
sovereignty, 58, 60, 167–168, 174; and ASEAN, 191; claims, 172, 174, 191; contested, 58; fragmented, 61, 70; and racialization, 71n3; and space, 168; state, 61, 167–168, 191, 193; and territory, 144, 168, 247. *See also* territoriality

spaces: atmospheric, 169; subterranean, 168, 247. *See also* landscapes
spatiality, 244
storytelling, as research method, 224
strategies: of accumulation, 170, 235; adaptive, 106; of defenders, 81; and fire, 169; legal, 25, 175; local, 214; mapping, 29, 167; for peace, 237; regional, 236; territorial, 166, 168, 169, 171–172, 248
structural violence, 222, 228, 230–231
subterranean: coal, 27, 29, 40, 44; and fire, 169–170; and forests, 164, 166, 175; impacts, 28–29, 40; landscapes, 171; life, 248; and peat fires, 171, 184; and peat soil, 184; resources, 168; spaces, 27–29, 40, 108, 119, 164, 168, 171, 247; and territoriality, 168; and verticality, 168
Suharto, 26, 29–30, 46n18, 112, 230; era, 170
Sulawesi: Konawe'eha River, 111–112; Southeast, 106, 114–115
Sumatra, Indonesia, 173, 181–185, 189; fires in, 181–184, 230; haze in, 163, 170, 173, 181, 185; peat lands in, 170, 230; smallholders in, 189
surveillance technologies, 13, 165, 167
sustainability: claims to, 153; and dams/hydropower, 148, 152–155; in planning, 148. *See also* development; hydropower
swidden, 114, 187, 189; bans of, 115; criminalization of, 114; and peatlands, 187; repression of, 169; *See also* agriculture
symbolic violence, a la Bourdieu, 201

technologies, 13, 165, 167; mapping, 167, 175. *See also* internet
temporality, 126, 129, 137, 244, 246; and volumes, 137–138
territorial: conflicts, 113; "trap," 3
territoriality, 164–166; claims based on, 168; dimensions, 166; economic, 174–175; and fire, 169; of forests, 167, 169; and haze, 174–175; and hydropower, 136; and mapping, 167; political, 168. *See also* transboundary

terrorism, 93; Anti-Terrorism Act (Philippines, 2020), 87, 93. *See also* activism; red-tagging
Thai-backed projects, 128, 130–131; coal-burning plants, 226
Thailand, 58, 60, 115, 172, 224; Chiang Khong, **141**; Chiang Saen, 149; energy companies, 131, 225; and haze, 226; Lancang cascade, 150; Mae Moh communities, 58; and the Mekong Basin, 142, 146, 149
THPA (Transboundary Haze Pollution Act, Singapore), 174–175
Tigyit coal mine/power plant, Myanmar, 56–70
timber. *See* forest products; wood
Timor Gap Treaty, 226
Timor-Leste, 226
Timor Sea, 226
Tonle Sap, Cambodia, 142–143, 149; "reverse flow," 149
topologies: of power, 142–153, 155; and topography, 142
transboundary: agreements, 144; haze, 189; legislation, 174; regimes, 154. *See also* territoriality
transnational: actors, 182; alliances, 147; companies, 26, 47n21, 182; criminal activity, 116; investment, 144; labor migration, 107; NGOs, 164; water governance, 155. *See also* foreign investment; transboundary
trans-scalar: approach, 182; conflict, 192; crisis, 14, 181; elites, 182; victims, 182, 190

UNFCCC (United Nations Framework Convention on Climate Change), 151, 215n1
United States: and migration, 116–117; San Francisco Bay Area, 243
U Thein Sein, 57, 61, 62, 63, 64
UXOs (unexploded ordnance), 133, 137

VCUs (verified carbon units), 203–204
verticality, 3, 7, 16n1, 28, 40, 44, 149, 166, 168–169. *See also* horizontality

Vientiane Times, 132
Vietnam, 105, 109, 233, 236; An Giang province, 110; Bac Lieu province, 234; Ca Mau province, 234; Dong Thap province, 110; Duyen Hai, 234; Ho Chi Minh City, 234; Mekong Delta, 105; projects in Laos, 114, 136; rice exports from, 110; as site of climate violence, 233–234
violence: and cattle, 228; cultural, 222, 228, 236; direct, 222, 230, 236; distanced, 184, 187; environmental, 136–137; everyday, 71; frontier, 227; as habitus, 128; more-than-human, 222, 229; as process, 222; quiet, 106; socionatural, 113; symbolic, 201; transformation, 220–236; and water, 126, 133. *See also* carbon violence; climate violence; direct violence; everyday violence; green violence; silent violence; slow violence

water, 125–126, 137, 147, 149; and catastrophe, 129; data sharing, 149; dewatering, 133; diplomacy, 142, 150, 154; politics of, 145; shortages, 64; systems, 112. *See also* rivers
waterscapes, 141, 145–146; anthropogenic, 145; contested, 146
Watts, Michael, book *Silent Violence*, 130
wetlands, drainage, 112, 232
Widodo, Joko, 31
wood, 186, 230–231; and carbon, 230–231. *See also* forest products
World Bank, 27, 147, 152, 234; funding, 234; reports, 104

Xayaburi Dam, Laos, 148
Xe Bang Fai River, Laos, 147
Xe Pian River, Laos, 133
Xe Pian Xe Namnoy Dam, Laos, 125, 136–137; collapse of, 126–127, 130–131, 132; and Heuny people, 131–133

yields: crops, 36, 38; maize, 108; rice, 109–110; fisheries, 150